The Political Research Experience

Third Edition

The Political Research Experience

Readings and Analysis

Third Edition

Marcus E. Ethridge

M.E. Sharpe
Armonk, New York
London, England

Library of Congress Cataloging-in-Publication Data

The political research experience: readings and analysis / [edited by] Marcus E. Ethridge—
3rd ed.
    p. cm.
    Includes bibliographical references and index.
    ISBN 0-7656-0756-5 (cloth: alk. paper)   ISBN 0-7656-0757-3 (pbk: alk. paper)
    1. Political science—Research. I. Ethridge, Marcus E.

JA86.P556 2002   2001032824
320′.072—dc21   CIP

Printed in the United States of America

The paper used in this publication meets the minimum requirements of
American National Standard for Information Sciences
Permanence of Paper for Printed Library Materials,
ANSI Z 39.48-1984.

BM (c) 10   9   8   7   6   5   4   3   2   1
BM (p) 10   9   8   7   6   5   4   3   2   1

For Annie

Contents

Preface

Political scientists are frequently confronted with nonscientific statements, speculations, and fervent assertions regarding the subjects they study. They often pick up a newspaper or watch a broadcast in which a journalist, politician, or activist, with virtually no data or careful thought, "explains" an issue or problem currently under study. After years of training in how to apply the scientific method to the study of politics, political scientists are often frustrated by the fact that so much of what they study is commonly approached in such nonscientific ways.

A recurring theme in this book is the superiority of scientific analysis over polemical, impressionistic, or journalistic efforts to understand political life. As zealous graduate students and earnest assistant professors, many political scientists took great pleasure in pointing out the errors of newscasters and essayists who analyze politics without a foundation in scientific method.

Experience has been a humbling teacher, however. Political scientists have learned that these nonscientific political scientists often have a great deal to offer. Many important questions cannot be resolved by scientific method. But experience has also demonstrated the scientific study of politics *is* valuable—not only for the specific knowledge it produces, but also because it suggests that political behavior is, ultimately, understandable. Sometimes, it is even roughly predictable. Political instability, shifts in public opinion, policy innovation patterns among states, and many other matters of political significance are not entirely random. The scientific approach to politics teaches us this important lesson, an idea that endures long after we become rusty on the technical details of our methodological training.

This third edition of *The Political Research Experience* is, like the previous editions, intended to help students develop a working understanding of political research. We can best appreciate both the basic importance of scientific political analysis and several important methodologies by seeing them in action, so to speak. Most instructors use published studies as illustrations, of course, but students typically find the works published by political scientists for their peers rather inaccessible. However, by exercising great care in selecting and editing articles and providing introductory and concluding essays that provide students with guidance, instructors can overcome this difficulty. This is the approach taken here, enabling students to read published research with real understanding.

In making revisions for the third edition, I have followed instructor and student feedback closely. Most of the excerpts are new to this edition. The most prominent change is the addition of a chapter on rational choice analysis, which includes an excerpt from Morris Fiorina. As explained in that chapter, rational choice analysis is not an alternative to scientific research, although some of its most passionate advocates sometimes imply that it is. Rational choice is best understood as a way to generate hypotheses using a well-developed theoretical foundation from economic reasoning. Since some form of rational choice analysis is now used in a large proportion of published political science articles, it is appropriate to include this topic (along with a particularly good illustration of it) in a book on research methods.

This edition contains excerpts exclusively from articles published in the *American Political Science Review* and the *American Journal of Political Science*. There are many other good political science journals, of course, but these two are commonly considered among the very best, and they also are known for their consistent emphasis on empirical inquiry. Although most of the articles excerpted are quite recent, I have included one from 1975 (Fred Greenstein's study of the political attitudes of children in several countries). This study remains an excellent illustration of univariate analysis, and students and instructors report that it deals with a fascinating and timely subject. Accessibility and clarity were the most important factors in selecting all the articles for the excerpts.

Several persons must be acknowledged as having contributed to the work on this book. William A. Boyd played a very special role, contributing a great deal to the planning and overall direction of the first edition. He also helped me to see that, above all, political science can be enormously entertaining. I also owe a great debt to Richard Kendrick, a methodologist in sociology whose spirited debates with me have ensured that I will never become complacent regarding my views about political life.

Irving Rockwood, currently a journal editor, helped to shape the first two editions, and his advice and encouragement resonate in this new one. My editors at M.E. Sharpe brought their experience and judgment to the planning, execution, and revision of this book, ensuring that it will be accessible and useful to students and instructors.

Finally, my wife, Judy, continues to be a source of support, encouragement, and companionship, the importance of which cannot be stated in a few words.

My daughter, who made no contribution at all, receives the dedication simply for being herself.

Marcus E. Ethridge
Milwaukee, Wisconsin

The Political Research Experience

Third Edition

1   Introduction: A Science of Politics

V.O. Key, Jr., one of the most renowned of all American political scientists, made the following assessment in his Presidential Address to the American Political Science Association in 1958:

> The burden of my argument may be stated briefly and bluntly. It is that the demands upon our profession have grown more rapidly than has the content of our discipline. We are, in a sense, the victims of our own success. The achievements of our profession arouse expectations that our discipline enables us to meet only imperfectly. If we are to narrow the gap between our knowledge and our responsibilities, we must devote greater resources in manpower and ingenuity to the systematic analysis of the phenomena of politics. (Key 1958, p. 961)

Most political scientists would agree that this statement applies today, nearly half a century later. Much has been learned from political research. New ideas and research techniques have been adopted, while others have been discarded. New sources of data have become available. Technological advances, particularly the personal computer and the Internet, have made some tasks in political science research more efficient and findings more easily disseminated. As a result, many politicians, journalists, and citizens expect a great deal from political science research.

And yet, most modern assessments still find that political science is a discipline that has not reached its promise. Political scientists hope to predict election results, give informed opinions on the chances for violent ethnic conflict in troubled regions, and explain the formation and breakup of important international alliances. With respect to these goals, the discipline has had only limited success.

Despite its incomplete achievements, political research is widely seen as a valuable undertaking. Many political scientists are motivated by a desire to contribute to the betterment of humankind. Sometimes the impetus for research is an intense curiosity about a specific political problem. In other cases, political inquiry is driven by a concern about ethical or moral values. Of course, political research is also carried out for personal gain, as when a candidate surveys his or her image among registered voters or when a multinational corporation hires a consultant to assess the political stability of a country selected as a potential site for a major new manufacturing facility. Common to all these efforts is an underlying belief that the information produced by scientific political research is worthwhile, that it has tangible value.

And so it does. Over the past several decades, the results of political science research have proven useful in a variety of settings. Political science research has played an important role in landmark judicial opinions, such as *Brown v. Board of Education of Topeka, Kansas*. Thanks to the work of political researchers, we have greatly expanded our understanding of the relative fairness of different voting and electoral systems and their impact on voters, parties, and government responsiveness.

Today, we are in an era of rapid political change. Although some developments have underscored the validity of the conclusions advanced by political research, other recent events have challenged well-established assumptions shared by generations of political scientists. Within the last two decades, we have witnessed the fall of the Berlin Wall, the decline of communism in the former Soviet Union and in most of eastern Europe, the end of apartheid in South Africa, and the rejection of military governments in much of Latin America. We have also seen the rise of intense ethnic conflicts in eastern Europe and Africa, and the persistence of uneven economic development around the world. In the United States, we have seen the president's party actually gain seats in the House of Representatives during a midterm election (1998), a phenomenon that had not occurred since 1934. Few political scientists accurately predicted this outcome.

These incidents and developments raise important doubts about how well we understand democratic government, the role of public policy in encouraging economic growth, the usefulness of competitive party systems, the permanence of totalitarianism, and many other fundamental political issues. Consequently, political scientists have begun a serious re-examination of some important ideas, highlighting the need for new scientific approaches. What appears to many of us to be a genuine worldwide explosion of democracy may be the beginning of a new age of reason and cooperation, or it could be a brief interlude before the world descends into increasingly violent ethnic and nationalist conflict, all too horribly exemplified by events in the former Yugoslavia and in central Africa. While pundits, journalists, and philosophers will surely contribute to our understanding of these events, they call for systematic political inquiry as well. According to a leading scholar, political science has a special responsibility to "enlighten the world about the current crisis of authoritarianism" (Pye 1990, p. 16). If we are to make sense of the dramatic and hopeful revolutionary changes that are now upon us, our most valuable tool is likely to be scientific political research.

Scientific Thinking and Politics

Most thinking about politics is not "scientific." Rather, we usually guess at the answers to political questions—Who will win the election? Will Ethiopia attain political stability?—using arguments or facts we happen upon. Of course, our thinking about politics and government is not the only area of human inquiry that has been unscientific. At least initially, we humans approach virtually everything we want to know about in a pre-scientific way, largely because real science demands a great deal of detailed work. Casual guessing is, in contrast, rather easy.

To appreciate the importance of a genuinely scientific approach to research, it is useful to consider how a very harmful, and ultimately wrong, conclusion in a very different field became widely accepted through prescientific analysis. Beginning as early as 1430, physicians in Europe and elsewhere believed that they could cure patients with high fevers by "bleeding" them. They accepted the conclusion because a plausible argument about it "made sense" to them and because casual observation seemed to confirm it.

Where did the idea of bleeding patients come from? When faced with patients with raging temperatures, some of whom died, many of these early physicians thought that reducing the amount of hot fluid in their patients' bodies would relieve the symptoms and prolong their lives. As "bleeding" therapy continued into the 1800s, some physicians' faith in the practice was probably reinforced by their observation of steam engines, which often broke down when excess heat could not escape. By the same logic, a feverish patient should be expected to cool down with the loss of a few pints of blood.

Many physicians acted on this entirely reasonable-sounding idea. And, after the treatment, many of their patients actually recovered from their illnesses. Because the logic of the idea was so compelling, it was natural that many physicians then attributed the recovery of their patients to the controlled loss of blood. Physicians were usually powerless at that time, desperately searching for steps they could take to save patients. The concept of "bleeding" was based on a straightforward, logical idea, and, in many cases in which it was applied, the patients got better. It is not difficult to see how the idea was quickly accepted.

How would a scientist evaluate the argument that bleeding cures fevers? Most important, the scientist would emphasize the need to control for other possible causes of the patients' recovery and the need for careful measurement. We now know that patients who recovered from their fevers during earlier times would have recovered without the bleeding treatment, and many of them would probably have recovered faster without it. According to many historians, George Washington actually died as a consequence of the bleeding administered by his physicians, rather than as a result of his final illness. If the physicians at that time had devised a controlled experiment, with a large number of feverish patients randomly assigned to two groups, one that would be given the treatment and another group that would not receive it, they would have discovered that the same percentage of patients recovered in both groups, indicating that the bleeding made no difference. Careful measurement would perhaps have revealed that the patients without the blood loss recovered somewhat faster. The absence of scientific method permitted the acceptance of a false conclusion, simply because it was (a) plausible and (b) appeared to be supported by a few cases.

It is arguable that at least some parts of the discipline of political science are as primitive, in scientific terms, as medicine was in 1795. We have accumulated some genuine knowledge, to be sure, but there are many, many instances in which researchers have accepted conclusions simply because they were based on plausible arguments that were apparently "proven" by unsystematic observations without controls.

During the 1996 U.S. elections, one widely respected journalist concluded that "the results of this election indicate that Americans simply want divided government." The conclusion made sense to her because she had spoken with some people who said that they wanted the president to act as a check on the Congress and who also thought that the White House would "go too far" if the Congress was in the hands of the same party. She also noted that some opinion polls found that a large majority of voters was concerned about extremists in both parties. Armed with these casual, but entirely reasonable bits of information, she concluded that the election results (which left both houses of Congress with a Republican majority and a Democrat in the White House) were *caused* by a general public preference for divided government.

Just as in the medical example, genuinely scientific research on this question would have to begin by exploring other explanations for the election results. A few obvious possibilities include the incumbency advantage (the fact that it is difficult for challengers to unseat candidates running for re-election), the poor campaigning skills of the Republican presidential candidate, and the general tendency of voters to stick with the status quo in good economic times. There were doubtlessly some voters who explicitly wanted a divided government to result from the election, but attributing the election outcome to this preference was not an example of scientific political thinking.

It is not only haphazard fact gathering and casual thinking that can produce lapses of scientific rigor, however. In many cases, the researcher's conclusions about moral or social values can displace his or her objectivity. Value questions are **normative** questions. Should government protect our privacy? Does government have an obligation to provide free medical care? These are questions that have not one but many answers depending on the views and values of the person responding. Science can give us information that can be helpful in making our value judgments about these kinds of questions, but it cannot settle normative questions directly. Yet, some analysts allow their convictions about normative values to affect their judgments about measuring variables, selecting cases, and other parts of the scientific process, leading to inaccurate conclusions.

Scientific thinking about politics is a special kind of political thinking. It is different from the offhand guesses that most of us engage in, and it is also different from purely normative analysis, no matter how sophisticated or well informed. Scientific thinking about politics is based on the principles used in scientific research. Science is best understood as a process in which reasoned propositions about the world are formulated, precisely stated, and then tested through empirical observation. Scientific thinking differs from our pre-scientific guesses in that it is systematic and thorough; it differs from normative analysis in its emphasis on **empirical** observation, its focus on what is, rather than on what ought to be. Political research based on such thinking is **scientific political research**.

Distinguishing Features of Scientific Political Research

Three distinguishing characteristics of scientific political research are **objectivity, verifiability**, and **quantification**. Scientific research is objective in that its methods are designed to produce results that are unaffected by the prejudices of the researcher. Results can be interpreted very differently, of course, but the results themselves should be a reflection of actual conditions, characteristics, or behaviors as observed by any careful researcher. If one researcher finds that states with competitive party systems spend more on welfare than other states, other researchers should be able to obtain the same result by studying the same data. In contrast, normative political analysis is inherently subjective; the values, opinions, and beliefs of each analyst become an intrinsic part of the analysis itself.

Scientific political research is also verifiable in that it is based on propositions that are supported by observable facts. The verifiability of findings from empirical research makes progress in our understanding of politics possible; inaccurate suppositions are discarded as they are disproved by observation. Verifiability is particularly crucial when our objective is to identify and explain a **causal relationship**. For this reason, we must be certain that we state propositions clearly and that they are falsifiable or capable of being disproved. Verifiability requires that empirical research focus on statements that are either true or false and which, if false, can be shown to be so by empirical evidence.

The third characteristic of scientific research is quantification. Unlike objectivity and verifiability, quantification is not an intrinsic part of science, but it is usually a characteristic of scientific research because of what it allows scientists to do. Many research questions involve comparisons of the magnitude of certain qualities or conditions or the frequency of certain behaviors. We want to know how voter turnout changes over time or varies with social class; the differences, if any, in the political attitudes and opinions held by different ethnic groups; and how levels of military preparedness vary from one country to another. The point is that we are normally not interested in simple yes or no questions ("Do poor people feel that the government is not responsive to their needs?") but in questions that have to do with how much or how much more (or less) ("Do fewer poor people than rich people believe that government is responsive?").

Quantification is also common in scientific political research because it facilitates the use of powerful statistical tools that can significantly enhance our understanding of politics. If we are interested in knowing the extent of a particular candidate's support within a particular district, for example, one way to determine this would be by talking with passers-by in a local mall or by reading the local newspaper. While this could prove somewhat valuable, we could make far more meaningful comparisons of the candidate's support over time and across different income and ethnic groups by employing modern survey research techniques featuring carefully designed questionnaires and scientifically constructed samples. Similarly, by employing such techniques for slightly different purposes, researchers are able to construct and test increasingly sophisticated models of the influences that shape public opinion, thus greatly extending our knowledge of politics. Quantification makes it possible for us to employ statistical techniques such as correlation, regression, and other measures of association that in turn facilitate more meaningful and precise findings than would otherwise be possible.

As we will discuss at greater length in the concluding chapter, these three distinguishing characteristics of the scientific study of politics—objectivity, verifiability, and quantification—are a continuing source of controversy. A common criticism is that the claim of objectivity is merely a cloak beneath which the researcher's biases, both conscious and unconscious, are hidden. Another complaint is that an emphasis on quantification leads to oversimplification and distortion of the concepts under study. In general, critics of scientific political research claim that politics is so complex and so intrinsically related to fundamental values that any effort to apply scientific methods ultimately produces nothing but confusion or unimportant truths. However, most political scientists feel that these problems are not insurmountable. They are issues of which we must be aware, but they do not make useful research impossible.

An Overview of the Research Process

Scientific political research is often designed to do more than simply describe facts. While it can help us determine, for example, whether some states adopted certain progressive policies before other states adopted them, such information is of limited value. We also need to know *why* this is true. When scientific research attempts to identify the underlying causes of observed facts or relationships, it moves from the descriptive to the analytical or explanatory.

Science is ultimately an attempt to explain: Its objective is to find out why something happens, not merely to describe what happens or measure its magnitude. Thus, while much scientific work involves observation and measurement, real scientific progress occurs when our findings are connected to larger theoretical questions about politics.

The Role of Theory

Theory has been defined as "a collection of interrelated, warranted assertions about something . . . [in which] at least two (and usually more) fairly abstract concepts are related to each other through a series of lawlike statements" (Leege and Francis 1974, p. 4). When researchers offer an explanation of some political phenomenon, that explanation often takes the form of a discussion of how their findings confirm, disprove, or amend theory. It is through the development of theory that science seeks to explain things.

Using our general understanding of politics, economics, and perhaps a bit of folk psychology, most of us could construct a preliminary theory of voter turnout. Our first step would probably be to list the factors we believe influence a person's decision to vote. Our second would be to attempt to identify and describe the significant relationships among those factors. The result would be a theory of voting behavior complete with a list of **variables** and lawlike statements linking them. While necessarily less sophisticated than the theories we might find in the literature on voting behavior, our "theory" would nonetheless possess the same basic attributes as its more sophisticated counterparts. It would also share with them the same basic purpose—to explain.

Of course, all theories are not created equal. One of the essential characteristics of a good theory is that its predictions must be clear and unambiguous. A vague theory, which can be reconstructed or interpreted so it always "explains" facts that appear to disprove it, is useless. As Abraham Kaplan explains, such a theory will tell "us nothing whatever about the world for it remains true no matter what is the case in the world" (Kaplan 1998 [1964], p. 100). As discussed above, scientific research must focus on statements which, in principle, are either true or false but not both.

Kaplan's point has to do with **hypothesis testing**. On the basis of theory, we are able to form a **hypothesis** about how one variable affects another, or how some condition leads to some effect. Empirical research involves the use of data to test the accuracy of our hypothesis. If the gathered data cannot lead us to accept or reject the hypothesis, then the hypothesis cannot be tested, and our understanding is not enhanced.

Consider, for example, the case of a therapist who, applying Freudian theory, diagnoses a disturbed boy as suffering from an Oedipal complex (a romantic attachment to his mother) and predicts the boy will attempt to kill or injure his father out of jealousy. The therapist then discovers that the boy is especially kind to his father. Instead of concluding that his prediction was false and that his diagnosis was not supported by the evidence, he then defends his original diagnosis by finding a way to "fit" the facts. He now explains that the boy's Oedipal complex, instead of leading him to commit patricide, has forced him to deny his feelings of jealousy by acting in an exemplary manner toward his father—thus allowing him to avoid confronting the awful fact of his love for his mother.

The net effect of this type of thinking is to make any hypothesis that we might construct about the boy's behavior nonverifiable. If the boy kills his father, it is because he is Oedipal. If he is kind to his father, it is because he is Oedipal. Facts about the boy's actual behavior cannot verify or refute the possibility that he has an Oedipal complex. He may or may not suffer from this malady, but research into his behavior was useless in finding out because the theory was constructed in a way that it appeared to explain whatever happened. Unfortunately, this problem of unscientific theory construction is not restricted to attempts to employ Freudian analysis.

Just prior to the Persian Gulf War (1991), some political analysts predicted that the United States and its allies would suffer 20,000 to 40,000 deaths and many other casualties. The prediction was based on the idea that the Iraqis would be fighting on their homeland with a defensive posture. When the war was over, and the Allied casualties were extraordinarily minimal, proponents of this prediction argued that they were still correct and that the result was a matter of U.S. advances in technology.

The point here is that the original prediction was not very helpful in scientific terms because the facts regarding the outcome were irrelevant to whether the proposition underlying the prediction was accepted as valid. As in the Freudian example, the analysts went on thoroughly believing in their notion that armies defending their homeland enjoy a tremendous military advantage, unperturbed by the facts in this case. The idea may or may not be accurate, but its scientific basis was not advanced by the "test" of the prediction.

Another important test of a good theory is its **generalizability**. Findings that apply to a single case are often a very useful beginning point that can suggest a great deal to us about the theoretical notions under consideration. Normally, however, the value of a theory is a function of its generality.

Analysis of voting behavior nicely illustrates the value of generalized theory construction. Political observers have long recognized that Republican candidates are more popular with voters in New Hampshire than in Massachusetts. This fact is interesting, and it is certainly useful when making election predictions in these two states. In and of itself, however, it is of little value in explaining voting behavior in general. If, however, we were to investigate further and to find that certain basic factors—say population density and industrialization—account for these states' differences in voting behavior, we would have increased the generality and the value of our results. Now our findings could be used to help us account for voting behavior not only in Massachusetts and New Hampshire, but in other states and at other times. By increasing the generalizability of our findings, we would have also enhanced the value of their contribution to theory.

Of course, theories vary in the extent of their generalizability. Our findings about the effects of population density and industrialization on partisan voting behavior in New Hampshire and Massachusetts, for example, might be relevant to an explanation of voting behavior in the United States but not to a general theory of voting behavior that applies to voters throughout the world. This is perfectly acceptable. While the ultimate aim of political science is to formulate a general theory of politics that would apply to all societies, most of our theories are far less general in scope. Nonetheless, they remain theoretical because they contain lawlike statements that identify and describe relationships between two or more concepts across some specified range of cases.

Theories do not simply appear spontaneously to the researcher. The theorizing that precedes the data gathering and analysis stages of scientific research consists of three important elements. First, the researcher must consider the problem in conceptual terms, identifying which of the dozens of events, influences, behaviors, etc., will be of theoretical importance. Second, he or she must develop operational measures for the key concepts to be studied and construct pertinent hypotheses. Finally, the research design must address the issue of causation.

Conceptualization

When we identify the basic elements that will be put together to form a theory, we are engaging in **conceptualization**. Political events and processes involve highly complex arrays of behaviors on the part of many people and institutions. A revolution, for example, comprises a wide range of actions and reactions, constraints, incentives, and consequences. Before anyone can construct a theory about the phenomenon we call "revolution," he or she must first identify which of the many behaviors, events, and factors surrounding the revolution were important. The journalist will simply report the facts (we hope); the scientist must determine which facts are of theoretical relevance.

Samuel Huntington's classic work on political instability in developing nations remains influential and controversial, and it is an excellent example of how a political scientist considers events in conceptual terms (Huntington 1968). We are always hearing of violent uprisings in troubled parts of the world, where one military leader gains or loses control of a toppled government, buildings are bombed, and people are killed. These governments seem never to get anything done, and violence appears a permanent feature of their citizens' lives. Huntington looked at these dismal conditions at a conceptual level rather than as unique incidents. In other words, he developed concepts that allowed him to classify what would otherwise be unique events and conditions. After looking at several dozen incidents of riots, property damage, and unscheduled changes in government, he worked to identify basic factors that might explain the causes of instability: How rapidly have the citizens become politically active? How old, or "institutionalized," is the government? Does political participation take place inside or outside official channels? Conceptualization involves extracting the basic elements that we think are involved in scientific explanation. Otherwise, we simply describe facts and end up with no theory at all.

Hypothesis Construction and Operationalization

Political research usually begins with a "hunch," an educated guess that some phenomenon is caused by some other phenomenon. Before we can analyze the idea scientifically, however, we must first delineate precisely the nature of our hunch, and we must decide how we are going to measure what we observe.

The first step in that process is **hypothesis construction**. Hypothesis construction is the translation of theories into testable propositions. The objective of scientific research is to determine if the hypothesis logically derived from our theory can be confirmed by observation. If so, our research findings will have supported our theory. If not, if our observations are inconsistent with our hypothesis, our theory will have to be revised or rejected.

In constructing a testable hypothesis, one of our first tasks is to translate the concepts that we have identified into variables for which we can devise a measurable **indicator**. Variables, as the name implies, are characteristics that vary. We can define them as characteristics that take on different values over time or across cases. Any characteristic that varies can become a variable. Size, shape, color, level of income, and standardized test scores are all examples of potential variables. Indicators are observable, measurable forms of variables.

The process of translation from concept to variable to indicator is known as **operationalization**. Consider the following hypothesis: "Republicans vote more regularly than Democrats." While this is a relatively straightforward hypothesis, it is not yet ready for testing. Consider what would happen if ten students were told to interview 100 randomly selected citizens, and, on the basis of the interview results, attempt to determine whether the hypothesis is accurate. Each student would have to decide how to tell if a person is a Republican or a Democrat and how to measure the regularity of voting. Some students would probably devise better methods than others, but, more importantly, the methods would be different. These different measurement strategies would lead to different results.

Researchers attempt to avoid this problem through careful and explicit operationalization procedures. A researcher confronted with the need to identify Democrats and Republicans, as in the above example, might use a simple multiple-choice item on a questionnaire, asking each respondent to select one of five possible responses: strong Democrat, weak Democrat, Independent, weak Republican, or strong Republican. (Questions of this type are commonly called **forced response items**.) By proceeding in this fashion, and describing the procedures used in the final report, our researcher would not only gather useful data, but would also make it possible for other researchers to duplicate his or her study at a later date.

More specifically, a good operational definition of a concept possesses two crucial qualities: **validity** and **reliability**. A valid measurement faithfully measures the concept it is meant to measure. The importance of validity can readily be seen in the controversy over intelligence testing. Critics claim that the tests involved do not really measure intelligence but, rather, something else, primarily how well a person has absorbed a particular set of cultural norms and values. Similarly, one could argue that the level of political participation in a country (a concept) cannot be fairly operationalized by measuring the level of voter turnout (an indicator) because such an indicator excludes other forms of participation. In such cases, the validity of a given operational definition is being challenged.

Reliability is equally important. An indicator is reliable if it produces consistent or dependable data. Put another way, reliable indicators are indicators that produce equivalent scores for equivalent cases. Reliability is low when a given measure works differently in different cultural contexts or at different times. For example, cross-national measures of per capita income may be seriously unreliable if they are based entirely on wage and salary figures. Such measures can work well in industrialized countries, but not in pre-industrial settings where significant proportions of people's personal income is derived from barter. If, therefore, we were to measure per capita income across both types of cultures by relying exclusively upon wage and salary figures, we would seriously underestimate personal income in some countries. Comparisons of the resulting figures across countries would not reveal the actual income differences. In short, our results would be unreliable.

The Special Problem of Causation

Confirming the existence of causal relationships is the ultimate objective of scientific research. This is a most difficult task. Nonetheless, there are ways in which the skilled researcher can maximize his or her ability to confirm the existence of causal relationships. In general, these involve the researcher's plan of attack, or **research design**, a concept that we will discuss in more detail in chapter 2.

In scientific research, a causal relationship involves two or more variables. There are two important types of variables in a causal relationship, independent and dependent. An **independent variable** is a factor or characteristic that causes changes in some other factor(s) or characteristic(s) under study. A **dependent variable** is a factor or characteristic that the independent variable presumably affects. To put it another way, the independent variable is the variable whose value is expected to influence (in whole or in part) the value of the dependent variable. Thus, if we were to hypothesize that a worker's salary level is determined by the level of his or her education, our independent variable would be the worker's level of education, and our dependent variable would be his or her salary.

Generally speaking, we can demonstrate **causation** if we can show that (a) the changes in the independent variable precede the predicted changes in the dependent variable; (b) the changes in the dependent variable are related in some nonrandom way to, or are associated with, the changes in the independent variable; and (c) no other independent variables are responsible for the observed changes in the dependent variable.

Meeting the first two of these requirements is relatively easy in most political research. Meeting the third is often profoundly difficult.

Consider, for example, a study of politically active citizens, all of whom have recently joined one or more political organizations and also display high feelings of political efficacy. (People with high feelings of political efficacy are people who have confidence in their own ability to understand and participate effectively in political affairs.) Observing such people, we might be tempted to conclude that joining a political organization leads to high feelings of political efficacy, in which case our independent variable would be the act of joining a political organization, and our dependent variable would be the level of political efficacy. Without further evidence, however, it would be equally plausible to assert the reverse, that a high level of political efficacy leads to joining a political organization. Clearly then, it is crucial to establish the sequence of events before we can be certain we have discovered a causal relationship.

Once we have established that changes in the independent variable occur prior to changes in the dependent variable, we can use relatively straightforward statistical procedures to determine whether the observed changes in our two variables are associated in some way. If, for example, we find that subjects in our study with high scores on the independent variable also have high scores on the dependent variable, we have discovered a **positive relationship**. If high scores on the independent variable are associated with low scores on the dependent variable, we have a **negative relationship**.

Of course, we also may discover that there is no apparent relationship between our two variables. If, for example, we find that the dependent variable scores for those cases scoring highest on our independent variable are about the same as the dependent variable scores of all other cases, we would be likely to conclude there is no relationship at all between the two variables.

It is important to meet all three of the criteria for causality before claiming to have discovered a causal relationship. Many studies have shown that people who are heavy smokers (the independent variable) have a high incidence of lung cancer (the dependent variable). As long as we can be certain that the smoking behavior normally occurs before the lung cancer develops, we have satisfied two of the three requirements for demonstrating causality.

As the Tobacco Institute is fond of reminding us, however, the discovery of a strong relationship between changes in the independent variable (level of smoking) and changes in the dependent variable (incidence of lung cancer) is not sufficient to establish causation, even when the changes in the independent variable clearly precede changes in the dependent variable. The association may be a **spurious relationship**.

A spurious relationship is one caused by some variable other than the independent variable (or variables) we have observed and measured. It is, in other words, always possible that a third variable (or variables) may be responsible for the changes we observe in both the independent and dependent variables. For example, insurance statistics regularly indicate that owners of Buick sedans have very few accidents. We might conclude from this that Buicks are inherently safer than other cars, that owning a Buick *causes* the low accident rate observed among Buick owners. General Motors could hardly be blamed for wanting us to think so.

However, after a moment's reflection, most of us might rightly suspect that the low accident rate is actually attributable to another variable—the driving habits of those who purchase different types of cars. After all, how likely is it that drivers with aggressive or dangerous driving habits will be attracted to Buick sedans? Thus, we might conclude that it is the varying safety-consciousness of the drivers involved (a third variable) that leads *both* to Buick ownership and to the driving habits that produce lower accident rates. The relationship between the car itself and the accident rate is apparent rather than real; in other words, it is spurious.

As we shall discuss at greater length in chapter 2, the task of ruling out spurious relationships is best dealt with at the research design stage. Good research designs deal with this problem in one of two ways. The first, **experimental design**, involves the creation of two comparable groups—an experimental and a control—to equalize any extraneous influences and thereby eliminate the possibility that something other than the independent variable is responsible for any observed changes in the dependent variable. Such designs are unfortunately uncommon in political research because of the difficulties encountered in controlling the wide range of influences on political behavior. The second, and far more common approach, is a **quasi-experimental design** that simulates experimentation either by gathering additional data or employing statistical methods to help the researcher control for spurious influences. Effectively employed, either approach makes it possible to identify the proportion of variation in a dependent variable that can be attributed to changes in the independent variable.

In the best political science research, careful and informed theorizing guides each of these steps. Skilled researchers do not determine which concepts to study or how to measure variables by whim or convenience, but by continuing attention to what makes sense in terms of the body of theory that they are trying to advance. Conceptualization, hypothesis construction and operationalization, and analysis of causation are thus basic elements in the process of scientific theorizing. After these steps are complete, the researcher is faced with problems having to do with observation and data analysis.

Data Collection

Useful data can be collected in a variety of ways. The most common sources are (a) questionnaires, (b) documents such as voting records, census data, and almanacs, and (c) content analysis.

Data collection strategies must be tailored to the problem at hand. Research questions concerning public opinion almost always involve survey research (chapter 5). Content analysis (chapter 7) employs detailed coding rules, and usually a panel of several coders, to convert written documents (newspaper stories, press releases, official speeches) into quantitative data.

Fortunately, there are several useful and easily available sources of data for political research, particularly public opinion surveys and census information. Other types of data that are readily available from official sources include voting results, data on per capita income, literacy rates, ethnic diversity figures, and many other such commonly studied socio-economic variables. However, some research projects call for a creative data collection strategy: for example, an attempt to measure the extent to which evening newscasts damage the popularity of the president (see chapter 7).

Sampling

In most instances, it is not practical for the researcher to study the entire **population** or **universe** of possible cases. Thus, the next step in the research process is to select the cases or subjects to be studied. This step is called **sampling**.

The idea of sampling is to limit the number of subjects for study to manageable proportions while ensuring that the results present a reasonably accurate picture of the population or universe in which we are interested. This is often accomplished by drawing a random sample from the larger set of cases being studied, but other types of samples are commonly employed as well, depending on the circumstances.

Measurement

Political data comes in many forms. One of the important ways in which data varies from study to study is the level of measurement employed. There are four basic levels of measurement in social science research—nominal, ordinal, interval, and ratio.

Nominal measurement is the simplest, or lowest, level of measurement. Nominal measures are measures that involve placing cases in specific categories, for example, a respondent's ethnic identity.

The next level of measurement is ordinal. **Ordinal measurement** involves ranking cases on some criterion. This level of measurement enables us to say that one case or subject is more conservative, unstable, disadvantaged, innovative, or has more or less of some other quality than another case. A great deal of political research makes use of ordinal measurement.

The two most precise levels of measurement are interval and ratio. **Interval measurement** is measurement that makes it possible to determine how much more of a given quality or characteristic one case has in comparison with another. Income is an example of a variable that can be measured at the interval level. If we know that Sally makes $40,000 a year and John makes $30,000, we not only know that Sally makes more than John, we know how much more—$10,000.

Finally, the highest level of measurement is **ratio measurement**. Ratio measures are interval measures that have a meaningful zero point, a point at which it can be said that none of the quality being measured exists. The distinction between interval and ratio measures is sometimes difficult to grasp. Temperature, for example, is an interval rather than a ratio measure. Even though most thermometers have a zero point, zero degrees does not indicate "no temperature." Age, on the other hand, can be measured at the ratio level since an age of zero does, in fact, mean no age. Fortunately, this difference is rarely of practical importance in political research.

Analysis

Following the collection and measurement of data comes the last major step in the research process, analysis. If a sufficient number of cases have been actually measured or observed, and if there is sufficient variation among them to make analysis possible, the researcher can proceed with hypothesis testing.

Much hypothesis testing in political research involves the use of **measures of association**, statistical techniques used to determine whether changes in one variable are in any way related to changes in another. As we shall see in later chapters, political researchers employ measures of association to determine such things as whether the frequency of voting increases as income increases, or whether a larger number of major political parties is in any way associated with political instability. Once the data have been analyzed, the resulting findings may be put to a variety of uses. At the very least, they should help the researcher either to confirm or reject his or her original hypotheses. In many instances, the researcher will interpret the findings further in terms of their implications for the theories from which the original hypotheses were derived. Finally, they may also be suggestive about policy choices facing political leaders.

The process of political research is fraught with opportunities for error. Vague hypotheses, invalid or unreliable operational definitions, unrepresentative samples, the application of analytic techniques inappropriate to the level of the data collected, and misinterpretation of results are just some of the potential pitfalls. Effective research designs help us to avoid these problems. The studies included in this volume were selected because they illustrate how careful attention to these potential problems can lead to research that is interesting and helpful in understanding political life.

A Checklist for Evaluating Political Research

There are several items to be considered when evaluating any piece of political science research. Some of these items are of greater or lesser importance in a given case, but each should be appraised in determining the soundness and the persuasiveness of a research project:

1. What are the study's hypotheses?
   - Are they verifiable?
   - Are they clear?
   - Are they generalizable?
   - How do they relate to a theory of political behavior?

2. What are the key variables in the hypotheses?
   - How are they operationalized?
   - Are the measures likely to be valid and reliable?

3. Did the research design properly specify how it would measure relationships among independent and dependent variables? Did it address the possibility of spurious relationships?

4. How did the researcher gather data?
   - Are the sources accurate?

5. If the study analyzes a sample, how was the sample selected?
   - Was it representative of the population in which we are interested?

6. What analytic method was employed?
   - Was it appropriate for the data and the research design?
   - Did it enable us to test the hypotheses?

The Purpose of This Book

The purpose of this book is to help you learn the basics of political research and to become a more informed consumer of other people's research.

To these ends, most of the chapters in this text—with the exception of this one and the concluding chapter—feature excerpts from published research articles accompanied by introductory and concluding essays. The purpose of these essays is to help you identify and appreciate the critical choices made by the researchers involved. Thus, the focus of this text is very much on political research as it is actually practiced.

The text is divided into several sections that correspond to the basic steps in the research process as described above. Chapter 2 examines research design and experimentation. Although political scientists rarely use actual experiments, the basic logic of research design is based on the principles of sound experimentation. The next two chapters cover measurement and operationalization (with separate chapters devoted to variables pertaining to individuals and variables pertaining to states or countries). After deciding how to measure concepts, the next step is gathering the data. Thus, the following chapters cover surveys, indexing, content analysis, and sampling. Although it is not an alternative to scientific research, rational choice analysis has become a centrally important part of political science, and chapter 9 is devoted to exploring its place in the discipline. Techniques for measuring association among variables are covered in chapters 10, 11, and 12. The final chapter addresses some basic and long-standing controversies surrounding the research process itself, including the issue of ethics in political research.

All of the excerpts included in the text are examples of high quality research. This should not be taken to mean that the editor believes each of them to be the very best piece of research available in its respective field, a judgment that would be hazardous in any case. Nor do they constitute a representative sample of research from all the major subfields of political science. Rather, each piece was selected for a combination of its overall quality, relevance to a particular topic, and accessibility. Insofar as possible, every attempt was made to select excerpts that are not only substantively interesting, but deal with issues that nonspecialist readers will be able to grasp and appreciate.

I hope that these excerpts and the accompanying discussions will stimulate your interest in and appreciation of political research. Each of the excerpts provides information which, if not the final word on the issues addressed, can help to make our views of political issues and problems more informed and useful. This is the ultimate objective of political science: not to replace political judgment or eliminate the need for discussion of political issues, but to make those judgments and discussions more informed, realistic, and meaningful.

2 The Logic of Research Design: Experiments and Quasi-Experiments

While some political inquiry is designed to identify opportunities for future research, or simply to gather data or design a measure, the most ambitious political research seeks to *explain* something. Such research involves the construction and testing of hypotheses via carefully established procedures, as discussed in chapter 1. Our focus here, and throughout most of this book, will be on this type of research.

After we determine what question or hypothesis we want to investigate, and after we design operational measures for the variables under study, we must devise a suitable plan of attack. That plan constitutes our research design.

There are many different types of research designs, each with a nearly infinite number of variations. Research designs are custom-made rather than mass-produced, and we will rarely find two that are identical. Further, each basic type of research design has its own distinctive strengths, weaknesses, and requirements. Some types of research designs are well suited only to particular types of research. When choosing a research design, our first task is to ensure that our research design matches our purposes.

Good research design follows the logic of **experimentation.** In fact, most of us think of experimentation whenever we think of science and scientists. True experiments involve carefully controlled observation of subjects that have been subjected to precisely measured effects. A well-designed experiment enables the scientist to isolate the impact of each independent variable, leading to useful conclusions. Experimental research provides us with a straightforward, effective way to determine the effect of one variable on another. When our purpose is to explain, experimentation is the ideal research strategy.

Unfortunately, most political behavior is difficult to study through experimentation. Experimental manipulation of the independent variables involved in political research is usually impractical, if not unethical or even illegal. We would not, for instance, want to allow researchers forcibly to remove a random sample of U.S. citizens to another country in order to study the impact of isolation from family on their political attitudes. We cannot deny the vote to a segment of citizens to see how the elimination of this basic political right affects the development of public opinion. Hence, most political research involves an effort to observe and analyze influences that cannot be controlled by the researcher.

But if true experimentation is seldom feasible in political research, its underlying logic exerts a powerful influence on the design of such research. It is the logic of experimentation that guides our choice of research design when studying politics, particularly when our purpose is to explain. The logic of experimentation represents, therefore, an ideal we seek to approximate when seeking answers to questions that preclude true experimentation. The fact that political research must often deviate from this ideal in no way diminishes its importance to the study of politics. Rather, the scientific study of politics requires a thorough mastery of the basic principles of experimentation. These are the principles that must guide us when designing the research we are able to undertake.

Experimental Designs

As we noted in chapter 1, one of the major hurdles researchers face when attempting to establish causation is the problem of spurious relationships. These are apparent relationships between independent and dependent variables that are actually caused by other variables not included in the study. For example, if we consider state party competition and state spending on education, we will find that these two factors are strongly correlated; the states with strong party competition spend more on education than states in which one party dominates state politics. Some analysts may be tempted to conclude, on the basis of this relationship between party competition and education spending, that the differences in party competition actually *cause* differences in state education spending. However, a more complete study will show that another variable, state per capita income, strongly influences both party competition *and* education spending. For states with a given level of per capita income, differences in party competition have virtually no effect on differences in state education spending. Research designs that do not anticipate and control for such relationships will produce untrustworthy results, leading us to believe that a variable explains something when it really does not.

Control Groups

The true experiment is the classic solution to the problem of spurious relationships. Experimental designs enable researchers to rule out spurious relationships as the cause of observed changes by making it possible for them to control the subjects' exposure not only to the independent variable, but also to any other variables that could account for any observed changes in the dependent variable. Under optimal circumstances, an experimental design thus controls for all potential spurious relationships (including those not anticipated by the researcher).

The key to controlling for spurious relationships is the proper use of a **control group.** Control groups enable the researcher to compare changes in a group of subjects that are exposed to the independent variable (the experimental group) to those observed in an otherwise identical set of subjects *not* exposed to the independent variable (the control group). It is, of course, essential that the two groups be equivalent in all important respects. This is usually achieved by randomly assigning subjects to the two groups.

The basic principle of experimental design is to structure the experiment so that factors other than the independent variable that could produce a measurable effect in the dependent variable(s) will equally affect the experimental and control groups. Any observed differences between the groups can then be logically attributable exclusively to the independent variable(s).

Sources of Erroneous Experimental Findings

Two of the most important potential sources of spurious relationships are **history** and **maturation effects.** History effects are external events that occur during the course of an experiment that might potentially affect the subjects. Maturation effects are changes in the subjects that occur during the course of the experiment as a result of the passage of time. For example, consider a long-term study of the effect of viewing war movies on attitudes about violence. If we assemble a group of college freshmen in January and then (a) measure their attitudes about violence at the beginning of a semester, (b) show them some war movies throughout January, and (c) measure their attitudes toward violence again in March, we would want to conclude that any differences in their attitudes were attributable to the movies. However, if the United States had become involved in a major international conflict during February, this event could have affected the subjects' attitudes, leading us to conclude incorrectly that the war films had caused the changes. The use of a control group enables us to remove this possibility because the control and experimental groups would *both* have been exposed to news about the historical event, and the only difference between the groups would be the fact that only the experimental group saw the films.

Both groups would also have "matured" by the same degree during the period, eliminating the possibility that we would incorrectly interpret any attitudinal changes produced by the subjects' physical or mental development during this passage of time as being caused by the films. If the subjects' maturation during the period covered by the experiment did produce attitudinal changes, they would have affected both the experimental and the control group subjects. Any *differences* between the two groups could then be attributed safely to the fact that only the experimental group saw the films.

History and maturation effects, along with a third threat that we shall discuss shortly—**testing effect**—are examples of threats to the **internal validity** of a research design. That is, they are examples of problems that can arise because of weaknesses in the logical structure of the research design itself. If left uncorrected, such weaknesses can call into question the interpretation of our study's results. To avoid such weaknesses, it is imperative that we ask ourselves whether there is anything in our research design that could leave our results open to multiple or conflicting interpretations.

Other potential problems threaten the **external validity** of our research design. Such problems threaten the generalizability of the results. External validity pertains to whether our results, even if the logical structure of the design enables us to conclude that the independent variable had a clear effect on the subjects, can be safely extrapolated to groups or subjects not included in our study. Perhaps the most obvious source of external validity problems is unrepresentative sampling (discussed in chapter 6). The unusual conditions of the experimental setting create another common source of external validity problems—our results could be attributable to the peculiar conditions endured by the subjects during the experiment, making it inappropriate to conclude that the experimental treatment would have the same impact in a more natural context. Similarly, if our experiment involves multiple treatments of subjects or multiple measurements of their opinions or behavior, their repetitive exposure to these aspects of the experiment may affect their responses, making it doubtful that the results can be generalized.

Researchers commonly distinguish between a **laboratory experiment** and a **field experiment.** Laboratory experiments are the type of experiment most likely to come to mind when we think of scientific research. Laboratory experiments provide the researcher with extensive control over the variables under study. Such experiments, however, are more common in the physical and life sciences than in the social sciences. Within the social sciences, field experiments, which take place outside a laboratory setting, are the most common form of experimentation.

Two Important Experimental Designs

In designing experiments, researchers employ a number of basic formats. While varying considerably in their details, all research designs share a common purpose, to produce results that will not be contaminated by threats to their internal or external validity. Two commonly employed types of design are the **classic experiment,** sometimes referred to as the "pre-test/post-test control group design," and the **Solomon four-group design.**[1]

In the classic experimental design, subjects are randomly assigned to one

---

1. See Leege and Francis (1974), chapter 3, for a fuller description of several experimental designs. Much of the following is drawn from their discussion.

of two equivalent groups, an experimental and a control group, and the scores of the two groups are then measured with respect to the dependent variable (the pre-test). The experimental treatment (or independent variable) is then applied to the experimental group only, after which the two groups' scores on the dependent variable are measured again (the post-test).

If the design has been properly executed, the control group will be equivalent to the experimental group in that it: (a) contains an equivalent set of subjects—normally as a result of random assignment; (b) has experienced the same passage of time between pre-test and post-test; and (c) has been subjected to the same environmental or historical events as the experimental group. If so, the two groups will be different *only* in that the subjects in the experimental group, and not those in the control group, will have been exposed to the experimental treatment. Under these conditions, changes in the dependent variable can almost certainly be attributed to the effects of exposure to the experimental treatment.

The classic experimental design can be depicted as follows, where X stands for the treatment or exposure to the independent variable, O represents an observation of the dependent variable, and the subscripts refer to the time order of the observations:

Experimental Group 1 O_1 X O_2
Control Group 1 O_1 O_2

One of the weaknesses of the classic experimental design is that we cannot always be certain the post-test scores of the two groups have not been influenced in some way by their exposure to the pre-test. Testing effects are a threat to both the internal validity and the external validity of an experiment. If exposure to the pre-test changes the subjects' sensitivity in some way, the pre-tested subjects could respond differently to the experimental treatment than would persons not exposed to the pre-test. If so, it would be misleading to conclude that the independent variable will generally have the observed effects on the population. Pre-testing may thus be a threat to external validity. However, it may also threaten internal validity. Perhaps the experimental treatment has no effect except when subjects are somehow changed by the pre-test. If so, we would observe differences between the control and experimental groups. But our conclusions that the experimental treatment caused the changes would be unsound *even for the subjects in the experiment* because the experimental treatment would not have caused the observed changes by itself. Thus, the internal validity could also be affected by testing effects.

The purpose of the Solomon four-group design is to help us rule out this possibility by adding two additional groups that do not receive the pre-test. It may be depicted as:

Experimental Group 1	O_1	X	O_2
Control Group 1	O_1		O_2
Experimental Group 2		X	O_2
Control Group 2			O_2

Again consider our hypothetical experiment designed to determine the effects of viewing violent war films on individual attitudes toward foreign policy. Using a classic experimental design, as described above, we would first administer a pre-test to the members of both the experimental and control groups to determine their existing foreign policy attitudes. The experimental group would then be shown war films depicting violence while the control group viewed nonviolent films (or no films at all). Finally, we would administer a post-test to both groups and compare the scores for the two groups to determine the attitudinal impact of the films.

The potential weakness in this procedure is that the experimental group's reactions to the films might be altered in some way by our pre-test. Answering a series of questions on a survey about violence, war, and conflict (the pre-test) could, for example, sensitize people to these issues and alter their thinking about them in either obvious or subtle ways *as they watch the films.* If so, this could result in different post-test scores than we would have seen if the subjects had not taken our pre-test. Of course, without a pre-test, we would not have a baseline from which to measure the films' effect on attitudes. Nevertheless, using a classic experimental design, we might mistakenly attribute changes in the attitudes of our subjects to their having watched the films, when the changes could actually have been produced by the effect of the pre-test. We could not be sure that the films would produce the attitudinal changes we observed in people who had not been exposed to the pre-test first.

The Solomon design addresses this problem by adding two additional groups that do not receive the pre-test. Thus, we can compare the post-test scores for the two experimental groups that watched the films—one that was pre-tested and one that was not. We can also compare the post-test scores for two control groups again, only one of which was pre-tested. If the groups receiving pre-tests are different, we can assume that a testing effect has occurred. The extent of this effect can be estimated from the difference in the post-test scores between the two groups, only one of which will have been exposed to the pre-test.

There are many other varieties of experimental designs. Similarly, there are many other ways of handling the several potential threats to the validity of our research design discussed in this chapter—as well as the many others not discussed here. Testing effects, for example, can sometimes be dealt with by simply extending the time between the pre-test and the exposure to the independent variable rather than adding the additional control group required for a Solomon four-group design.

Quasi-Experimental Design

As useful as experimentation is, true experiments require a degree of control that can seldom be realized in political research. For this reason, much political research involves an alternative class of research design that approximates experimental logic. These designs are often referred to as quasi-experimental. Cook and Campbell (1979, p. 6) offer the following definition:

> Quasi-experiments [are] experiments that have treatments, outcome measures, and experimental units, but do not use random assignment to create the comparisons from which treatment-caused change is inferred. Instead, the comparisons depend on nonequivalent groups that differ from each other in many ways other than the presence of a treatment whose effects are being tested.

The major difference between experimental and quasi-experimental designs is that in quasi-experimental designs, the researcher is unable to meet one or more of the conditions required to conduct a true experiment. As O'Sullivan and Rassel (1989, p. 59) note:

> True experiments require the manipulation of at least one independent variable, the random assignment of subjects to groups, the random assignment of the independent variable to groups, and the exposure of the experimental group or groups to the treatment in isolation from other factors. If one of these conditions cannot be met, the appropriate research design is a *quasi-experimental* one. [emphasis in original]

In a quasi-experimental design then, the researcher attempts to meet as many of the conditions for experimentation as possible and adopts a variety of other methods to offset threats to the validity of the research design. Quasi-experimental designs typically involve the collection of additional data—above and beyond that which would be required for an experiment—or the use of certain data analysis techniques that help the researcher isolate the effects of the independent variable. Properly executed, the result is a research design that, in the words of Manheim and Rich (1991, p. 82), allows us to proceed "as if we had exercised all the control characteristics of a true experiment, and . . . provide[s] a sound logical basis for causal inferences."

The two most common quasi-experimental designs are the **ex post facto design** and the **time-series design**. The ex post facto design is quite common in political research. Using this approach, the researcher makes a single observation, collecting information about all relevant variables. For example, a researcher interested in the effect that one's regional location has on one's attitudes toward civil rights could administer a national opinion survey that would include questions on civil rights attitudes and the regional location of each subject. Since variables other than region could affect civil rights attitudes, the researcher would make sure that the survey included questions about income, education, religion, political party affiliation, age, and other variables. Using appropriate statistical techniques, the researcher would control for the effects of these other variables to determine whether region has any effect on the dependent variable, attitudes toward civil rights.

Chapter 12 is devoted to multivariate analysis, the methods used primarily to isolate the effects of independent variables in ex post facto research designs. However, the idea is conceptually simple. If we think that an apparent relationship, for example, a relationship between region and civil rights attitudes, is really caused by the influence of income (perhaps those citizens in the region with negative civil rights attitudes have particularly low incomes), then we can "control" for this possibility in a multivariate analysis. In effect, we would use statistical analysis to determine whether subjects with a given level of income tend to have different attitudes depending on their region. If regional differences are associated with attitudinal differences regardless of region, we would be on firm ground in concluding that the independent variable affects the dependent variable.

This study would not be a true experiment, however. We could not be sure that some variable we had not considered was really responsible for any relationship between region and attitudes, even after we control for the effects of the variables that we think could be relevant. The ex post facto design is, however, typically the best we can do, and, if the researcher is careful and thorough, the results can be sound. The Oliver/Mendelberg article, excerpted below, and the Oliver article excerpted in chapters 8 and 12, are good examples of ex post facto designs.

Time-series designs are a second type of quasi-experiment. Such designs involve a series of observations both prior to and following the introduction of the independent variable. When employing such designs, we make the assumption that external influences are constant and that any trends identified prior to the introduction of the independent variable will continue. Thus, if we discover a clear trend in the values of the dependent variable prior to the introduction of the independent variable, we can then project this trend forward in time to predict the expected values of the dependent variable. If the values observed after the introduction of the independent variable are different from the trend that we projected, we may be able to attribute the difference to the independent variable. The essence of time-series designs lies in this comparison (Cook and Campbell 1979, p. 6).

For example, a time-series design could be employed to determine whether or not stricter criminal penalties for drunk driving actually reduce highway fatalities. We would gather data on the number of highway fatalities for each of several years prior to and after the establishment of the stricter penalties. If the upward trend in fatalities continues undiminished after the stricter penalties went into effect, we could conclude that the new laws had no effect. A downturn in fatalities coinciding with the stricter penalties would suggest that they did have an impact. As with other quasi-experimental designs, this kind of study would require that we eliminate the effect of other variables (the introduction of safer cars, changes in the availability of alcohol to teenagers, etc.) that could have coincided with the stricter laws, producing a downturn in fatalities that had nothing to do with the laws.

The basic logic of experimental design is apparent in both true experiments and quasi-experiments. Sound research requires a clear understanding of this logic. In this chapter, we have excerpts from one example of a field experiment and one example of a quasi-experimental design.

———————— Excerpt 1 ————————

Television news has been the primary news source for most Americans for many years. While many Americans appear to be generally satisfied with local news broadcasts, a common complaint about local news programming is that it tends to emphasize visual spectacle rather than real substance.

Violent crime is thus inevitably a major topic on local newscasts. Detailed inquiry into city budgets and the successes and failures of the welfare department may be more important to the lives of citizens, but video footage of shootings, wounded crime victims, and handcuffed suspects apparently makes for much better television.

Some analysts and activists have argued that the over-emphasis on crime stories on local newscasts should not only be criticized for stressing the sensational over the substantive, it also may have a negative impact on race relations. In cities in which African Americans are disproportionately seen in video footage of violent crime scenes, the fact that crime stories are so prominent on local news broadcasts may tend to worsen racial prejudice.

Franklin Gilliam and Shanto Iyengar strongly suspected that local television news has such an impact. Designing a research project to shed light on the problem is, however, a difficult undertaking. After a moment's reflection, it is clear that a researcher cannot simply send a questionnaire to a sample of city residents, asking them to indicate whether or not local television news strengthens or weakens racist attitudes; the answers to such questionnaires would doubtlessly reflect the respondents' existing attitudes about racism, television, and so forth.

These authors felt that the best research design for this problem was an experiment. As they pointed out, "Experiments have the well-known advantage of greater precision in estimating causal effects." Gilliam and Iyengar wanted to expose their subjects to a range of newscasts and then measure their reactions in ways that would allow them to make inferences about the effects of the newscasts on attitudes about race.

Prime Suspects:
The Influence of Local Television News
on the Viewing Public

Franklin D. Gilliam Jr., *University of California, Los Angeles*

Shanto Iyengar, *Stanford University*

American Journal of Political Science 44, no. 3 (July 2000): 560–573. Copyright ©
2000 by the University of Wisconsin Press. Reprinted with permission.

Local television news is America's principal window on the world. Surveys
of television viewing (e.g., Roper-Starch 1994), hours of daily programming
(Papper and Gerhard 1999) and the actual share of the viewing audience captured by local newscasts (Hess 1991), all demonstrate the dominance of local
news. In fact, people can watch live local news almost anytime—mornings,
afternoons, evenings, prime time, and late night. As the amount of news time
has increased, so too has competition between stations. The drive for audience ratings pushes local news organizations to favor an "action news" format.

Stories about crime provide several necessary ingredients for the successful
marketing of news—concrete events with powerful impact on ordinary people,
drama and emotion, and, above all, attention-getting visuals. The special attraction of television to crime is reflected in the content of local television news. In a
recent study of fifty-six different cities, crime was the most prominently featured
subject in the local news (Klite, Bardwell, and Salzman 1997). In some cities,
crime accounted for more than 75 percent of all news coverage.

We argue that local news coverage of crime follows a standard script that
features two distinct elements. First, crime is violent. Armed bank robberies,
homicides, "home invasions," carjackings, and gang-related activities are now
staples of local news. The second element of the crime script is the presence
of a particular suspect. Episodic reporting requires a regular "cast" of charac-
ters the most prominent of which is the suspect. Given the visual nature of the
medium, the importance of the suspect to the script means that crime news is
often accompanied by racial imagery (Campbell 1995; Entman 1990, 1992;
Entman et al. 1998; Gilliam et al. 1996; Gilliam and Iyengar 1997; Graber
1976; Hurwitz and Peffley 1997; Peffley, Shields, and Williams 1996; Romer,
Jamieson, and de Coteau 1998; Worthy, Hagan, and MacMillan 1997).

Our objective in this article is to evaluate the relative contribution of each
element of the crime news script—the focus on violent crime and the inclusion of racial imagery—on public opinion. In general, we find that the latter

is more influential. Viewers exposed to the "racialized" element of the script become more supportive of capital punishment, mandatory sentencing, and other deterrent measures. Not unexpectedly, exposure to this version of the script also serves to substantiate negative attitudes about racial minorities. In closing we consider the implications of these results for intergroup relations, electoral politics, and the practice of journalism.

The Crime Story as a Narrative Script

The theoretical basis for our expectations concerning the effects of crime news on the viewing audience derives from the concept of "scripts." As developed by cognitive psychologists, a script is "a coherent sequence of events expected by the individual, involving him either as a participant or as an observer" (Abelson 1976, 33; also see Abelson 1981; Schank 1990; Schank and Abelson 1977; Mandler 1984). In their pioneering work, Schank and Abelson (1977) described "behavioral" scripts such as going to a restaurant: people "know" that they eat first and pay later. Other researchers have expanded the concept to embrace "narrative" or text-based scripts which appear in fiction, humor, advertising and, of particular interest to us, television news reports (see Sulin and Dooling 1974; Black, Galambos, and Read 1984; Graesser et al. 1980). Indeed, scripts are characteristic of all forms of story telling. In the case of mystery novels, for example, the "Agatha Christie" script leads readers to expect (in order) a murder, the appearance of assorted suspects and clues, and the final denouement (orchestrated by Monsieur Poirot or Miss Marple) in which all is explained.

All scripts, either behavioral or narrative, facilitate comprehension by distilling experience and knowledge. Because they provide an orderly and quite predictable set of scenarios and roles, scripts allow the "reader," quite effortlessly, to make inferences about events, issues, or behaviors. Because the "target" actions are marked by sequence, there is a clear sense of what is to come. We do not need to see the customer paying the bill or ordering the food to know that this follows the reading of the menu. We do not need to see police officers at the crime scene to be aware of their presence. In many cases script-based expectations are so well developed that when people encounter incomplete versions of the script, they actually "fill in" the missing information and make appropriate (that is, script-based) inferences about what must have happened. In the case of the restaurant script, for instance, the sight of an individual seated at a table reading a text leads observers to understand that this is a customer attempting to decide what to eat. Our evidence indicates that for viewers in Los Angeles and across the country, the expectations prompted by the crime script have achieved the status of common knowledge. Just as we know full well what happens in a restaurant, we also know—or at least think we know—what happens when crime occurs.

As told by television news, the crime news script unfolds in three ordered segments. It usually begins with the anchorperson's terse announcement that a crime has occurred. The viewer is then transported to the scene of the crime for a first-hand look supported by accounts from bystanders, relatives of the victim, or other interested parties. Finally, the focus shifts to the identity and apprehension of the perpetrator and the related efforts of law enforcement officials.

The following example, taken from a recent report aired by Los Angeles Channel 9 (KCAL), is typical:

Anchor's introduction: "A man was shot this afternoon in broad daylight while sitting in his jeep."

Crime scene coverage: pictures of jeep and cordoned-off street; concerned neighbor comments ("Imagine something like this happening just in front of your house; I mean, it's really scary.")

Apprehension of suspect: "Police are looking for this man last seen driving away in a blue Honda Accord (picture of suspect on screen). Police believe the suspect may have argued with the victim before he was shot."

Within this brief presentation (the entire story runs for 90 seconds) there are several underlying regularities. First, as seen in the news, crime is violent (Elias 1994; Crispin-Miller 1998). Second, coverage is episodic in the sense that the news focuses on discrete events rather than collective outcomes or general context (Iyengar 1991). Third, crime episodes require a central causal agent, namely, a "prime suspect." Typically, what viewers learn about suspects is limited to visual attributes, most notably their race or ethnicity. As depicted in the local news, crime is violent, and criminal behavior is associated with race/ethnicity.

In the next section we present a detailed content analysis that examines the prevalence of the crime news script in the Los Angeles television news market. We then report the results of several experiments in which viewers encountered different versions of the crime script. Finally, we corroborate the experimental results using a survey of Los Angeles County residents.

Crime Coverage in Los Angeles Local News, 1996–1997

The centrality of violent crime to local news programs was readily apparent in our study that encompassed all English-language commercial television stations operating in the LA market.[1] These stations aired a total of 3014 news stories on crime during 1996 and 1997 (when we administered our studies) of which 2492 (83 percent) were about violent crime.[2] The crime of murder, which accounts for less than 1 percent of all crime in Los Angeles County, was the focus of 17 percent of crime stories in the newscasts sampled. In fact, the number of murder stories (510) is equivalent to the *total* number of nonviolent crime stories (522) during the period sampled. While brutal acts of violence are understandably newsworthy, they represent but a small portion of the actual crime rate. This is important because most people get their information about crime from the media, not from personal experience.

Table 1

Content of Television Crime Coverage (Los Angeles, 1996–1997)
(Total Crime Stories = 3,014)

	Number of violent stories	Murder stories	Nonviolent stories
Total	2,492	510	522
Total number of perpetrators	52%	56%	53%
	(1,297)	(287)	(276)
White perpetrators	41%	33%	61%
	(529)	(96)	(169)
Black perpetrators	29%	36%	21%
	(370)	(104)	(58)
Hispanic perpetrators	22%	22%	16%
	(291)	(64)	(43)
Asian perpetrators	8%	8%	2%
	(107)	(23)	(6)

As shown in Table 1, the racial element of the crime script is clearly less prominent than the violence element. Nevertheless, over one-half of all crime reports made *explicit* reference to the race or ethnicity of the suspect.[3] Minorities accounted for 56 percent of all suspects and 59 percent of suspects in violent crime cases. The comparable figures for white suspects were 44 percent and 41 percent, respectively. Thus minorities are more likely to be depicted in the role of the suspect. Regardless of the type of crime, African-Americans comprised the largest group of *minority* suspects.[4] In short, the content analysis documents the scripted nature of crime news; crime is invariably violent and more often than not, stories make reference to the race/ethnicity of a particular suspect(s).

Obviously, the particular racial cues present in television crime coverage are partly a reflection of the disproportionate representation of particular racial groups in criminal activity. The prominence of blacks in crime news, for example, is not that much out of line with the actual black arrest rate in Los Angeles County—although blacks do not account for the largest number of murders (California Department of Justice 1997). However, the media's near exclusive focus on violent crime distorts the real world in the following way: when viewers encounter a suspect in the news he is invariably a violent perpetrator, when in reality the greatest number of felony arrests are for *property* crimes (Gilliam 1998). To the extent that people do see nonviolent crime stories, the perpetrator is most typically white (recall the data in Table 1). In the real world, however, minorities actually account for the largest share of nonviolent (property) felonies (Gilliam 1998). Clearly, the news is not an accurate reflection of the real world of crime.

In the next section we appraise the impact of the violent crime and race of the perpetrator elements of the crime script on attitudes about crime and race, respectively. We begin this section with a description of our experimental design. We move on to discuss the measurement of our dependent variables. We end the section by developing three competing hypotheses about the effect of the crime news script on the viewing public.

Assessing the Impact of the Crime Script on Viewers' Attitudes

Design

We rely primarily on experimental methods to assess the effects of the crime news script. Experiments have the well-known advantage of greater precision in estimating causal effects. We designed the experiments in this study so that the only differences between any two groups of viewers concerned the relevant aspects of the crime news script—the presence or absence of violent crime and the race of the alleged perpetrator. Since all other properties of the news presentation were identical we can attribute the observed differences between conditions, if any, to the cues conveyed by the crime script.

Of course, experiments are not without their limitations. Most experiments are administered upon "captive" populations—college students who must participate in order to gain course credit. Experiments also require a somewhat sterile, laboratory-like environment which bears little resemblance to the cacophony of the real world. Our own research was designed to overcome the artificial nature of the experimental method. As described below, our participants represented a fair cross-section of Los Angeles metropolitan area residents, our experimental manipulation consisted of an actual (and typical) news report on crime, and the experimental setting closely emulated the typical citizen's encounter with local news.

The principal objective of our manipulation was to manipulate the main elements of the crime news script. *Four* levels of the manipulation were established. First, some participants watched a story in which the alleged perpetrator of a murder was an African-American male. Second, other subjects were given the same news report, but this time featuring a white male as the murder suspect. A third set of participants watched the news report edited to exclude information concerning the identity of the perpetrator. Finally, a control group saw no crime news story at all.

The most innovative aspect of this design concerns our ability to vary the race of a "target" face (in this case, the alleged perpetrator) while maintaining all other visual characteristics. The original "input" was a local news report which included a close-up "mug shot" of the suspected perpetrator of the crime in question. The picture was digitized, then "painted" to alter the perpetrator's skin color, and then reedited into the news report. Beginning with two different perpetrators (a white male and a black male), we were able to produce altered versions of each individual in which their race was reversed, but all other features remained identical.[5] Thus, the perpetrator featured in the "white" and "black" versions of the story was equivalent in all respects but race.[6] Using this method, any differences in the responses of the subjects exposed to the white or black perpetrators can only be attributed to the perpetrator's race.

Participants watched a fifteen-minute videotaped local newscast (including commercials) described as having been selected at random from news programs broadcast during the past week. The objective of the study was said to be "selective perception" of news reports. Depending upon the condition to which they were assigned (at random), they watched a news story on crime that sometimes included a close-up photo of the suspect. Using the method described above, the photo either depicted an African-American or white male. The report on crime was inserted into the middle position of the newscast following the first commercial break. Except for the news story on crime, the newscast was identical in all other respects. None of the remaining stories on the tape concerned crime or matters of race.

On their arrival, participants were given their instructions and then completed a short pretest questionnaire concerning their social background, party identification, and political ideology, level of interest in political affairs, and media habits. They then watched the videotaped newscasts. The viewing room was furnished casually, and participants were free to browse through newspapers and magazines, snack on cookies, or chat with fellow participants. At the end of the videotape, participants completed a lengthy questionnaire that included questions about their evaluations of various news programs and prominent journalists, their opinions concerning various issues in the news, their reactions to particular news stories and, depending on the study, questions tapping their beliefs about the attributes of particular racial/ethnic groups. After completing the questionnaire, subjects were debriefed in full and were paid the sum of fifteen dollars.

Using this basic design, we have administered five separate studies between April 1995 and November 1997. Study 1 was administered at the UCLA Media Research Laboratory (which consists of a two-room suite on campus). Studies 2 and 3 were conducted at a major shopping mall in the city of Los Angeles. Studies 4 and 5 were conducted at a smaller mall in an outlying section of the metropolitan area known as Simi Valley which is located in Ventura County. Each study was designed (in part) to evaluate different attitudes about crime and race. Studies 1, 2, and 4 addressed attitudes towards the criminal justice process in general. Study 3 focused on questions of juvenile crime. While Studies 2 and 3 focused on traditional racial stereotypes, Studies 4 and 5 were designed to investigate the effects of the crime news script on more subtle racial attitudes. Finally, participants in Studies 1, 3, and 4 completed measures of "free recall" of the crime news story that enable us to validate the experimental manipulation and assess viewers' reconstruction of the news story. To maximize the reliability of the analysis, we pooled all five experiments. However, because some indicators were not common to all five studies, the number of cases varies across analyses.

The experimental "sample" consisted of 2331 residents of the Los Angeles metropolitan area who were recruited through flyers and announcements in newsletters offering $15 for participation in "media research." The age of the participants ranged from 18 to 74. Fifty-three percent were white, 22 percent were black, 10 percent were Asian, and 8 percent were Latinos.[7] Fifty-two percent were women. The participants were relatively well educated (49 percent had graduated from college) and, in keeping with the local area, more Democratic than Republican (45 percent versus 25 percent) in their partisan loyalty.

In order to assess the validity of our manipulation, we began by examining participants' ability to recall the details of the news story. As noted above, a subset of subjects were asked to recall the content of the crime report. At the end of the questionnaire subjects completed a section which began with the following instructions: "Now we want to know what you remember and how you felt about some of the stories you just saw. On the next page, some of the stories are briefly described." Subjects were asked to recall what the story was about, their thoughts and reactions to the story, and to identify the race, age, and gender of the "suspect in the story." The question about the race of the suspect was used to construct a test of accuracy in recall by comparing across the three experimental conditions.

Table 2 presents the results of these comparisons. While subjects were generally accurate in their recall of the presence of a perpetrator (an average of about 67 percent), they responded more accurately in the black perpetrator condition (70 percent) than in the white perpetrator condition (64 percent). This difference is statistically significant at the .05 level. Similarly, subjects in the white perpetrator condition were about 50 percent less likely to recall having seen a suspect than subjects in the black perpetrator condition ($p < .10$). This pattern is in keeping with the extensive literature in social and cognitive psychology indicating that people are more likely to attend to information that confirms their prior beliefs (see, for example, Graesser, Singer, and Trabasso 1994; Roediger and McDermott 1995).

Turning to the especially interesting case of the condition that did not feature a perpetrator, Table 2 shows that over 60 percent of the respondents who watched the story with no reference to a perpetrator falsely recalled having seen a perpetrator. Even more striking, in 70 percent of these cases, the perpetrator was identified as African-American. Taken together, these data reveal that the crime script generates strong expectations about crime, allowing viewers to fill in gaps in the script. Lacking concrete evidence about the perpetrator, viewers infer what must have happened. Overall, the recall data validate the notion that the crime script is no mere journalistic device; instead, it is a powerful filter for observing daily events.

Table 2

Manipulation Check: Recall of Suspect by Experimental Condition

	Black suspect	No suspect	White suspect
Percent recalling	70	44	10
suspect as black	(182)	(56)	(21)
Percent recalling	13	19	64
suspect as white	(34)	(24)	(137)
Percent unable to	17	37	26
recall suspect	(45)	(46)	(56)

Notes

1. We selected newscasts aired during the evening, prime time, and late-night time periods from the three major network affiliates in Los Angeles (KCBS, KABC, and KNBC), the Fox (KTTV), and Warner Brothers (KTLA) stations, in addition to two independent stations KCAL and KCOP.

2. We also found that violent crime was no more or less visible in the offerings of the six television stations studied. Moreover, violent crime was just as newsworthy in the late afternoon, early evening, prime time, and late-night newscasts. The prominence of violent crime is a systematic phenomenon.

3. Suspects were identified either visually (in the form of a composite sketch or actual photograph) or verbally (in the form of a spoken reference).

4. African-Americans, do not, however, comprise the largest (absolute) number of murder suspects (California Department of Justice 1997).

5. The validity of this inference, of course, depends on the assumption that experimental participants recognized the racial manipulations. We tested the ability of participants to recognize the race of the original and transformed versions of the two different male suspects (one white, one black) in a pilot study. UCLA students ($N = 90$) were shown the four pictures (on a computer screen) along with a series of other pictures. As part of a "facial memory" test, the students were asked to indicate the ethnicity of each individual presented. In addition to accuracy of racial identification, we measured response latency on the assumption that lower latency would indicate greater confidence in the "target" individual's race. The results of this pretest revealed that in both cases the level of accuracy for the original and painted versions of the target were equivalent (.93 versus .87 and .84 versus .83 respectively). Response latency was also uniform across the original and altered faces. Latency was slightly higher in the case of the altered photos, but in neither case was the difference significant. In short, the manipulations "worked."

6. This represents a significant methodological advance over previous work in which researchers have manipulated racial cues using different stimulus individuals. For example, Iyengar (1991) showed his participants news reports of an unemployed black man and unemployed white man and news stories about crime featuring either a white or black perpetrator. Since the individuals featured in these stories differed in several respects other than race or ethnicity, Iyengar's studies provided only weak tests of the effects of race.

7. Because our interest in this set of studies was on black/white differences, we oversampled black subjects. The downside of this strategy is that we "undersampled" other minority groups. Our sample, therefore, does not fully match the general demographics for the Los Angeles metropolitan area. On the other hand, this approach does allow for a more refined analysis of our black subjects, which, as we will see shortly, is important in evaluating competing hypotheses.

References

Abelson, R.P. 1976. "Script Processing in Attitude Formation and Decision Making." In *Cognition and Social Behavior*, ed. J.S. Carroll and J.W. Payne. Mahwah, N.J.: Lawrence Erlbaum Associates.

Abelson, R.P. 1981. "The Psychological Status of the Script Concept." *American Psychologist* 36:715–729.

Allport, G.W. 1954. *The Nature of Prejudice.* Garden City, N.J.: Doubleday.

Belden, M., and J. Russonello. 1997. *Reporting of Existing Public Opinion Data on Juvenile Justice Issues.* Washington, D.C.: Belden and Russonello.

Bienenstock, E.J., P. Bonacich, and M. Oliver. 1990. "The Effect of Network Density and Homogeneity on Attitude Polarization." *Social Networks* 12:153–172.

Black, J.B., J.A. Galambos, and S.J. Read. 1984. "Comprehending Stories and Social Situations." In *Handbook of Social Cognition*. Vol. 3, ed. R.S. Wyer Jr. and T.K. Skrull. Mahwah, N.J.: Lawrence Erlbaum Associates.

California Department of Justice. 1997. *Crime 1997 in Selected California Jurisdictions.* Sacramento: Division of Criminal Justice Information Services.

Campbell, A., P.E. Converse, W.E. Miller, and D.E. Stokes. 1960. *The American Voter.* New York: John Wiley and Sons.

Campbell, C. 1995. *Race, Myth and the News.* Thousand Oaks, Calif.: Russell Sage.

Crispin-Miller, M. 1998. *Crime News in Baltimore: The Economic Cost of Local TV's Bodybag Journalism.* New York: Project on Media Ownership.

Dovidio, J.F., and S.L. Gaertner. 1986. *Prejudice, Discrimination, Racism: Theory and Research.* New York: Academic Press.

Dyson, M.E. 1996. *Race Rules: Navigating the Color Line.* Reading: Addison-Wesley.

Elias, R. 1994. "Official Stories: Media Coverage of American Crime Policy." *Humanist* 54:3–8.

Entman, R.M. 1990. "Modern Racism and the Images of Blacks in Local Television News." *Critical Studies in Mass Communication* 7:332–346.

Entman, R.M. 1992. "Blacks in the News: Television, Modern Racism, and Cultural Change." *Journalism Quarterly* 69:341–362.

Entman R.M., B.H. Langford, D. Burns-Melican, I. Munoz, S. Boayue, C. Groce, A. Raman, B. Kenner, and C. Merrit. 1998. *Mass Media and Reconciliation.* Cambridge: John F. Kennedy School of Government.

Gilliam, F.D., Jr. 1998. "Race and Crime in California." In *Racial and Ethnic Politics in California*, ed. M.B. Preston, B.A. Cain, and S. Bass. Berkeley: University of California.

Gilliam, F.D., Jr., and S. Iyengar. 1997. "Prime Suspects: The Effects of Local News on the Viewing Public." Presented at the Annual Meeting of the Western Political Science Association, Portland.

Gilliam, F.D. Jr., S. Iyengar, A. Simon, and O. Wright. 1996. "Crime in Black and White: The Violent, Scary World of Local News." *Harvard International Journal of Press/Politics* 1:6–23.

Graber, D. 1976. *Verbal Behavior and Politics.* Urbana: University of Illinois Press.

Graesser, A.C., S.B. Woll, D.J. Kowalski, and D.A. Smith. 1980. "Memory for Typical and Atypical Actions in Scripted Activities." *Journal of Verbal Learning and Verbal Behavior* 18:319–332.

Graesser, A.C., M. Singer, and T. Trabasso. 1994. "Constructing Inferences during Narrative Text Comprehension." *Psychological Review* 101:371–395.

Guensburg, C. 1999. "Taming the Beast." *American Journalism Review* 21:1–10.

Hess, S. 1991. *Live from Capital Hill: Studies of Congress and the Media.* Washington, D.C.: Brookings Institute.

Holley, J. 1996. "Should the Coverage Fit the Crime?" *Columbia Journalism Review* May/June:27–32.

Hunt, D. 1997. *Screening the Los Angeles "Riots": Race, Seeing, and Resistance.* New York: Cambridge University Press.

Hurwitz, J., and M. Peffley. 1997. "Public Perceptions of Crime and Race: The Role of Racial Stereotypes." *American Journal of Political Science* 41:375–401.

Iyengar, S. 1991. *Is Anyone Responsible? How Television Frames Political Issues.* Chicago: University of Chicago Press.
Jackman, M., and M. Muha. 1984. "Education and Intergroup Attitudes: Moral Enlightenment, Superficial Democratic Commitment, or Ideological Refinement?" *American Sociological Review* 49:751–769.
Kinder, D.R., and L.M. Sanders. 1996. *Divided by Color: Racial Politics and Democratic Ideals.* Chicago: University of Chicago Press.
Klite, P., R.A. Bardwell, and J. Salzman. 1997. "Local TV News: Getting Away with Murder." *Harvard International Journal of Press/Politics* 2:102–112.
Mandler, J.M. 1984. *Stories, Scripts, and Scenes: Aspects of Schema Theory.* Mahwah, N.J.: Lawrence Erlbaum Associates.
McAdam, D. 1982. *Political Process and the Development of Black Insurgency, 1930–1970.* Chicago: University of Chicago Press.
McConahay, J.B. 1986. "Modern Racism, Ambivalence, and the Modern Racism Scale." In *Prejudice, Discrimination, Racism: Theory and Research*, ed. J.F. Dovidio and S.L. Gaertner. New York: Academic Press.
Morris, A.M. 1984. *The Origins of the Civil Rights Movement: Black Communities Organizing For Change.* New York: Free Press.
Newby, I.A. 1965. *Jim Crow's Defense.* Baton Rouge: Louisiana State University Press.
Neuman, W., M. Just, and A. Crigler. 1992. *Common Knowledge: News and the Construction of Political Meaning.* Chicago: University of Chicago Press.
Oliver, M.L. 1988. "The Urban Black Community as a Network: Toward a Social Network Perspective." *Sociological Quarterly* 29:623–645.
Papper, R., and M. Gerhard. 1999. *Issues and Trends: 1999 Newsroom Workforce Survey.* Washington D.C.: Radio and Television News Directors Association.
Peffley, M., T. Shields, and B. Williams. 1996. "The Intersection of Race and Crime in Television News Stories: An Experimental Study." *Political Communication* 13:309–328.
Pettigrew, T.F., and R.W. Meertens. 1995. "Subtle and Blatant Prejudice in Western Europe." *European Journal of Social Psychology* 25:57–75.
Roediger, H.L. III, and K.B. McDermott. 1995. "Creating False Memory: Remembering Words Not Presented in Lists." *Journal of Experimental Psychology* 21:803–814.
Romer, D., K.H. Jamieson, and N.J. de Coteau. 1998. "The Treatment of Persons of Color in Local Television News—Ethnic Blame Discourse or Realistic Group Conflict?" *Communication Research* 25:286–305.
Roper-Starch Worldwide. 1994. *Roper Reports* 93:22–23.
Schank, R.C. 1990. *Tell Me a Story: A New Look at Real and Artificial Memory.* New York: Scribners.
Schank, R.C., and R.P. Abelson. 1977. *Scripts, Plans, Goals, and Understanding.* Mahwah, N.J.: Lawrence Erlbaum Associates.
Schuman, H., C. Steeh, and L. Bobo. 1985. *Racial Trends in America: Trends and Interpretations.* Cambridge: Harvard University Press.
Sears, D.O. 1988. "Symbolic Racism." In *Eliminating Racism: Profiles in Controversy*, ed. P.A. Katz and D.A. Taylor. New York: Plenum.
Sidanius, J., F. Pratto, and L.D. Bobo. 1996. "Racism, Conservatism, Affirmative Action, and Intellectual Sophistication: A Matter of Principled Conservatism or Group Dominance?" *Journal of Personality and Social Psychology* 70:1–15.
Smith, R.C. 1996. *We Have No Leaders: African Americans in the Post-Civil Rights Era.* Albany: State University of New York Press.
Sniderman, P., and T. Piazza. 1993. *The Scar of Race.* Cambridge: Harvard University Press.
Sulin, R.A., and Dooling, D.J. 1974. "Intrusion of a Thematic Idea in Retention of Prose." *Journal of Experimental Psychology* 103:255–262.
Tajfel, H. 1978. *Differentiation Between Social Groups: Studies in Intergroup Relations.* London: Academic Press.
Worthy, S., J. Hagan, and R. Macmillan. 1997. "Just Des(s)erts? The Racial Polarization of Perceptions of Criminal Injustice." *Law and Society Review* 31:637–676.

Discussion Questions

1. What are some of the alternative research designs Gilliam and Iyengar might have employed to study this particular problem? In what way, if any, would the results produced by these alternative strategies be likely to differ from those obtained here?
2. What steps did the authors take to ensure that the experimental setting had minimal impact on their ability to draw conclusions about the effect of television newscasts?
3. To what extent did the nature of the experimental design undercut the authors' ability to generalize their findings to the broader population?
4. Can you think of any history or maturation effects that could have confounded the results?
5. How did the authors introduce the concept of "control" into their experimental design?

Commentary

Gilliam and Iyengar designed an experiment to test an interesting and important research question about the effect of local television news programming. Although the design involved some controversial features, their conclusions provide a compelling confirmation that viewers have been significantly influenced by the content of local newscasts.

Their experimental approach had clear advantages over other approaches. Consider how a conventional survey research design to address the same research question may have worked. Instead of using an experimental design, we could ask a random sample of persons about their attitudes toward crime and race, along with some questions regarding their television viewing habits. We would then determine if there were any correlations between the prevalence of racist attitudes regarding violent crime suspects and the amount of local newscasts our respondents actually viewed. Following the notions that led Gilliam and Iyengar to undertake their study, we would hypothesize that persons watching more local newscasts would have the most racist attitudes.

Although such a study could be worthwhile, the key problem is that we would not be able to deal with the very real possibility that pre-existing racist attitudes were somehow the cause of viewing habits. Perhaps some people who are unusually interested in local stories about violent crime are obsessed with their images of racial differences. It would be very difficult, without the experimental approach used here, to determine the influence of newscasts. Gilliam and Iyengar's experimental design, however, allowed them to compare the perceptions of subjects who saw different newscast content, *when every other influence to which they were exposed was identical, and when the groups of subjects seeing the different newscasts were otherwise identical*.

Several features of the research design are noteworthy. First, the authors went to great lengths to produce a "normal" setting for the subjects. Since the experiment was designed to test the impact of viewing local newscasts on television, it was important to arrange for the subjects to view the newscasts in the way they typically view them. In the experiment, the subjects had access to newspapers and magazines, snacks, and the opportunity to interact with other subjects, allowing them to behave as most people normally do in their homes. If the design had called for showing the newscasts to the subjects in a setting with no distractions (e.g., in a classroom while sitting in a hard chair), they would be experiencing the newscasts in a highly artificial way. Perhaps the content of the newscasts would have a different impact on people if they viewed them in such an unnatural setting. If so, designing the experiment that way would have produced misleading conclusions about the real-world effect of such newscasts. Because newscasts probably have less influence on people when they are surrounded by family members, friends, and other distractions, the design used here attempted to mimic these conditions as much as possible.

Strictly speaking, Gilliam and Iyengar's design did not incorporate a control group. There was no group whom they exposed to everything *except* the experimental treatment. Instead, the authors had separate groups of subjects that saw slightly different newscasts, some with a black suspect, and others with a white suspect, and others where the suspect was not depicted. In a sense, we could argue that those seeing newscasts that did not include the black suspect were the "control" group. Perhaps there would have been some value in assigning a group of subjects to a room in which they saw no newscast at all but instead had a television showing a sporting event or a sitcom. The attitudes of this group could have been measured before and after their time in the experiment (which would ideally have been the same amount of time that the experimental subjects were in their rooms).

However, the essential comparison was the attitudes and perceptions of subjects after seeing newscasts that were different in terms of their racial content. By randomly assigning subjects to see different newscasts, the authors were on firm ground in attributing measured differences between the otherwise similar groups of subjects to the differences in the content of the newscasts.

Another important strength of the study is the fact that the authors based their conclusions on experiments with subjects in different areas of town and from different ethnic and educational backgrounds. They point out that the pool of subjects was not perfectly representative of citizens in the Los Angeles metropolitan area, but they provided information on their subjects so that the reader is able to make judgments about the representativeness of the experiment.

The findings excerpted here are compelling. The authors showed that people apparently make assumptions about the racial identity of suspects in violent crime stories and that their assumptions are not prompted by the facts in the particular case they just heard about. Perhaps racial stereotyping has been generated by decades of local news coverage, by the entertainment media, or by other influences, but this political science experiment provides strong confirmation that such stereotyping is a reality.

——————————— Excerpt 2 ———— ——

As noted earlier, true experiments are relatively rare in political science. The underlying principles of experimentation, however, can be detected in typical quasi-experimental designs. In order to generate an explanation regarding the effect of an independent variable on a dependent variable, it is necessary to find that the two variables are correlated and that the correlation is not attributable to something else. While experiments provide the best way to control for other variables that may explain changes in the dependent variable, quasi-experimental design can accomplish the same thing, depending on the quality and completeness of the design. A recent study by J. Eric Oliver and Tali Mendelberg is a good example of this kind of research.

These authors were also interested in the problem of race in America. There is a great deal of social science research indicating that racial hostility on the part of white citizens is greatest in areas in which there is a large black population. This is known as the "power-threat" hypothesis, which suggests that whites engage in racist behavior in response to a perceived threat from a large black population. According to the hypothesis, whites living in areas with sparse black populations do not develop racist attitudes because they never feel threatened.

Oliver and Mendelberg constructed a quasi-experimental design to address this question. They felt that there were several factors other than the proportion of blacks in a given area that could account for differences in racist attitudes on the part of white citizens. Education level, income, age, partisanship, and other aspects of a person's background could also influence racist attitudes and behavior. An experiment to determine the effect of living in different areas would obviously not be possible, so the authors designed a quasi-experiment.

Reconsidering the Environmental Determinants of White Racial Attitudes

J. Eric Oliver, *Princeton University*

Tali Mendelberg, *Princeton University*

American Journal of Political Science 44, no. 3 (July 2000): 574–589. Copyright ©
2000 by the University of Wisconsin Press. Reprinted with permission.

In recent years, scholars have begun to reexamine the role of social environments as a determinant of whites' racial attitudes. Most of this research focuses on the "power-threat" hypothesis, which states that white racial animosity
increases with the percent of blacks in an environment (Blalock 1967; Key
[1949] 1984). According to this hypothesis, whites engage in racial violence,
resist desegregation, vote for racist candidates, and switch political parties
partly in response to the threat that living among many blacks poses to their
political and economic privilege. Over the past two decades, numerous studies have validated this claim: whites' negative racial attitudes increase with
higher percentages of blacks in the county, metropolitan area, and state, and
not just in the South (Bobo 1988; Fossett and Kiecolt 1989; Giles and Hertz
1994; Giles and Evans 1986; Glaser 1994; Huckfeldt and Kohfeld 1989;
Matthews and Prothro 1966; Wright 1977). In perhaps the most thorough test,
Taylor (1998), using national cross-sectional data from the past twenty years,
finds consistent patterns of prejudice and opposition to race-targeted policies
among whites as the black percentage in a metropolitan area increases. Across
all of these works, a large body of evidence supports the argument that white
racial hostility rises in direct proportion to the size of the surrounding black
population.

   As compelling as these findings are, they leave many unanswered questions about the relationship between whites' social surroundings and their
racial attitudes. To begin with, these studies conceptualize racial threat solely
in terms of racial environments. The originators of the threat hypothesis, however, also paid attention to socio-economic contexts. For example, in *Southern Politics,* V.O. Key noted that the political differences between the black-belt
counties of Alabama and North Carolina arose not from their racial populations (which were equally large) but from their distinct class arrangements
([1949] 1984, 217). Despite this fact, the research of the past several decades
has consistently ignored the socio-economic status of whites' environments—
none of the contemporary studies of white racial attitudes considers their economic contexts.[1]

The nation's high levels of residential segregation also call for another look at the ways in which interracial competition affects white racial attitudes. The vast majority of whites live in highly segregated communities: nearly 75 percent of all whites live in municipalities that are less than 5 percent black. Because most whites are sequestered in predominantly white, suburban municipalities, they are removed from local political arenas where their power or privilege is contested by African Americans or where the effects of race-targeted policies are felt. While many important race-targeted policy decisions are made at the state and federal levels, their implementation often hinges on locally based decisions and their effects may only be felt at the neighborhood or municipal level. In other words, one type of policy may be contested within the county, another across a metropolitan area, and a third within a municipality. For example, inter-racial competition for jobs takes place across counties or the metropolis, but competition for housing and primary education may occur within municipalities or special districts. Although previous research typically measures threat with large contextual units, such as counties, it is not self-evident that the black percentage in a geographic unit as large as a county or metropolitan area is a sufficient threat to any given privilege, much less all privileges (for related arguments see Voss [1996] and Forbes [1997]).[2]

Given these considerations, alternative explanations for the contextual variation in racial attitudes are in order. Scholars have long noted that intergroup hostility does not come solely from "realistic" conflict over power or material resources (Levine and Campbell 1972; Sherif 1966) but is also influenced by psychological responses to economic and physical duress (Bettelheim and Janowitz [1950] 1964; Fromm 1941; Sales 1973). If these hypotheses are correct, the social environment can influence racial attitudes in ways that have little to do with racial composition or with interracial competition for resources. These alternative theories, however, have not been adequately tested with cross-sectional data that measure both individual and environmental characteristics.

Thus, despite a flurry of recent research, the environmental determinants of whites' racial attitudes are still unclear. Identifying them requires three modifications to the study of social environments and racial attitudes: (1) attention to the context's socio-economic composition as well as its racial composition; (2) distinctions among different contextual levels and their correspondence to interracial competition for geographically distributed resources; and (3) a fuller exploration of alternative hypotheses to realistic competition. With these three goals in mind, we reexamine the threat hypothesis and test some alternatives.

Reconsidering the Threat Hypothesis

The impact of racial threat on whites' racial attitudes is typically demonstrated with an elegant, bivariate relationship: the greater the percentage of blacks in an environment, the more racially antagonistic whites seem to be.[3] But while intuitively appealing, this formulation overlooks the impact of the environment's socio-economic composition. Recent studies of racial threat have not neglected the impact of social status per se, but they have operationalized it only as an *individual-level* variable (Giles and Hertz 1994; Huckfeldt and Kohfeld 1989). Yet the socio-economic characteristics of the *environment* may be just as important for shaping interracial competition. For example, tipping models predict that housing values are affected more adversely by racial integration in lower-status white neighborhoods than in affluent ones (Massey and Denton 1993). As racial integration is a greater material threat to residents of low-status neighborhoods, racial animosity in these settings may be higher. Low-status white neighborhoods also are more likely to be located in racially heterogeneous cities, in which competition between racial groups for public services, jobs, and contracts is likely to be more frequent and intense. To properly gauge white vulnerability to black political and economic advancement, one must take into account the *interaction* between socio-economic and racial contexts. Neighborhood tipping, for example, may be more likely in low-status neighborhoods, but it is only possible if sufficient numbers of minorities are nearby. If interracial competition for resources is the source of white racism, then the greatest levels of white racial hostility should be at the intersection of racial and socio-economic contexts.

Given the reality of white residential patterns, however, we may question whether this interaction still takes place. In today's metropolis, most whites are politically and spatially separated from blacks by municipal jurisdictions. White suburbanization has not only increased the racial and economic segregation of the population (Massey and Eggars 1993; Schneider and Logan 1984) but solidified these differences with municipal boundaries (Danielson 1976). Because a municipality's social composition shapes its tax burdens, home values, and the quality of education and other public services (Boger 1997; Danielson 1976; Schneider 1989), politically bounded racial segregation drastically curtails the racial competition for both public and private goods. Although interracial competition may still exist in state or national politics, the effects of many race-targeted policies are determined by local jurisdictions. For most whites, these local political jurisdictions are so racially segregated as strongly to reduce the interracial competition for political and economic resources.

But if segregation undercuts realistic group conflict, do social contexts still shape whites' racial attitudes? We believe they do. In particular, socio-economic contexts may influence racial attitudes independent of racial contexts. Most American cities and suburbs are not simply divided along racial lines; they are highly distinguishable by their socio-economic status. While high levels of racial segregation may eliminate much of the racial competition for resources, high levels of economic segregation may affect racial attitudes in other ways.

For example, socio-economic environments may foster distinct racial *norms,* particularly when socio-economic status is measured by education. According to Huckfeldt and Kohfeld (1989), citizens' racial opinions are shaped in part by informational cues from their social environment. If less educated whites tend to have racially antagonistic views, then living among many people with such views is likely to produce "spatially structured patterns of preference" (Huckfeldt and Kohfeld 1989, 57). Conversely, highly educated settings may encourage greater racial tolerance.

Socio-economic environments also may influence racial attitudes as part of a larger psychological response to stressful collective circumstances. Research on authoritarianism and on ethnic conflict has generally found that out-group animosity is heightened by conditions of economic stress or status anxiety (Bettelheim and Janowitz [1950] 1964; Feldman and Stenner 1997; Gurr 1968; Horowitz 1985; Konecni 1979; Sales 1973; but see Green et al. 1998). Low-status settings, defined by low rates of education and employment, expose residents to a daily dose of petty crime, concentrated physical decay and social disorder, such as abandoned buildings, verbal harassment, and public drug consumption (Skogan 1990). This exposure in turn leads to a constellation of negative psychological states which are experienced by residents: feelings of anxiety and fear, alienation from neighbors, lack of trust in others, and suspicion toward out-groups in general. In settings characterized by general anxiety and fear, anti-black affect may arise because African Americans are a salient target in a racially divided society. The stigma and stresses of living in a low-status environment also may propagate more racial animosity from feelings of relative deprivation (Tajfel and Turner 1979). In other words, whites in low-status settings may seek to denigrate out-groups as a means of maintaining their own sense of well-being (Brown 1985; Rieder 1985). By increasing negative psychological states, these collective circumstances foster racist sentiments for reasons that have little to do with interracial material competition. The collective circumstances hypothesis has usually been tested with historical records or experimental data, often times with weak or inconsistent results (Konecni 1979). Researchers have not utilized cross-sectional survey data to examine whether individuals have systematic psychological responses to the status composition of their surroundings, leaving the relationship between social environments, psychological states, and racial attitudes undetermined.

Measuring Social Contexts

To test these propositions, we use data from the 1991 National Race and Politics Study (NRPS), a nationwide random-digit telephone survey conducted by the Survey Research Center at the University of California, Berkeley.[4] The NRPS is one of the richest data sources for American attitudes on race, carrying scores of items measuring racial predispositions and policy preferences.

Because we are interested primarily in the effects of context on white attitudes, we analyze only non-Hispanic whites (1,854 of the original 2,223 respondents). We constructed the contextual measures for the 1,681 white respondents with identifiable zip codes by extracting data on the zip code and metropolitan area levels from the 1990 Census (Summary Tape File 3B).

Identifying a context's boundaries is essential for understanding its potential effects. An environment's racial composition can vary widely depending on what geographic unit or level is measured. The impact of the geographical unit on a given policy is also likely to be contingent on the extent to which that unit affects the implementation of the policy. We take these differences into account by measuring two levels of racial context: the percent black at the zip-code level and percent black at the metropolitan level.[5]

Measuring the environment's socio-economic composition represents a different set of challenges. Unlike racial contexts, socio-economic contexts must be measured primarily in smaller units, such as zip codes, because larger units, like metropolitan areas, have too much internal heterogeneity and too little external variation.[6] While the racial percentage of a metropolitan area may provide some indication of interracial proximity, the educational level of the metropolis will be a very poor indicator of what any particular socio-economic context is like. Unlike racial contexts, socio-economic status environments also can be measured by any number of indicators such as income, unemployment, occupation, and education. We chose educational composition, measured by the percent of residents in a zip code with a college degree. As Huckfeldt, Skogan, and others have shown, education is often a more reliable indicator of an area's socio-economic status than its median household income, is better distributed than unemployment, and is more easily ordered than occupational categories (Huckfeldt 1986; Skogan 1990).[7] At the individual level, education and income are only moderately correlated ($r = .38$), but at the contextual level they are highly correlated ($r = .68$).

The NRPS also allows us to measure racial predispositions with a variety of sophisticated measures. These include "modern" or "symbolic" racism (Kinder and Sanders 1996). Following Alvarez and Brehm (1997), we measure symbolic racism with a three-point Likert scale asking respondents to rate the amount of attention government pays to minorities and two eleven-point scales assessing respondent anger at "special advantages" for blacks in jobs and schools and minority spokesmen who are "always complaining" about discrimination.[8] We also use a traditional measure of racial prejudice composed of five positive and five negative stereotypes of blacks.[9] Sniderman and Piazza (1993) and Feldman and Stenner (1997) suggest the importance of two other predispositions that are not directly racial but may be related to racial attitudes: authoritarianism and anti-Semitism. Authoritarianism is measured with a composite scale of five items on the importance of "preserving traditional ideas of right and wrong," "respect for authority," "standards of politeness," "strengthening law and order," and "maintaining respect for

America's power in the world."[10] The anti-Semitism scale is comprised of four questions measuring the extent to which respondents agree or disagree that Jews use "shady practices," believe themselves to be "better than others," are "more loyal to Israel than America," and "do not care about non-Jews."[11] All four predisposition measures were rescaled on a zero-to-one interval scale for comparability.[12] The mean scores (and standard deviations) are .59 (.24) for symbolic racism, .47 (.14) for negative stereotypes, .36 (.24) for anti-Semitism, and .73 (.21) for authoritarianism.

Finally, the 1991 NRPS has a battery of questions regarding race-targeted policy preferences. We selected the items that best capture materialistic competition between races: support for government efforts at housing desegregation, job programs for minorities, and university affirmative action.[13] In the first policy item, respondents were asked about "blacks buying houses in white suburbs." Respondents who were in favor (either strongly or mildly) were then asked a follow-up question about their support for programs to encourage blacks to buy homes in white suburbs. Responses to the follow-up question were used to create a single four-point Likert scale.[14] The second item is a three-point measure of support for federal programs to help blacks get jobs and eliminate discrimination.[15] The third item is a four-point measure of support or opposition to giving blacks preference in university admissions.

Social Contexts and Racial Predispositions

We begin with the bivariate relationships between predispositions and contexts. Figure 1 depicts mean scores on the four predisposition items across quartiles of the percent black in the zip code and of the metropolitan area, and across quintiles of zip-code education.[16] In the crosstabulations, the greatest environmental effects come from education—not race. Whites' racial predispositions stay relatively constant across a zip code's racial composition. The average stereotype score is nearly identical in zip codes that are more than 10 percent black (.49) as it is in zip codes with no blacks (.48), with the same pattern holding for the symbolic racism, authoritarianism, and anti-Semitism predispositions (for similar findings see Kinder and Mendelberg, 1995). Across the larger context—metropolitan areas—white racial prejudice increases with larger percentages of blacks. Residents of metropolitan areas that are more than 20 percent black score, on average, six percentage points higher on symbolic racism and four percentage points higher on the negative stereotype scale than do residents of metropolitan areas that are under 5 percent black—small but statistically significant differences.

But where opinions vary only sporadically and mildly with the racial composition of the environment, they vary quite sharply with its level of education. The mean score on all four predispositions steadily declines between people in the least and most educated contexts. Between zip codes with less than 15 percent college educated and those with more than 45 percent college educated, the average score decreases by nine percentage points for symbolic racism, by six points on the stereotype scale, by fourteen points on the authoritarianism scale, and by ten points on the anti-Semitism scale.[17]

Thus, a simple, bivariate analysis suggests that: (1) the greatest contextual difference lies in an environment's educational and not its racial composition; and (2) the negative effect of racial composition occurs in the largest setting. Of course, such results may reflect individual-level characteristics and have little to do with the environment. After all, respondents in more educated zip codes are themselves more educated, which may explain their more liberal predispositions. To control for these and other factors, we employed a series of Ordinary Least Square (OLS) regressions that include relevant contextual and individual demographic variables. Table 1 presents coefficients from the first set of equations, regressing each of the four racial predispositions on zip-code education, zip-code racial composition, two dummy variables measuring the racial composition of the metropolitan area, southern residence, and several individual-level characteristics that might influence racial attitudes, including education, income, age, sex, length of residence, and dummy variables for Republicans and political independents (Kinder and Sanders 1996; Sniderman and Piazza 1993).[18]

Even controlling for individual education, income, partisanship, and other characteristics, the relationships depicted in Table 1 are remarkably similar to the bivariate pattern. As in Figure 1, no significant differences exist among whites based on their zip code's racial composition.[19] In larger contexts, however, the racial environment does have a small effect. Like earlier studies using multivariate equations (Taylor 1998; Fossett and Kiecolt 1989), we find that whites in heavily black metropolitan areas exhibit greater negative stereotypes about blacks. Our model predicts that residents of predominantly black metropolitan areas (more than 17 percent) score three percentage points higher on the stereotype scale than whites in metropolitan areas with few blacks (under 7 percent). Unlike past research, however, we find no statistically significant relationships between the percentage of blacks in the metropolitan area and other indicators of racial hostility.[20]

Once again, the largest contextual effects arise from the zip code's level of education, even when taking individual education and income into account. The model predicts that residents of zip codes with fewer than 5 percent college-educated residents score 27 percentage points higher on the symbolic racism scale, twenty-five percentage points higher on the authoritarianism scale, 11 percentage points higher on the anti-Semitism, and 9 percentage points higher on the negative stereotype scales than residents of the most educated zip codes (i.e., zip codes with more than 70 percent of residents with a college degree). These differences are much larger than those across *any* of the racial context measures.[21]

Given that interracial threat is typically characterized in terms of competition for economic resources and political power, these findings, while new,

Table 1

The Effects of Racial and Economic Contexts on White Racial Predispositions
(with Individual-Level Controls)

	Symbolic racism	Negative stereotypes	Anti-Semitism	Authoritar-ianism
Environmental variables				
Education—zip code	−.274**	−.089**	−.106*	−.248**
	(.054)	(.031)	(.057)	(.040)
Percent black—zip code	−.072	−.039	−.064	−.028
	(.072)	(.033)	(.056)	(.044)
Medium black metro	.020	.015	.009	.004
	(.020)	(.010)	(.017)	(.014)
High black metro	.034	.031**	.030	.019
	(.019)	(.012)	(.018)	(.014)
Rural	.015	−.005	.021	.004
	(.018)	(.010)	(.016)	(.013)
South	.037**	.032**	.025	.027*
	(.016)	(.009)	(.015)	(.012)
Individual-level variables				
Education	−.025**	−.021**	−.045**	−.056**
	(.006)	(.004)	(.006)	(.005)
Income	.005**	−.001	−.004*	−.001
	(.002)	(.001)	(.002)	(.002)
Age	.001	.001*	.000	.001**
	(.000)	(.001)	(.000)	(.000)
Length of residence	−.004	−.000	.002	.003
	(.006)	(.004)	(.006)	(.005)
Female	.000	−.020**	−.067**	.001
	(.013)	(.008)	(.013)	(.011)
Republican	.070**	.015	.016	.061
	(.014)	(.009)	(.014)	(.011)
Independent	−.021	−.050*	−.068*	−.031
	(.034)	(.021)	(.034)	(.026)
Adjusted R^2	.07	.08	.11	.20
N	1,476	1,416	1,389	1,469

Source: 1991 Race and Politics Survey/1990 Census.

** $p < .01$, * $p < .05$.

seem consistent with the threat hypothesis. A zip code's education level is probably a better indicator of white material vulnerability than its racial composition. For instance, less educated white neighborhoods are more likely to be poor than black neighborhoods. Yet this consideration also implies that the above test is incomplete. If the material vulnerability of whites in low-status neighborhoods is much greater when those neighborhoods are situated in heavily black areas, then the greatest racial animosity should occur at the

Table 2

The Interdependent Effects of Racial and Economic Contexts on White Racial Predispositions (with Individual-Level Controls)

	Symbolic racism	Negative stereotypes	Anti-Semitism	Authoritar-ianism
Environmental variables				
Education—zip code	−.219**	−.114*	−.257**	−.210**
	(.091)	(.057)	(.095)	(.075)
Percent black—zip code	−.092	−.022	−.056	−.022
	(.055)	(.034)	(.056)	(.044)
Medium black metro	.023	.001	−.027	.022
	(.033)	(.021)	(.034)	(.027)
High black metro	.059	.014	−.014	.008
	(.032)	(.020)	(.033)	(.026)
Rural	.007	−.013	−.027	.010
	(.030)	(.019)	(.031)	(.024)
Zip educ. × md. blk. metro.	−.045	.054	.172	−.083
	(.729)	(.081)	(.134)	(.440)
Zip educ. × hi. blk. metro.	−.116	.036	.201	.045
	(.120)	(.075)	(.125)	(.099)
Zip educ. × rural	.019	.046	.245	−.033
	(.140)	(.089)	(.147)	(.114)
South	.037**	.032**	.026	.026*
	(.014)	(.009)	(.015)	(.012)
Individual-level variables				
Education	−.025**	−.021**	−.046**	−.053**
	(.006)	(.004)	(.006)	(.005)
Income	.005**	−.001	−.004*	−.001
	(.002)	(.001)	(.002)	(.002)
Age	.001	.001*	.000	.001**
	(.000)	(.001)	(.000)	(.000)
Length of residence	−.004	−.000	.002	.003
	(.005)	(.004)	(.006)	(.005)
Female	.000	−.027**	−.067**	.001
	(.012)	(.008)	(.012)	(.009)
Republican	.068**	.015*	.008	.068
	(.012)	(.008)	(.012)	(.010)
Independent	−.092	−.052**	−.059*	−.038
	(.029)	(.021)	(.029)	(.023)
Adjusted R^2	.07	.08	.11	.20
N	1,476	1,416	1,389	1,469

Source: 1991 Race and Politics Survey/1990 Census.

** $p < .01$, * $p < .05$.

Figure 1   **Average Racial Predisposition Scores by Three Social Contexts**

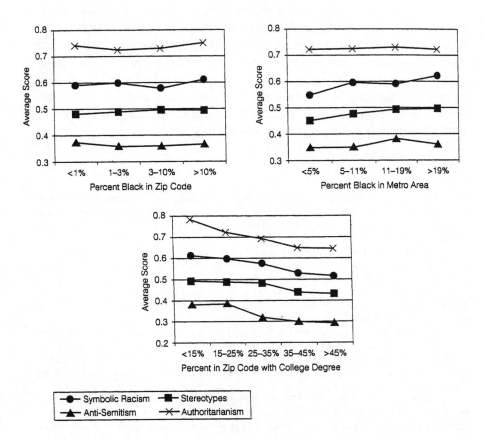

Source: 1991 Race and Politics Study and 1991 U.S. Census, Summary Tape File B.

intersection of race and status contexts. In other words, if the threat hypothesis is true, then whites in low-education zip codes in highly black metropolitan areas should be more racist than those in low-education zip codes in sparsely black environments.

To test for these effects, we reestimated the equations in Table 1 with interaction terms between the percent black in the metropolitan area and the zip-code education measures. Using the three categories of metropolitan area, two interaction terms were created by multiplying the dummy variables representing medium and high black metropolitan areas with the zip-code education measure. Another interaction term measuring the effects of zip-code education in rural areas was also included, leaving the dummy variable for a low black metropolitan area as the excluded term. The results are depicted in Table 2.

Contrary to the threat hypothesis, the effect of educational composition does not change with the racial environment. Whites in low-education zip codes in predominantly black metropolitan areas were no more racially antagonistic than whites in low-education places in largely white metropolitan areas. In none of the equations listed in Table 2 are the interaction effects between zip-code education and metropolitan racial composition large or statistically significant. Quite simply, the effects of zip-code education are the same irrespective of the surrounding racial environment. Nor are the effects different when the racial context is the zip code. When similar equations were estimated with interactions between zip-code education and racial composition, the same results emerged: the effects of zip-code education are no greater in microcontexts with larger percentages of blacks.

Notes

1. Other, nonattitudinal research has supported Key's claim. For example, James (1988) found that depressed black registration was caused not so much by a large black population as by repressive economic arrangements that required white farm owners to keep black farm workers politically quiescent.

2. Carsey (1995) and Wright (1977) also compare different levels of context but focus largely on electoral behavior. The difficulty in drawing conclusions from these works comes from the substantial differences between the determinants of voting behavior and racial attitudes, particularly with respect to context; for instance, rural and urban counties may have different voting procedures or mobilization efforts that could affect voting choice in a way that does not shape racial attitudes.

3. Many of these studies differentiate between political threat, economic threat, or status threat and some (Blalock 1967) specify curvilinear relationships between black populations and white racial animosity. In taking these works as a whole, however, it seems clear that all types of threat are closely linked and most view threat increasing as a linear function of the black population.

4. Alvarez and Brehm (1997, 349) describe the sample: "The survey was a telephone interview based on random-digit dialing using a stratified two-phase sample selection procedure. The first phase sampled from known area codes and prefixes, appending a four-digit random number to generate a complete ten-digit telephone number. The second phase drew disproportionately from sample strata containing at least one known residential number, although drawing also from strata where there was no known residential number. . . . The target population consisted of all English speaking adults over 18 years old, residing in households with telephones within the contiguous 48 states."

5. Zip-code level data may not precisely measure a respondent's immediate neighborhood, but they provide a much better indicator of the respondent's immediate context than county or metropolitan area data. Most zip codes in our study contain between 10,000 and 40,000 inhabitants.

6. The average percent black across 265 metropolitan statistical areas is 10 percent with a standard deviation of .09; it is 19 percent (a standard deviation of .06) for percent with a college degree. For smaller contextual units the averages and standard deviations for race are about the same but much higher for education: the average percent black across zip codes is 8 percent with a standard deviation of .13; the average percent with a college degree across zip codes is 22 with a standard deviation of .14.

7. Many zip codes with low to moderate incomes may be comprised of middle- to upper-class residents who are either in school, retired, live in southern or rural areas, or simply work in low-paying professions (see Massey and Eggars 1993; Huckfeldt 1986). While the percent with a college degree ranges from 5 to 75 percent in our sample, unemployment only varies from 2 to 23 percent. Occupational categories are not so easily ranked (not all administrative jobs are necessarily middle class; some are low-skill, low-paid work). The possibility that zip-code education may nevertheless capture effects that are distinct from zip-code income is explored in Appendix A [not included here], which suggests that the effects are in fact quite similar.

8. Three items were averaged, summed, and rescaled from 0 to 1 to create the symbolic racism measure. First, respondents were asked, "Taking everything into consideration, do you think the government has been paying too much attention to the problems of minorities, about the right amount of attention, or do you think they haven't been paying enough attention to these groups?" Then respondents were asked to rate their anger from 0 (no anger) to 10 (extremely angry) on a variety of items. The two used in the symbolic racism measure were "How about giving blacks and other minorities special advantages in jobs and schools?" and "spokesmen for minorities who are always complaining that blacks are being discriminated against?"

9. Respondents were asked, "How about (STEREOTYPE)? On a scale of 0 to 10, how well do you think it describes most blacks?" with 0 being a "very inaccurate" and 10 being a "very good" description, where STEREOTYPE is a characteristic. Negative characteristics included aggressive or violent, lazy, boastful, irresponsible, and complaining. Positive characteristics were dependable, intelligent in school, determined to succeed, hardworking, and good neighbors. A composite scale was created by subtracting the sum of the positives from the sum of the negatives. This score was then rescaled from 0 to 1.

10. Respondents were asked to rate the importance of these values on a scale from 0 to 10. These five items were drawn after a principle component analysis of an original group of twelve indicators that might capture the elements within Adorno et al.'s (1950) "F scale." The five items we chose all had a factor loading above .7. The excluded items measured questions on important values in raising children, tolerance of different groups, and questioning rules and authority.

11. Respondents were read a series of statements about Jews and asked how much they agreed or disagreed (strongly or somewhat) to each. Responses were combined in an unweighted average to generate a four-point scale.

12. All predispositional measures have alpha scores over .57.

13. The NRPS made heavy use of wording experiments in asking about policy preferences. Because of the limited sample size in some of the contexts, we combined different versions of questions. As a check, we first estimated our equations separately within each experimental condition. In all cases, the size and direction of the contextual coefficients were approximately the same as when the experimental conditions are combined, although they would typically lose statistical significance, a product of the reduced sample size.

14. The question asked, "How do you feel about blacks buying houses in white suburbs?" While 88 percent of white respondents initially reported being in favor of blacks buying homes in white suburbs, only 50 percent of this subgroup, when asked in identically worded follow-up questions, were in favor of efforts by either government, religious, or business groups to encourage blacks to buy homes in white suburbs.

15. The question asked, "Some people feel that the government in Washington should (increase spending for programs to help blacks get more jobs/do more to make sure that blacks are not discriminated against in getting jobs). Others feel that blacks should take care of their own problems. How do you feel?"

16. Not surprisingly, the racial composition of the zip code mirrors the hypersegregation found in most American cities and neighborhoods (Massey and Denton 1993). Roughly a quarter of white Americans live in zip codes that are less than 1 percent black. The next quartile live in zip codes under 3 percent black and the third quartile in zip codes under 10 percent black. Only a quarter of all white respondents live in zip codes that contain at least the same percentage of blacks as live in the country as a whole. The distributions across the other contextual measures are not so imbalanced: for example, 50 percent of whites live in a metropolitan area that is at least 10 percent black. There are no systematic variations in the standard deviations of the mean scores.

17. The standard errors for the means did not vary consistently across values for any of the predisposition items or for any of the three contextual measures.

18. In order to measure the racial composition of metropolitan areas without excluding rural residents, we divided metropolitan areas into three categories: under 7 percent black, 7–16 percent black, and over 16 percent black. This allows us to include all respondents by making two dummy variables from the later categories (medium black metro, high black metro), one variable for rural residence, and treating the metropolitan areas with few blacks as the excluded category. We found little variation in the racial composition of the rural areas—in

comparing the percent black in the county of our rural respondents, we found that over 85 percent lived in counties under 5 percent black. Consequently, most of the rural areas in this sample are predominantly white. Individual education is a six-category scale, income a thirteen-category scale, length of residence a five-category scale, and age is coded directly from 18 to 94.

19. Nor are there any significant effects from the percent black in the county. When a term measuring the percent black in the county was substituted for both the zip code and metropolitan area racial measures, no statistically significant coefficients emerge. Because metropolitan areas are comprised of counties, this finding is generally not surprising.

20. Given the correlation between the percent black in the zip code and metropolitan area (i.e., metropolitan areas with more blacks are more likely to contain zip codes with more blacks), high multicollinearity was obviously a concern for the multivariate estimates. Multicollinearity, however, does not appear to be influencing the results. When separate equations were run with only one of the racial contextual indicators used at a time, the results were virtually the same. For instance, including percent black in the zip code as the only contextual measure of race did not yield large or statistically significant coefficients for that measure. Nor could we find any interactive effects among the racial contexts. In other words, the effects of living in a predominantly black zip code were no different in a metropolitan area with more blacks. Finally, given the low number of cases per context, multi-level estimation procedures like HLM cannot be used.

21. Similar results are attained when the median household income is used in place of zip-code education: the equations predict that residents of zip codes with higher incomes will score lower on the symbolic racism, negative stereotype, and authoritarianism scales, although the size of the coefficients is lower and their relative standard errors greater, reflecting the noisy character of median household income. Nevertheless, the consistency of these results shows that zip-code education is not fundamentally different from income as an indicator of zip-code socio-economic status. This does not distinguish among the three rival hypotheses—threat, norms, and collective circumstances—because zip-code education may be a more reliable measure of material circumstances than is zip-code income. Additional tests (not depicted) with both the education and income level of the metropolitan area included failed to yield any significant results, the consequences of metropolitan economic contexts being so diffuse.

References

Adorno, T.W., Else Frenkel-Brunswik, Daniel Levinson, and R. Nevitt Sanford. 1950. *The Authoritarian Personality*. New York: Wiley.

Alvarez, R. Michael, and John Brehm. 1997. "Are Americans Ambivalent Toward Racial Policies?" *American Journal of Political Science* 41:345–374.

Bettelheim, Bruno, and Morris Janowitz. [1950] 1964. *Social Change and Prejudice*. New York: Macmillan.

Blalock, Hubert M. 1967. *Toward a Theory of Minority-Group Relations*. New York: Wiley.

Bobo, Lawrence. 1988. "Group Conflict, Prejudice, and the Paradox of Contemporary Racial Attitudes." In *Eliminating Racism: Profiles in Controversy*, ed. Phyllis Katz and Dalmas Taylor. New York: Plenum Press.

Boger, John Charles. 1997. "Race and the American City: The Kerner Commission Report in Retrospect." In *Race, Poverty, and American Cities*, ed. John Charles Boger and Judith Welch Wegner. Chapel Hill: University of North Carolina Press.

Brown, Roger. 1985. *Social Psychology*. 2nd ed. New York: Free Press.

Carsey, Thomas. 1995. "The Contextual Effects of Race on White Voter Behavior: The 1989 New York Mayoral Election." *Journal of Politics* 51:221–228.

Danielson, Michael. 1976. *The Politics of Exclusion*. New York: Columbia University Press.

Feldman, Stanley, and Karen Stenner. 1997. "Perceived Threat and Authoritarianism." *Political Psychology* 18:741.

Forbes, Hugh. 1997. *Ethnic Conflict*. New Haven: Yale University Press.

Fossett, Mark A., and K. Jill Kiecolt. 1989. "The Relative Size of Minority Populations and White Racial Attitudes." *Social Science Quarterly* 70:820–835.

Fromm, Eric. 1941. *Escape from Freedom*. New York: Holt, Rinehart, & Winston.

Giles, Michael, and Arthur Evans. 1986. "The Power Approach to Intergroup Hostility." *Journal of Conflict Resolution* 30:469–485.

Giles, Michael, and Kaenan Hertz. 1994. "Racial Threat and Partisan Identification." *American Political Science Review* 88:317–326.

Glaser, James. 1994. "Back to the Black Belt: Racial Environment and White Racial Attitudes in the South." *Journal of Politics* 56:21–41.

Green, Donald Phillip, Dara Strolovich, and Janelle S. Wong. 1998. "Defended Neighborhoods, Integration, and Hate Crime." *American Journal of Sociology* 104:372–403.

Gurr, Ted. 1968. "Psychological Factors in Civil Violence." *World Politics* 20:245–278.

Horowitz, Donald. 1985. *Ethnic Violence.* Cambridge: Harvard University Press.

Huckfeldt, Robert. 1986. *Politics in Context: Assimilation and Conflict in Urban Neighborhoods.* New York: Agathon Press.

Huckfeldt, Robert, and Carol Kohfeld. 1989. *Race and the Decline of Class in American Politics.* Urbana: University of Illinois Press.

James, David R. 1988. "The Transformation of the Southern Racial State: Class and Race Determinants of Local-State Structures." *American Sociological Review* 53:191–208.

Key, V.O. 1984 [1949]. *Southern Politics in State and Nation.* New York: Knopf.

Kinder, Donald R., and Tali Mendelberg. 1995. "Cracks in American Apartheid: The Political Impact of Prejudice Among Desegregated Whites." *Journal of Politics* 57:402–424.

Kinder, Donald R., and Lynn Sanders. 1996. *Divided by Color: Racial Politics and Democratic Ideals in the American Republic.* Chicago: University of Chicago Press.

Konecni, Vladimir. 1979. "The Role of Aversive Events in the Development of Intergroup Conflict." In *The Social Psychology of Intergroup Relations,* ed. William Austin and Stephen Worchel. Monterey, CA: Brooks/Cole Publishing Company.

Levine, Robert, and Donald Campbell. 1972. *Ethnocentricism: Theories of Conflict, Ethnic Attitudes, and Group Behavior.* New York: Wiley.

Massey, Douglas, and Nancy A. Denton. 1993. *American Apartheid: Segregation and the Making of the Underclass.* Cambridge: Harvard University Press.

Massey, Douglas, and Mitchell Eggers. 1993. "The Spatial Concentration of Affluence and Poverty During the 1970s." *Urban Affairs Quarterly* 29:299–315.

Matthews, Donald, and James W. Prothro. 1966. *Negroes and the New Southern Politics.* New York: Harcourt, Brace and World.

Rieder, Grant. 1985. *Canarsie: The Jews and Italians of Brooklyn Against Liberalism.* Cambridge: Harvard University Press.

Sales, S. 1973. "Threat as a Factor in Authoritarianism: An Analysis of Archival Data." *Journal of Personality and Social Psychology* 28:44–57.

Schneider, Mark. 1989. *The Competitive City: The Political Economy of Suburbia.* Pittsburgh: University of Pittsburgh Press.

Schneider, Mark, and John Logan. 1984. "Racial Segregation and Racial Change in American Suburbs, 1970–1980." *American Journal of Sociology* 89:874–888.

Sherif, Muzafer. 1966. *Group Conflict and Cooperation: Their Social Psychology.* London: Routledge and Kegan Paul.

Skogan, Wesly G. 1990. *Disorder and Decline: Crime and the Spiral of Decay in American Neighborhoods.* Los Angeles: University of California Press.

Sniderman, Paul M., and Thomas Piazza. 1993. *The Scar of Race.* Cambridge: Belknap Press of Harvard University.

Tajfel, Henri. 1982. *Social Identity and Intergroup Relations.* Cambridge: Cambridge University Press.

Tajfel, Henri, and John Turner. 1979. "An Integrative Theory of Intergroup Conflict." In *The Social Psychology of Intergroup Relations,* ed. William Austin and Stephen Worchel. Monterey, CA: Brooks/Cole Publishing Company.

Taylor, Marylee. 1998. "Local Racial/Ethnic Proportions and White Attitudes: Numbers Count." *American Sociological Review* 63:56–78.

Voss, Stephen. 1996. "Beyond Racial Threat: Failure of an Old Hypothesis in the New South." *Journal of Politics* 58:1156–1170.

Wright, Gerald. 1977. "Contextual Models of Electoral Behavior: The Southern Wallace Vote." *American Political Science Review* 71:497–508.

Discussion Questions

1. The "power-threat" hypothesis holds that the proportion of blacks in a given community is the central determinant of white racism in that community. What other factors could arguably be responsible for differences in the degree of racism, according to the authors?
2. Why were the authors unable to fashion a field experiment to test their hypotheses?
3. How did the authors measure black geographic concentration? Did their measure make sense?
4. What was the unit of analysis in this study?

Commentary

Oliver and Mendelberg began with a well-known, widely accepted premise and then proceeded to undermine it with a strong research design. Many of the most important advances in social science, and in all scientific fields for that matter, begin this way. Conventional wisdom often turns out to be wrong, or at least incomplete, but solid empirical inquiry is required to demonstrate its weakness. The study excerpted here made a significant contribution by showing that the "power-threat" hypothesis is not necessarily the last word on the subject.

The authors began by looking at the differences among racial attitudes of the survey respondents living in different metropolitan areas or zip codes with different percentages of black residents. They also looked at how these attitudes vary depending on the average educational attainment in each zip code area. This *bivariate* analysis (see chapter 11) suggests that racist attitudes decline when there is greater educational attainment in an area, but that the percentage of black residents in a given area has little impact. These are interesting findings, but the fact that more than a single variable could affect differences in racist attitudes required the use of a multivariate study.

The Oliver/Mendelberg study is an ex post facto design because the independent variables and the dependent variables were measured at one time, and the "control" was achieved through statistical analysis rather than by the creation of control and experimental groups of subjects. Ideally, the authors would like to have been able to select a random sample of citizens, assign them randomly to two groups, one of which would be exposed to life in an area with a high black concentration and the other exposed to life in an area without a high black concentration. If such a study could be implemented, we would be able to see if differences between the two groups of subjects with respect to their racist attitudes emerged, and, if so, we could say that the differences were attributable to the fact that only one of the groups lived in an area with a high concentration of black residents. Obviously, such an experiment would not be possible.

As in all ex post facto designs, Oliver and Mendelberg thus tried to determine which factors *other than the independent variable* (the percentage of black residents in one's area) could possibly affect the development of racist attitudes. In a genuine experiment, the researcher does not have to know what other factors could affect the subjects because, whatever they are, they will equally affect the subjects in the control and experimental groups, and, thus, any differences between the groups will be attributable to the fact that only one group was exposed to the independent variable. In this multivariate analysis, the authors used their judgment and their understanding of the subject to select education level, age, income level, gender, partisan affiliation, and length of residence as variables that should be included.

As we will discuss in chapter 12, when all the variables are considered together in a multivariate analysis, we are able to see what effect a given independent variable has on the dependent variables *when the other independent variables are held constant.* The results in Table 2 show, for example, that "whites in low-education zip codes in predominantly black metropolitan areas were no more racially antagonistic than whites in low-education places in largely white metropolitan areas." The effect of being in a low-education area apparently increases racist attitudes, and this effect obtains regardless of variations in the concentration of black residents in the area. Although the authors did not use an experimental design, their study provides strong evidence that racism has more to do with education than with the concentration of black residents in a given area. This is an important finding about a perennially critical problem for American society.

3 Measurement and Operationalization I: Variables Pertaining to Aggregate Units

Research usually begins with imagination: what factors account for some behavior or pattern or condition? Political scientists usually read journalists' stories, editorial essays, and research reports of various kinds in generating their ideas. As mentioned in chapter 1, ideas that actually evolve into research projects require that the researcher consider the problem in *conceptual* terms. That is, he or she must identify the basic factors that transcend a specific incident or observation and that should be examined closely in the research design.

The next step is deciding how to measure the concepts that will become the elements of our hypothesis. No matter how sophisticated or impressive our analytic tools, our results are meaningless unless the concepts we study are measured accurately.

Concepts and Variables

Simply put, operationalization is the process of translating abstract concepts into observable indicators. Until operationalized, concepts like literacy or economic development or political participation have imprecise and diverse meanings. Most of us know how to explain the meanings of these terms, but they are not yet operationalized for scientific research.

Operationalization is often a painstaking process in political science. The fact that the concepts studied are generally familiar is, ironically, a serious obstacle to clear operational definitions. Most readers and many researchers quickly assume that the operational definition of a given concept is essentially given by its familiar meaning. For example, most of us could understand the thrust of this statement: "There is great inequality in land ownership in Latin America." However, an operational definition of "inequality in land ownership" is not as simple as we might expect. Even a concept such as "the age of a state" is often open to several different meanings. In scientific research, the analyst must design operational definitions that not only have recognizable meanings to readers, but that also produce usable data. Unless this is done successfully, any attempt at hypothesis-testing will fail.

The Criteria for Useful Operationalizations

As discussed in chapter 1, the empirical indicators we employ must be both valid and reliable. They must meaningfully measure the concept in question, and they must do so consistently across different subjects and at different times. Unfortunately, these two criteria are often in conflict. The most reliable measures may not be valid. Most students have encountered an example of this problem in connection with testing and grading procedures. Multiple-choice tests are highly reliable in that each answer is graded in exactly the same way. If "d" is the correct answer to a question, all students selecting this answer will receive exactly the same credit. However, as is widely recognized, multiple-choice exams fare less well when it comes to validity. Students who understand a particular concept fairly well may nonetheless select the wrong answer from the list of available choices because of ambiguous wording or because they do not understand one specific point. When they receive zero credit, the score inaccurately indicates zero understanding, despite the fact that the student has learned something about the subject of the question.

Essay exams have less of a validity problem. Such exams allow the instructor more freedom to evaluate the student's response and, where appropriate, to give partial credit, thus reflecting more accurately the actual level of the student's mastery of the material. The potentially greater validity of the essay test is secured at some cost to reliability, however, since the scores awarded will inevitably be affected by the student's interpretation of the questions, the instructor's response to different student writing styles, or simple fatigue. In testing and grading, as in many other areas, it is difficult to devise measurement strategies that are both highly valid and highly reliable.

Successful operationalization must also produce indicators that can be measured in an objective manner. This requirement is implicit in the ideas of validity and reliability, but it deserves special notice. Many political concepts are particularly difficult to deal with objectively; we have strong notions of what is meant by democracy, human rights, or even economic development. The indicators we employ as measures of our variables must be constructed in ways that eliminate the influence of the researcher's prejudices on the data collection process.

Finally, our operational definitions of concepts must be practical. Most political scientists have, at one time or another, considered research ideas that are conceptually interesting but involve impractical measurement strategies. Prepared surveys and census data are often used because operational variables based on them are usually practical. This kind of material is available in government documents or in similar sources, and the researcher only has to choose items that validly represent the concepts at hand. Operational variables that require generation of raw data can be very ingenious, but, unfortunately, projects employing such operationalizations are often abandoned because of time or resource constraints.

For example, a colleague and I once attempted to analyze a large number of legislative enactments in terms of the degree of administrative discretion that each enactment contained. We wanted to give each legislative enactment a "score" corresponding to how much discretion it gave to agency officials in that area of public policy. This seemingly straightforward effort quickly bogged down as we attempted to devise a "scoring" formula for profoundly complex and varied documents. The project may yet succeed, but its operationalization has proven to be a monumental task.

Our focus in this chapter is on the operationalization of **aggregate variables**, that is, variables that pertain to states, countries, or other collective entities. Such variables often figure prominently in political research, as when we argue that "free-market countries protect human rights more effectively than socialist countries," or propose that "states with especially competitive party systems spend more for welfare and education than other states." These and similar propositions require that we operationalize concepts involving state-to-state or country-to-country comparisons.

The following selections illustrate how aggregate-level concepts that may at first appear simple are really quite complex. These two examples were selected because they demonstrate how the researchers' thorough substantive understanding of the problem enabled them to select appropriate indicators for their concepts.

———————————— Excerpt 3 ————————————

As election results show us every two years, the American states vary considerably with respect to ideology. Some states are likely to support conservative Republicans while others are usually safe havens for liberal Democrats. This information figures prominently in the electoral strategies devised by political consultants in both parties.

Ideological differences among states may also help to account for state-to-state differences in terms of the policies and programs they adopt. Some states are reluctant to spend much money on education, welfare, and environmental protection, while other states are eager to take an activist stand on such issues. Some states embrace the death penalty, while others have rejected it for more than a century. While many factors are obviously involved in leading states to adopt different policy choices, it is clear that the predominant ideology of each state's citizens is one of them.

However, it is also clear that a state's elected political leaders may have ideological positions that do not accurately reflect the prevailing ideology of their citizens. Sometimes, a conservative politician may have electoral success in a liberal state, or vice versa, because he or she is personally charismatic, or because the other party was hobbled by scandal or a weak candidate. In some cases, politicians may effectively conceal their real ideological positions until after the election is over.

There are several important political science questions that require us to consider the differences among states, and among the political leaders in the states, with respect to ideology. Explaining differences in policy, and analyzing the extent to which leaders actually represent their citizens, are simply the two most crucial questions to consider. If we find that the ideological differences among the states have little impact, it would raise fundamental doubts about the democratic quality of our governmental system.

The authors of the following excerpt constructed inventive measures of the ideology of each state and of each state's elected leaders, an important step toward making it possible to address some of these questions. Their study is a fascinating example of how the difficulties encountered in measuring basic political science concepts lead analysts to adopt creative, and perhaps controversial, operational definitions.

Before reading the excerpt, it is important to appreciate the goals that the authors had for their measures. They were not interested in creating a measure that would give them a complete, detailed, and fully informative picture of each state's predominant political ideology, or a comprehensive assessment of each individual politician's worldview. Instead, they wanted to create a data set that would enable them to make comparisons across states. If we want to acquire a deep understanding of the dominant ideology in Utah and Minnesota, for example, we would want to spend several months doing surveys, reading textbooks adopted in local schools, digesting local newspapers, attending religious ceremonies in the most prevalent denominations, and taking in the content of political advertisements that the residents find persuasive. Our report would doubtlessly make interesting reading. However, the authors of the following excerpt wanted measures that would allow them to make quantitative comparisons across states so that certain important research questions could be tested. Their study reveals that achieving this goal calls for an approach to measurement that is quite different from what we would use for other purposes.

Measuring Citizen and Government Ideology in the American States, 1960–1993

William D. Berry, *Florida State University*

Evan J. Ringquist, *Florida State University*

Richard C. Fording, *University of Kentucky*

Russell L. Hanson, *Indiana University Bloomington*

American Journal of Political Science 42, no. 1 (January 1998): 327–348. Copyright © 1998 by the University of Wisconsin Press. Reprinted with permission.

Democracy requires a strong correspondence between popular preferences, the ideological orientations of elected representatives, and government policies. Many scholars focus on these connections at the state level in American politics. Two concepts are critical to their analyses. One is *state citizen ideology*, generally conceived as the mean position on a liberal-conservative continuum of the "active electorate" in a state (Erikson, Wright, and McIver [hereafter EW and M] 1993, 14). The other may be termed *state government ideology*—the mean position on the same continuum of the elected public officials in a state, weighted according to the power they have over public policy decisions (e.g., Berry and Berry 1992; Brown 1995; Plotnick and Winters 1985).

The two concepts are difficult to operationalize. Several analysts use political culture as a surrogate for citizen ideology (e.g., Grogan 1994; Taggart and Winn 1993). Others simulate public opinion using models that associate demographic characteristics with issue orientations (Weber and Shaffer 1972). A third group measures citizen ideology with the vote share received by a liberal candidate in a particularly ideological election, e.g., McGovern in 1972 (Klingman and Lammers 1984; Nice 1986). A fourth camp relies on respondents' ideological self-identification; Wright, Erikson, and McIver [hereafter WE and M] (1985) combine dozens of *New York Times*/CBS News polls to create samples large enough to estimate the average ideological position of a state's citizens.

Except for the simulation-based indicator, all of these measures ignore longitudinal variation in citizen ideology. This may not seem problematic in cross-sectional analysis, where *all* variables are static. But measures of citizen ideology quickly become outdated. Elazar's (1984) maps of political culture date from 1965, and the McGovern vote share is a quarter century old. Similarly, the WE and M (1985) measure has been used to account for variation in policies observed in the late 1980s and early 1990s (Clingermayer and Wood 1995; Hill, Leighley, and Hinton-Andersson 1995), even though the measure is based on surveys between 1976 and 1982.

The operationalization of state government ideology is less eclectic than that of citizen ideology. The simplest indicator focuses on the party in control of a single institution, assuming that Democrats are liberal and Republicans are conservative (Hedge and Scicchitano 1994). But majority control of an institution does not confer absolute power over decision-making (Smith 1997). Thus, a measure based on parties' share of seats in the state legislature is an improvement (Scholz and Wei 1986). Other refinements use information about the party in control of each chamber of the legislature, as well as the governor's office (Berry and Berry 1992; Brown 1995). All such indicators neglect, however, important ideological distinctions among parties with the same label, e.g., the difference between Southern and Nonsouthern Democrats (Brown 1995; Jennings 1979; Paddock 1992).

A New Strategy for Measuring State Citizen and Government Ideology

The deficiencies of current indicators of ideology could be eliminated if we had direct access to citizens' and leaders' political orientations. Unfortunately, surveys of citizens' attitudes are only available for some states, and then only in selected years. Comparable assessments of the ideology of state legislators and governors are not available on a regular basis, either. Hence, we must forge a different strategy for constructing annual measures of citizen and government ideology in each of the 50 states. Specifically, we propose measures based on interest group ratings of members of Congress, supplemented by two other sources of information: election returns for congressional races, and data on the party composition of state legislatures and party affiliation of governors.

Apparently, Rabinowitz, Gurian, and MacDonald (1984) were the first to measure state *citizen* ideology using interest group ratings of members of Congress. They combined information from Americans for Democratic Action (ADA) and Americans for Constitutional Action (ACA), computing an average ideology score for each state's congressional delegation. Others followed suit, using ratings from a variety of organizations (e.g., Barrilleaux and Miller 1988; Campbell 1992; Holbrook-Provow and Poe 1987). Regrettably, none of these scholars addressed a basic flaw in the original measure. In the typical congressional election, competing candidates have different ideological positions. Thus, a measure based solely on roll call votes by the *winning* candidate misrepresents "average" citizen ideology in the district by ignoring the ideological preferences of citizens who vote for losing candidates. Our measure rectifies this error by estimating the ideological positions of unsuccessful challengers and combining these scores with those of elected representatives.

Congressional roll call data have been used to measure state *government* ideology, too. For example, Piskulich (1993) treats a state's average congressional delegation ADA score as an indicator of state elites' ideology. This yields a continuous measure of government ideology, and allows for geographic differences in the "same" party; Republicans in Vermont tend to have very different ADA scores than their counterparts in Idaho, for example. There is still room for improvement, however. National and state legislators from the same party may have similar ideologies, but the strength of the party's congressional delegation can differ substantially from its strength in the state legislature. Hence the average voting score in a state's congressional delegation may not reflect the mean ideological position of the state's legislature. This problem can be solved by computing mean voting scores separately for Democratic and Republican congressional delegations, and calculating a weighted average that reflects the strength of each party in the state legislature (Plotnick and Winters 1985).

Whether a state legislature's ideology is measured by the percentage of seats held by each party, or by congressional party delegation ideology scores weighted by these percentages, extant measures unrealistically assume that the power of a party within a chamber is linearly related to the proportion of seats it controls. We modify this assumption and construct a new indicator of government ideology, after developing a measure of citizen ideology. The measures rely on nine specific assumptions about the behavior of voters, politicians, congressional rating organizations, political parties, and government institutions. We defend these assumptions following an abbreviated presentation of our methodologies.[1]

Citizen Ideology

To measure citizen ideology, we identify the ideological position of each member of Congress in each year using interest group ratings (see Assumption 2, discussed below). Next, we estimate citizen ideology in each district of a state using the ideology score for the district's incumbent, the estimated ideology score for a challenger (or hypothetical challenger) to the incumbent, and election results that presumably reflect ideological divisions in the electorate (see Assumption 1). Finally, citizen ideology scores for each district are used to compute an unweighted average for the state as a whole.

Thus, the major challenge is estimating citizen ideology in a congressional district in a given year.[2] Our measure averages the ideology scores for major party candidates, using weights that are proportional to each candidate's share of support in the district:

$$\text{CITIDEO}_{d,t} = (\text{INCSUPP}_{d,t})(\text{INCIDEO}_{d,t}) + (\text{CHALSUPP}_{d,t})(\text{CHALIDEO}_{d,t}) \qquad [1]$$

where $\text{CITIDEO}_{d,t}$ denotes citizen ideology in district d in year t. $\text{INCSUPP}_{d,t}$ is the (estimated) proportion of the electorate in year t preferring district d's incumbent, and CHALSUPP is the (estimated) proportion of the electorate preferring the challenger (or a hypothetical challenger). $\text{INCIDEO}_{d,t}$ is the ideology score for district d's incumbent in year t, and CHALIDEO is the (estimated) ideology score for the challenger (or hypothetical challenger).

The ideology of the incumbent is observed and measured by a rating organization. The ideology of the challenger is not directly observable; to estimate $\text{CHALIDEO}_{d,t}$ we presume that the ideology score of the challenger is equal to the average ideology score of all incumbents in the state from the same party (relying on Assumption 4).[3]

If elections were annual, we could observe citizens' support for the incumbent and challenger each year. As it is, we must estimate support for the incumbent and a "hypothetical challenger" in off-years using results from the previous and following elections; we give greater weight to the election that is closer in time to the year of analysis, and we assume that public support for an incumbent changes gradually throughout his/her term (see Assumption 5).[4] For cases in which a district's incumbent does not compete in the following general election, we assume (#3, below) that voters perceive the ideological position of the candidate from the incumbent's party to be similar to that of the incumbent so that the election can still be viewed as a referendum on the incumbent's ideology.

Government Ideology

To measure the ideological position of a state government, we need ideology scores for the governor and the major party delegations in each house of the state legislature. These scores can then be aggregated on the basis of certain assumptions about the distribution of power among policy-makers.

Some labor organizations rate state legislators according to their voting records, just as the AFL-CIO Committee on Political Education [COPE] rates members of Congress, but the practice is not widespread. Hence we use information about the ideology of members of Congress to estimate the ideological positions of state legislators, on the assumption (#6, below) that the average ideological position of a party in a state's legislature is the same as the average position of that party's members of the state's congressional delegation.[5] Also, by construction the ideology of a state's governor is equal to the estimated average ideology score of state legislators from the same party (see Assumption 7).

Thus, our methodology yields annual ideology scores for five major actors in state government (the governor, and two major parties in each legislative chamber). To measure the ideological orientation of state government, these scores must be combined in a way that reflects the relative power of these five actors. In choosing weights, we stipulate that the governor and the legislative branch are equally powerful, and that within the legislative branch, the two chambers have equal strength (see Assumption 8).

Our assumption about the distribution of power between parties *within* a single chamber (see Assumption 9) is specified in Figure 1. There is a qualitative difference in the powers of the majority and minority parties. Even when the majority is slight, the maximum power that a minority party can attain is well below .50. For specificity we assume this value equals .40, which implies that the minimum share of power wielded by any majority party (regardless of its size) is .60. We further assume that a majority achieves total power when its share of seats reaches 60%. Finally, the arrowhead on the line in the upper right quadrant of Figure 1 reflects the property that as the majority's share of seats declines from .60 and approaches .50, power approaches .60, but drops abruptly to a value of .50 when seat share reaches one-half. Similarly, as the majority's share of seats increases from .40 and approaches .50, party power gradually increases from zero and approaches .40.

The relation depicted in Figure 1 can be used to determine the power of the Democratic and Republican delegations within a state's lower and upper chambers in any year, using data on party seat shares. To compute our ultimate measure of state government ideology we use these intra-chamber power share measures along with our assumptions about the inter-institutional distribution of power to compute a weighted average of the ideology scores for the five institutional actors:

$$\begin{aligned}
\text{GOVTIDEO}_{s,t} = (.25)[(&\text{POW:DEM:LOW}_{s,t})(\text{ID:DEM:LOW}_{s,t}) + \\
(&\text{POW:REP:LOW}_{s,t})(\text{ID:REP:LOW}_{s,t})] + \\
(.25)[(&\text{POW:DEM:UPP}_{s,t})(\text{ID:DEM:UPP}_{s,t}) + \\
(&\text{POW:REP:UPP}_{s,t})(\text{ID:REP:UPP}_{s,t})] + (.50)[\text{ID:GOV}_{s,t}]
\end{aligned} \qquad [2]$$

where $\text{GOVTIDEO}_{s,t}$ is the overall ideology of government in state s in year t. $\text{POW:DEM:LOW}_{s,t}$, $\text{POW:REP:LOW}_{s,t}$, $\text{POW:DEM:UPP}_{s,t}$, and $\text{POW:REP:UPP}_{s,t}$ are the Democrats' and Republicans' shares of power within a state's lower and upper chambers, respectively (the shares sum to 1 in each chamber). $\text{ID:DEM:LOW}_{s,t}$, $\text{ID:REP:LOW}_{s,t}$, $\text{ID:DEM:UPP}_{s,t}$, and $\text{ID:REP:UPP}_{s,t}$ are the average ideology scores of Democrats and Republicans in a state's lower and upper chambers, respectively (all of which are assumed to equal the average ideology of the corresponding state Democratic or Republican congressional delegation). $\text{ID:GOV}_{s,t}$ is the governor's ideology, equal to the average ideology score of all members of the state legislature in the governor's party.

The terms on the first two lines of equation 2 reflect the ideology of the lower chamber (weighted one-fourth), the terms on the third and fourth lines reflect the ideology of the upper chamber (weighted one-fourth), and the last line reflects the governor's ideology (weighted one-half).[6] Together these terms

Figure 1   **Assumed Relationship Between the Proportion of Seats in a Legislative Chamber Controlled by a Political Party and the Proportion of Power Within the Chamber Controlled by the Party**

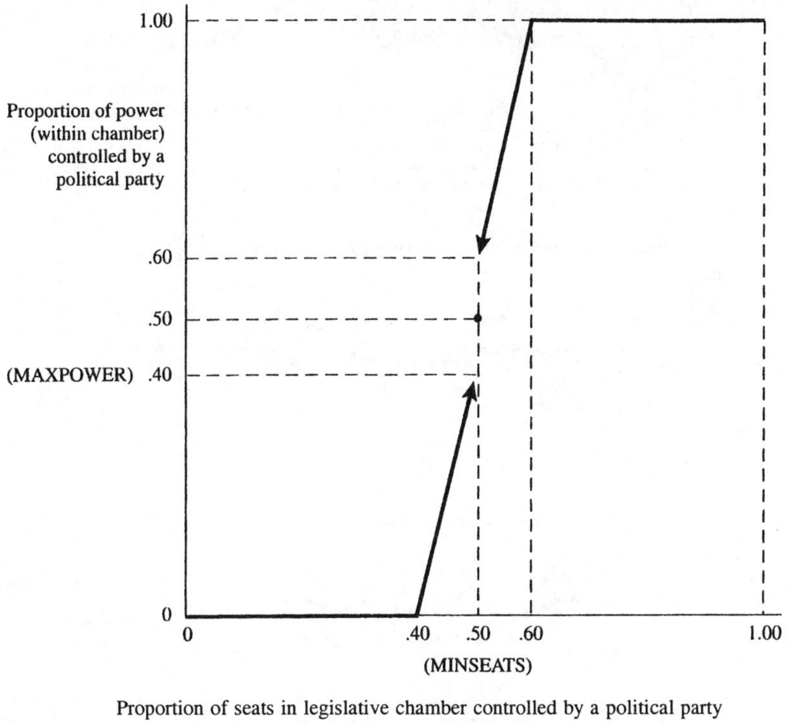

Proportion of seats in legislative chamber controlled by a political party

locate the ideological center of gravity in state government at a particular moment in time.

Implementing the Measures

To measure citizen ideology and government ideology we need interest group ratings reflecting the ideology of members of Congress. Several good candidates are reported annually by *Congressional Quarterly*, but only ADA and COPE scores are available for the entire period from 1960 to 1993.[7] Consequently, for each state in each year our indicators are based on an average of ADA and COPE scores, with zero representing the most conservative value, and 100 the most liberal position.

   In some states, citizen and government ideology track each other very closely over time. Graph A of Figure 2 shows that this is true in a populous liberal state—Massachusetts—and a smaller conservative state—Alabama. In other states, citizen and government ideology diverge substantially. Citizen ideology has been stable in Ohio, but frequent changes in party control have brought dramatic shifts in state government's ideological position, as is apparent in graph B.[8]

Figure 2   **Trends in Citizen and Government Ideology in Selected States, 1960–1993**

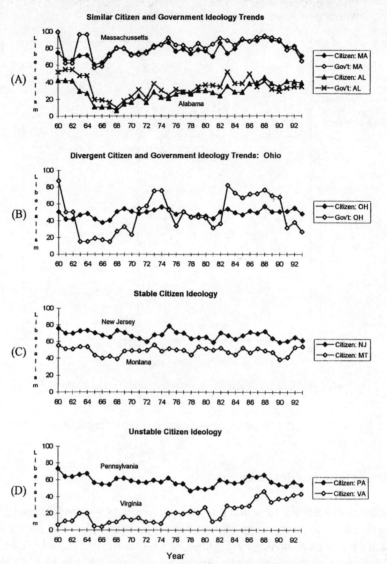

Annual measures shed new light on WE and M's assertion that state citizen ideology is stable over time. Graph C shows this is true for some states: between 1960 and 1993, citizen ideology in New Jersey has a relatively narrow range of 19.4 and a standard deviation of 4.8. (Illinois has the smallest range: 14.0.) Even some very small states like Montana, for which we would expect more temporal variation due to measurement error, exhibit a high degree of stability. Elsewhere, though, citizen ideology varies substantially over time (see graphs D and A). In Pennsylvania, citizen ideology has a range of 26.7 and a standard deviation of 5.7. The comparable statistics in Massachusetts are 33.0 and 8.2. For Virginia, they are 42.8 and 12.3. In none of these states are the large range and variance the result of a stochastic process. A simple regression of our indicator on time uncovers a statistically significant "change" coefficient in each case; the wide variation signals real shifts in the ideology of citizens and elites.[9] In fact, the range of ideology values exceeds one-fourth of the maximum potential range (100) for the citizen ideology indicator in 34 of the 50 states. Evidently, EW and M (1993) are wrong about the general stability of citizens' ideological orientations in the American states—if our measures are sound. We now proceed to that demonstration.

Reliability and Validity of Our Ideology Measures

The reliability of our indicators can be assessed by treating scores from different organizations as alternative measures of legislators' ideology. In a test of parallel forms, we constructed distinct measures of state *citizen* ideology based on ADA scores and COPE scores, respectively. When the data are pooled across the states and years, the two indicators are correlated at .85. A pure ADA measure of state *government* ideology correlates with a pure COPE measure at an even higher level of .90.[10] These results confirm our measures' high degree of reliability.[11]

We assess the validity of our ideology indicators in three ways. Our measures are based on a set of explicit assumptions, so we indirectly analyze our measures' validity by assessing the accuracy of these underlying assumptions. Then we determine the convergent validity of our citizen indicator, correlating it with an accepted measure of ideology. Finally, we assess the construct validity of our measures by examining their relation to other variables linked to ideology in theories of state politics.

Assessing the Validity of Our Assumptions

Underlying our measures are nine assumptions that we now articulate and defend. Wherever possible, we include empirical tests of the accuracy of these assumptions.

> *Assumption 1:* **Voters are arrayed on a liberal-conservative ideological continuum, and in two-candidate elections they vote for the candidate whose ideology is closest to their own.**

Early studies discounted the ideological capacity of voters, but measurement error marred the analyses (Achen 1975). Later researchers detected an increase in ideological thinking among the American electorate. Not all scholars are convinced of the change, but the preponderance of evidence supports Jacoby's (1995) conclusion that a large majority of the electorate displayed some degree of ideological thought by the 1980s. The impact of ideology on voting behavior is generally conceded. Mann (1980) shows that ideology plays a significant role in voters' evaluation of congressional candidates. In turn, these evaluations are strongly related to vote choice in congressional elections (Brown and Woods 1991). Thus, the "Downsian" model of voting is appropriate for our purposes.

Assumption 2: **On at least some bills legislators' votes are guided primarily by ideology. Moreover, "raters" can identify a set of bills that accurately reflects legislators' ideology.**

Members of Congress have enduring ideological dispositions, which accounts for the relative stability of their voting records (Poole and Rosenthal 1991). Various groups provide reliable and valid measures of the ideological dispositions of members of Congress (Herrera, Epperlein, and Smith 1995; Smith, Herrera, and Herrera 1990). Our analysis confirms this finding; the correlation between members' ADA and COPE scores for 1960–93 is .88, strongly implying that rating organizations are tapping a common dimension of ideology.

Assumption 3: **When a seat is open, voters perceive the ideological position of the new candidate from the incumbent's party to be similar to that of the incumbent.**[12]

In the absence of survey data on voter perceptions, this assumption cannot be tested directly. We also lack information about the ideological position of unsuccessful candidates. We can measure, however, the ideological distance between incumbents and party members who replaced them. We examined all districts with the same boundaries before and after any election conducted in the period 1961–92, and computed the average of ADA and COPE scores for representatives in the pre- and post-election years. Where the incumbent was not renominated, but was succeeded by a member of the same party (n = 387), the average absolute difference between pre- and post-ideology scores was 13.8. The average absolute change in ideology scores for 4,349 reelected incumbents was 8.6, a value only 5.2 units less than 13.8. Thus, incumbents are generally replaced by party members with similar ideological positions, and it would be surprising if voters did not notice such a pronounced tendency.

Assumption 4: **Voters perceive the ideological position of a challenger to resemble the typical ideological position of incumbents from the same party in the same state.**

A direct test of this assumption is impossible because we lack data on voter perceptions, and interest groups rate challengers only if they win. We can observe, however, successful challengers during their first year in office, and compare their ideological positions to the average position of all non-first-year incumbents from the same party in the same state. For 1961–93, the average absolute difference between the ADA/COPE score for a freshman member of Congress and the mean ideology score for nonfreshmen incumbents of the same party and state is 11.9 (n = 745). In contrast, the mean absolute difference between the ideology score for a freshman and the average score for nonfreshmen incumbents of the opposing party in the same state is 53.6. Therefore, challengers' ideological positions are similar to the positions of incumbents of the same party and state.

> *Assumption 5:* **The proportion of voters who prefer the incumbent's ideology to that of a "hypothetical challenger" changes linearly from the proportion of votes received by the incumbent at the start of a term to the proportion of votes received by the incumbent (or the successor candidate from his or her party) in the next election.**

With no information about support for incumbents during their terms, we must interpolate between elections. This oversimplifies reality, especially in Senate "districts" where there is a six-year gap between elections. The vast majority of districts we analyze, however, are in the House and have a shorter interval between elections. Judging from the positive results of our battery of reliability and validity tests, the distortion associated with this simplifying assumption must be small.

> *Assumption 6:* **The mean ideological position of the members of a party in a state's legislature is similar to the mean position of the party's U.S. representatives and senators.**

Some labor organizations rate state legislators in the same fashion as national organizations rate members of Congress. We obtained ideology scores for state legislators from 18 state AFL-CIO federations for various years, and calculated 142 average party delegation AFL-CIO scores.[13] These average scores correlate very highly (r = .95) with average ADA/COPE scores for the comparable congressional delegations.[14] Also, when the average state score is regressed on the average congressional score, the intercept estimate is near zero (1.778) and the slope estimate is close to one (.934), meaning the regression line approximates a 45-degree angle through the origin.[15] This is very strong evidence of the ideological similarity of state and national legislators of the same party, although the data are drawn from a nonrandom sample of state-years.

Information about the ideological positions of state legislators is also available from Uslaner and Weber's (1977) survey, from which EW and M (1993, 98–9) derive mean scores for legislators from each state party delegation in 1974. The cross-sectional correlation between these scores and the average ADA/COPE scores for the parallel congressional delegation in 1974 is .78.

Assumption 7: **The expected ideological position of a governor is equal to the average ideological position of state legislators from the same party.**

Because of a lack of information about governors, Assumption 7 cannot be tested directly. There is evidence, however, that state political elites from the same party, but different institutions, have similar ideological positions (Nice and Cohen 1983). Using an ideological self-identification item in Cotter et al.'s (1984) survey, EW and M (1993) calculate average ideology scores for county chairpersons in each party in all states for 1979–80. The correlation between this score and the average ADA/COPE score for the comparable congressional delegation is .83. EW and M (1993) also report an elite ideology measure based on Miller and Jennings's (1987) survey of delegates to the 1980 Democratic and Republican presidential nominating conventions. The measure correlates with the average 1980 ADA/COPE congressional delegation score at .78.

Assumption 8: **The governor and the legislative branch have equal power over the policy decisions of state governments. Within the legislature, chambers have equal power.**

Measures of government ideology that average scores for different institutions typically employ weights of .50, .25, and .25 for the governor and the two legislative chambers, respectively (e.g., Berry and Berry 1992). The most common alternative weights the governor and each legislative chamber equally (e.g., Brown 1995). When our government ideology measure is recalculated using these weights, ideology scores change only slightly; the correlation between the two sets of scores (pooled for all states from 1960 to 1993) is .98. Our measures are insensitive to this assumption.

Assumption 9: **If parties have the same number of seats in a chamber, their power over policy is equal. Otherwise, the majority party controls at least 60% of the power. This power grows until the majority has 60% of the seats, when it obtains complete policy control.**

Two variables must be considered here. One is the maximum proportion of power that a *minority* party can attain (denoted MAXPOWER in Figure 1). The other is the minimum proportion of seats that gives a *majority* party virtually total power (MINSEATS). We calculated the government ideology measure nine different ways, using all combinations of MINSEATS values of .55, .60, and .65, and MAXPOWER values of .35, .40, and .45. The correlation matrix showing the relationships among the nine measures contains entries above .99 in all cells. Thus, our measure of government ideology is insensitive to minor changes in Assumption 9. We chose the intermediate values of .60 and .40.

Assessing Convergent Validity (with a Note on Reliability)

The most widely accepted indicator of state citizen ideology is WE and M's (1985; see also EW and M 1993) measure of public opinion liberalism. We compared our measure of citizen ideology to their original measure of conservatism (based on data from 1976 to 1982), and their updated measure of liberalism (which covers 1976–88). To insure comparability, we averaged our measure over the same periods analyzed by WE and M and excluded Alaska and Hawaii from the analysis. The correlation between our measure and WE and M's is a healthy –.68 for the 1976–82 period, and an even stronger .80 for 1976–88.

We expect a weaker fit between our citizen measure and EW and M's in less populous states. In small states, there are fewer congressional representatives whose scores can be used to estimate citizen (or government) ideology, and hence there is more random noise in the measure. The EW and M (1993) measure is similarly affected by low population. Their state samples range from 13,369 in California to only 292 in Wyoming. This means that both measures of citizen ideology are less reliable, and the correlation between them should be weaker in small states.

To test our expectation, we excluded the 13 states averaging two or fewer House districts during the 1970s and 1980s, and recalculated the correlation between our citizen measure and EW and M's across the remaining 37 states. The correlation rises to a very strong .90. Since the two indicators are based on fundamentally different methodologies, a correlation of .90 indicates that apart from the random error introduced when our indicator is measured for the smallest of states, there is a remarkably slim amount of additional systematic error.

Notes

1. A full description of the methodologies is in a supplement that accompanies the replication data set.

2. Each senator in a state is assumed to be elected in a separate (state-wide) district.

3. When there is no congressional delegation from one party in a given year, we estimate the score for the missing delegation using information about the other party in the same state, and the same party in neighboring states. See the unpublished supplement for details.

4. For uncontested elections, we linearly interpolate the vote share of the incumbent between the most recently contested election and the next contested election. To that value we add a "bonus" equal to 10% of the share estimated to be won by the challenger. We assume, however, that all incumbents in uncontested elections would have won at least 60% of the vote had they been challenged. The unpublished supplement gives the rationale for these assumptions and details of our methodology.

5. See note 3.

6. For years in which Minnesota and Nebraska have nonpartisan legislatures, GOVTIDEO is an unweighted average of the governor's ideology and the mean ideology score for all members of Congress from state s in year t.

7. The American Conservative Union and the American Civil Liberties Union [ACLU] did not begin rating members until 1964 and 1977, respectively. ACA stopped doing so in 1984.

8. The divergence of citizen and government ideology in states like Ohio shows that the two measures are distinct, even though they are derived in part from the same ADA/COPE ratings. Nevertheless, because of the overlap we do not advocate using our measures to investigate the causal relationship between citizen and government ideology.

9. For Virginia, the t-score for time is 8.74. The t-scores are 4.68 and -2.53 for Massachusetts and Pennsylvania, respectively. Similar regressions for the stable states of New Jersey and Montana produce estimates that are statistically indistinguishable from zero, as they should be.

10. We also constructed citizen and government ideology measures for 1977–92 using ACLU scores. For this period the correlation between our measure of citizen ideology and the ACLU-based measure is .85; it is .92 for our indicator of government ideology and one based on ACLU scores.

11. Our test of reliability is limited in scope. We demonstrate consistency in our measures when the rating organization is varied, while the remaining features are held constant.

12. This situation, as well as that described in Assumption 4, could arise because voters have little information about a new candidate's positions, or because new candidates actually tend to have ideologies similar to those of incumbents from the same party in the same state.

13. We obtained ratings for Arkansas (1987, 1989, 1991, 1993); California (1990, 1991, 1992, 1993); Colorado (1987–88, 1989–90, 1991–92); Connecticut (1992, 1993); Illinois (1991, 1993); Indiana (1991, 1992, 1993); Iowa (1991, 1992, 1993); Michigan (1991–92); Minnesota (1991, 1992, 1993); Missouri (1985, 1986, 1987, 1988, 1989, 1990, 1991, 1993); Montana (1977, 1981, 1983, 1985, 1987, 1989, 1991, 1993); North Dakota (1989, 1991, 1993); Oregon (1979, 1981, 1983, 1985, 1987, 1989, 1991, 1993); Pennsylvania (1991–92); Vermont (1989, 1991, 1992, 1993); Washington (1993); West Virginia (1983, 1984, 1985, 1986, 1987, 1988, 1989, 1990, 1991, 1993); and Wisconsin (1987–88, 1989–90, 1991–92).

14. State legislative scores reported on a two-year basis are compared to the corresponding two-year average ADA/COPE scores. Otherwise, the comparisons are annual.

15. In our regression, every state is weighted equally. A state's overall weight is divided equally across observations for which information is available. Thus, the observations for legislative party delegations in Washington each carry a weight of one, since data are available for a single year. Three years of ratings are available for Iowa, so each observation carries a weight of one-third. This compensates for the uneven availability of AFL-CIO scores over time.

References

Achen, Christopher H. 1975. "Mass Political Attitudes and the Survey Response." *American Political Science Review* 69:1218–31.

Barrilleaux, Charles, and Mark Miller. 1988. "The Political Economy of State Medicaid Policy." *American Political Science Review* 82:1089–107.

Berry, Frances Stokes, and William D. Berry. 1992. "Tax Innovation in the States: Capitalizing on Political Opportunity." *American Journal of Political Science* 36:715–42.

Brown, Robert. 1995. "Party Cleavages and Welfare Effort in the American States." *American Political Science Review* 89:23–33.

Brown, Robert D., and James A. Woods. 1991. "Toward a Model of Congressional Elections." *Journal of Politics* 53:454–74.

Campbell, James E. 1992. "Forecasting the Presidential Vote in the States." *American Journal of Political Science* 36:386–407.

Clingermayer, James, and B. Dan Wood. 1995. "Disentangling Patterns of State Debt Financing." *American Political Science Review* 89:108–20.

Cotter, Cornelius P., James L. Gibson, John F. Bibby, and Robert J. Huckshorn. 1984. *Party Organizations in American Politics.* New York: Praeger.

Elazar, Daniel. 1984. *American Federalism: A View from the States.* 3rd ed. New York: Harper.

Erikson, Robert S., John McIver, and Gerald C. Wright, Jr. 1987. "State Political Culture and Public Opinion." *American Political Science Review* 81:797–814.

Erikson, Robert S., Gerald C. Wright, Jr., and John McIver. 1989. "Political Parties, Public Opinion, and State Policy in the United States." *American Political Science Review* 83:729–50.

Erikson, Robert S., Gerald C. Wright, Jr., and John McIver. 1993. *Statehouse Democracy.* New York: Cambridge University Press.

Grogan, Colleen M. 1994. "Political-Economic Factors Influencing State Medicaid Policy." *Political Research Quarterly* 47:589–623.

Hedge, David, and Michael J. Scicchitano. 1994. "Regulating in Space and Time: The Case of Regulatory Federalism." *Journal of Politics* 56:134–53.

Herrera, Richard, Thomas Epperlein, and Eric R.A.N. Smith. 1995. "The Stability of Congressional Roll-Call Indexes." *Political Research Quarterly* 48:403–16.

Hill, Kim Quaile, and Jan Leighley. 1992. "The Policy Consequences of Class Bias in State Electorates." *American Journal of Political Science* 36:351–65.

Hill, Kim Quaile, Jan Leighley, and Angela Hinton-Andersson. 1995. "Lower Class Mobilization and Policy Linkage in the United States." *American Journal of Political Science* 39:75–86.

Holbrook, Thomas M. 1991. "Presidential Elections in Space and Time." *American Journal of Political Science* 35:91–109.

Holbrook-Provow, Thomas M., and Stephen C. Poe. 1987. "Measuring State Political Ideology." *American Politics Quarterly* 15:399–416.

Jacoby, William G. 1995. "The Structure of Ideological Thinking in the American Electorate." *American Journal of Political Science* 39:314–35.

Jennings, Edward T., Jr. 1979. "Competition, Constituencies, and Welfare Policies in the American States." *American Political Science Review* 73:414–29.

Klingman, David, and William W. Lammers. 1984. "The 'General Policy Liberalism' Factor in American State Politics." *American Journal of Political Science* 28:598–610.

Kmenta, Jan. 1986. *Elements of Econometrics.* 2nd ed. New York: Macmillan.

Mann, Thomas. 1980. *Unsafe at Any Margin: Interpreting Congressional Elections.* Washington, DC: American Enterprise Institute.

Meier, Kenneth J., and Deborah R. McFarlane. 1992. "State Politics on Funding of Abortions: A Pooled Time-Series Analysis." *Social Science Quarterly* 73:690–98.

Miller, Warren, and M. Kent Jennings. 1987. *Parties in Transition: A Longitudinal Study of Party Elites and Party Supporters.* New York: Russell Sage.

Morgan, David R. 1994. "Tax Equity in the American States." *Social Science Quarterly* 75:510–23.

Nice, David. 1986. "State Support for Constitutional Balanced Budget Requirements." *Journal of Politics* 48:134–42.

Nice, David, and Jeffrey Cohen. 1983. "Ideological Consistency among State Party Delegations to the U.S. House, Senate, and National Conventions." *Social Science Quarterly* 64:871–9.

Paddock, Joel. 1992. "Inter-Party Ideological Differences in Eleven State Parties: 1956–80." *Western Political Quarterly* 45:751–60.

Page, Benjamin, and Robert Shapiro. 1992. *The Rational Public: Fifty Years of Trends in America's Policy Preferences.* Chicago: University of Chicago Press.

Piskulich, C. Michelle. 1993. "Toward a Comprehensive Model of Welfare Exits: The Case of AFDC." *American Journal of Political Science* 37:165–85.

Plotnick, Robert D., and Richard F. Winters. 1985. "A Politico-Economic Theory of Income Redistribution." *American Political Science Review* 79:458–73.

Poole, Keith T., and Howard Rosenthal. 1991. "Patterns of Congressional Voting." *American Journal of Political Science* 35:228–78.

Rabinowitz, George, Paul H. Gurian, and Stuart E. MacDonald. 1984. "The Structure of Presidential Elections and the Process of Realignment, 1944 to 1980." *American Journal of Political Science* 27:611–35.

Scholz, John T., and Feng Heng Wei. 1986. "Regulatory Enforcement in a Federalist System." *American Political Science Review* 80:1249–70.

Smith, Eric R.A.N., Richard Herrera, and Cheryl Herrera. 1990. "The Measurement Characteristics of Congressional Roll-Call Indexes." *Legislative Studies Quarterly* 15:283–95.

Smith, Mark A. 1997. "The Nature of Party Governance: Connecting Conceptualization and Measurement." *American Journal of Political Science.*

Stimson, James A. 1991. *Public Opinion in America: Moods, Cycles, and Swings.* Boulder, CO: Westview.

Stimson, James A. 1994. "Domestic Policy Mood: An Update." *The Political Methodologist* 6:20–2.

Taggart, William A., and Russell G. Winn. 1993. "Imprisonment in the American States." *Social Science Quarterly* 74:736–49.

Uslaner, Eric M., and Ronald E. Weber. 1977. *Patterns of Decision-Making in State Legislatures.* New York: Praeger.

Weber, Ronald E., and William R. Shaffer. 1972. "Public Opinion and American State Policy Making." *Midwest Journal of Political Science* 16:633–49.

Wright, Gerald C., Jr., Robert S. Erikson, and John McIver. 1985. "Measuring State Political Ideology with Survey Data." *Journal of Politics* 47:469–89.

Wright, Gerald C., Jr., Robert S. Erikson, and John McIver. 1987. "Public Opinion and Policy Liberalism in the American States." *American Journal of Political Science* 31:980–1001.

Discussion Questions

1. What are some alternative ways to measure differences among states with respect to the prevailing ideology of their citizens? What are some other ways to measure the prevailing ideology of the elected leaders in each state?

2. Ideology and party identification are factors that do not change quickly over time. For what period of time do you think the authors' measures would be of practical usefulness before they should be updated? How would you make such a judgment?

3. How would you judge the *validity* and the *reliability* of the measures described in the excerpt? Did the authors sacrifice some of one for increases in the other?

4. What are the limits of these measures' application? Would you feel confident in using them to discuss differences in state political culture with representatives of each state? Why or why not?

5. How do the measures created here compare to the measures used in previous studies, such as using "the state's vote for McGovern in 1972" as a measure of a state's citizens' ideology?

Commentary

Some readers have reacted negatively to the measures designed in this study. We often consider differences among states in great richness of detail and historical context, and we evaluate the partisan and ideological positions of members of Congress as if each individual politician is unique. Each state and each elected leader is, in fact, unique in terms of ideology, and a full description of the ideology of either states or their politicians would require a comprehensive, multifaceted investigation, along with seasoned judgment.

This article illustrates that the objectives of scientific measurement and detailed description are often quite different. If we were writing a modern history of the politics of Tennessee or of Senator Fred Thompson, for example, we would approach our task very differently from the approach taken in this study. Scientific measurement almost always involves tremendous simplification. In some cases, the simplification produces superficial measures that are essentially worthless. In others, the simplification may be startling to casual observers, but the measures can still be useful to political scientists for the purpose of comparisons across a large number of cases. We may not have great confidence that our measure genuinely distinguishes between two very similar states, but we can be confident that *most* states with "very liberal" scores really are different, as a group, than *most* states with "very conservative" scores. If we are sufficiently confident of the overall comparisons, we will find that the measure is useful for the purpose at hand.

Put another way, the measures in this excerpt are quite reliable, but perhaps the fact that they simplify complex concepts would lead some readers to doubt their validity. This is not to say that there is no basis for seeing the measures as valid; the authors would probably respond that they are interested in state government and citizen ideology *as they are manifested in voting choices*, and, if understood in this somewhat limited way, the information used in the measures is quite sound. If a more detailed, historically based description of each state leader's politics or of each state's citizens' ideas would, potentially, provide a more complete picture, such a method could never be reliable. Different readers would judge the fine details of each state or leader in different ways; some would emphasize views on one kind of issue, while others would emphasize different issues in their efforts at comparison. Some would emphasize votes on bills, while others would emphasize speeches. The information produced this way could be interesting, but not scientifically useful. The method here created a reliable measure, generally unaffected by the biases of the researchers, and therefore useful for hypothesis testing.

The foundation of the measurement approach used in the article is a set of scores regularly given by the Americans for Democratic Action (ADA) and the AFL-CIO's Committee on Political Education (COPE). These groups compute scores based on the voting records of each member of congress. Those who consistently vote for bills that are considered "liberal" or "pro-labor" and who vote against bills that are "conservative" or "pro-business" get high scores from these groups. Legislators voting against labor/liberal bills and for conservative/business bills get low scores. The scores range from 0 to 100.

However, the ADA and COPE ratings of members of Congress do not automatically provide a picture of the ideology of the citizens who elect them. The authors wanted to devise a way of comparing states with respect to the prevailing ideology of their citizens. Perhaps the most obvious way to proceed would be to give each congressional district a "score" based on the rating received by the person elected from that district. Such an approach would seem logical, given that liberal candidates usually have greater electoral success in liberal districts than in conservative districts. Then one could simply average the ADA or COPE ratings received by the elected representatives in each district of each state to compute the ideology score for each state.

The authors of this study wanted a more precise measure. They reasoned that a district's ideology is not indicated simply by the ideology of the person elected, but also by the *strength of that candidate's electoral support* and by the *ideology of the defeated competitor*. For example, a district in which a very liberal candidate soundly defeated a moderately conservative one probably has a more liberal population than a district in which a similarly liberal candidate barely defeated a very conservative candidate. Both districts may have elected representatives with similar ADA or COPE ratings, but they would be quite different in the extent to which liberal ideology predominates.

Let's look at three hypothetical districts, one in Minnesota, one in Oregon, and one in Mississippi. In our Minnesota district, a representative with an ADA rating of 94 won a resounding victory over a challenger with a 54 ADA rating. She won with 62 percent of the popular vote, to 38 percent for the loser, a landslide triumph. In our Mississippi district, a decidedly conservative politician with an ADA rating of 13 defeated a moderate candidate with a 59 ADA rating. In this district, the winner received 53 percent of the vote, and the loser 47 percent. Finally, in the district in Oregon, the representative had an extremely liberal 95 ADA rating, defeating a challenger with a conservative ADA rating of 27. This race was quite close, with the liberal candidate winning 51 percent of the vote and the loser receiving 49 percent.

Again, the authors' goal is to produce a measurement of the ideology of each congressional district's citizens (which are then averaged across each state to get a state score). For each district, they multiply the proportion of the popular vote received by the winner times the ADA or COPE score for the winner, and then they add this product to the product of the proportion of the popular vote won by the loser times his or her ADA or COPE score. Thus, with our hypothetical examples:

$$\text{The Minnesota District's Ideology} = (.62 \times 94) + (.38 \times 54)$$
$$\text{The Mississippi District's Ideology} = (.53 \times 13) + (.47 \times 59)$$
$$\text{The Oregon District's Ideology} = (.51 \times 95) + (.49 \times 27)$$

Doing the math, we get a score of 78.8 for the Minnesota district, 34.62 for the Mississippi district, and 61.68 for the Oregon district.

Note that the Oregon district receives a *lower* score, indicating a less liberal population, than the Minnesota district, *even though the person elected from the Minnesota district was rated more liberal than the person elected from the Oregon district*. This is a consequence of the fact that the liberal politician from Oregon was almost defeated by a decidedly conservative challenger, a sign that the Oregon district contained a large number of conservative voters. In Minnesota, the very liberal representative coasted to victory over a moderate, providing strong evidence that this district is largely made up of rather liberal voters.

The authors of the article took this basic approach and then applied it in several different ways to produce measures. Although their measures may be questioned in terms of how fully they provide a sense of each state's ideological makeup, they are based on a large amount of clearly relevant information, and they incorporate that information in a consistent and thus reliable way.

It is important to note that the measures developed in this excerpt are for *aggregate* data. That is, the unit of analysis is the state citizenry or the state legislature or executive branch. The measures are computed on the basis of information obtained about individuals (voting scores for each member of Congress, votes by individual citizens, etc.), but the actual measures are applied to the aggregate units. The key point is to recognize the unit of analysis because this is what determines whether the measure is at the individual or aggregate level.

The authors' criticism of previously existing measures explains why they felt that a new set of measures was warranted, but considering these other approaches helps to illustrate the problems encountered in measuring political concepts. One of the most striking alternatives was the use of the percentage of each state's vote for George McGovern in 1972 as a measure of the liberalness of each state's citizens. It is true that the 1972 election was one of the most ideologically divided presidential elections since the 1930s (although 1964 also provided a stark contrast). It is also true that the data for this measure were easily obtained. However, using a measure based on how a state's voters behaved in 1972 as an indicator of *current* differences among states with respect to ideology is rather doubtful. Ideology does not change quickly, but this measure was probably out of date before it was no longer used.

—————————————— Excerpt 4 ——————————————

Viva Zapata! is a classic film about revolutionary politics in Mexico. Released in 1952, the film stars Marlon Brando in the title role. *Viva Zapata!* depicts the desperate poverty of Mexican peasants and the opulent wealth of the rich plantation owners. The large estates made these wealthy men influential, and they used their influence to ensure that elected leaders and courts did their bidding. The story makes one central point: When nearly all of the land is in the hands of the rich, the poor will not only be poor—they will also be denied political power and basic rights under law.

The idea that severe inequality in land ownership is the basic source of poverty and instability in Latin America is not simply a Hollywood vision. For many analysts of Latin American politics, land inequality has been the central factor in explaining persistent civil violence and political instability. Although we know a great deal about the problem from historical and even journalistic accounts, the effect of land inequality on political instability in Latin America has also been a subject of scientific research.

Determining whether inequality in land ownership is associated with political violence may seem to be a straightforward project. We simply gather data on land ownership and on political violence and see if the countries with the most violence have the greatest inequality. However, operationalizing these seemingly uncomplicated concepts is difficult, and the errors that are commonly made have cast doubt on the conclusions that many researchers have reached.

In the following excerpt, Charles Brockett examines operationalization problems in the typical approaches to measuring both political violence and land inequality in the five nations of Central America. His analysis suggests that the measurement of political violence is distorted by inaccurate data, and that the measurement of land inequality is distorted by the use of indicators that do not faithfully correspond to the relevant concept of land inequality. In short, the first operational measure suffers from *unreliability* and the second suffers from *invalidity*. Brockett argues convincingly that better operationalization is needed if we are to understand the effect of land inequality on political violence.

Measuring Political Violence and Land Inequality in Central America

Charles D. Brockett, *University of the South*

American Political Science Review 86, no. 1 (March 1992): 169–176. Copyright © 1992 by the American Political Science Association. Reprinted with permission.

Land is the most important resource in rural societies, and access to sufficient land is invariably the fundamental desire of most peasants. Accordingly, it has long been thought that the maldistribution of land is the key determinant of rural unrest, particularly unrest in its most dramatic forms, rebellion and revolution. Land maldistribution can have different manifestations. The most common aspects cited are landholding patterns so concentrated that either (1) many peasants are left with *minifundios* too small for family support (the *minifundización hypothesis*) or (2) that many peasants own no land at all (the *landlessness hypothesis*). In the most current literature the first position is argued by Midlarsky (1988) and the second by Prosterman and Riedinger (1987).

However, Muller and Seligson claim that this conventional wisdom is wrong (1987, 433–34). Their cross-national longitudinal data analysis of 85 states finds both that landlessness is irrelevant as an explanation for political violence and that land inequality (as measured by the Gini index*) has only weak predictive value. Instead, they discover a stronger relationship for mass political violence with national income inequality (again measured by the Gini index).[1] They conclude, therefore, that agrarian inequality is relevant to mass political violence "only to the extent that it is associated with inequality in the nationwide distribution of income" (p. 443).

This controversy has important policy ramifications, as the various authors point out. Land redistribution (and associated support programs) is often promoted as a prophylactic against rural disorder and instability.[2] Muller and Seligson's sophisticated analysis appears compelling, thereby questioning the adequacy and wisdom of land redistribution. However, in reality, their study is flawed because of the meaningless data used to measure their dependent variable, mass political violence. The same flaw also negates Midlarsky's analysis, as in fact it does most empirical data analyses on this subject.[3] Their shared deficiency is their reliance on the grossly inaccurate data set provided by the *World Handbook of Political and Social Indicators* (Taylor and Jodice

---

Editor's note: The Gini index is a widely-used measure of inequality. See the Commentary following the excerpt for an explanation of this important measure.

1983). In addition, I shall also argue that previous studies are inadequate in their conceptualization of the independent variable. Land inequality cannot be adequately captured in a single dimension no matter how sophisticated the measure but must be understood instead as multidimensional in nature.[4] It is my argument, then, that the empirical relationship between land inequality and political violence remains undetermined.

Measuring Mass Political Violence

> February [1977] An army base is set up near San Juan Cotzal [Guatemala]. Since 1976, killings have included 68 cooperative leaders in the Ixcán, 40 community leaders in Chajul, 28 in Cotzal, and 32 in Nebaj. In one community, the presidents of Catholic Action, Caritas and the local cooperative and community development committee, as well as five sacristans and four bilingual teachers, have been killed. (Davis and Hodson 1982, 47)

> Guatemalan deaths from political violence, 1976–77, according to the *World Handbook:* 0.

The most complete and most widely used cross-national longitudinal data set on political protest and violence is provided by the *World Handbook of Political and Social Indicators* (Taylor and Jodice 1983). A prodigious undertaking, providing annual events data for 1948–77, it is not good enough. The data are mortally flawed for Central America and (I suspect) for the rest of Latin America and the Third World more generally.

The primary source for the data set is the *New York Times Index,* supplemented for Latin America by *Keesing's Contemporary Archives.* Taylor and Jodice point out (p. 12) that *Keesing's* draws from nine basic sources (all European, with the exception of the *New York Times*), supplemented, for Latin America, with six additional sources—again, not located in Latin America itself.

Obviously, cost factors cannot be ignored; it is certain that to incorporate truly regional—if not national—sources into the *Handbook* would present tremendous, and perhaps insurmountable, difficulties. However, the validity of the data set rests not on financial considerations but on accuracy. In response to criticisms of "imprecision" in the 1972 edition of this data set (as well as in others), Gurr has argued that "the kinds of inferences drawn in quantitative macropolitics are not likely to be affected by anything less than gross and systematic error" (1974, 250). And that is precisely the charge. If valid, this claim has serious implications. As Lichbach has noted, the *World Handbook*'s indicator has been settled upon by scholars as the common dependent variable in cross-national statistical studies of political conflict (1989, 451).

> On November 23, 1974, National Guard troops with tanks and bazookas attacked a group of peasants in La Cayetana, San Vicente, [El Salvador,] killing six and arrest-

ing twenty-six (later thirteen were found to have disappeared).[5] These peasants had occupied sixty *manzanas* of idle land belonging to an absentee owner, after repeated attempts to rent the land had failed. . . . By some accounts, the military met . . . and decided that to allow the land occupation would be setting a dangerous precedent, and so they decided to attack the area. (Berryman 1984, 110)

New York Times and *Keesing's:* event not reported.

The *Handbook* grossly understates Central American deaths from political violence. For example, standard estimates for deaths and disappearances from political violence in Guatemala for 1966–68 are 3 thousand to 8 thousand, with another 15 thousand for 1970–75 (Brockett 1988, 106–7); the *Handbook* gives only 207 deaths for the overall period.[6] Similarly, for Nicaragua, it has been estimated that over a thousand peasants were killed during the 33 months of martial law beginning at the end of 1974 (Brockett 1988, 168); the *Handbook* gives only 59 deaths for the encompassing five-year period. Although the death toll in El Salvador was far less for the period under examination than in the first two countries, those acquainted with Salvadoran events will agree that the 22 deaths reported by the *Handbook* for 1973–77 substantially underreports the tragic reality.[7] Even allowing for wild exaggerations in the "standard" estimates for these countries, the *Handbook* is clearly in gross error.[8]

Probably the most striking anomaly in the data set is that the *Handbook* reports political deaths in Honduras during the mid-1970s as twice as numerous as in either El Salvador or Guatemala! In reality, Honduras would rank fourth with Guatemala far ahead for all five. The unavoidable conclusion, then, is not just that the *Handbook* scores seriously underreport various countries but, more seriously, that a more accurate reporting would alter both the rankings between countries and the magnitude of the intervals between country scores, thereby substantially altering quantitative analyses utilizing this data set.

There are undoubtedly systematic factors at work producing the gross errors in the data reported by the *Handbook*'s sources. Political violence directed at peasants in remote sections of countries without permanently stationed *New York Times* correspondents is much less likely to be reported than urban violence in countries with permanent correspondents. Simply said, remote rural disappearances are harder to tabulate than assassinations in city streets. Other factors are at work, as well. The *Handbook*'s Honduran data for 1975 are surprisingly complete.[9] This was probably a coincidence, however, resulting from a systematic bias. The Honduran "bananagate" scandal of 1975 reached right into Wall Street, generating unparalleled coverage of Honduran affairs in the U.S. press.[10] As a result, the six people killed in June of that year at a peasant training center received mention by the *New York Times,* although the six peasants killed in 1972 in La Tlanquera were missed, their deaths having preceded the scandal.

Finally, there can be discrepancies between the *New York Times Index* and the news story itself:

> While a worldwide television audience saw El Salvador's sunny beaches before the "Miss Universe" finals July 19 [1975], off-camera heavily armed troops were called out to halt demonstrations by students protesting the Government's expenditure of $4 million on the contest. . . .
>
> Then on July 30 about 3,000 students demonstrating in San Salvador against repression of . . . earlier marches were stopped by machine-gun and automatic-rifle fire from soldiers.
>
> According to the military Government, which contended that the march was part of a "Communist plot," *one person was killed,* five wounded and 11 arrested. But according to the students, *at least 12 persons were killed,* 20 wounded and 40 arrested. Witnesses said that about 50 persons, some apparently dead and others bleeding, had been taken away in army ambulances and trucks.[11]

The index lists only the one death claimed by the Government in the July 30 shootings, ignoring the higher number reported by witnesses.

Measuring Land Inequality

Land inequality is often just measured by the Gini index,[12] which is so simplistic and misleading that it is of limited utility for meaningful cross-national comparisons. Indeed, as Table 1 indicates, the Gini land inequality scores for the Central American countries are virtually identical. For such reasons, Midlarsky (1988, 1989) argues, instead, for a measure of "patterned inequality," by which he means a comparison of the pattern of concentration of land holdings between smallholders and largeholders. In turn, however, Muller, Seligson, and Fu convincingly demonstrate that Midlarsky's measure is "interesting conceptually but so flawed in construction as to be of little utility" (1989, 586).[13] They create instead an "index of bifurcated inequality." This measure is constructed from the proportion of small farms and from the average sizes of small farms compared to large farms.

Both sets of authors are attempting to measure what might be termed *minifundización,* that is, to devise a measure that captures the discontent of the smallholder without enough land to support a family yet confronts other farms that are of vast and "unjust" size. The Muller, Seligson, and Fu approach appears adequate for this purpose on the lower end of the land distribution scale. However, it would seem that what is most relevant to the smallholder about large estates is not their average size but rather the extent to which they dominate the local land supply. Beyond a certain size, an "unjustly" huge farm is just that—a large farm unjustly dominating the land supply, be it four hundred or four thousand hectares in size. Furthermore, the subdivision of large farms within the elite (by inheritance, sale, or subterfuge to avoid land reform laws) has no effect on land inequality from the perspective of the smallholder but could have a substantial impact on the bifurcation measure if the subdivisions were sufficiently prevalent. Accordingly, the share of total agricultural land dominated by the largest farms would be a better indicator of the role of the upper end of the land distribution scale in creating land inequality and peasant discontent than is the average size of "large" farms.[14]

Unlike the Gini index, these measures indicate substantial differences between the Central American countries. As row 2 of the table shows, *minifundios* are much more prevalent in Guatemala and El Salvador—in fact, twice as prevalent in the former than in Costa Rica. Similarly, the countries vary in the average size of the smallholder's land. Row 4 reports a score created by combining these two measures, which demonstrates *minifundización* to be the worst in El Salvador, followed by Guatemala and then Honduras, with Costa Rica and then Nicaragua grouped at the bottom. At the top end of the land distribution scale, essentially the same rankings obtain: Guatemala is closely followed by El Salvador, with the greatest concentration of land in the largest estates, and Nicaragua and Costa Rica with the least.[15]

Land distribution data are important indicators of rural inequality but are insufficient by themselves because of the increasing prevalence of landlessness among peasants. In fact, the landless of Central America constitute about one-third of the total population (prior to the agrarian reforms of the 1980s), with the exception of Costa Rica. Prosterman and Riedinger (1987, 10–11, 25) define landlessness as the lack of "ownership or ownership-like rights" among "those who cultivate the land." The landless include tenants, since they lack secure use of the land and face landlord extractions, amounts over which they usually have little control. The figures reported in Table 1, however, mask significant differences in the situation of the landless. Tenants vary widely in the security of their tenancy and the income-generating potential of "their" land. It is probable, for example, that the higher landless score of Honduras is less a source of intense discontent than the lower score of Guatemala, where the seasonal migration of Indians from the highlands to work on plantations was the largest migratory-labor-force-as-a-percentage-of-total-population in the world during the 1970s—and under extraordinarily oppressive circumstances (Paige 1975, 361).

These various indicators can be combined into an overall measure of land inequality. Row 7 reports such an inequality score, which combines, with equal weight, the three dimensions: *minifundización*, land concentration in the largest estates, and landlessness. By this measure, the worst land inequality in the early 1970s in Central America was found in El Salvador and then Guatemala, with a larger gap between them and Honduras, followed (by a large gap, again) with Nicaragua and Costa Rica. If land inequality translates into political action and conflict, it might be argued that the relative size of the rural population could be an important factor. Accordingly, row 9 takes this factor into consideration, giving a score for "the relative rural disruption potential" (with largely the same country rankings but a closing of the gap

Table 1

Land Inequality and Disruption Potential

Measures of land inequality	Costa Rica	El Salvador	Guate- mala	Hon- duras	Nicara- gua
1. Gini index of land concentration	.81	.81	.82	.78	.80
2. Smallholders[a] as % of all operators	43	74	87	64	51
3. Average size of small- holder farm (hectares)	1.7	1.2	1.8	1.9	2.6
4. Minifundización score[b]	25	62	48	34	20
5. % of all land in largest farms[c]	54	64	69	56	54
6. Landless score	20	36	32	32	27
7. Inequality score[d]	99	162	149	122	101
8. % rural population	59	62	66	72	51
9. Relative rural disruption potential[e]	59	100	99	87	52

Sources:

Row 1: Muller and Seligson 1987, Table A-1 for early 1970s except Guatemala (1964) and Nicaragua (1963).

Rows 2–3: Muller, Seligson, and Fu 1989, Table 2 for early 1970s except Guatemala (1964) and Nicaragua (1963); substituting data for Guatemala 1979 and Nicaragua 1971 made little difference.

Row 5: Brockett 1988, Table 4.1; also United Nations, Food and Agriculture Organization 1981, Table 3.3; for further discussion, see my n. 15.

Row 6: Prosterman and Riedinger's data for early 1970s (as reported by Muller and Seligson 1987, Table A-1) does not include Honduras or Nicaragua; Prosterman and Riedinger's later efforts (1987, Table 2) are for the early 1980s (except for El Salvador and Nicaragua, which are for the period just prior to their reforms). The data used here are an estimate for the mid-1970s, using the midpoint of the two data sets (and the mid-point for the 1987 data set where a range was given). Mid-1970 scores for Honduras and Nicaragua were estimated by reducing the score for the later date by the same amount as the average of El Salvador and Guatemala (Costa Rica is less comparable).

Row 8: United Nations 1976, 171–72 for early 1970s.

Notes:

[a] Smallholders are those with five hectares or less.

[b] Row 2 divided by row 3.

[c] Amount of total land held by largest 3.5–4% of farms in early 1970s (1979 for Guatemala). Cut-off sizes in hectares: Costa Rica, 200; El Salvador, 20; Guatemala, 22.4/44.8; Honduras, 50; Nicaragua, 345/690.

[d] Sum of rows 4–6.

[e] Row 7 times row 8.

between the top three countries). Regardless of which score is used, the essential point is that a multidimensional measurement of land inequality demonstrates substantial differences between the five countries of Central America.

Devising adequate measures of land inequality, however, takes us only a short distance, since it is unlikely that there is any direct relationship between land inequality and political violence. A major weakness of statistical analyses of comparative political violence is that they are largely devoid of any theoretical link between macro-economic processes and structures and either individual or collective behavior.[16] For example, much of the case literature suggests that changes for the worse in economic status are more likely to lead to discontent and violence than would a constant misery.[17] It is conceivable, then, that countries and regions with high but stable levels of land inequality might be less prone to rural unrest than would others with lower levels of land inequality but where the economic security of the peasantry is markedly deteriorating.

Bringing in Social Complexity

To make the point more concretely, imagine two countries with similar land distribution patterns and landlessness rates. In country A, the agrarian system has remained fairly stable for decades; but high population growth rates have steadily driven up the levels of landlessness. Country B also experiences population growth; but, in addition, the commercialization of agriculture has rapidly transformed its agrarian system. Profit-motivated commercial farmers in country B use their superior resources (monetary and coercive) to dispossess peasants of lands to which they had long enjoyed ownershiplike use and to break long-term tenancy relationships. In both countries there will be mass poverty, but deprivation alone seldom leads directly to mass mobilization. In country B, which is the superior approximation of the Central American reality, discontent has a target.[18] It is not so much poverty alone, Prosterman and Riedinger point out, "as it is *blamable* poverty that seems to serve as a predictor of violence" (1987, 9). When the disadvantaged live in dangerous political environments, assertion of their demands is risky. To overcome this discouraging environment, mass collective action usually requires "not only a sense of misery but also a sense of outrage and injustice" (Huntington and Nelson 1976, 102).[19] A good illustration of this point is provided by White's explanation of peasant mobilization in Honduras:

> The brutality of many of these evictions [of semisubsistence farmers by larger landholders] proved to be the catalyst in breaking down the friendly dependence on helpful patrons and developed a profoundly emotional opposition. The evictions were the sudden, sharp deprivation which moved campesinos to risk their lives in organizing to counter rural elites and protest before government authorities. . . . It was the small farmers who became the leaders in the national mobilization of campesinos. The evictions or other means of blocking access to land to which campesinos thought they had a legitimate right also became the basis for the land occupations or recuperations (1977, 181–82).

Conclusion

This research note has discussed a number of hypotheses concerning the relationship between land inequality and mass political violence. Empirical social science teaches well the importance of rigorous hypothesis testing with the appropriate evidence. Regrettably, it sometimes unintentionally reminds us of the necessity of ensuring the validity of the empirical data utilized for such testing. If the *World Handbook*'s data set provided reasonably accurate measurements of the cross-national levels of mass political violence, it would allow for the meaningful testing of the relationships I have examined. However, the *World Handbook* cannot be used for this purpose. The data for at least Central America are grossly inaccurate. Since the data set is not valid for this region, the burden of proof falls on future users to demonstrate that it is sufficiently accurate for the regions of their study. The appropriateness of this data set for cross-national studies that wish to generalize globally, however, is another matter. Since at least part of the *World Handbook*'s data is the product of gross and systematic error, valid cross-national statistical tests of global hypotheses and theoretical models concerning political violence must await the construction of better data sets.

The compilation of the *World Handbook*'s data set on political protest and violence was an extraordinary undertaking and accomplishment; but by the standard of accuracy, it was an unjustifiable shortcut for Central America and (probably) for the rest of the Third World. The construction of reasonably accurate data sets for these countries will probably have to be done on the basis of a substantial division of labor, with small regions researched by different scholars. Instructive for these future efforts would be Tarrow's (1989) use of national newspapers for his study of Italy and Tilly, Tilly, and Tilly's (1975) use of truly multiple sources in their comparative study of France, Italy, and Germany. Of course, as we move from institutionalized democracies to most Third World countries, censorship becomes a major obstacle to the development of accurate data sets.[20] A notable attempt to address this problem for a Central American country through the use of both national and international sources is the chronology of political violence in the Guatemalan highlands for 1976–82 compiled by Davis and Hodson (1982). They utilized five Guatemalan and four Mexican newspapers; one Costa Rican newspaper; North American newspapers and magazines; and reports from human rights, governmental, and religious organizations.

Future scholarship also must take social complexity into account better than heretofore. First, land inequality is multidimensional, involving, at a minimum, landlessness, insufficient land, and land concentration. Second, a more general concept of rural *inequality* would add to these dimensions other factors, such as income inequality and the security of tenancy and paid labor arrangements. Third, subjective experience is critical to mobilization. Similar levels of inequality can correlate with various levels of political mobilization and violence because of differences in the perception of the sources of that inequality. The available case material suggests that the most explosive situations arise when peasants believe they have been "unjustly" dispossessed of land. Finally, there is no direct relationship between rural discontent based on the perception of unjust inequality with levels of peasant mobilization, political conflict, and political violence. Instead, this relationship is mediated by the always-changing political context.

Notes

An earlier version of this study was presented at the fifteenth international congress of the Latin American Studies Association, Miami, 1989. I thank Mitchell Seligson for his helpful comments.

1. Midlarsky (1988, 503–4) appropriately objects that the Gini index is an invalid measure of what I have called here the *minifundización* hypothesis, of which his "patterned inequality" hypothesis is an example. Additional objections to the Gini index are provided by Prosterman and Riedinger (1987, 24–25). Midlarsky's debate with Muller and Seligson continued in more recent publications.

2. The underlying arguments vary from the inherent value of stability, to reform as preemptive of more radical movements and changes, to stability as the by-product of doing what is just (i.e., reallocating to peasants what they deserve).

3. These two studies are among the best of those that have examined the relationship between economic inequality and political conflict. For critical reviews of this literature, both highlighting the disappointing lack of theoretical progress, see Zimmerman 1980 and, almost a decade later, Lichbach 1989.

4. Although the focus here will remain on land inequality, a fuller account of the sources of rural violence would include other dimensions of rural inequality, such as income. There is, of course, a thriving literature on the socioeconomic determinants of rural collective action, among them McClintock 1984, Migdal 1984, Paige 1975, Poplin 1979, Scott 1976, Tutino 1986, and Wolf 1969.

5. The names of the murdered and of 10 of the disappeared can be found in the congressional testimony of Fabio Castillo, former president of the National University of El Salvador (U.S. House, Committee on International Relations 1976, 41).

6. A small story reporting the Amnesty International charge of some 20 thousand deaths and disappearances in Guatemala during the prior decade appeared in the *New York Times* on 12 December 1976. Although it is obvious that this kind of data could not be included in the events data set, it is curious that it did not lead to a reexamination of the validity of the Guatemalan data compiled for the *Handbook*.

7. To his credit, Midlarsky (1988) realizes that there are serious problems with the Central American data. His "solution," however, is inadequate. He uses the entire 1948–77 data set, dividing the Latin American countries into quintiles. However, because "El Salvador and Nicaragua . . . are known to have experienced intense violence in this period," they are artificially moved into the top quintile (El Salvador all the way from the bottom). Guatemala, where the most deaths actually occurred, is left in the third quintile (when it belongs in the first); nor are the scores of any of the other countries reconsidered. In response to the excellent critique by Muller, Seligson, and Fu (1989) of his handling of the dependent variable, Midlarsky (1989, 589) refers to the "arguments developed" in note 7 of his 1988 article. These "arguments" however, consist solely of a quick reference to LaFeber's *Inevitable Revolutions* (1983). The cited page in LaFeber makes no reference to El Salvador at all; its discussion of Nicaragua is in terms of the tens of thousands of deaths in the war against Somoza, almost all of which occurred after 1977, that is, after the end date of the data set.

8. If the data are erroneous for one region, similar problems would presumably be found elsewhere as well. Just a quick glance at the annual country scores shows the following examples of underreporting of political deaths: Chile 1973, 537 deaths; Brazil 1968–72, 36; and Uruguay 1973–77, 14.

9. The data for 1976, however, are another matter. The *Handbook* reports 15 Honduran deaths for 1976. The only relevant *New York Times* story (24 July 1976) lists 14 deaths—but of Salvadoran soldiers killed in a border conflict with Honduran armed forces. The *Keesing's* editon of 30 April 1976 (p. 27708) does list 15 peasants killed in Honduras; however, the deaths are reported as having occurred on 8 November 1975 (and are already included in the *Handbook* total for 1975). In fact, the process by which *Keesing's* was utilized by the compilers of the *Handbook's* scores is a mystery. For example, the *Handbook* reports 22 deaths for Guatemala in 1973; the *New York Times,* 17; so *Keesing's* (6–12 August, 1973, p. 26025) total of 22 must have been utilized. Yet in the following year *Keesing's* (18–24 March, 1974, p. 26419) mentions 8 Guatemalan deaths but the *Handbook* only lists 1. Similarly, the *Handbook's* total for El Salvador during 1974–75 is only 3 political killings but *Keesing's* (10 September, 1976, p. 27938) lists 26 killings just for November 1974–September 1975.

10. The *New York Times'* first 1975 story on Honduras appeared on 10 April with the U.S. Security and Exchange Commission's charge that United Brands (the successor to United Fruit) had paid a $1.25-million bribe to the Honduran president to obtain favorable tax treatment on its banana exports. In April and May, the *Times* ran some 24 stories related to Honduras, all involving the scandal and its aftermath. The rest of the year had 17 more stories, including several concerning the escalating rural unrest in the country. During the previous three years the *Times* had run only nine stories on Honduras, none of which involved the considerable unrest in the countryside. Meanwhile in 1975, the rest of Central America was largely ignored in the *Times.* For El Salvador there were but three stories and for Guatemala only one. Costa Rica did have nine articles; but five were scandals related to the United States, and the remainder were short pieces. Similarly, four of Nicaragua's seven stories ran in January following the audacious Christmas party attack by the Sandinistas; and two of the remainder concerned the new U.S. ambassador.

11. "Unrest Growing in El Salvador" *New York Times,* 10 August 1975 (emphasis added). Other sources give a higher death toll—for example, Berryman at least 20 dead (1984, 111); Montgomery at least 37 dead and "several dozen" more disappeared (1982, 89), Webre at least 37 dead and "many more" disappeared (1979, 189).

12. Muller and Seligson, for example, use the Gini index for measuring inequality in the distribution of land, which is then combined with the proportion of the labor force employed in the agricultural sector to yield an "agrarian inequality" score (1987, 435).

13. Indeed, this statement can be aptly applied to the whole study. Most of its weaknesses are identified by Muller, Seligson, and Fu (1989). Although still critical, Lichbach sees more merit in Midlarsky's work, praising it as "the most sophisticated and relevant formal models of the [economic inequality-political conflict] nexus" (1989, 452).

14. Another advantage is that this approach avoids the impossible task of deciding what constitutes a "large" farm. For a discussion of these difficulties, see Muller, Seligson, and Fu 1989, 580–81.

15. The decision of how to operationalize "the largest farms" was an artifact of the data sources. The available land distribution data are reported by size categories, whose number varies between countries but is usually around 10–12. The procedure was to find breaks between categories that yielded approximately the same cutoff point for "the largest farms" for each country (which turned out to be between the largest 3.5–4% of all farms). This could be done for three of the countries, but the percentage of land held by the largest farms had to be extrapolated for two (Guatemala and Nicaragua). As note c to Table 1 indicates, the cutoff point in hectares varied substantially between countries—another manifestation of the large difference between them in the extent of land concentration.

16. Lichbach discusses this deficiency insightfully (1989, 448–55).

17. Eckstein is a recent example of the argument that "economic relationships, especially changing economic relationships [are] the principal cause of protest and pressure for change" (1989, 4; also 16–17).

18. Midlarsky accounts for *minifundización* almost entirely in terms of population growth (1988, 494–95). He gives virtually no consideration to the other factors discussed for country B, which scholars have identified as crucial to accounting for the political conflict in the region (Brockett 1988; Williams 1986).

19. Similarly, see Gurr 1970, 155–231; Jenkins 1985, 5–6; McAdam 1982, 34; Moore 1978, 459–71; and Scott 1977, 236.

20. Illustrative of the problem is Lindenberg's discovery concerning social discontent coverage in Central American newspapers: "Precisely at the moments when historical sources indicate that there was the most discontent, evidence of the volume of that discontent disappears in countries whose newspapers were censored" (1990, 405).

References

Berryman, Philip. 1984. *The Religious Roots of Rebellion.* Maryknoll, NY: Orbis.
Brockett, Charles D. 1988. *Land, Power, and Poverty: Agrarian Transformation and Political Conflict in Central America.* Boston: Allen & Unwin.
Brockett, Charles D. 1991. "The Structure of Political Opportunities and Peasant Mobilization in Central America." *Comparative Politics* 23:253–74.
Davis, Shelton H., and Julie Hodson. 1982. *Witnesses to Political Violence in Guatemala: The Suppression of a Rural Development Movement.* Boston: Oxfam America.
Doran, Charles F., Robert E. Pendley, and George E. Antunes. 1973. "A Test of Cross-national Event Reliability: Global Versus Regional Data Sources." *International Studies Quarterly* 17:175–204.
Eckstein, Susan, ed. 1989. *Power and Popular Protest: Latin American Social Movements.* Berkeley: University of California Press.
Gurr, Ted R. 1970. *Why Men Rebel.* Princeton: Princeton University Press.
Gurr, Ted R. 1974. "The Neo-Alexandrians: A Review Essay on Data Handbooks in Political Science." *American Political Science Review* 68:243–52.
Gurr, Ted R., and Raymond Duvall. 1973. "Civil Conflict in the 1960s: A Reciprocal Theoretical System with Parameter Estimates." *Comparative Political Studies* 6:135–70.
Huntington, Samuel P., and Joan M. Nelson. 1976. *No Easy Choice: Political Participation in Developing Countries.* Cambridge: Harvard University Press.
Jackman, Robert W. 1978. "The Predictability of Coups d'État: A Model with African Data." *American Political Science Review* 72:1262–75.
Jackman, Robert W., and William A. Boyd. 1979. "Multiple Sources in the Collection of Data on Political Conflict." *American Journal of Political Science* 23:434–58.
Jenkins, J. Craig. 1985. *The Politics of Insurgency: The Farm Worker Movement in the 1960s.* New York: Columbia University Press.
Kuper, Leo. 1981. *Genocide.* New Haven: Yale University Press.
LaFeber, Walter. 1983. *Inevitable Revolutions: The United States in Central America.* New York: Norton.
Lichbach, Mark I. 1989. "An Evaluation of 'Does Economic Inequality Breed Political Conflict?' Studies." *World Politics* 41:431–70.
Lindenberg, Marc. 1990. "World Economic Cycles and Central American Political Instability." *World Politics* 42:397–421.
McAdam, Douglas. 1982. *Political Process and the Development of Black Insurgency, 1930–1970.* Chicago: University of Chicago Press.
McClintock, Cynthia. 1984. "Why Peasants Rebel: The Case of Peru's Sendero Luminoso." *World Politics* 37:48–84.
Midlarsky, Manus I. 1988. "Rulers and the Ruled: Patterned Inequality and the Onset of Mass Political Violence." *American Political Science Review* 82:491–509.
Midlarsky, Manus I. 1989. "Land Inequality and Political Violence." *American Political Science Review* 83:587–95.
Midlarsky, Manus I., and Kenneth Roberts. 1985. "Class, State, and Revolution in Central America: Nicaragua and El Salvador Compared." *Journal of Conflict Resolution* 29:163–93.
Migdal, Joel S. 1984. *Peasants, Politics, and Revolution: Pressures toward Political and Social Change in the Third World.* Princeton: Princeton University Press.
Montgomery, Tommie Sue. 1982. *Revolution in El Salvador.* Boulder: Westview.
Moore, Barrington. 1978. *Injustice: The Social Basis of Obedience and Revolt.* Armonk, NY: M.E. Sharpe.
Muller, Edward N., and Mitchell A. Seligson. 1987. "Inequality and Insurgency." *American Political Science Review* 81:425–52.

Muller, Edward N., Mitchell A. Seligson, and Hung-der Fu. 1989. "Land Inequality and Political Violence." *American Political Science Review* 83:577–86.

Paige, Jeffery M. 1975. *Agrarian Revolution: Social Movements and Export Agriculture in the Underdeveloped World.* New York: Free Press.

Popkin, Samuel L. 1979. *The Rational Peasant.* Berkeley: University of California Press.

Prosterman, Roy L., and Jeffrey M. Riedinger. 1987. *Land Reform and Democratic Development.* Baltimore: Johns Hopkins University Press.

Russett, Bruce M., Hayward R. Alker, Jr., Karl W. Deutsch, and Harold D. Lasswell. 1964. *World Handbook of Political and Social Indicators.* New Haven: Yale University Press.

Scott, James C. 1976. *The Moral Economy of the Peasant: Rebellion and Subsistence in Southeast Asia.* New Haven: Yale University Press.

Scott, James C. 1977. "Peasant Revolution: A Dismal Science." *Comparative Politics* 9:231–48.

Tarrow, Sidney. 1989. *Democracy and Disorder: Social Conflict, Protest, and Politics in Italy, 1965–1975.* New York: Oxford University Press.

Taylor, Charles L., and Michael C. Hudson. 1972. *World Handbook of Political and Social Indicators.* 2d ed. New Haven: Yale University Press.

Taylor, Charles L., and David A. Jodice. 1983. *World Handbook of Political and Social Indicators.* 3d ed. Vol. 2, *Political Protest and Government Change.* New Haven: Yale University Press.

Tilly, Charles, Louise Tilly, and Richard Tilly. 1975. *The Rebellious Century, 1830–1930.* Cambridge: Harvard University Press.

Tutino, John. 1986. *From Insurrection to Revolution in Mexico: Social Bases of Agrarian Violence, 1750–1940.* Princeton: Princeton University Press.

United Nations. 1976. *Demographic Yearbook.* New York: UN.

United Nations. Food and Agriculture Organization. 1981. *1970 World Census of Agriculture: Analysis and International Comparison of the Results.* Rome: FAO.

U.S. House. Committee on International Relations. 1976. *Human Rights in Nicaragua, Guatemala, and El Salvador: Implications for U.S. Policy.* Hearings before Subcommittee on International Organizations. 94th Cong., 2d sess.

Webre, Stephen. 1979. *José Napoleón Duarte and the Christian Democratic Party in Salvadoran Politics, 1960–1972.* Baton Rouge: Louisiana State University Press.

Weede, Erich. 1986. "Income Inequality and Political Violence Reconsidered." *American Sociological Review* 51:438–45.

White, Robert A. 1977. "Structural Factors in Rural Development: The Church and the Peasant in Honduras." Ph.D. diss., Cornell University.

Williams, Robert G. 1986. *Export Agriculture and the Crisis in Central America.* Chapel Hill: University of North Carolina.

Wolf, Eric R. 1969. *Peasant Wars of the Twentieth Century.* New York: Harper & Row.

Zimmerman, Ekhart. 1980. "Macro-comparative Research on Political Protest." In *Handbook of Political Conflict,* ed. Ted Robert Gurr. New York: Free Press.

Discussion Questions

1. Brockett argues convincingly that existing data sources for political violence are shoddy. In what ways do unreliable data about political violence disturb the research results? Are unreliable data better than no data at all?

2. A researcher reading Brockett's article may suggest that the problem of unreliable data on political violence could be obviated by assuming that the scores for each country are low by, say, 50 percent. How would this correction address the reliability problems Brockett identifies?

3. Brockett's subject was a study of five countries. Would the reliability problem be worse or less severe if he wanted to examine the relation-

ship between violence and land inequality in a much larger number of countries?

4. Table 1 reveals that the five Central American nations are almost identical with respect to the "Gini index of land concentration," but that they are quite different with respect to other measures of land inequality. The differences among the measures would enable a researcher to "pick and choose" among them, selecting a measure that would tend to "prove" his or her hypothesis. What would be part of a legitimate basis for choosing which measure to use as an operational definition of land inequality?

5. In his discussion of "social complexity," Brockett suggests that poverty alone seldom leads to mass mobilization and violence. To promote violence, the poor must feel that there is someone or something that has caused their poverty. How can an operational definition of land inequality take this factor into account?

Commentary

Political scientists have been eager to study the effect of land inequality on political violence in Latin America. Hard evidence that land inequality leads to violence could be used to support demands for meaningful land reform and for other policies that could enable the poor in these countries to be self-sufficient. Such evidence would also be useful in developing a general theory to explain the origins of political instability in poor countries.

Brockett suggests that perhaps political scientists have been *too* eager to apply their statistical methods to this problem. The data on political violence are, in his view, so unreliable that studies using them are worthless.

This problem raises a perplexing question. Should researchers simply do nothing at all with the *World Handbook* data? If Brockett's assertions are accurate, this may be the wisest course. However, a constructive step would be to look for indicators that may only indirectly measure the key concept but which have greater reliability. For example, if our study incorporated a sufficiently lengthy time span, we might consider measuring political instability in terms of "extra-constitutional changes of government." Such a measure would not tell us how many people died in each violent episode, but it would tell us how often the government was brought down by instability. This measure would also certainly be more reliable. If we could determine that land inequality is associated with more incidents of this kind of political instability, we would have a useful finding.

The most interesting operationalization problems that Brockett discussed had to do with land inequality. As shown in Table 1, the Gini index for land inequality indicates that all of the countries have roughly the same amount of inequality, while other measures reveal dramatic differences. Which measure is valid?

Figure 3.1   **The Gini Index of Land Concentration**

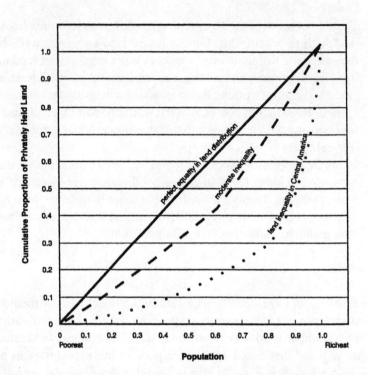

The Gini index is a basic measure that can be used to indicate how equally anything (income, land, legislative seats, etc.) is distributed among the members of a population. See Figure 3.1. In this illustration, the vertical axis is the cumulative proportion of privately held land in some country. The horizontal axis represents the country's population, arranged in equal segments of 10 percent each from the poorest tenth to the richest tenth.

The straight diagonal line indicates perfect equality. If this line represented the distribution of land for an actual country, it would mean that the first 10 percent of the population owned 10 percent of the land, the next 10 percent owned 10 percent, and so on. Every segment of the population, no matter how rich or poor, would have an equal share of the nation's land. The two curved lines represent realistic distributions, neither of which is perfectly equal. The dashed line shows moderate inequality. The poorest 40 percent of the population own about 30 percent of the land. The dotted line corresponds to the reality of land inequality in Central America. Reading from the figure, this line indicates that the poorest 60 percent of the population own just over 10 percent of the land. Most of the land is owned by a small number of very wealthy citizens.

While the mathematics of calculating the Gini coefficient are beyond our purview here, the figures are easily interpreted. Generally speaking, a score of zero indicates perfect equality, and scores approaching one indicate severe inequality. (The coefficient measures deviation from the ideal of perfect equality.)

Brockett points out that most ideas linking land inequality and violence focus on the particular economic conditions of the poorest citizens. However, even with the same level of poverty, the violence potential may be much greater if many people are completely landless than if many poor people own some land. The Gini index simply reveals the *overall* inequality of land ownership. It therefore gives virtually the same score for each of these countries, despite the fact that, for example, landlessness is nearly twice as high in El Salvador than in Costa Rica. The percentage of the landowners who have less than five hectares also varies tremendously: 43 percent in Costa Rica and 87 percent in Guatemala. In short, while the Gini index can be a valuable measure of inequality, it tells us about the degree of inequality that characterizes the society as a whole, not about the specific conditions of the poorest segment of the population.

The researcher's job is to determine which measure is the most valid indicator of land inequality, given the way in which land inequality is conceptualized and used *in that study*. If our understanding of the probable spurs to violence in these countries leads us to predict that unrest stems from many poor farmers having impossibly small plots of land, then we should use a measure that indicates the proportion of the population with no land or with very small holdings. If, on the other hand, we expect that it is resentment about how much larger the big plantations are than the typical poor person's farm, then a measure of relative land shares would be used. The appropriate measure is the measure that captures the aspect of inequality (landlessness, or size of poor farms as compared to large ones, or something else) that is relevant to the researcher's conceptualization. Only that measure is valid.

Brockett's article helps us understand both the importance of reliability in measurement, and the importance of choosing indicators that are appropriate for the hypotheses actually being tested. In the best research, these choices are not arbitrary, but are based on a sound theoretical foundation.

4 Measurement and Operationalization II: Variables Pertaining to Individual Behavior

Individual behavior is a basic subject of political science research. Individuals vote, hold opinions, make policy, and participate in politics in many ways, and an understanding of these behaviors is important to politicians and citizens alike.

Although there is an enormous body of research devoted to individual political behavior and public opinion, unsound conclusions about these subjects are common. In part this may be because we observe individual behavior every day and because we have definite ideas about the motivations and circumstances surrounding our own behaviors. We may come to believe, for example, that "poor people are more likely to vote than rich people," or "women who are successful professionals are likely to hold more liberal views on foreign policy than their male counterparts."

It is easy to accept such propositions, especially when they seem to be both plausible and consistent with what we often call common sense or a reasoned argument. Unfortunately, many plausible ideas are erroneous. Even in the realm of individual behavior, common sense alone is inadequate to allow us to distinguish the possible from the misleading, the true from the false. Here, as in other areas, scientific research remains our most reliable method for determining whether our ideas are consistent with the facts.

In this chapter, we focus once again on operationalization. In contrast with the previous chapter, however, our primary focus here is on operationalizing variables pertaining to individual behavior.

There are at least two reasons for treating such variables separately from those that have to do with aggregate data. The first is that there are differences in the way the two types of data are normally obtained. The aggregate data used in research is normally obtained from almanacs, state blue books, and other official sources. In such cases, operationalization involves adapting available data to suit the researcher's purposes. With individual level variables, however, our primary data source is apt to be surveys and interviews. Although survey results are often obtained through official compilations, the researcher has more control over data collection because he or she can be more selective about the items and the cases to be included in a given study. This greater control and flexibility allows the researcher to tailor the type of data collected to fit specific needs, but it also creates opportunities for error.

The second reason for their separate treatment is more subtle. When testing hypotheses that have to do with individuals, it is important to avoid the error of improperly drawing inferences about their behavior or characteristics from aggregate level data. When we confuse findings about aggregates with properties of individuals, we commit what is known as an **ecological fallacy**. If, for example, we found that congressional districts with a high proportion of older voters tended to support Democratic candidates, and concluded, on the basis of this finding, that individual voters become more supportive of the Democratic party as they get older, we would be guilty of an ecological fallacy. The fallacy stems from the fact that we have drawn an inference about individuals from data regarding the aggregates that contain them. It may be that it is the *younger* voters in districts with a high proportion of older voters who are actually responsible for the high Democratic party support in those districts. Because we cannot rule out this possibility using data pertaining to the overall percentage of older voters in each district (aggregate data), our inference is unwarranted and unproven. It may be true, or it may not. Our evidence cannot tell us. The solution, clearly, is to obtain individual level data.

Unfortunately, ecological fallacies are not uncommon in political science. The best way to guard against them is to be certain that we base our inferences about individuals on data pertaining to those individuals rather than on data about aggregate level units *containing* those individuals.

Operationalizing individual level variables often presents a challenge. Individual level variables such as age, height, weight, and gender are clear, unambiguous, and relatively simple to measure. Unfortunately, with the exception of age and gender, they are also of little political importance. Devising ways to measure more important variables, such as poverty, partisanship, or alienation, can be a complex task. Even when simple at a conceptual level, such variables are often difficult to measure. Others, such as the extent to which a person is career-oriented, professional, or Marxist, are difficult even to define conceptually, let alone operationalize.

Consider the simple question of party identification. We are accustomed to talking about Republicans and Democrats, but how do we determine whether someone (other than an officeholder with a declared party affiliation) is a Democrat or a Republican? If we asked five political science students to devise a way to measure this seemingly simple concept, they might well come up with five very different approaches to the problem. One possible approach would be to ask people to indicate the candidates for whom they voted in a recent election. Another would be to ask their opinions on a selected set of policy issues and compare those views to the stated positions of the parties. A third would be simply to ask people to rate themselves as Democrats, Republicans, or none of the above.

Whatever the approach taken, one important measure of its success is whether other researchers employing the same operational definition obtain similar results. If so, we can have some confidence in the reliability of our operationalization.

This requirement, however, tends to require significant simplification and specificity in the operationalization of our variables. As a result, we run the risk of diluting the richness or complexity of the concepts involved, although this risk is often more apparent than real. The critical test here is whether our operationalization generates data that is appropriate to the question at hand. One could argue, for example, that a complete understanding of the extent of an individual's ideology requires a thorough and lengthy examination of his or her beliefs including, perhaps, a discussion of selected works from Marx, Aristotle, Locke, and Hobbes. Perhaps so, but when our objective is to understand aggregate trends in public opinion, we will undoubtedly find that standardized, quantitative measures can be extremely helpful (and much more practical!).

As the following excerpts demonstrate, even difficult concepts can be operationalized in ways that produce sound and convincing results. When the concepts involved are ambiguous or multifaceted, as is so often the case in political research, we may need to make use of a **composite indicator**, that is, a measure that combines sets of measurements into a single indicator (e.g., see the Brockett excerpt in chapter 3). We also often make extensive use of indexes (see chapter 6).

In the case of liberalism, for example, we may find that there are, in fact, any number of satisfactory ways to operationalize this complex concept short of engaging the subjects whose attitudes we wish to measure in extensive discussions of liberal philosophy. The key point is that many individual level variables relevant to political research cannot satisfactorily be measured by a single indicator. Like conservatism, they are complicated and multifaceted, requiring that we devise a variety of indicators to tap several essential aspects. This in turn requires that the researcher thoroughly understand the concepts he or she wishes to measure and their role in the theory or proposition being tested. The excerpts below illustrate these principles in action.

———————— Excerpt 5 ————————

One of the most disturbing trends in contemporary American politics is persistently low voter turnout, particularly in congressional elections. Historical data indicate that turnout was much higher during the last decades of the nineteenth century, despite the fact that literacy rates were lower, transportation was more difficult, and registration rules were more restrictive in that era. Today, it is easier to vote than ever, and yet no more than 35 percent of those eligible actually vote in elections for the House of Representatives and the Senate, and just over 50 percent voted in the extremely close 2000 presidential election.

As one would expect, most research on the phenomenon of nonvoting focuses on the differences between those who vote and those who do not. The conventional wisdom is that nonvoters are simply less educated, less informed, and less involved than citizens who do vote. Moreover, according to the dominant image, the nonvoter is also poor. The assumption is that nonvoters stay away from the polls because they are not interested in politics, because poverty makes it difficult for them to get to the polls, or because they do not understand political issues.

If this general idea is correct, measures to increase voting turnout should emphasize getting information to nonvoters and removing registration obstacles that make it difficult for the poor to vote. However, if some people do not vote because they are dissatisfied with the political system, or because they feel that the outcome of a given election is not in question, these measures will have only a small effect.

Ragsdale and Rusk set out to examine the nature of the nonvoting population. They began with the assumption that nonvoters are a diverse lot. If research could indicate what varieties of nonvoters exist, we would be in a much better position to understand why so many Americans fail to vote.

The theoretical foundation that Ragsdale and Rusk constructed suggested that nonvoting could be a consequence of four distinguishable voter traits: ignorance, indifference, dissatisfaction, and inactivity. Although these are fairly simple concepts, measuring them with quantitative indicators was a complex, painstaking process. The researchers decided on a strategy employing multiple indicators drawn from survey results. As you read the excerpt, consider whether or not the concepts were measured appropriately.

Who Are Nonvoters? Profiles from the 1990 Senate Elections

Lyn Ragsdale, *University of Arizona*

Jerrold G. Rusk, *University of Arizona*

American Journal of Political Science 37, no. 3 (August 1993): 721–746. Copyright © 1993 by the University of Wisconsin Press. Reprinted with permission.

A high wooden fence surrounds a vacant lot at the end of a narrow dusty street of row houses in Baltimore, Maryland. On the fence amidst various spray painted gang slogans and teenage graffiti is a declaration scrawled brightly in red: "Don't Vote! Prepare for Revolution!" Whether Americans are following the second edict seems questionable, but in high numbers they exuberantly follow the first. In 1990 only 35% of those eligible to vote turned out in Senate elections and gubernatorial races; fewer still (33%) voted in House contests.

Scholars offer four main explanations for why Americans do not vote: demographic, psychological, contextual, and rational. First, researchers outline a personal "resources" explanation for nonvoting. They argue that social, educational, and financial attributes in individuals' demographic backgrounds give them the resources to participate in politics. Those with limited personal resources—little formal education, low income, no job, or marginal occupational status—are less likely to vote than others (Wolfinger and Rosenstone 1980; Rosenstone 1982).

A second explanation postulates that individuals' long-standing psychological involvement in politics affects turnout (Campbell et al. 1960; Shaffer 1981; Abramson and Aldrich 1982). General political interest and partisanship—or the lack thereof—may affect people's decisions to go to the polls. Scholars also maintain that alienation, defined as a global dissatisfaction with the political system, accounts for nonvoting. Individuals with low political efficacy, trust, and civic duty are more likely to stay away from the polls than others.

A third explanation stresses the electoral context: campaign mobilization, the competitiveness of the race, and registration laws influence participation (Patterson and Caldeira 1983; Caldeira, Patterson, and Markko 1985; Rusk 1974). Caldeira, Patterson, and Markko conclude that "old-fashioned efforts to get out the vote do in fact translate into increased turnout at the polls" (1985, 500). Conversely, when races are lopsided and laws restrictive, nonvoting increases.

Finally, researchers present formal theories of participation that consider nonvoting as rational abstention. Citizens rationally abstain when they perceive that the costs of voting outweigh the benefits gained from seeing one candidate win over another (Downs 1957, 266). The decision to abstain "depends upon the citizen's comparative evaluation of the candidates" (Davis, Hinich, and Ordeshook 1970, 429). These theories posit two conditions of nonvoting: indifference—when citizens see little difference between the candidates—and alienation—when citizens dislike all candidates (Downs 1957; Garvey 1966). Unlike the view of alienation espoused in the psychological explanation, the rational approach maintains that the perceived inadequacies of the candidates produce alienation. Some empirical work finds that nonvoters are more likely to be indifferent and alienated than voters (Brody and Page 1973).

Each of these four explanations offers some insights into the nature of nonvoting. But, for two reasons, no one explanation is compelling. Most fundamentally, the corpus of work on turnout does not provide an understanding of the differences *among* nonvoters. Each explanation only distinguishes nonvoters *from* voters. Results reveal that nonvoters are more likely than voters to be young, poorly educated, low-income individuals who are indifferent about the candidates, have little interest in politics, and face registration barriers. A portrait of a stereotypic nonvoter emerges: one who pays little attention to politics and who lacks the motivation and personal resources to be more attentive. Yet this leaves nonvoters as a large monolith. An underlying assumption of much of this work is that nonvoters respond (or fail to respond) to politics in the same way. None of the explanations analyze factors that permit distinctions among nonvoters. Some nonvoters may pay little attention to politics, while others may pay a great deal of attention, but fail to vote for other reasons. Scholars have categorized different types of political participants, including voters (Verba and Nie 1972). Yet no effort has ascertained whether there may be different types of nonvoters.

Second, there is little agreement among the studies about conditions that may prompt nonvoting. The demographic and psychological explanations emphasize factors largely exogenous to a given election. The individual characteristics are held to be, or indeed are, largely immutable. The two explanations eclipse consideration of how individuals' knowledge about and evaluations of candidates and issues influence nonvoting. The third and fourth explanations, however, suggest that such short-term endogenous campaign factors, which change from election to election, do affect nonvoting. Yet the third explanation stops short of ascertaining how citizens' knowledge of and opinions about the campaign will affect their decisions to vote. The fourth explanation acknowledges citizens' views of the campaign but does not satisfactorily resolve how indifference and alienation are involved in the campaign process. Certainly, indifference and alienation presume campaign knowledge, which not all nonvoters may possess. Too, the fourth explanation does not detail the specific elements of the campaign—issue positions, personal characteristics, achievements in office—which may bring citizens to the polls or keep them at home.

A Campaign Attention Model of Nonvoting

This study seeks to remedy these problems with an examination of nonvoters in the 1990 midterm Senate elections. It develops a campaign attention model of nonvoting in two parts. First, the model proposes that variations in individuals' campaign attention create several conditions for nonvoting. Such variations involve both the amount of specific information individuals have about the candidates and issues of a campaign and the degree to which individuals form concrete judgments about these candidates and issues. Second, the model specifies that other factors, such as demographic characteristics, general political interest, and the electoral context, may work to heighten or lessen variations in information and opinion. Together these various elements help to identify several profiles or types of nonvoters.

Variations in Campaign Attention

Students of voter turnout note that citizens have two decisions to make at election time: whether to vote and for whom to vote. We argue that campaigns press the second decision to precede the first. People decide for whom (if anyone) to vote before they decide whether to vote. Both answers depend on individuals' attention to the campaign. Increasing levels of campaign attention prompt individuals to gather information about candidates and issues, form judgments about them, establish preferences between the candidates, and then decide whether to vote. This suggests a continuum of campaign attention among nonvoters, ranging from no attention to high attention. Some nonvoters may pay little, if any, attention to the campaign and thus satisfy the stereotype of nonvoters as oblivious to politics. Other nonvoters' attention levels may be more similar to those of voters. They may have knowledge of the campaign, opinions about the candidates and issues, and make comparisons between the candidates.

We conceptualize citizens' decisions about which (if any) candidate to support as resulting from one of four decision scenarios, each of which involves a different level of campaign attention. These scenarios describe conditions for nonvoting: political ignorance, indifference, dissatisfaction, and inactivity.

Political Ignorance

Some individuals may pay little, if any, attention to the campaign. They gather little or no specific information about the candidates and the issues and therefore can form few concrete judgments about them. With little basis upon which to evaluate the candidates, these individuals are unable to decide for whom to vote and usually, as a result, do not vote. This scenario describes a condition of political ignorance among individuals who do not vote because they are insufficiently aware of one or both candidates or the issues.

Indifference

Other individuals may gather some information about the candidates and issues of the campaign. But they may not form opinions about the candidates, or, alternately, they may have opinions about the candidates but see no difference between them. Either situation leads to a condition of indifference: individuals are unable to decide for whom to vote and, hence, do not vote. In neither case do individuals see any meaningful differences between the candidates or their issue stands. Individuals' campaign attention is greater than that under the political ignorance condition, but the information they obtain does not motivate them to vote.

Dissatisfaction

Still other individuals may gather more information about the campaign than in the scenarios above. This information leads to the formation of definite opinions about the candidates and their issue stands, but the candidates are evaluated negatively. This scenario illustrates a condition of dissatisfaction where individuals do not vote because they dislike the candidates for whatever reasons. Rather than vote for the candidate they dislike least, individuals stay home.

Inactivity

Finally, some individuals do not regularly participate in elections. They may have some information about the candidates and issues and even form opinions about them, but because they often stay away from the ballot box, for whom to vote and whether to vote are moot concerns. This scenario portrays a condition of political inactivity among those individuals who vote infrequently, if at all.[1]

Individual Characteristics and the Electoral Context

The second feature of the model indicates that these four conditions for nonvoting are associated with individuals' demographic characteristics, their political interest, and the electoral context. Individual demographics are likely to be highly variable across nonvoters. Generalizations distinguishing voters from nonvoters can easily create the impression that all nonvoters are alike. Yet to say that people who are older, with higher incomes, better educations, and stable residences are more likely to vote than others does not mean that nonvoters are young, poor, uneducated drifters. Demographics augment or minimize the four conditions. They do not per se reveal why individuals do not vote. For instance, very few low-income individuals do not vote literally because they have too little money to get to the polls. Instead, difficulties associated with low incomes may prevent individuals from paying attention to the campaign. The combination of low income and political ignorance creates a situation for nonvoting.

Too, individuals' political interest will vary widely among nonvoters. Scholars often assume that nonvoters as a lot are politically disinterested and nonpartisan. Yet only some nonvoters may fit this description. Other nonvoters may have participated in the past and have firm partisan preferences. Political interest and partisan preferences may heighten or mute the four conditions for nonvoting. As one example, some nonvoters may be keenly interested in politics, but are equally dissatisfied with the candidates.

Finally, the electoral context creates various situations that make different conditions for nonvoting more or less likely. The competitiveness of the race, the amount of money spent, and the competition faced in other races create different contexts for nonvoters. For instance, a highly competitive race may create a context of mobilization within which ignorance and indifference are lessened. By contrast, a lackluster contest that receives little media attention may exacerbate these nonvoting conditions.

Thus, different patterns of association among the conditions for nonvoting, individual characteristics, and electoral contexts distinguish types of nonvoters. Analyzing these various patterns is necessarily a descriptive, not an explanatory, exercise. The investigation below shows that (1) different types of nonvoters can be identified and (2) levels of campaign attention, individual characteristics, and electoral contexts help to describe these nonvoter types. The cluster analysis employed distinguishes types of nonvoters, although the technique cannot gauge the extent to which different individual characteristics and electoral contexts affect the four conditions for nonvoting.

Data and Measurement

We analyze nonvoters in the 1990 midterm Senate incumbent and open seat elections. Senate elections provide an appropriate, and previously unstudied, setting within which to examine the nature of nonvoting. Electoral participation has been studied in presidential races (Shaffer 1981), gubernatorial elections (Patterson and Caldeira 1983), contests for the House of Representatives (Caldeira, Patterson, and Markko 1985), state legislative races (Austin et al. 1991), and Senate primaries (Kenney 1986). Yet participation in Senate general elections has not been investigated. Senate races, along with contemporaneous governors' contests, are statewide campaigns that are apt to set the level of salience for midterm contests. Citizens are likely to have information and to form opinions about Senate (and gubernatorial) candidates and issues to a greater degree than for other candidates (Hinckley 1980; Wright and Berkman 1986). If people choose to go to the polls in midterm elections, visible statewide Senate campaigns are likely to be instrumental in those decisions.

Analyzing Nonvoters

Our inquiry employs the 1990 Senate Election Study (SES). This data set is uniquely suited to measure the attention of nonvoters to campaign issues and images in very specific terms. The study asks respondents about campaign issues, name recognition of the candidates, ratings of the Senate candidates on overall and ideological grounds, and impressions of incumbents' activities. The study also provides a range of questions to ascertain citizens' social characteristics and psychological involvement in politics.[2]

Yet, there is a difficulty in using the SES data. As with all public opinion surveys, including the National Election Studies, the Senate Election Study overestimates turnout. On average, the election studies' data tend to overestimate turnout by about 15 percentage points (Katosh and Traugott 1981). A vote validation study has accompanied many of these election studies to ascertain whether in fact respondents voted. Unfortunately, this was not performed for the 1990 Senate Election Study. The key question, then, is whether the turnout inflation present in the study is a general pattern of misreporting across the population or is most prevalent in certain subpopulations.

To examine this, we compared SES voters with voters as reported by the Bureau of the Census on four dimensions: race, education, age, and sex. The greatest turnout inflation was among nonwhites whose reported turnout in the SES survey was 56%, while the reported Census Bureau turnout was only 43%. The smallest turnout inflation was among men. Their reported turnout in the SES survey was 51%, while the Census reported 46% of men voting. The difference, however, between the greatest and smallest inflation is not dramatic, suggesting that individuals throughout the population misreport their vote to some degree. Subpopulations are not then significantly overrepresented among reported nonvoters. As a final supplemental test, we conducted an analysis of Senate nonvoting using the voter validation data from the 1990 postelection National Election Study. The results of this modified analysis were similar to those presented below.[3] The analysis that follows using the SES data, therefore, is not inappropriate (for a similar conclusion, see Sigelman 1982).[4]

Indicators of Campaign Attention

From the Senate Election Study, we devised measures of the four conditions for nonvoting—ignorance, indifference, dissatisfaction, and inactivity—as well as individuals' background characteristics, their psychological involvement in politics, and the results of electoral mobilization efforts.

Ignorance

The model includes three measures to test individuals' level of information on issues and candidates: issue awareness, name recognition, and incumbents' accomplishments. First, Senate candidates spend considerable time putting forth issue messages to their state audiences. Some nonvoters may pick up on these messages, while others may not. Issue awareness is measured by whether citizens recalled an issue discussed by the candidates during the campaign.[5] Second, candidates expend energy and money to get their names across to potential voters. Name recognition for candidates challenging venerable incumbents and those competing in open seat races can be crucial to their campaigns. Some nonvoters may recognize the names of the Senate candidates, while others may fail to do so. Name recognition is measured by respondents' ability to identify Senate candidates correctly when presented with their names.[6] Third, senators spend considerable amounts of their own time and their staff's time to accomplish something memorable for the folks back home. The campaign becomes a convenient vehicle through which to remind citizens of such visible accomplishments. Nonvoters' recollections of these efforts are measured by whether they remembered anything special the senator had done for the state.[7]

Indifference

The model also incorporates three measures of nonvoters' opinions on issues and candidates: senators' voting records, candidates' perceived ideological differences, and overall candidate evaluations. First, senators often worry about how they present their voting records and what an opponent may make of them (Fenno 1978). Nonvoters' reactions to senators' voting records are measured by their agreement or disagreement with the way the incumbent has voted on bills before Congress.[8]

Second, candidates may pledge their positions on an array of state and national issues and attempt to line up citizens' support accordingly. Issues often capture individuals' attention in different ways and degrees (Rusk 1987). Some individuals may prefer a candidate because of his or her position on a single issue. Others may assess several different issues. To capture this amalgamation of issue positions, we measure nonvoters' views of the ideological proximity (distance) between the two candidates.[9] This is likely to reflect the issue positions known by the nonvoters, weighted most heavily for the issues of greatest salience.

Third, Senate candidates work to convey positive images to citizens. These images may be based on a variety of factors, including personal characteristics, issue positions, political qualifications, and accomplishments. Nonvoters may form and compare summary evaluations of the candidates drawn from these images. The absolute value of the difference between nonvoters' ratings of the two candidates on a feeling thermometer measures these comparative evaluations.[10] A large score approaching 100 means there is considerable difference perceived between the two candidates. A score approaching zero means little difference is seen.

Dissatisfaction

Some campaigns, however, are ugly battles in which individuals feel they are choosing between the lesser of two evils. Negative advertising, questions of qualifications, personal conduct, or issue stands may leave people disgruntled toward the candidates. The comparative measure above does not capture whether people are favorable or unfavorable, merely how much difference they see between the candidates. A dissatisfaction indicator measures when nonvoters perceive one or both candidates negatively.[11]

Inactivity

Finally, to capture individuals' overall participation in politics, we include an indicator of whether nonvoters have voted in the previous election.[12] Unfortunately, the SES does not include questions on civic duty, political trust, and efficacy that could provide additional information about attitudes toward political involvement. The indicator of past voting does serve as a suitable omnibus measure of inactivity. People's past voting gives some indication of their belief in the importance or effectiveness of participation at the polls.

Demographic, Psychological, and Electoral Factors

We employ five measures of individuals' background characteristics: education, income, age, residential mobility, and unemployment, each measured in a straightforward fashion.[13] Scholars have found education and income to be important determinants of turnout (Wolfinger and Rosenstone 1980). Low education and low income constrain individuals' opportunities to increase their awareness of politics. Thus, nonvoters with low education and low income are less likely to pay attention to the campaign than other nonvoters. Some may have little information about the campaign; others may have somewhat more information, but see no differences between the candidates. These personal characteristics may help describe the profiles of politically ignorant and indifferent nonvoters. Nonvoters with higher education and income may pay more attention to the campaign, form concrete judgments about the candidates, but may be unhappy with the choices offered. Higher education and higher income, then, may help characterize the profile of dissatisfied nonvoters.

Researchers consistently observe that age influences participation. Some have found a curvilinear relationship in which the young and the old are less likely to vote than others (Caldeira, Patterson and Markko 1985). Among nonvoters, then, these two age groups may be less likely to pay attention to the campaign than other nonvoters. In addition, studies observe that people who are mobile—those who have moved from one residence to another—find it difficult to reregister and participate (Squire, Wolfinger, and Glass 1987). Nonvoters who have moved recently may be less aware of the campaign than other nonvoters. Among the young, the old, and the mobile, some may have little information about the campaign; others may be modestly informed, but may not distinguish between the candidates. Youth, old age, and residential mobility may help describe both the profiles of politically ignorant and indifferent nonvoters.

Finally, researchers observe that unemployment suppresses turnout (Rosenstone 1982). The unemployed may find it difficult to pay any attention to the campaign. Unemployment, then, may help describe the profile of politically ignorant nonvoters. Yet it is also conceivable that the unemployed pay some attention to what politicians say and do about the economy. Thus, unemployed nonvoters may find it difficult to get to the polls, but may still know the candidates and issues of the campaign. Under this logic, unemployment may help characterize a profile of politically inactive nonvoters.

We also incorporate two indicators of individuals' psychological involvement in politics. First, we measure nonvoters' overall knowledge of the campaign, independent of any specific knowledge they have of candidates and issues.[14] Nonvoters with little overall knowledge of the campaign may be less aware of specific candidates and issues or less able to form opinions distinguishing between the candidates. This lack of general campaign knowledge may help describe the profiles of politically ignorant and indifferent nonvoters. By comparison, nonvoters with higher overall campaign knowledge may be more aware of specific candidates and issues, but may dislike what they see. General campaign knowledge, then, may further detail the profile of dissatisfied nonvoters. Second, the absence of partisanship may influence individuals' psychological involvement in the election. Studies show that many (although not all) independents have limited interest in politics (Jacobson 1992). Independent nonvoters, then, are less likely to pay attention to the campaign than partisan nonvoters.[15] Political independence may help describe both the profile of politically ignorant nonvoters, who know little, and the profile of indifferent nonvoters, who know something but not a great deal.

We also include five measures of the electoral context. First, research observes that candidates' campaign expenditures influence citizens' recognition of and decisions about candidates (Jacobson 1992). Nonvoters facing a race with spending skewed in favor of one candidate may pay less attention to the campaign than nonvoters observing a race with fairly even campaign spending between the candidates. Second, studies hypothesize that a runaway race for one candidate is more apt to decrease turnout than a close race. In a fashion similar to campaign spending, nonvoters who face an uncompetitive race are less likely to pay attention to the campaign than nonvoters observing a highly competitive race. Third, the closeness of the gubernatorial election outcome also is measured. Among nonvoters, a one-sided governor's race may be associated with limited campaign awareness.[16] Thus, lopsided campaign expenditures and uncompetitive senatorial and gubernatorial races may help define the politically ignorant and indifferent nonvoter profiles.

Fourth, we measure the effect of voter registration on nonvoting by the number of days before the election a person must register in order to qualify to vote.[17] Nonvoters faced with registration impediments may see little reason to pay attention to the race at all. Finally, we measure citizens' perceptions of economic conditions.[18] Nonvoters who see good economic conditions may believe that the government is in good order and find little reason to follow the campaign. Hence, stringent closing dates and positive economic conditions may help define the politically ignorant nonvoter profile.

It should be noted that demographic characteristics, psychological interests, and electoral contexts do not occur in isolation from one another. For instance, older people with low education and low income who face a fairly uncompetitive race may not pay attention to the campaign in the same way as older people with high education and high income viewing a more competitive campaign. The unemployed facing a race with roughly equal campaign spending by the two candidates and no registration closing date may respond differently to the campaign than the unemployed facing lopsided spending by one candidate and registration barriers. These different combinations of factors, not individual factors, are likely to help identify several types of nonvoters.

Profiles of Nonvoters

To identify several profiles of nonvoters, a cluster analysis was performed on reported nonvoters in the 1990 Senate Election Study.[19] Cluster analysis is a search technique for locating groups of individuals who have similar scores on a series of variables (Aldenderfer and Blashfield 1984). In the present case, this results in relatively homogeneous groups of nonvoters. The characteristics that the members of one group share can be compared to those characteristics that make them different from the other groups.

Cluster analysis has the advantage that coefficients are easily interpreted. The cluster centers presented in Table 1 are simply the standardized mean values of the variables for cases in the cluster. Since the variables are in standard form (with mean 0 and standard deviation 1), it is easy to judge how far above or below the mean a cluster of individuals is on a given variable. Summary results from the cluster analysis reported in Table 1 reveal five distinct profiles of nonvoters in Senate elections. To clarify these profiles, Table 2 presents a comparison of unstandardized means for all variables across nonvoters and voters. Once the cluster analysis has categorized individuals into one of the five clusters, it is appropriate to obtain unstandardized mean scores for each of the clusters.[20] This offers a more substantively meaningful interpretation of the cluster analysis results. It also permits an analysis of how subsets of nonvoters differ from voters in 1990 Senate races. The discussion below refers to the unstandardized values found in Table 2, although the same conclusions can be drawn from analyzing Table 1.

Political ignorance characterizes the profile of nonvoters found in cluster 1. Individuals in this cluster have little information about the campaign. They do not recognize the name of either the Democratic or Republican candidate. Results in Table 2 show an unstandardized mean score of .010 for Democratic name recognition. With this score just slightly above 0 (the value for no recognition), it is clear that, as a group, the politically ignorant barely know the name of the Democratic candidate. They are only slightly more aware of the name of the Republican candidate ($X = .205$). These scores are sharply below the nonvoter grand means for Democratic and Republican name recognition across the other clusters of nonvoters. In addition, the politically ignorant nonvoters are unaware of campaign issues or anything special the incumbent has done. Among the politically ignorant nonvoters, the unstandardized value for issue awareness of .222 is far less than the nonvoter grand mean of .546. In addition, the value for incumbent special effort of 0 is below the nonvoter grand mean of .153. The ignorant nonvoters also see little difference between the candidates, either in their ideological stances or their overall evaluations. In both instances, the unstandardized means for the politically ignorant are markedly below the means for any of the other nonvoter clusters. The ignorant nonvoters are political independents who pay little overall attention to the current campaign but who have voted at average levels in the past.

The results also describe how individual demographics contribute to this political ignorance. As shown in Table 2, these uninformed nonvoters are less educated (some high school), older (mean age = 61), with below-average income (between $20,000 and $30,000), and stable residences (on average 22 years as compared with 12 years for nonvoters overall and 14.5 years for voters).[21] Indeed, ignorant nonvoters are older and more stable residents than voters as well as the other groups of nonvoters. The electoral context also helps describe this profile of political ignorance. These nonvoters face contests with lopsided campaign expenditures and weak competition between the two candidates. Such a context presumably inhibits the attention individuals pay to the campaign.

Indifference defines the next profile of nonvoters found in cluster 2. Unlike the politically ignorant, these nonvoters have some political knowledge. Although they do not follow the campaign closely, they do recognize the names of the candidates. Indeed, as the results in Table 2 indicate, mean Democratic name recognition for these indifferent nonvoters is close to that of voters (compare $X = .799$ for indifferent nonvoters with $X = .818$ for voters) and Republican candidate name recognition actually exceeds that of voters (compare $X = .881$ to $X = .850$, respectively). Yet, most important, the indifferent nonvoters see few differences between the candidates. These nonvoters see below-average differences between the candidates on overall comparisons (compare $X = 18.224$ for the indifferent to $X = 21.477$ for all nonvoters), negative evaluations ($X = .240$ for the indifferent; $X = .456$ for all nonvoters), and ideology ($X = .818$ for the indifferent; $X = 1.210$ for all nonvoters). The demographic attributes of these indifferent nonvoters indicate that, unlike the uninformed nonvoters, they are younger (average age = 39), somewhat mobile (less than 10 years at current residence), highly educated (some college) individuals who have above-average incomes (over $40,000). Indifferent nonvoters have higher education and income than voters as well as the other groups of nonvoters. They face a campaign with average competition and fairly equal spending between the candidates.

Selective awareness describes the profile of nonvoters found in cluster 3, which is a variant of indifference. These selectively aware nonvoters recognize only one of the two candidates in the race. They know the Democratic candidate at a level higher than that for any other group of nonvoters and even higher than that for voters (compare $X = .909$ for the selectively aware nonvoters with $X = .818$ for voters), but they do not know the Republican candidate ($X = .030$ for the selectively aware nonvoters). Checks reveal that 86.1% of the selectively aware faced races with a Democratic incumbent and a Republican challenger.[22] The selectively aware also recall something special that their senators have achieved. Yet because they lack information on one of the candidates, they do not make strong comparative judgments between the candidates, thus leading to indifference and nonvoting. This information skew is clarified by examining the electoral context: a well above-average gap in expenditures combined with below-average competition presumably favors the incumbent. These selectively aware nonvoters are partisans who have voted in the past. They are individuals of average age (46 years old) who are fairly stable residents (11 years at same residence) with below-average education (high school) and below-average income (between $20,000 and $30,000).

Dissatisfaction identifies the profile of nonvoters in cluster 4. These nonvoters are more informed than others but perceive candidates negatively, prompting dissatisfaction and nonvoting. They are aware of the Senate campaign on a general level and also are aware of specific issues and candidates in the campaign. The dissatisfied nonvoters recognize the Democratic and the Republican candidates more clearly than do voters. They also are more aware of the issues and are able to recall more clearly the incumbent's special effort than are voters or the other groups of nonvoters. Dissatisfied nonvoters also see greater ideological distances between candidates than those seen by voters or the other nonvoter groups. They also see greater overall differences between candidates than those seen by the other nonvoters, although they perceive slightly smaller differences than those perceived by voters. Yet greater information and more clearly perceived candidate differences do not mean that dissatisfied nonvoters prefer one candidate to the other. Instead, they view the candidates in a distinctly unfavorable light. Their mean score of 1.519 on the negative evaluation measure in Table 2 indicates that many see one or both candidates negatively.[23] (This compares with $X = .456$ for all nonvoters and $X = .340$ for voters.) Also, they strongly disapprove of the incumbent's voting record. The demographics of these dissatisfied nonvoters reveal that they are somewhat mobile (eight years at current residence), younger (average age = 41 years old) individuals with slightly above-average income (between $30,000 and $40,000) and education (some beyond high school). The races they observe involve a moderate gap between candidates' expenditures and roughly average competition.

Finally, *conditional inactivity* defines the fifth profile of nonvoters. These nonvoters are less likely to have voted in the past than other nonvoters. This inactivity is associated with financial hardship. These nonvoters are unemployed (as seen by the unstandardized value for unemployment of 1.000) and see far worse economic conditions than do either voters or any other group of nonvoters but the selectively aware. They are younger people (average age = 35) who have below-average education (high school) and income (between $20,000 and $30,000). Thus, it appears that their inactivity is conditioned by their economic circumstances. If these circumstances improve, they might participate in politics. This speculation is bolstered by observing that these nonvoters pay some attention to the campaign: they know the candidates, see differences between the candidates' ideologies, and find average differences between their overall candidacies. They also are slightly dissatisfied with the candidates. They are likely to be political independents who face "average" races: average competition for both senator and governor and a slightly below-average campaign spending gap.

The results lend credence to our argument that only the combination of demographic, psychological, and contextual factors helps detail nonvoter profiles. Examining one factor in isolation from the others reveals little about differences among nonvoters. For example, indifferent nonvoters and conditionally inactive nonvoters are younger than other nonvoters. Yet nothing is learned about how age associates with nonvoting from this observation alone. We gain greater insight by recognizing that relative youth is associated with high education, high income, and neutral perceptions of economic conditions for indifferent nonvoters; but it is associated with low education, low income, unemployment, and negative perceptions of the economy for conditionally inactive nonvoters. These two groups, although both fairly young, are mirror opposites in education, income, employment status, and contextual perceptions of the economy. This illustrates that no one characteristic alone is sufficient to describe a profile of nonvoters.

Table 1

Cluster Analysis of Nonvoters, Senate 1990

	Cluster				
	1	2	3	4	5
Campaign attention					
Issue awareness	−.650	−.109	.230	.462	−.092
Democrat name recognition	−3.645	.193	.274	.233	.155
Republican name recognition	−2.671	.256	−3.436	.253	.193
Incumbent special effort	−.394	−.404	.295	1.170	.015
Voting record	−.159	−.151	.017	−.504	−.128
Ideological distance	−.768	−.287	−.075	.681	.256
Candidate comparison	−.860	−.153	−.178	.381	.018
Negative evaluation	−.466	−.231	−.531	1.368	.049
Past voting	.097	−.091	.636	.060	−.394
Demographics					
Education	−.553	.770	−.235	.194	−.279
Income	−.554	.697	−.205	.157	−.378
Age	.885	−.513	.046	−.221	−.513
Residential stability	.680	−.153	−.082	−.250	−.148
Unemployment	−.211	−.226	−.226	−.226	4.419
Psychological involvement					
Campaign awareness	−.556	−.122	.297	.617	−.087
Independence	.216	.150	−.169	.089	.170
Election contest					
Campaign money	.272	−.196	1.142	.152	−.066
Competitiveness	.208	.007	.235	−.033	.011
Gubernatorial race	−.372	.324	−.478	.332	.092
Closing date	.138	−.153	.160	.013	−.045
Economic conditions	.348	.089	−.356	.089	−.250
Cases (total = 948)	170	229	114	389	46
Percentage of total cases	18.0	24.1	12.1	41.0	4.8

Note: Entries are standardized mean values for cases in the cluster. [See note to Table 2 (p. 115) for meaning of cluster numbers.]

Notes

1. We expressly avoid the term "alienation" to apply to either the dissatisfaction or inactivity condition, since it has been previously applied to both. The rational explanation has applied alienation narrowly to candidate dissatisfaction, while the psychological explanation has applied it broadly to system dissatisfaction. It seems most appropriate to avoid the semantic and substantive controversy by adopting more narrowly descriptive terms: dissatisfaction for individuals who do not like the candidates and inactivity for individuals who do not participate. Moreover, inactivity involves people's actual participation in politics, distinct from their feelings about the merit of this participation, which is implied in the broader definition of alienation. In addition, we lack the necessary variables to measure alienation when it is conceived as a diffuse rejection of the political system.

2. The 1988 Senate Election Study is also available, but it does not include several questions that the 1990 study uses to measure candidates, issues, social characteristics, and psychological involvement. Consequently, the analysis here is confined to the 1990 study. It is also

Table 2

Comparison of Means Across Nonvoters and Voters, Senate 1990 (Unstandardized Entries)

	Voter mean	Nonvoter grand mean	Nonvoter clusters[a]				
			1	2	3	4	5
Campaign attention							
Issue awareness	.757	.546	.222	.491	.661	.776	.500
Democrat name	.818	.697	.010	.799	.909	.851	.754
Republican name	.850	.704	.205	.881	.030	.870	.792
Incumbent effort	.305	.153	0	-.004	.268	.608	.159
Voting record	.366	.090	.032	.035	.107	-.051	.046
Ideology	1.682	1.210	.160	.818	1.107	2.141	1.560
Compare candidates	31.125	21.477	3.148	18.224	17.688	29.601	21.856
Negative evaluation	.340	.456	.094	.240	.043	1.519	.494
Past voting	.938	.618	.666	.429	.928	.647	.427
Demographics							
Education	3.046	2.046	.977	3.536	1.592	2.421	1.506
Income	3.825	3.497	2.689	4.514	3.198	3.726	2.946
Age	49.301	44.714	61.091	39.379	45.565	40.635	35.229
Resident stability	14.459	12.010	22.371	9.683	10.756	8.199	9.759
Unemployment	.040	.049	.003	0	0	0	1.000
Psychological involvement							
Campaign awareness	1.983	1.384	.794	1.069	1.254	2.039	1.292
Independence	.373	.422	.535	.496	.339	.466	.506

Election contest						
Campaign money	1,760	1,897	2,419	1,521	4,090	2,188	1,770
Competitiveness	208	219	271	221	361	211	222
Gubernatorial race	74	38	12	61	6	62	45
Closing date	24	25	26	22	26	25	23
Economic conditions	-.741	-1.952	-.806	-1.660	-3.091	-1.860	-2.775

[a]Cluster 1. Ignorance
Cluster 2. Indifference
Cluster 3. Selective awareness
Cluster 4. Dissatisfaction
Cluster 5. Conditional inactivity

difficult to apply the campaign model to a comparison of midterm Senate and gubernatorial races. No study asks questions about gubernatorial campaigns in any depth.

3. Three variables described below were not measured with the postelection data: issue awareness, senator's voting record, and senator's special effort. The measure of campaign awareness used in the SES survey also is not available in the postelection study. A substitute measure counts the total number of stories individuals recalled reading about the campaign in newspapers or hearing about the campaign on television. All other measures are identical to those discussed below using the SES data. The results reveal that for the 1990 postelection study five clusters best fit the data.

4. Abramson and Claggett (1986) also find that nonwhites overreport voting more than whites. This result differs, however, from that of Silver, Anderson, and Abramson (1986), who find, in an examination of voter validation studies for 1964, 1976, and 1980, that the highly educated tend to be those most inclined to overreport their voting. The difference in results may be because Silver, Anderson, and Abramson focus on presidential years and Sigelman and we focus on midterm election years. During presidential races, there may be a stronger desire on the part of educated people to report socially desirable behavior.

5. The specific question asks: "In your state, what issue did the candidates talk about most during the campaign for the Senate?" From this question, a dummy variable is constructed, coded 1 for respondents who recalled a specific issue and 0 for respondents who could not recall a visible campaign issue.

6. The variable is coded 1 if respondents recognized the candidate and 0 if they did not.

7. The measure is coded 1 if respondent remembered "anything special that [the incumbent] has done for the people in this state while he has been in Congress," 0 if respondent did not remember anything special, and −1 if respondent said the incumbent had done nothing special.

8. The measure distinguishes among those who said they generally agreed with the senator's votes (coded 2), those who agreed and disagreed about equally (coded 1), those who did not know or had not paid much attention (coded 0), and those who generally disagreed with the senator's votes (coded −2).

9. Questions ask respondents to place the two candidates on a seven-point liberal-conservative scale, which ranged from very liberal to very conservative. The measure calculates the absolute value of the difference between respondents' placement of one candidate on the scale and their placement of the other.

10. The feeling thermometer question asks respondents to give their evaluations of the candidates on a scale ranging from 0 (very unfavorable) to 100 (very favorable), where 50 is a neutral midpoint.

11. This variable is constructed as follows. If an individual rates both the Democratic and Republican candidates negatively (less than 50 degrees) on the feeling thermometer, the variable is scored 2. If the respondent rates only one candidate negatively, the variable is coded 1. If the individual rates both candidates at or above 50 degrees, the variable is scored 0.

12. The question employed asks whether respondents voted in the 1988 election for president. This recalled turnout is likely to be inflated, as is current reported turnout, but it is the best measure available for capturing people's past political involvement.

13. Education is measured on an ordinal scale ranked for the highest degree the individual has received: no high school degree is coded 0; high school degree or equivalent, 1; two-year technical school, 2; two-year associate degree, 3; bachelor's degree, 4; a master's degree, 5; and a doctorate, 6. Income is also measured ordinally, with a low-income category of less than $10,000 coded 1; $10,000–$19,999, coded 2; $20,000–$29,999, coded 3; $30,000–$39,999, coded 4; $40,000–$59,999, coded 5; and $60,000 and above, coded 6. Age is measured on an interval scale from 18 to 97 years old. Residential stability is measured on an interval scale according to how long a respondent has lived at his or her present address. Some studies have concluded that the key dividing line between residential mobility and stability is between individuals who resided at the same address for two years or less and those who have resided there longer (Squire, Wolfinger, and Glass 1987). In preliminary analyses, we incorporated such a measure in the cluster analysis estimated below. This measure did not perform as well as the interval measure adopted. Unemployment is measured by a dummy variable coded 1 for those individuals who reported they were unemployed or temporarily laid off, and 0 for all others.

14. This is measured by the number of stories respondents heard, saw, or read about the Senate campaign: "none," coded 0; "just one or two," coded 1; "several," coded 2; "a good many," coded 3. Those who did not know the number of stories are coded 0.

15. A dummy variable is coded 1 for respondents who reported that they were independents or apolitical and 0 for those who reported a party affiliation. A measure of partisan intensity also was devised, coded for strong partisans, weak partisans, and nonpartisans (including the apolitical). The results using this measure were not as strong as those for the measure of independence.

16. The campaign expenditures variable is measured by the absolute value of the difference between expenditures by the Democratic candidate and expenditures by the Republican candidate. The competition variable for Senate and governors' races is the absolute value of the difference between the total votes received by the Democratic candidate and the total votes received by the Republican candidate. All variables are expressed in thousands. Unstandardized entries for the gubernatorial measure may, in part, be lower than those for the Senate measure because not all states with Senate races also had governors' races.

17. This closing date variable ranges from 31 days for Virginia to election day registration for such states as Maine, Minnesota, and Wisconsin (and no registration for North Dakota).

18. The measure combines in an additive index respondents' impressions of the state and national economies (whether the economies are much better off, somewhat better off, the same, somewhat worse off, much worse off).

19. Verba and Nie (1972) employed cluster analysis to ascertain different types of participators; for another use of cluster analysis, see Lewis-Beck, Hildreth, and Spitzer (1988).

20. Standardization is used only to calculate the Euclidean distances across the cases. Once these are calculated and the clusters are formed, standardization is no longer necessary. The newly formed clusters of individuals can then be assigned unstandardized mean values for each variable. This indicates more precisely how individuals who have been categorized in one cluster differ from individuals categorized in another cluster.

21. To translate the means for the education and income variables found in Table 2 into these categories, refer to note 13. For example, politically ignorant nonvoters' unstandardized mean score for education is .977. This is close to the value 1 for the high school education category.

22. There were numerous examples of strong Democratic incumbents in 1990, including Joseph Biden of Delaware, David Boren of Oklahoma, Al Gore of Tennessee, Howell Heflin of Alabama, Sam Nunn of Georgia, and David Pryor of Arkansas.

23. The variable ranges from 0 to 2, where 2 indicates that both candidates are perceived negatively.

References

Abramson, Paul, and John Aldrich. 1982. "The Decline of Electoral Participation in America." *American Political Science Review* 76:502–21.

Abramson, Paul, and William Claggett. 1986. "Race-Related Differences in Self-Reported and Validated Turnout in 1984." *The Journal of Politics* 48:412–22.

Aldenderfer, Mark, and Roger Blashfield. 1984. *Cluster Analysis.* Beverly Hills: Sage.

Austin, Erik, Jerome Clubb, William Flanigan, Peter Granda, and Nancy Zingale. 1991. "Electoral Participation in the United States, 1968–1986." *Legislative Studies Quarterly* 16:145–64.

Brody, Richard, and Benjamin Page. 1973. "Indifference, Alienation, and Rational Decisions." *Public Choice* 15:1–17.

Caldeira, Gregory, Samuel Patterson, and Gregory Markko. 1985. "The Mobilization of Voters in Congressional Elections." *The Journal of Politics* 47:490–509.

Campbell, Angus, Philip Converse, Warren Miller, and Donald Stokes. 1960. *The American Voter.* New York: Wiley.

Davis, Otto, Melvin Hinich, and Peter Ordeshook. 1970. "An Expository Development of a Mathematical Model of the Electoral Process." *American Political Science Review* 64:426–48.

Downs, Anthony. 1957. *An Economic Theory of Democracy.* New York: Harper and Row.
Fenno, Richard. 1978. *Home Style.* Boston: Little, Brown.
Garvey, Gerald. 1966. "The Theory of Party Equilibrium." *American Political Science Review* 60:29–38.
Hinckley, Barbara. 1980. "House Reelections and Senate Defeats: The Role of the Challenger." *British Journal of Political Science* 10:441–60.
Jacobson, Gary. 1992. *The Politics of Congressional Elections.* 3d ed. New York: Harper/ Collins.
Katosh, John, and Michael Traugott. 1981. "The Consequences of Validated and Self-Reported Voting Measures." *Public Opinion Quarterly* 45:519–35.
Kenney, Patrick. 1986. "Explaining Primary Turnout: The Senatorial Case." *Legislative Studies Quarterly* 11:65–74.
Lewis-Beck, Michael, Anne Hildreth, and Alan Spitzer. 1988. "Was There a Girondist Faction in the National Convention, 1792–1793?" *French Historical Studies* 15:519–48.
Patterson, Samuel, and Gregory Caldeira. 1983. "Getting Out the Vote: Participation in Gubernatorial Elections." *American Political Science Review* 77:675–89.
Rosenstone, Steven. 1982. "Economic Adversity and Voter Turnout." *American Journal of Political Science* 26:25–46.
Rusk, Jerrold. 1974. "The American Electoral Universe: Speculation and Evidence." *American Political Science Review* 68:1028–49.
———. 1987. "Issues and Voting." In *Research in Micropolitics,* vol. 2, ed. Samuel Long. Greenwich, CT: JAI Press.
Shaffer, Stephen. 1981. "A Multivariate Explanation of Decreasing Turnout in Presidential Elections, 1960–1976." *American Journal of Political Science* 25:68–95.
Sigelman, Lee. 1982. "Nonvoting in Voting Research." *American Journal of Political Science* 26:47–56.
Silver, Brian, Barbara Anderson, and Paul Abramson. 1986. "Who Overreports Voting?" *American Political Science Review* 80:613–24.
Squire, Peverill, Raymond Wolfinger, and David Glass. 1987. "Residential Mobility and Voter Turnout." *American Political Science Review* 81:45–65.
Verba, Sidney, and Norman Nie. 1972. *Participation in America.* New York: Harper and Row.
Wolfinger, Raymond, and Steven Rosenstone. 1980. *Who Votes?* New Haven: Yale University Press.
Wright, Gerald, and Michael Berkman. 1986. "Candidates and Policy in U.S. Senate Elections." *American Political Science Review* 80:567–88.

Discussion Questions

1. The authors measured "ignorance" in three ways: They considered the respondents' information on issues, the extent to which the respondents were able to recognize candidates' names, and respondents' recollection of actions taken by incumbents to help constituents. Did the inclusion of all three measures validate their operationalization of the ("voter ignorance") concept?

2. Two of the measures of "indifference" were quite different. One indicator measured respondents' "agreement or disagreement with the way the incumbent has voted on bills before Congress," while the other measure was "the absolute value of the difference between nonvoters' ratings of the two candidates on a feeling thermometer." Both measures attempt to assess the extent to which potential voters are likely to care about the election. Which measure is better (more valid), and why?

3. The researchers measured the "dissatisfaction" variable in terms of how negatively the respondents' felt about the candidates. According to footnote #11, if the respondent rated both candidates below 50 on the 100 point "feeling thermometer," that respondent was given a score of 2 on "dissatisfaction"; respondents rating one candidate negatively were given a score of 1; and respondents rating neither candidate negatively received a score of 0. Note that this scoring procedure disregarded a considerable amount of information. For example, "feeling thermometer" readings of 11 and 47 were both counted as "negative" appraisals. Would a more elaborate scoring procedure have been better? Why?

4. "Inactivity" was measured entirely in terms of whether or not the respondent voted in the previous election. Can you think of a more valid measure, one that would perhaps include the respondent's participation in several previous elections? If such a broader measure had been used, would we expect it to be as reliable as the one used here?

5. This study was an effort to determine the characteristics of nonvoters in a single election. If a researcher wanted to determine the factors that could account for declining turnout over time, how would he or she have to adjust the operationalization of the independent variables? What other variables could be considered as helping to explain declining turnout?

Commentary

Ragsdale and Rusk demonstrated that nonvoters are not a uniform mass of apathetic citizens. Some people apparently actively decide not to vote on the basis of disgust with the candidates (or their advertisements), or because they have lost faith in the system itself. Many of these people presumably *would* vote if certain conditions were changed. Discovering the differences among nonvoters is potentially of great political and practical importance.

Designing operational definitions for the key concepts used in this study was a crucial part of the research enterprise. As always, the researchers' findings were only relationships among the *indicators* of the variables in which they were interested. If the indicators had not faithfully represented the variables, the results would not tell us anything important.

The key finding—that there are identifiable varieties of nonvoters—was made possible by the use of multiple indicators. As the authors explained, "cluster" analysis is a method for discovering groups of cases or individuals that have similar scores on certain variables. Although the use of multiple indicators was appropriate given the complex and multifaceted nature of the concepts involved, it also enabled the researchers to use this analytic tool. Like all good research, this study suggests possibilities for future inquiry: Will a reduction of "negative" campaigning increase turnout among the "dissatisfied" nonvoter? What effect will expanded media coverage of elections have on turnout? What are the partisan or ideological characteristics of different kinds of nonvoters? As research on voting behavior advances, it is clear that further study of the nonvoter will continue to be important.

—————————— Excerpt 6 ——————————

The study of women in politics has focused attention on a wide range of issues that were neglected by political scientists in earlier decades. Many of us have heard of the "gender gap," the tendency of contemporary male and female voters to differ somewhat with respect to their support for Democrats and Republicans. Many political scientists have also noted that men and women are interested in somewhat different political issues. Although the political differences between men and women are often overstated, there are some real contrasts, and these differences have considerable practical importance.

Many feminists have long argued that contrasts in status and power in the home have an impact on the different ways that men and women approach public pursuits, such as the worlds of work and politics. Perhaps men are more likely to develop an interest in politics as a result of being dominant at home, or by virtue of the fact that they observed such dominance in their fathers when they were children. On the other hand, some have argued that men tend toward more individualism and competition, while women are oriented more strongly to community and nurturing, and that men therefore will be relatively uninterested in public affairs, while women will see the political arena as an opportunity to pursue broader public interests.

Although there is certainly no consensus on the matter, it is highly likely that the roles we play in our family relationships may influence the way we participate in politics, and gender differences in family life may promote differences between the sexes in this respect. Burns, Schlozman, and Verba set out to explore the issue through an empirical study designed to investigate the factors that determine gender differences in political involvement.

The research question explored in the article is essentially about the effect on political participation of *attitudes* and *perceptions* that men and women acquire in family life. Thus, the authors had to devise ways of measuring the respondents' feelings or judgments about themselves, their spouses, and their families. Moreover, they were primarily interested in the differences between the perceptions of male and female respondents. For example, when they considered the possibility that respect for one's spouse could be a factor affecting political participation, they were interested primarily in the *difference* between the tendency of men and women to *rate* their spouses as having good judgment.

Pay special attention to the many different kinds of information that the authors needed in order to address their research question. Their approach to measuring the attitudes of individual husbands and wives was critical to the credibility of their often surprising findings.

The Public Consequences of Private Inequality: Family Life and Citizen Participation

Nancy Burns, *University of Michigan*

Kay Lehman Schlozman, *Boston College*

Sidney Verba, *Harvard University*

American Political Science Review 91, no. 2 (June 1997): 373–389. Copyright © 1997 by the American Political Science Association. Reprinted with permission.

One theme of recent feminist theory is that, until women are equal at home, they cannot be equal in the polity. In her pathbreaking study, Susan Okin (1989, 22) argues that, although patriarchal domestic relationships have consequences for women's ability to participate fully as citizens, theorists of justice have either neglected the family or exempted the family from the principles by which the polity must be evaluated. "In a just society, the structures and practices of families must give women the same opportunities as men to develop their capacities, to participate in political power and influence social choices, and to be economically secure."

An especially important variant of this line of reasoning emphasizes the way that an unequal division of labor at home—with women assuming a disproportionate share of the domestic responsibilities—deprives women of the essential political resource of time and, thus, compromises their ability to be active in politics. Anne Phillips (1991, 96–7) offers a particularly articulate statement of this point of view:

> Women are prevented from participating in public life because of the way their private lives are run. The division of labor between women and men constitutes for most women a double burden of work. . . . The mere pressures of time will keep most women out of any of the processes of decision-making . . . the way our private lives are organized promotes male involvement and reduces female participation. Who collects the children and who makes the tea is [sic] a vital political concern. . . . Whether at the simplest level of having no free time, or as a more complex consequence of always being told what to do, women's experiences in the home continually undercut the possibilities for democracy.

For the student of political participation, this theoretical formulation presents several difficulties. First, theorists who characterize the family as an incubator of citizen inequality draw out the implications for women's participation in politics but ignore the effect of domestic inequalities on *men's* participation. In this article we allow for the possibility that domestic hierarchy of various kinds may affect men's as well as women's comportment in politics.

Second, this formulation offers only a limited view of the multiple possibilities for inequality at home and is insufficiently specific as to how each aspect may operate to influence the political activity of the members of a couple. In our analysis we broaden the formulation and give it greater clarity, testing the following possibilities.

Resources: Resource constraints with respect to either time or money may depress participation. That is, differing positions in the labor market or differing responsibilities at home may leave either spouse in the position of having a greater stockpile of leisure time or personal income, resources that may facilitate political activity.

Family Social Structure: Implicit within the distribution of tasks or authority in the household are lessons that might have implications for the predisposition to take part in politics. Role differentiation and patterns of authority within the family may affect political activity in either or both of two ways:

A. Those who do not share fully in authority over family decisions or who find that they do not enjoy equal respect may extrapolate from their experiences and feel less efficacious in the political realm.
B. Those who assume the burden for running the household and rearing children may receive the implicit message that their energies are to be focused inward on the home rather than on the public world outside.

Our analysis leaves open the possibility that, on any particular dimension, husbands and wives may be equal or unequal and, if the latter, either spouse may be advantaged. Furthermore, we do not assume that the implications for political activity of inequality with respect to any of these dimensions must be the same for wives and husbands.

Third, in emphasizing the resource constraints imposed on women by the traditional family, feminist theory is silent as to the potential effects on political activity of ideology, that is, the role played by *beliefs* about appropriate gender roles. There has long been a tension within the social sciences—dating back to differences between the successors to Marx and Weber—over whether social action springs from material conditions or whether values and beliefs have an independent influence on behavior. Recent scholarship argues that ideas about gender roles operate on their own to shape family life, above and beyond the influences of relative resources, and affect the behavior of both men and women (e.g., Brines 1994; Thompson and Walker 1989; West and Zimmerman 1987). Working from a similar perspective, political scientists (Sapiro 1983; Tolleson-Rinehart 1992) argue that ideas about women's proper roles affect women's political behavior.

A final difficulty is that, by the theorists' own admission, the empirical evidence on which this theory is predicated is slender. Phillips—who asserts (1991, 97) "I consider the argument won almost as soon as it is stated"— seems to find the connection between inequality at home and inequality in politics to be so obvious that the absence of empirical confirmation is hardly a liability. To us, however, the lack of evidence is problematic.

Inside the Household: The Multiple Dimensions of Inequality

The literature yields numerous insights about gender inequalities in the family and in politics. This article attempts to provide the missing empirical link between the two domains by assessing the effect of domestic inequalities on the political participation of married men and women. Our understanding of political participation is quite broad, encompassing not only voting and making contributions of time or money to campaigns but also nonelectoral forms of participation that are sometimes, though not always correctly, considered to be more congenial to women: contacting public officials, attending protests, participating in informal community efforts, serving on local governing boards, and becoming involved in political organizations.

We also construe inequalities between wife and husband quite broadly. Drawing on Weber's (1958) insight that societies are stratified on multiple bases, we consider several kinds of hierarchy *within* the household. That is, we conceptualize the family as a microeconomy, micropolity, and microsociety and consider asymmetries along various dimensions: the relative position of wives and husbands in their resources, their voice in family decisions, and the respect they accord each other. We are concerned not simply with differences on any of these dimensions but with their hierarchical nature and with the effect of relative advantage of the husband or wife on the participation of either member of the couple.

Before proceeding to the dimensions of inequality, it is important to differentiate what we are attempting from the well-known SES model of participation. According to that model, those who are well endowed with socioeconomic resources are more likely to be active in politics.[1] Our enterprise is to apply this logic to the private domain of the family, not to the world outside the home. We want to ascertain for each marriage partner whether relative advantage within the family—that is, privilege in terms of the amount of free time or money enjoyed, autonomy in decision making, or respect—facilitates political activity.

Our first concern is with resources. It is well known that family income is a crucial resource for participation in politics, especially for the ability to make political contributions. Yet, the SES model treats family income as equally enabling to each marriage partner regardless of whose wages, inheritance, or lottery ticket brought it into the household. Because we are looking inside the household, we ask whether relative contributions to total family income have similar implications for the ability of husband and wife to take part. Hence, we include measures gauging the relative economic wherewithal of the husband and wife, that is, who brings money into the household.[2]

Given the emphasis in the literature upon the way differential responsibilities for household chores constrain the time women have available for politics, we are particularly interested in probing the role of time. Therefore, we include in our analysis measures of the relative amount of time each partner contributes to household management.

What is known about time as a resource for political activity is somewhat surprising. The availability of leisure time, in general, plays an unexpectedly weak role in fostering political activity. How much leisure time people command, that is, how many hours they have left after accounting for time devoted to paid work, household tasks, and school, has much less effect on their political activity than does, say, their level of education or interest in politics (Brady, Verba, and Schlozman 1995). Nevertheless, given the emphasis placed upon time constraints in explanations of gender differences in political activity, it is important to look closely at these constraints in the domestic context.

We also consider several aspects of inequality related to family social structure. Closely related to having money or time is decision-making autonomy—the power to make independent decisions—with respect to the allocation of whatever money or time is available to the family. What may really count is not the amount of resources available but the *control* over these resources. Furthermore, individuals may generalize from their experiences with decision making in the family to their roles in the polity. Exercising power in the family, either as an equal partner or as the dominant partner in decisions, may enhance feelings of political competence, an expectation supported by work on the family as an agent of socialization (Almond and Verba 1963, 324–35; Sapiro 1983). Thus, control over money or time may have an effect on both actual political resources and the motivation to use them in politics.

We are also concerned with respect within the family. There may be stratification at home, just as in the world outside, in terms of social respect. Couples differ in the level of respect accorded each partner and in the extent to which that respect is mutual or asymmetrical. Enjoying relative respect may have the consequence of enhancing the confidence with which a family member confronts the wider political world.

We are unsure what to expect regarding the effects of a traditional division of labor upon the ability to take part in politics, apart from the consequences for access to such resources as time and money. A disproportionate share of the responsibility for vacuuming and grocery shopping may negatively affect participation, perhaps by constricting the opportunities to develop the capacities critical for political activity or by reinforcing the stereotype that those who mind the hearth should not venture into the public world of politics.

Alternatively, the critical factor may be time: So long as the partners are equally busy, it may not matter who does what. That is, separate but equal may be genuinely equal when it comes to the division of labor at home.

In addition to assessing the consequences for political activity of inequalities in class, status, and power at home, this inquiry addresses another issue: the role of beliefs about appropriate gender roles in enhancing political activity. As we mentioned, recent scholarship on the family has returned to socialization theory to ask whether ideas about gender roles shape marital interactions above and beyond the influences of relative resources. We are interested in whether views about gender roles have consequences for political activity, above and beyond their effect on the division of labor within the household.

The Data

The data we report derive from the third wave of a major study of citizen participation. The first wave involved a telephone screening interview with 15,000 randomly selected respondents from across the country. A second wave consisted of face-to-face interviews with 2,500 respondents selected from those 15,000 in a manner to provide larger numbers of political activists as well as members of minority groups. For the third wave we conducted telephone interviews with 609 of the respondents from the second wave, using items about social characteristics and voluntary activity from the initial questionnaires as well as new items about family characteristics. (See Appendix A for a fuller description of the samples for the first and second waves.) Of this group, 380 were married at the time of the third interview.[3] For married respondents we also conducted separate interviews—using special techniques to ensure that the members of the couple could not monitor each other's answers—with their spouses.[4] These data provide basic information on the members of the couples sample who were entering our study for the first time and up-to-date information on the people interviewed in the first and second waves. In addition, we have independent reports from each spouse about family and household matters. Thus, we are able to combine information from wife and husband to typify the family. We can also consider inconsistencies in reports from partners and incorporate any discrepancies into our characterization of the family.

The Measures of Family Equality: Descriptive Data

Because issues of family equality are not ordinary fare for political scientists, we consider it important to describe in detail the variables used to measure it. For each of the several dimensions on which there might be family hierarchy, we present the views of both husband and wife. These data can be presented in several ways: as a comparison of the aggregate characteristics of husband

and wife, as a measurement of the level of agreement within couples,[5] and as typifying the joint characteristics of both spouses within a couple. We shall use one or more of these modes of data presentation where appropriate.

Resources: Money and Time

Table 1 presents data about two resources essential for running a household: money and time. The top row shows the average estimates reported by wives and by husbands of the proportion of family income brought in by the wife by virtue of her wages and other sources of income (such as child support, rental income, or dividends) attributable to her.[6] There is, in the aggregate, remarkable agreement between women and men that the wife brings in about one-third of the household income, a figure which accords with that found in other surveys (Thompson and Walker 1989, 850). That wives contribute less than an equal share to the family exchequer is related, presumably, to the fact that, compared to men, women are less likely to work for pay and earn less when they work full time. In short, women seem to be at a disadvantage when it comes to command of family financial resources. The person who brings income into the family may be able to exercise greater control over its uses for family or individual purposes (an issue to which we shall return shortly).

In addition to the averages for wives taken together and husbands taken together, Table 1 presents data about whether marriage partners agree about these matters. Members of married couples seem to be in rough, though not perfect, agreement as to the proportion of the family exchequer contributed by the wife. On average, spouses differ by 18% in their estimate of the proportion of family income attributable to the wife.[7] The correlation between their estimates is .44, which is significant at the .001 level.

Table 1 also contains data on the wife's share of total hours devoted by both members of the couple to necessary household work. Respondents were asked to estimate for themselves and their spouse how much time each spent on a variety of activities in an average day: gainful employment, including commuting and work taken home; necessary household tasks (with childcare as a subset); taking courses for credit (and studying for them); and sleeping. As before, we present figures for wives taken together and husbands taken together. There is relatively little difference between the average estimate by husbands and by wives of the proportion contributed by the wife to the total hours devoted to housework. Interestingly, the average estimates for contributions of household time and money are mirror images: Wives contribute about one-third of the income and just under two-thirds of the housework time.[8] In addition, there is significantly more variability in the assessments of the proportion of household income contributed by the wife than in the assessments of the proportion of household labor she contributes.[9] Table 1 also presents information about the level of agreement within married couples about how much of the total housework the wife does. Once again, the data show rough but not perfect agreement between spouses.

It must be noted, however, that despite the fact that they contribute more time to household chores than do men, women, on average, do not appear to have less free time than men. Among married respondents—the subjects of this study—men and women reported an identical amount of free time per day: six hours.[10] Among those married respondents with full-time jobs and children at home, women have, on average, less free time (3.05 hours) than do similarly situated men (3.45 hours). Yet, the difference is smaller than might have been expected on the basis of the division of labor at home because men with full-time jobs and children at home tend to put in longer hours at work. In sum, men and women differ little in the amount of time they have available after they have honored their commitments to job, household, and school.[11]

We can amplify these findings about who does what at home. For several common household chores—cleaning, grocery shopping, paying bills, taking care of the car, and caring for the children—we asked each partner whether s/he did all, most, some, little, or none of that task. Table 2 shows the distribution of the aggregate responses for wives and for husbands. Overall, a similar division of labor is reported, with wives doing more when it comes to cleaning, shopping, caring for the children, and, to a lesser extent, paying bills, and with men taking primary responsibility for the car. When we consider couples and compare spouses, we find some tendency toward claiming credit: Ordinarily, each partner makes a more generous assessment of his or her own effort than, by inference, does the spouse. Yet, the proportion of couples in which the spouses give contradictory answers—each claiming to do all or most of a particular chore—is relatively low. For each of the tasks, except for repairing the car, couples give contradictory reports less than one-tenth of the time. The fewest contradictory responses are found in relation to traditional female chores: taking care of the children and cleaning the house. Most wives—and few husbands—claim to do all or most of these tasks.

We can also embellish the data in Table 1 on the relative economic position of the spouses. As a corollary to the data about relative contributions to family income, we have included in Table 3 information about the occupational levels of respondents. The data in the upper portion of the table show the distribution on a scale measuring respondents' assessments of the amount of education and on-the-job training required for their jobs. Considering just those who are currently in the work force, wives are less likely than husbands to be in high-level occupations. In the lower portion of the table we present data, for those in the work force, comparing the job levels of members of couples (the husband's job level minus the wife's). The preponderance of positive numbers shows the expected result: husbands are likely to have higher status occupations than their wives.

Table 1

Resource Equality: Proportion of Total Household Income and Housework Attributable to Wife

	Wives' report	Husbands' report	Average difference between spouses[a]	Correlation between spouses
Income (percentage of family	33%	31%	18%	.44
income contributed by wife)	(26)	(27)	(21)	
Housework (percentage of total	69%	62%	15%	.45
hours of housework wife does)	(18)	(18)	(13)	
Number of cases				
Income	367	344		
Housework	372	348		

Note: Standard deviations in parentheses.

[a]Average of the absolute values of the difference in the responses of the members of a couple.

Table 2

Division of Household Chores

	All	Most	Some	Little	None		N	Contra-dictory responses[a]
Housecleaning								
Wives say they do	41%	34%	17%	3%	5%	= 100	374	7%
Husbands say they do	1	10	46	31	12	= 100	349	
Grocery shopping								
Wives say they do	47	34	14	2	4	= 100	374	9%
Husbands say they do	9	13	38	25	15	= 100	349	
Paying bills								
Wives say they do	48	17	13	12	11	= 101	374	9%
Husbands say they do	21	20	14	20	25	= 100	348	
Repairs/car								
Wives say they do	7	13	29	27	24	= 100	374	17%
Husbands say they do	69	24	5	1	1	= 100	349	
Taking care of the children								
Wives say they do	11	63	22	1	4	= 101	230	5%
Husbands say they do	[b]	7	75	10	9	= 101	224	

[a]Both members of a couple claim to do all or most of the chore.
[b]Less than 1%.

Table 3

Job Levels of Husbands and Wives

A. Education and on-the-job training required

| | | Work force members[a] | |
		Wives	Husbands
Least education and on-the-job training	1	15%	9%
	2	32	14
	3	13	34
	4	31	17
Most education and on-the-job training	5	9	26
		100%	100%
N		313	333

B. Comparative job levels of members of couple:
   Husband's job level minus wife's job level

−4	−3	−2	−1	0	+1	+2	+3	+4		N
b	b	6	18	29	32	7	6	3	= 101%	274

[a]Eighteen percent of the wives and 13% of the husbands have not had a job for as long as one year.

[b]Less than 1%.

Control Over Money and Time

Beyond the amount that each spouse contributes to the family is the issue of who controls the use of the family stockpile of time or money. We asked both a question about how much responsibility each takes for "bigger financial decisions"[12] and a series of questions about whether they can make a decision on their own to give "a few hours" to a charity drive, political cause, or something they enjoy doing or whether their spouse would have some say in a decision to use time in these ways. Table 4 presents the responses. Financial decision making is a domain in which husbands report, on average, that they exercise greater control than is reported by wives. Nearly three-quarters of the husbands indicated taking all or most of the responsibility for big financial decisions, whereas only one-quarter of the wives made such a claim.[13] The agreement between spouses is fairly high; in only 15% of the couples do both spouses claim to make all or most of the big financial decisions.

With respect to control over time, we were surprised to find a very different pattern. Compared with husbands, wives were more likely to report being able to give time to voluntary activities—charitable, political, or social—without consultation. We guessed that this unexpected finding might reflect the fact that those who are not in the work force, a group that is disproportion-

Table 4

Control Over Money and Time

A. Responsibility for the larger financial decisions, by sex

	All	Most	Some	Little	None		N	Contradictory responses[a]
Wives say they have	7%	19	65	7	2	= 100%	373	15%
Husbands say they have	17%	55	26	1	[b]	= 99%	348	

B. Comparative control of free time of husbands and wives[c]

	Combined report of wife and husband
Husband has more freedom	7%
Members of couple have equal freedom	62%
Wife has more freedom	31%
	100%
N	329

Number of times out of three respondent reports that spouse would have some say in respondent's decision about how to spend a few hours

	Wives' report	Husbands' report
0	62%	42%
1	23%	19%
2	10%	20%
3	6%	19%
	101%	100%
N	368	340

[a]Both members of couple say they have all or most of the responsibility.

[b]Less than 1%.

[c]Based on answers to the following question: "Would your spouse have some say about how you spend a few hours (on a charity drive, on something you enjoy, on a political campaign or cause)?"

ately female, would exercise particular control over their time. When we looked at the data, however, this hypothesis was discredited: Women who work full time are as likely as women at home to make autonomous decisions about the use of small amounts of time.

Respect

Measuring the relative respect of husband and wife for each other is extremely difficult. In a series of questions adapted from the General Social Survey, we asked respondents to choose, in order, three people (e.g., their husband or

Table 5

Beliefs About Equality in the Family

	Primacy of domestic role for wife[a]		Belief in gender equality in sharing household chores[b]		Primacy of husband in decision making[c]	
	Wives	Husbands	Wives	Husbands	Wives	Husbands
Strongly agree	15%	11%	34%	24%	2%	2%
Agree somewhat	28	34	56	66	5	5
Disagree somewhat	45	45	10	10	35	67
Strongly disagree	12	10	[d]	[d]	58	26
	100%	100%	100%	100%	100%	100%
Contradictory responses[e]	37%		19%		12%	
N	364	341	375	349	373	348

[a]"A wife should give up her job whenever it interferes with her role as a wife and mother."

[b]"Husbands and wives should share household chores equally."

[c]"It's best if just the husband is in charge of making family decisions."

[d]Less than 1%.

[e]One member of the couple agrees strongly or somewhat; the other member of the couple disagrees strongly or somewhat.

wife, a friend, a member of the clergy) whose judgment they really trust and with whom they might be likely to discuss important matters. Substantial majorities—73% of the wives and 68% of the husbands—listed their spouse first. Our measure of mutuality of respect involves comparing the responses of husbands and wives to ascertain whether they rank each other at the same place on the list or whether one partner places the other higher on the list than vice versa. This measure indicates considerable symmetry in the rankings of spouses. Sixty percent of the couples put each other at the same point on this list.[14] In 22% of couples, she ranks him higher than he ranks her; in 18% of couples the situation is reversed. In short, there is a good deal of mutual respect in these couples. Asymmetries—one spouse accords the other more respect than she or he receives in return—are relatively rare and relatively balanced. There is a tilt in favor of the husband, but it is quite small.

Beliefs About Gender Equality

Finally, we consider beliefs about equality between the sexes. Reflecting our concern with the implications of domestic inequalities for political participation, we asked several questions about attitudes toward equality at home between husband and wife: whether a woman should quit her job if it conflicts with her roles as wife and mother; whether household chores should be shared equally between spouses; and whether it is best if just the husband is in charge of family decisions. We deliberately chose these items because they ask about gender roles at home and are devoid of explicit political content.

Table 5, which presents the responses, shows that the three items elicited, on average, surprisingly similar expressions of support for gender equality at home from wives and husbands, although wives seem to have somewhat stronger views on these issues.[15] Fifty-seven percent of wives and 55% of husbands reject the idea that a woman should quit her job if it interferes with her roles at home; 90% of husbands and of wives agree with the statement that household chores should be shared equally; and 93% of wives and of husbands disagree with the idea that men should make the family decisions. Once again, marriage partners tend to, but do not inevitably, agree on these matters. A substantial minority of couples—37%—find themselves on the opposite side of the fence, with one spouse agreeing and the other disagreeing when it comes to whether a wife should quit her job. For the other two items, the proportion of couples who disagree is much lower. And very few couples— less than 1% in each case—have opposing opinions that are strongly held. Although the data suggest a widespread belief in equality at home, we must remember the lessons of tables 2, 3, and 4, which showed considerable stereotyping in the actual division of labor. For instance, though more than nine out of ten wives and husbands disagree with the idea that just the husband should be in charge of making family decisions (Table 5), 72% of husbands but only 26% of wives report that they have responsibility for major financial decisions (Table 4). These findings are consistent with longitudinal data showing that, when it comes to gender equality in the division of household chores and responsibilities, beliefs appear to have outrun practice (Scanzoni and Fox 1980).

Equality at Home: Summary

The data in tables 1–5 do not lend themselves to simple summary. There is considerable evidence of traditional arrangements. Husbands bring in a disproportionate share of the family income and are more likely to exercise power in managing it. In addition, there is stereotyping in who is responsible for which family chores, with wives assuming a greater share of the household work—relatively egalitarian beliefs of both husbands and wives to the contrary. Nevertheless, although women spend more time on housework, in the aggregate they do not lack free time. Moreover, wives seem to exercise greater autonomy than husbands in making decisions about the use of small amounts of time. Finally, husbands and wives do not differ in the way they rank the other in the list of those they really trust.

Equality at Home and Activity in Politics

Our goal is to assess the effect of inequalities at home on the political activity of marriage partners. To do so, we use separate ordinary least-squares (OLS) regressions to ascertain the factors that predict political participation for wives and husbands. This will permit us to understand the extent to which, all else being equal, various family patterns affect the participation of each partner. In interpreting these results it is important to distinguish between, on the one hand, the distribution of a particular factor between husbands and wives and, on the other, the size and direction of its effect on participation for either set of marriage partners. For example, neither husbands nor wives are, in the aggregate, advantaged in terms of the relative respect they receive at home, but enjoying respect at home might give a boost to the activity of either wives or husbands, or both, or neither.

The dependent variable in this analysis is an overall summary of an individual's political activity, an additive scale based on eight activities: voting, working in campaigns, making campaign contributions, contacting public officials, taking part in protests, working informally with others to solve community problems, belonging to local governing boards, and affiliating with political organizations. (For scale construction and its characteristics, see Appendix B.) On average the wives in our sample engage in 2.27 acts (s.d. = 1.62), and the husbands in 2.42 (s.d. = 1.76) on this scale (one-tailed $p < 0.05$).

For explanatory variables, we begin with a set of basic participatory factors—resources and engagement—and add to them measures of the various aspects of family equality just discussed. Measures of the participatory resources are education (coded from 1 to 6, ranging from 8th grade or less to graduate school) and family income in tens of thousands of dollars (0 to 25 that is, $0 to $250,000). To capture an individual's engagement with politics, we include as well a measure of political interest (coded from 1 to 4, ranging from not at all interested to very interested). These variables have been shown to be significant predictors of political participation (Verba, Schlozman, and Brady 1995), and they should provide controls to ensure that any seeming effects of inequalities between wife and husband do not merely reflect characteristics of the individual or other social characteristics of the family.

To this base, we add five variables measuring family hierarchy, that is, the *relative position* of husband and wife with respect to class, status, and power *within the home*. (1) Money and time: the proportion of family income attributable to the wife (0 to 100) and the proportion contributed by the wife of the total hours devoted by the couple to housework (0 to 100). (2) Occupation status: the difference between the job levels of the wife and husband (–5 to 5). (3) Decisional control over money and time: relative control over major financial decisions (–1 to 1) and relative discretion with respect to use of small blocks of time (–1 to 1). (4) Respect: relative ranking of husband and wife on the list of trusted advisors (–2 to 2). (5) We also include a measure of beliefs about gender equality: both spouses' views about appropriate domestic roles for husband and wife (1 to 4, ranging from most traditional to least traditional).[16]

Table 6

Equality at Home: Overall Political Activity by Individual and Family Variables, OLS Regression Results

	Wives			Husbands		
	B	Standard error	Beta	B	Standard error	Beta
Participatory factors						
Education[a]	.29	(.09)**	.21	.28	(.08)**	.21
Family income[b]	.11	(.03)**	.24	.04	(.03)	.03
Political interest[a]	.36	(.12)**	.17	.54	(.14)**	.21
Domestic hierarchy: relative family resources						
Percentage of family income brought in[a]	.005	(.004)	.08	.004	(.004)	.05
Advantage in job level over that of spouse[c]	−.02	(.05)	−.02	.07	(.06)	.08
Percentage of household work done[a]	.005	(.006)	.05	−.01	(.007)	−.10
Domestic hierarchy: relative family power						
Discretion with respect to small amount of time[c]	−.15	(.15)	.05	.41	(.17)*	.14
Control over major financial decisions[c]	−.68	(.73)	.05	1.52	(.77)*	.11
Domestic hierarchy: relative respect						
Gets more respect as advisor from spouse than gives in return[c]	.21	(.10)*	.11	−.02	(.11)	−.01
Beliefs in gender equality at home						
Wife's beliefs	.66	(.32)*	.13	.11	(.33)	.02
Husband's beliefs	−.08	(.50)	.00	−.04	(.54)	−.00
Constant	−2.97	(1.66)		−1.43	(1.74)	
N		271			270	
Adjusted R^2		.24			.20	

$* p < .05, ** p < .001$.
[a]Separate measure for each spouse.
[b]Same measure for each spouse.
[c]Same relative measure in each column; direction reversed to favor each spouse (e.g., wife's job level minus husband's for her; husband's minus wife's for him).

Thus, we seek to learn how hierarchy within the home with respect to such matters as resources brought in, control over resources available within the home, and relative respect as well as both spouses' beliefs about equality at home affect the participation of each member of the couple—over and above the effect of the basic participatory factors. Since we are concerned to understand how domestic hierarchy is related to political participation for each partner in the couple, we estimate separate models for wives and husbands. To help clarify what we are doing in these models, we code the relative variables in a direction favorable to the husband (e.g., the proportion of money he brings into the household) in the husbands' model and in a direction favorable to the wife in the wives' model. Table 6, which contains the results of these analyses, confirms that education and political interest are participatory factors for both husbands and wives, as is family income for wives. Our main concern, however, is with how various kinds of inequality between spouses, as indexed by our relative measures, build upon participatory predispositions rooted in an individual's education, income, and political interest.

Domestic arrangements do have implications for political activity. These implications, which are different for husbands and wives, do not conform to what we anticipated. Many of the factors that we expected to enhance wives' activity—for example, bringing in a high proportion of family income, dividing the housework relatively equally, or exercising authority over family time or money—seem not to affect their participation. Yet, wives do get an extra participatory boost from the relative respect they command within the household, that is, by being ranked higher on their husband's list of trusted advisors than they rank their husband. In addition, a wife who believes in equality at home is likely to be more active in politics, regardless of what her husband believes about domestic roles.

The pattern is very different for husbands. Neither their own beliefs about appropriate domestic arrangements nor their wives' views have consequences for husbands' political activity. When it comes to the husband's participation, what seems to matter is whether he is boss at home. Husbands who exercise greater power over the family exchequer and who have relative autonomy in the use of small amounts of time are more likely to be active in politics.[17] In short, an egalitarian arrangement does not empower a husband for politics; exercising power at home does.

Since the results reported in Table 6 are central to our argument, we estimated the model that produced those results in various ways to test for its robustness, that is, to ensure that the signs for variables remain the same and the relationship of coefficients to their standard errors also remain similar though various specifications. We used a number of different indicators for the independent variables. For example, we estimated versions of the model in which we included measures of two additional participatory resources: job level and leisure time. As expected, neither variable has a significant effect on the activity of either husbands or wives, and the results presented in Table 6 were unchanged. We also included a measure of the traditional division of labor, defined as a situation in which the wife does a disproportionate share of the shopping and cleaning. In none of the various specifications we tried did traditional division of labor have a significant effect either for women or men. Moreover, inclusion of this variable leaves other results unchanged.

Appendix A: The Sample

The data for the first two waves of the sample come from a two-stage survey of the voluntary activity of the American public. The first stage consisted of 15,053 telephone interviews of adult (18 years old or older) Americans conducted by the Public Opinion Laboratory of Northern Illinois University and the National Opinion Research Center (NORC) during the last six months of 1989. These interviews were between 15 and 20 minutes in length, and they provided a profile of political and nonpolitical activity as well as basic demographic information. Respondents were selected randomly from telephone exchanges matched to the primary sampling units of the NORC national, in-person sampling frame. This clustered sample was designed to be representative of the American population. Within each household, adults were chosen at random using a Kish table.

The sample for the second wave was designed to incorporate distinctive features that meet the particular requirements of studying participation and representation. To assess how well the activists reflect the citizenry, a representative sample of the public is essential. Yet, ordinary representative samples contain very few of the most interesting activists—those who engage in relatively rare but important activities, such as giving large donations, serving on local governing boards, or taking part in protests. Similarly, they contain few cases of activists drawn from politically relevant racial and ethnic minorities —African Americans and Latinos—groups of particular interest in an investigation of participatory representation. To select respondents for the second stage of in-person interviews, the sample of 15,053 was first reweighted to adjust for the fact that the screener had yielded a slightly disproportionate share of women. The sample was then stratified by race and ethnicity (African American, Latino, and "all other") and by level and type of political participation. African Americans, Latinos, and political activists were oversampled, with weights ranging from 1 (inactive Anglo-whites) to 16 (highly active Latinos). In spring 1990, NORC conducted in-person interviews averaging almost two hours each with 2,517 of the original 15,000 respondents. With appropriate sampling weights, these data can be treated as a national random sample.

The data from the first two waves are deposited at the Inter-university Consortium for Political and Social Research at the University of Michigan (Verba et al. 1990). A code-book is available for each survey, along with extensive information on sampling and other technical matters.

For the third wave, we interviewed all traceable respondents from the second wave. When they happened to be married, we interviewed their spouse as well. We were able to reinterview 609 of the second-wave respondents, 380 of whom were married at the time of the third-wave interview. For married respondents, we conducted separate full interviews with the spouse. With appropriate sampling weights, the data from the third wave can be treated as an ordinary random sample. As for the previous two waves, this is a national sample.

Appendix B: Question Wording and Scales

Time Spent on Household Chores

"About how many hours per day do you spend on necessary work for your home and family, including cooking, cleaning, taking care of children or other relatives, shopping, house and yard chores, and so forth? About how many hours in total do you spend in an average day on such necessary activities for home and family?" We asked a parallel question about the respondents' estimates of their spouse's time spent on household chores.

For the wife's report of the percentage of the household time she contributed, we used the number of hours she ascribed to her own work expressed as a percentage of the total number of hours she estimated that she and her husband spent, individually, on household work; for example, a wife who reported that she spent four hours and her husband spent one hour was coded $100 \times (4/(4 + 1))$, or 80.

For the husband's report of the percentage of the household time his wife contributed, we used the number of hours he ascribed to her work expressed as a percentage of the total number of hours he estimated that he and his wife spent, individually, on household work; for example, a husband who reported that he spent four hours and his wife spent one hour was coded $100 \times (1/(4 + 1))$, or 20.

For the combined measure that we used in the regressions, we used the number of hours that she ascribed to her work expressed as a percentage of the total number of hours she estimated that she spent and he estimated that he spent, individually, on household work; for example, a wife who reported that she spent four hours and a husband who reported that he spent four hours was coded $100 \times (4/(4 + 4))$, or 50.

Income

"Now, look at response card H. (The income categories from response card H are as follows: A. Under \$5,000; B. \$5,000–9,999; C. \$10,000–14,999; D. \$15,000–19,999; E. \$20,000–24,999; F. \$25,000–29,999; G. \$30,000–34,999; H. \$35,000–39,999; I. \$40,000–49,999; J. \$50,000–59,999; K. \$60,000–74,999; L. \$75,000–99,999; M. \$100,000–124,999; N. \$125,000–149,999; O. \$150,000–199,999; P. \$200,000 and over.) Which of the income groups listed on this card includes the *total income* before taxes of all members of your family living in your home? Please include salaries, wages, pensions, dividends, interest, and all other income. Please tell me the letter for the correct category.

"Look, again, at card H. In which of these groups did *your own* total earnings from your occupation fall last year [1992] before taxes. Just tell me the letter.

"Besides income from wages, did you *yourself* bring other income into the household this past year, for example, from child support, alimony, governmental benefits, interest earnings on your own accounts, rent on your own real estate, any inheritances, or the like?

"[If other income] Look at card H one more time. Which letter best represents the amount of money you *yourself* brought into the household, from these sources *other than your wages* in 1992?"

We recoded these variables to indicate tens of thousands of dollars.

For the descriptive statistics, we used information from each spouse to calculate each spouse's estimate of the wife's contribution to family money.

For the wife's estimate of her contribution to the family income, we used the income that she ascribed to herself from her job and from other sources as a percentage of her estimate of the total family income, for example, a wife who reported bringing in $10,000 from her job and $10,000 from other sources and who reported a family income of $40,000 was coded $100 \times ((1 + 1)/4)$, or 50.

For the husband's estimate of his wife's contribution to the family income, we used the income that he ascribed to himself from his job and from other sources as a percentage of his estimate of the family income; to calculate his estimate of her contribution, we subtracted his estimate of his contribution from 100. So a husband who reported bringing in $10,000 from his job and $10,000 from other sources and who reported a family income of $40,000 was coded $100 - (100 \times ((1 + 1)/4)) = 100 - 50$, or 50.

For the combined measure of the wife's contribution to the family income, we used the income that she ascribed to herself from her job and from other sources as a percentage of that total income plus the income that he ascribed to himself from his job and from other sources; for example, a wife who reported bringing in $10,000 from her job and $10,000 from other sources and a husband who reported bringing in $20,000 from his job and $20,000 from other sources would be coded $100 \times ((1 + 1)/(1 + 1 + 2 + 2))$, or 33.

Division of Household Chores

"Now I'd like to ask you some questions about activities around the house. I am going to read you a list of some chores that usually need to be done in a household. After I read each one, please refer to response card E and reply with the *letter* that best represents your answer. If nobody does it, or if you pay someone to do it, just tell me.

"What about grocery shopping? How much responsibility do you take for this? All, most, some, a little, or none? Just read me the letter.

"What about paying family bills, that is, actually writing the checks? How much responsibility do you take for this? Just read me the letter.

"How about repairing the car or taking the car in for repair? How much responsibility do you take for this? Please read the letter from card E that describes your choice.

"What about house-cleaning chores such as vacuuming, dusting, and cleaning the bathroom? How much responsibility do you take for this? Please read a letter from card E that is next to your choice.

"[If there are children at home] What about taking care of children, that is, all child-related activities, including taking care of them, driving them places, and helping them with homework, for example? How much responsibility do you take for this? Please read me the letter from card E next to your choice."

Control Over Time and Money

"Think about bigger financial decisions—things like how much your family can afford to spend on housing or how much, and what kind, of insurance to buy. How much responsibility do you take for this? Please read me the letter from card E next to your choice."

For the regressions, we combined the two spouses' responses such that 1 indicated that he had more control (and the two spouses agreed about that), 0 indicated that they were equally in control (or that there was credit claiming), and –1 indicated that she had more control (and the two spouses agreed about that). We cleaned this measure as we describe in Appendix C.

"Now I'd like to ask you a few questions about things families usually have to make decisions about. For each question use response card G to tell me whether this is a decision you would make on your own or whether your husband (wife) would have some say in the decision. What about whether to give a few hours (commit time on a regular basis) to a charity drive (something you enjoy that doesn't involve your husband [wife]/a political campaign or cause)?"

For the regressions, we combined the two spouses' responses such that 1 indicated that he had more autonomy than she did, 0 indicated equality, and –1 indicated that she had more autonomy than he did.

Respect in the Family

"From time to time, most people seek out other people whose judgment they trust to discuss important matters. Think about three people whose judgment you really trust, and with whom you might be likely to discuss important matters. Please use the categories on response card C.

"Think of the *first* (second/third) person you'd be likely to talk with. Which category on card C describes that person? Please read the letter next to your choice.

    A. An advisor—for example, a lawyer, a doctor, or a priest, minister, or rabbi

B. A friend or neighbor
C. A co-worker
D. Your wife (husband)
E. Another close relative besides your wife (husband) (e.g., mother, father, or one of your siblings or children)
F. Someone else"

We first took each respondent's combined responses to the three questions to create a variable that we coded 1 if the respondent would turn first to the spouse, 2 if the respondent would turn second or third to the spouse, and 3 if the respondent would not turn to the spouse first, second, or third. Then we combined the two spouses' scores such that 2 indicated that he would turn to her before she would turn to him, 0 indicated equality, and –2 indicated that she would turn to him before he would turn to her.

Beliefs About Gender Equality

"Now, on a different topic, I am going to read you a series of statements and for each one, please use card F to tell me whether you agree strongly, agree, disagree, disagree strongly, or have no opinion.

A. A wife should give up her job whenever it interferes with her roles as a wife and mother.
B. Husbands and wives should share household chores equally.
C. It's best if just the husband is in charge of making family decisions."

For the regressions, we recoded the three variables such that higher numbers indicated a stronger belief in gender equality. We calculated an average score (on the four-point scales) for each respondent. We cleaned the variables as we describe in Appendix C.

Job Level Scale

The job level variable is based on the amount of education and on-the-job training the respondent believes is needed for the respondent's job. It has five levels. The lowest level jobs require no more than a high school diploma and no more than one month of on-the-job training for mastery. At the other end of the scale (level 5) are jobs requiring either a college degree and at least two years of training on the job or a graduate degree.

The questions asked were: "(In general) How much formal education does somebody need to do a job like (yours/the one you had)—no special formal education, a high school diploma, technical school, a college degree, a graduate degree, or what?" and "How long does a person have to spend in training on the job to be able to handle a job like yours?"

Although the job level classifications are based on what respondents told us rather than upon objective assessments, examination of actual cases suggests that respondents make judgments fairly accurately. Examples of occupations at each level include:

1. Dishwasher, janitor, cashier
2. Bank teller, mail carrier, machine operator
3. Electrician, machinist, construction inspector
4. Insurance agent, engineer, elementary school teacher
5. Physician, architect, attorney

To calculate job level difference, we subtracted her job level from his.

Education

The education variable has six categories:

1. 8th grade or lower
2. 9–12
3. graduated high school or GED
4. some college
5. college graduate
6. graduate school

The following questions were used to create the categorization.

"What is the highest grade of regular school that you have completed and gotten credit for? (IF NECESSARY, SAY: By regular school we mean a school which can be counted toward an elementary or high school diploma or a college or university degree.)

"Did you get a high school diploma or pass a high school equivalency test?

"Do you have any college degrees, that is, not including degrees from a business college, technical college, or vocational school?

"What is the highest degree that you have ever received?"

Political Interest

The political interest scale is based on the following question: "How interested are you in politics and public affairs? Are you very interested, somewhat interested, only slightly interested, or not at all interested in politics and public affairs?" The variable is coded 1 to 4, with 4 indicating very interested.

Political Activity Scale

Eight political acts were added together to form our overall scale.

Voting

A voter is defined as someone who voted in the 1992 presidential election. The following questions were asked.

"Are you currently registered to vote?

"In talking to people about elections, we find that they are sometimes not able to vote because they're not registered, they don't have time, or they have difficulty getting to the polls. Think about the presidential elections since you were old enough to vote. Have you voted in all of them, in most of them, in some of them, rarely voted in them, or have you never voted in a presidential election?

"Thinking back to the national election in November 1992, when the presidential candidates were Bill Clinton, the Democrat, and George Bush, the Republican, did you happen to vote in that election?"

Campaign Work

"Since January 1992, the start of the last national election year, have you worked as a volunteer, that is, for no pay at all or for only a token amount, for a candidate running for national, state, or local office?"

Campaign Contributions

"(We have been talking about campaign activity.) Now we would like to talk about contributions to campaigns. Since January 1992 did you contribute money to an individual candidate, a party group, a political action committee, or any other organization that supported candidates?"

Community Activity

"Now some questions about your role in your community. In the past *two years,* since [current month] have you served in a voluntary capacity, that is, for no pay at all or for only a token amount, on any official local governmental board or council that deals with community problems and issues, such as a town council, a school board, a zoning board, a planning board, or the like?

"Aside from membership on a board or council or attendance at meetings, I'd like to ask also about informal activity in your community or neighborhood. In the past twelve months, have you gotten together *informally* with or worked with others in your community or neighborhood to try to deal with some community issue or problem?"

Contacting

"In the past five years, since [interview date 1992], have you initiated any contacts either in person, by phone, or by letter with a government official on the national, state, or local level about a problem or an issue of concern to you? Was this [most recent] contact in the past twelve months?"

Protesting

"In the past two years, since [current month], have you taken part in a protest, march, or demonstration on some national or local issue (other than a strike against your employer)?"

Political Organization

"There are many kinds of organizations that people join, for example, unions or professional associations, fraternal groups, recreational organizations, political issue organizations, community or school groups, and so on. *Not including* membership in a local church or synagogue, are you a member of any organizations? Do any of these organizations ever take stands on any public issues, either local or national?"

We asked a parallel question of those who were members of a single organization. We coded the respondent as belonging to a political organization if s/he answered yes to the question about whether any of the organizations take stands in politics.

The Overall Political Activity Index

One point was given for each act. The additive scale runs from 0 to 8.

The various items of the index are all positively related to one another, as the following correlation matrix shows:

Items in Overall Political Activity Index[a]

	Correlation coefficients						
	Campaign work	Campaign contribution	Contact	Protest	Community board	Informal community	Political organization
Vote	.15	.28	.22	.04	.10	.13	.26
Campaign work		.27	.21	.13	.16	.13	.18
Campaign contribution			.26	.15	.13	.15	.37
Contact				.15	.16	.23	.31
Protest					.08	.10	.16
Community board						.15	.12
Informal community							.19

Note: All correlations are significant at $< .05$.

[a]Cronbach's $\alpha = .6192$.

Appendix C

Our survey contained a number of different measures of the equality dimensions discussed in this article. We used LISREL to determine the measure of each of these constructs with the highest validity (in other words, the measure with the largest coefficient on the underlying construct) (Bollen 1989). In four cases, no single measure was able to capture the construct sufficiently: percentage of housework hours put in by the wife, control over major financial decisions, his belief in gender equality, and her belief in gender equality. As a consequence, we developed measurement models for these four variables. To construct these cleaned measures, we first used LISREL to select the measure with the highest validity. We then regressed that variable on the other measures of the construct; the predicted values from those equations are the variables we used here. Our goal was to take advantage of the common variance across the measures for each construct. We chose this path instead of the creation of a scale in order to keep the variables in their original scales. The consequent measures do retain their original scales, but they contain less measurement error than their original versions.

For the measure of the percentage of housework hours put in by the wife (described in Appendix B), we regressed her percentage of the hours using information from both the husband and the wife on the difference between the wife's hours and the husband's hours using combined estimates, the wife's percentage using only information from the wife, the wife's percentage using only information from the husband, a combined report of who does the housecleaning, and a combined report of who does the grocery shopping. The resulting estimation had a corrected R^2 of .81. The coefficients and standard errors for the equation were:

Difference in hours	−2.85	(.16)
Wife's estimate	0.13	(.03)
Husband's estimate	0.25	(.03)
Housecleaning	0.004	(.86)
Grocery shopping	−1.09	(.75)
Constant	30.42	(.03)

For the measure of control over family finances, we regressed a combined measure of that control on a combined measure of who pays the bills and relative autonomy with respect to spending small amounts of money. The corrected R^2 was .07. The coefficients and standard errors for the equation were:

Paying bills	0.13	(.03)
Relative autonomy with respect to spending small amounts of money	0.06	(0.035)
Constant	0.19	(0.02)

For the two measures of his belief in gender equality and the measure of her belief in gender equality, we used an average of each spouse's responses on three questions as the dependent variable in the measurement equation: whether a wife should give up her job whenever it interferes with her roles as wife and mother, whether husbands and wives should share chores equally, and whether it is best if just the husband is in charge of making family decisions. For each spouse, we regressed this averaged variable on whether a woman's place is in the house, whether the government should help women, whether men have more of the top jobs because they are born with more drive and ambition, whether an employed mother can establish just as warm and secure a relationship with her children as a mother who is at home full time, whether a mother of young children should work if the family does not need the money, whether the husband should have major responsibility for making financial plans, and whether it is anyone else's business if a husband hits his wife from time to time. The adjusted R^2 for this equation was .38 for women and .17 for men. The coefficients and standard errors are given below.

	Her belief		His belief	
Should have equal role	.08	(.02)	.04	(.02)
Women should help themselves	−.03	(.01)	.00	(.01)
Men have top jobs because they are more ambitious	−.07	(.02)	−.05	(.02)
Employed mother cannot have warm relationship with children	.07	(.03)	.04	(.03)
It is others' business if husband hits wife	.15	(.05)	.16	(.05)
A mother of young children can work if she wants	.12	(.02)	.10	(.03)
Man should not have the major responsibility for the couple's financial plans	.05	(.02)	.07	(.03)
Constant	1.63	(.22)	1.69	(.24)

Appendix D

Since it could be argued that the correct measures would be individual-level measures rather than the relative measures that we used in the article, we report an analysis using individual measures here. For all but one of the relative measures, we also have individual-level measures. Our goal in these equations was to choose the set of measures that demonstrated the highest level of stability across different specifications. The contextual measures were significantly more stable than were the individual-level measures. Thus, they won out in our specification efforts. Nevertheless, we wish to provide a sense of the extent to which the individual-level measures drive the results we report here. In this appendix, we report the individual-level coefficients and their standard errors. We use the model reported in Table 6 for these estimations. We substitute the particular individual-level variables for the contextual variable in the equation. We do this one variable at a time.

For income, we added her income from all sources to the model; the variable for the family income is already in the model. For her equation, the coefficient on this variable is 0.15, with a standard error of .07. For his equation, the coefficient on this variable is −.20, with a standard error of .07. These significant coefficients are not highly stable (see Burns 1995).

For job level, we included each spouse's job level. In her equation, the estimate for his job level is .01 (.07) and for her job level is .05 (.08). In his equation, the estimate is .08 (.09) for his job level and −.06 (.07) for hers. These are not systematic.

For time spent in housework, we included the number of hours each spouse said s/he contributed each day. In her equation, the estimate for his contribution is −.07 (.05) and for her contribution is −.004 (.03). In his equation, the estimate for his contribution is .002 (.05), while the estimate for her contribution is .05 (.03). These are not systematic.

For autonomy with respect to time, we used each spouse's report of her or his own autonomy. In her equation, the estimate for her lack of autonomy is −.09 (.11) and for his is −.10 (.08). In his equation, the estimate for her lack of autonomy is −.06 (.12) and for his is −.23 (.08). While the combined report is more stable, this result suggests that the effect of the autonomy measure for men is driven by their own lack of autonomy and not by the comparison between the two spouses' autonomy.

For consulting with the spouse, we used each spouse's report of her or his consulting behavior (0–2, with 2 indicating that the spouse is the first person turned to). In her equation, the estimate for his behavior is .002 (.14) and for hers is −.42 (.14). In his equation, the estimate for his behavior is .008 (.15) and for hers is −.03 (.15). Again, while the combined report generates the most stable coefficient, this result suggests that the effect of the confiding measure for women may be driven by women's own behavior. The relationship is complex. Women who confide in their spouse tend to believe in and practice equality at home. In general, then, because women who confide in their spouse tend to believe in equality, the effect is a wash (the combination of this coefficient and the coefficient on belief in equality). Yet, when women who do not believe in equality confide heavily in their husband, they participate less. The first group of women mentioned practices a companionate marriage. The second group confides because these women believe in inequality. The consequences are quite different for the two groups of women.

Notes

1. The relationship between SES and political participation is well documented. See, for example, Bennett and Bennett 1986, Conway 1991, Milbrath and Goel 1977, and Verba and Nie 1972. For extended discussion of the SES model and a much more elaborated model based on resources, see Verba, Schlozman, and Brady 1995, especially chapters 9, 12, and 15.

2. Blumberg and Coleman (1989) develop a theory of gender power within the family that stresses the importance of who brings money into the home, rather than the job per se. They do not, however, consider the implications of economic control for political participation.

3. It is important to note that the respondent's marital status at the time of the second wave was not a criterion in interviewing spouses. Thus, we did not specifically select couples who were married in both waves, which would have overrepresented those with marriages of longer duration.

We considered interviewing the domestic partners of unmarried, heterosexual, and homosexual respondents, but there were simply too few respondents in these categories to pursue this approach. A study that seeks comparisons of married and unmarried couples would need to follow a strategy analogous to ours, a large initial screener followed by oversampling of respondents in "living-together" arrangements, and probably would require an even larger screener sample to begin with.

4. We mailed respondents a series of cards, analogous to those used to inquire about family income in the personal interview. These cards contained the alternative answers for many items, especially sensitive ones. When answering a question, the respondent was directed to say the letter corresponding to the response category rather than to express the response in words. In this way, someone else in the room would have difficulty knowing what the respondent was saying to the interviewer over the phone. Thus, we added to the existing advantages of surveying couples by telephone: "By telephone, others present in the room cannot hear the questions and may have little information upon which to guess the meaning of the answers. Telephone interviews may feel more private, since third parties only hear one side" (Aquilino 1993, 375).

5. Where there are discrepancies between the reports of each spouse, we make no assumption as to which partner should be trusted.

6. Question wording for these and all items can be found in Appendix B.

7. This figure is an average of absolute values. Thus, a couple in which the wife's estimate of her contribution is, say, 15% *higher* than the husband's estimate of her contribution is not balanced by a couple in which her estimate of her contribution is 15% *lower* than his estimate of her contribution.

8. Although it would have been preferable to base our data on time diaries, we are encouraged that our findings about the proportion of time given to household tasks are consistent with those of other studies. For example, Schor (1992) estimates that women contributed 72% of the household time in 1967 and 63% in 1987. Using a range of methods for ascertaining relative contributions of household labor, numerous studies (Huston and Geis 1993, 94; Lennon and Rosenfield 1994; South and Spitze 1994) arrive at similar results.

9. For the combined estimates of household time and money used below (see appendices B and C for explanation of the construction of these variables), women contribute 32% of the household money, with a standard deviation of 25. In contrast, women contribute 61% of the household labor, with the smaller standard deviation of 16.

10. Gender parity in access to free time also has been noted in the family studies literature. See Thompson and Walker (1989, 850) and Zick and McCullough (1991, 471).

11. Secondary analysis of data using similar questions from a study conducted four decades earlier shows substantial change in some respects, not so much in others. In 1955, women reported bringing in 13% of the family income compared with 33% in the recent study, but their contribution to household work has not diminished proportionately. In the earlier study, they reported doing 69%, more recently 69% (Axelrod and Blood [1955] 1974).

12. Vogler and Pahl (1994, 273–4) use a similar measure of control over large household decisions as an indicator of "strategic control over household finances."

13. Reanalysis of the earlier survey shows that wives were even less likely to make financial decisions forty years ago. In 1955 nearly two-thirds of wives reported having little or no

responsibility for major financial matters, in contrast to only 9% who made this assessment in the recent survey (Axelrod and Blood [1955] 1974).

14. We are concerned with the relative respect accorded by members of the couple. Hence, low but equal levels of respect count as equality in this measure: We define the circumstance in which neither partner confides in the other (the case for three couples in our sample) as conferring no relative disadvantage. The overwhelming share of the equal-respect couples (88%) are at the highest level of mutual respect.

15. Huston and Gels (1993, 93) find this same similarity between husbands and wives. Data from the Detroit Area Study reported in Thornton and Freedman (1979) indicate that the views of women have moved in a more egalitarian direction over the past three decades.

16. Our survey contains a number of different measures of these constructs. We used LISREL to determine the measure with the highest validity among those for a particular construct (Bollen 1989). We use that variable here to measure the construct. In three instances, we used regression measurement models to help reduce the amount of measurement error in the variables. In these three instances, no single measure was able to capture the construct sufficiently. These three variables—time given to work at home, control over money, and beliefs about gender equality—retain their original scales but contain less measurement error than their original versions. See Appendix C for elaboration.

17. In this context recall from Table 4 that, compared to wives, husbands are more likely to be dominant over family money than over their own time.

References

Almond, Gabriel A., and Sidney Verba. 1963. *The Civic Culture.* Princeton: Princeton University Press.

Aquilino, William S. 1993. "Effects of Spouse Presence during the Interview on Survey Responses Concerning Marriage." *Public Opinion Quarterly* 57 (Fall):358–76.

Axelrod, Morris, and Robert Blood. [1955] 1974. Detroit Area Study, 1955: A Description of Urban Kinship Patterns and the Urban Family. [Computer file.] Conducted by University of Michigan, Department of Sociology. ICPSR study #7319. Ann Arbor, MI: Inter-university Consortium for Political and Social Research [producer and distributor].

Beckwith, Karen. 1986. *American Women and Political Participation.* New York: Greenwood.

Bennett, Stephen Earl, and Linda L. M. Bennett. 1986. "Political Participation." In *Annual Review of Political Science,* ed. Samuel Long. Norwood, NJ: Ablex Publishing.

Bird, Gloria W., Gerald A. Bird, and Marguerite Scruggs. 1984. "Determinants of Family Task Sharing: A Study of Husbands and Wives." *Journal of Marriage and the Family* 46 (May):345–55.

Blood, Robert O., Jr., and Donald M. Wolfe. 1968. *Husbands and Wives: The Dynamics of Married Living.* New York: The Free Press.

Blumberg, Rae Lesser, and Marion Tolbert Coleman. 1989. "A Theoretical Look at the Gender Balance of Power in the American Couple." *Journal of Family Issues* 10 (June):225–50.

Blumstein, Philip, and Pepper Schwartz. 1983. *The American Couple: Money, Work, and Sex.* New York: Morrow.

Bollen, Kenneth A. 1989. *Structural Equations with Latent Variables.* New York: John Wiley.

Brady, Henry E., Sidney Verba, and Kay Lehman Schlozman. 1995. "Beyond SES: A Resource Model of Participation." *American Political Science Review* 89 (June):271–94.

Brines, Julie. 1994. "Economic Dependency, Gender, and the Division of Labor at Home." *American Journal of Sociology* 100 (November):652–88.

Browning, Martin. 1992. "Children and Household Economic Behavior." *Journal of Economic Literature* 30 (September):1434–75.

Burns, Nancy. 1995. "The Choices and Constraints of Gender." Presented at the annual meeting of the Midwest Political Science Association, Chicago.

Conway, Margaret. 1991. *Political Participation in the United States.* 2d ed. Washington, DC: CQ Press.

Douhitt, Robin A. 1989. "The Division of Labor within the Home: Have Gender Roles Changed?" *Sex Roles* 20 (June):693–704.

Epstein, Cynthia Fuchs. 1988. *Deceptive Distinctions: Sex, Gender, and the Social Order.* New Haven: Yale University Press.

Goode, William J. 1971. "Force and Violence in the Family." *Journal of Marriage and the Family* 33 (November):624–36.

Hochschild, Arlie. 1989. *The Second Shift.* New York: Viking.

Huston, Ted L., and Gilbert Geis. 1993. "In What Ways Do Gender-Related Attributes and Beliefs Affect Marriage?" *Journal of Marriage and the Family* 49 (Fall):87–106.

Lennon, Mary Clare, and Sarah Rosenfeld. 1994. "Relative Fairness and the Division of Housework: The Importance of Options." *American Journal of Sociology* 100 (September):506–31.

Milbrath, Lester W., and M.L. Goel. 1977. *Political Participation.* 2d ed. Chicago: Rand McNally.

Oakley, Ann. 1974. *The Sociology of Housework.* New York: Pantheon.

Okin, Susan Moller. 1989. *Justice, Gender, and the Family.* New York: Basic Books.

Pahl, J.M. 1989. *Money and Marriage.* New York: St. Martin's.

Phillips, Anne. 1991. *Engendering Democracy.* Cambridge, UK: Polity.

Rubin, Lillian B. [1976] 1992. *Worlds of Pain.* New York: Basic Books.

Sapiro, Virginia. 1983. *The Political Integration of Women.* Urbana: University of Illinois Press.

Scanzoni, John, and Greer Litton Fox. 1980. "Sex Roles, Family and Society: The Seventies and Beyond." *Journal of Marriage and the Family* 42 (November):743–58.

Schlozman, Kay Lehman, Nancy E. Burns, and Sidney Verba. 1994. "Gender and the Pathways to Participation: The Role of Resources." *Journal of Politics* 56 (May):963–90.

Schor, Juliet. 1992. *The Overworked American: The Unexpected Decline of Leisure.* New York: Basic Books.

South, Scott J., and Glenna Spitze. 1994. "Housework in Marital and Nonmarital Households." *American Sociological Review* 59 (June):327–47.

Starrels, Marjorie E. 1994. "Husbands' Involvement in Female Gender-Typed Household Chores." *Sex Roles* 31 (October):473–91.

Stoker, Laura, and M. Kent Jennings. 1995. "Life-Cycle Transitions and Political Participation: The Case of Marriage." *American Political Science Review* 89 (June):421–33.

Thompson, Linda, and Alexis J. Walker. 1989. "Gender in Families." *Journal of Marriage and the Family* 51 (November):845–71.

Thornton, Arland, and Deborah Freedman. 1979. "Changes in the Sex Role Attitudes of Women, 1962–1977: Evidence from a Panel Study." *American Sociological Review* 44 (October):831–42.

Tolleson-Rinehart, Sue. 1992. *Gender Consciousness and Politics.* New York: Routledge.

Verba, Sidney, and Norman H. Nie. 1972. *Participation in America: Political Democracy and Social Equality.* New York: Harper and Row.

Verba, Sidney, Kay Lehman Schlozman, and Henry E. Brady. 1995. *Voice and Equality: Civic Voluntarism in American Politics.* Cambridge, MA: Harvard University Press.

Verba, Sidney, Kay Lehman Schlozman, Henry E. Brady, and Norman Nie. 1990. "American Citizen Participation Study" [Computer file]. ICPSR version. Chicago, IL: University of Chicago, National Opinion Research Center (NORC) [producer], 1995. Ann Arbor, MI: Inter-university Consortium for Political and Social Research [distributor], 1995.

Vogler, Carolyn, and Jan Pahl. 1994. "Money Power, and Inequality within Marriage." *Sociological Review* 42 (May):263–88.

Weber, Max. 1958. "Class, Status, and Party." In *From Max Weber: Essays in Sociology,* ed. H. H. Gerth and C. Wright Mills. New York: Oxford University Press.

Welch, Susan. 1977. "Women as Political Animals? A Test of Some Explanations for Male-Female Political Participation Differences." *American Journal of Political Science* 21 (November):711–31.

West, Candace, and Don Zimmerman. 1987. "Doing Gender." *Gender and Society* 1 (June):125–51.

Zick, Cathleen D., and Jane L. McCullough. 1991. "Trends in Married Couples' Time Use: Evidence from 1977–78 and 1987–88." *Sex Roles* 24 (April):459–87.

Discussion Questions

1. How did the authors choose the items they expected would have an impact on male and female differences with respect to political involvement? Were their choices well-grounded in theory?
2. The key concern that prompted the researchers to undertake this study was the problem of inequality in family life. What kinds of inequality did they measure?
3. Virtually all the data focused on the respondents' judgments and perceptions about family life. Ideally, it would have been helpful to have had some objective information about such things as which spouse has responsibility for financial decisions and which spouse has more free time, but such data would require scientific observation of behavior that is literally behind closed doors. Given this fact, was the authors' use of survey data appropriate?
4. Do you consider the measures here to be valid and reliable?

Commentary

Burns, Schlozman, and Verba attacked a very controversial and very complicated research subject in this article. As they noted, there is a substantial literature on the question of how family life affects men and women in the political arena, but very little empirical evidence is contained in it. One writer even concluded that the matter is so obvious that "I consider the argument won as soon as it is stated." The authors of this study, following a firm adherence to the principles of rigorous social science, felt that even strong opinions must be backed up with careful research.

Their conclusions may strike some readers as unsettling, or at least rather surprising. Perhaps the most consistent finding is that husbands and wives are remarkably similar in their perceptions about family life and about the proper roles of spouses. Moreover, contrary to some expectations, women appear to have no shortage of free time, and they seem to have more freedom than their husbands in deciding how to spend it. Thus, family life does not appear to diminish women's political participation by constraining their time.

These and other conclusions were based on a wide range of important measurement decisions. Although the questions respondents were asked required them to engage in a considerable amount of subjective estimation, the persuasiveness of the study was strengthened by virtue of the fact that the questions were fairly specific. For example, when discussing the division of household chores, the questionnaire included items on housecleaning, grocery shopping, paying bills, repairing the car, and taking care of the children. If the authors had operationalized this item simply with a general question about "doing household chores," different responses could have been created by respondents interpreting the phrase differently. The measure was thus made more reliable by virtue of the authors' specific focus in the questions.

The measure of the "mutuality of respect" required the authors to consider the differences between husbands and wives in terms of the respect that each gives the other. The original survey asked the respondents to list the three persons whom they most trusted to discuss important matters with. A large majority of both husbands and wives listed their spouse first. The most interesting cases, however, were those in which a husband or wife listed his or her spouse as the person he or she trusted most, while the spouse did not return the same level of respect. The authors were interested in this asymmetry, because it would possibly indicate some degree of dominance in family life. This is an interesting and inventive measurement choice. Clearly, we would not expect to get useful or candid answers if respondents were asked "which spouse in the family is dominant?" Instead, the authors calculated for each respondent the degree to which he or she received more respect than he or she granted in return. It is reasonable to suppose that this is a better measure of "domestic hierarchy" than a more direct question would have provided.

The authors measured the dependent variable, "political activity," by adding up how many of several kinds of political participation each respondent reported doing (voting, working on campaigns, contributing to campaigns, contacting public officials, protesting, working with a community board, and informal community work). Respondents received scores on this variable based on the number (0–8) of the activities in which he or she reported being engaged.

One obvious weakness of the dependent variable is the fact that it is based on self-reports; many people can be expected to report having voted when they really did not vote, for example, and the same may apply to the other kinds of participation as well. One may also raise questions about the fact that all forms of participation are rated equally. Two respondents can both receive a score of 5 by engaging in a rather different combination of political activities.

Nevertheless, the measure is sound for the purpose of comparing respondents. It is intuitive that a person engaging in many of these activities should be rated higher in terms of political participation than a person at the low end of the measure. Even given the fact that some over-reporting could be involved, it is highly likely that persons with higher scores are, generally speaking, more active in politics. We have reason to be interested in determining what kinds of factors are associated with different scores on this dependent variable.

As shown in Table 6, the variables that most strongly influenced participation, by both husbands and wives, are education level and interest in politics. People with more education and more political interest participate more actively in politics, regardless of gender. (Look at the coefficients with the single or double asterisks; as we will discuss in later chapters, these are the coefficients that we can be very confident were not produced as a result of the sample being unrepresentative of the broader population. The "beta" of .21 for the education variable means that there is some tendency for respondents with higher levels of education to have higher levels of political participation, but a coefficient in this range does not indicate a very strong relationship.)

There are some gender differences, but the differences are not very large. For example, political participation is apparently not affected by differences in the percentage of family income brought in by husbands and wives. These conclusions disturb some assumptions that many writers make about family life and the role of gender in politics. Clearly, Americans differ greatly with respect to their interest and activity in politics, but family life does not appear to be the primary determinant of those differences.

5 Surveys

The public opinion survey has become a basic tool of modern social research. Surveys are conducted to determine why certain cars sell better than others, why television programs gain or lose popularity, and which groups of voters are most likely to support a given candidate. Political scientists make extensive use of surveys to obtain data about political behavior and attitudes. Such information may be valuable in and of itself. (Which candidate will be our next president?) In other cases, survey research helps us to analyze and interpret the influences affecting political behavior.

Surveys can be among the most powerful tools used by political scientists, but they are also vulnerable to errors that can profoundly distort research findings. If the sample is in any way unrepresentative or the questions poorly constructed, our results will invariably be misleading or inaccurate. Consequently, survey research requires great attention to detail in planning and design.

Gathering Survey Data

There are three main ways to gather survey data: the face-to-face method, the mailed survey, and the telephone survey. Each of these three approaches has its own strengths and weaknesses. No one of the three is ideal for all research problems.

The two most important considerations in selecting the method by which to gather data are cost and **response rate**, or the proportion of subjects who actually respond to the survey. Face-to-face surveys usually produce a very high response rate—often over 90 percent—but are the most expensive and time consuming to conduct. The mail survey is the least expensive method but usually has the worst response rate—seldom better than 50 percent. Telephone surveys fall between mail and face-to-face surveys with respect to cost and, properly conducted, will also have respectably high response rates, frequently as much as 70 percent. Perhaps for this reason, most public opinion polls today are conducted by telephone. The cost of the face-to-face method makes it prohibitive for most academic researchers. Political scientists typically rely on mail or telephone surveys, although even these methods normally require success in obtaining a research grant from outside sources.

A third factor to be considered when designing a survey is whether the method chosen is likely to be effective in reaching a representative sample of the population under study. Telephone surveys have limitations in this regard. Some people do not have telephones. Further, among those who do, certain kinds of people are more likely to be available for phone calls than others at any given time. Mail surveys also have weaknesses with respect to representativeness. It is relatively easy to mail questionnaires to a random sample of individuals. However, not everyone is equally likely to respond to such a survey. As a result, the results may or may not be adequately representative of the target population. If it is critical that responses be obtained from many different types of people, the face-to-face method is by far the best approach.

The face-to-face survey is inferior to the other approaches in only one respect: It involves the risk of bias or distortion resulting from the respondent's reactions to the interviewer. The inflection, speaking style, personality, and even body language of the interviewer can affect the respondent's answers. The mailed survey is normally best at minimizing problems induced by the interaction of the respondent and the interviewer, while telephone surveys again fall somewhere in between.

When selecting a method for data collection, the researcher must weigh all of these considerations—cost, response rate, the relative effectiveness of the method as a means of reaching a representative sample of the population involved, and possible interviewer/respondent reactions. The importance of the last concern is often heavily influenced by the nature of the research question involved. Some kinds of questions are much more likely than others to produce false responses when the respondent is concerned about what may be done with his or her answers.

Writing the Questions

Once a survey design has been selected, the next task is to prepare the questions to be asked. This is a critical stage in the design of any survey, and all survey questions must be constructed with great care.

First, the questions should be designed to gather evidence that bears directly and as conclusively as possible on the research problem under investigation. This may seem an obvious point. It is an important one nonetheless. Unless written carefully, survey questions can easily produce results that seem to bear on the research problem but are, in fact, misleading. Consider, for example, a researcher who is interested in determining the proportion of city residents who would *prefer* to live in the suburbs. If he or she asks whether the respondent *plans* to make such a move, it is possible—perhaps even likely—that many respondents who would prefer to make such a move would answer "no," for the simple reason that they could not afford a house in the suburbs. As a result, the researcher's results would almost surely be misleading as evidence regarding citizen preferences. A failure to ask the right question is a common failing in survey research.

Second, the meaning of the questions must be clear to the respondent. The researcher cannot assume that respondents will interpret ambiguous or uncertain questions in the way the researcher intends. A question like "Did you vote in the last election?" could refer to almost any recent election. The answers given, therefore, will differ depending on the respondent's interpretation.

Legal and social science terminology is notoriously unclear to lay persons and a potential source of confusion for survey respondents. Political scientists may have a fairly definite idea of what it means to "participate in politics," for example, but most survey respondents would find the phrase rather vague. Questions also become vague when they contain awkward negatives (e.g., "Do you feel that the governor should not pardon Al Capone?"). The meaning of a "yes" answer will not be easily understood by the respondent. "Double-barreled" questions are also notoriously unclear (e.g., "Do you support President Bush, or do you think that the Republicans do a poor job in the White House?"). Again, the respondent may agree with the first part of the question while disagreeing with the second part; we cannot be sure what part of the question the respondent has answered.

Ambiguity is best avoided by being specific, direct, and simple, and providing alternatives or examples when necessary to ensure that the question will be properly understood. "Do you approve of government welfare policy?" could refer to state, local, or federal policy, or even a particular local agency with which the respondent is familiar. Moreover, the idea of approval is rather nebulous. A more specific question such as the following would be more likely to obtain accurate results. "Last year the federal government spent (x number of) dollars on the construction of low-income housing. Do you believe this amount is too much, about right, or too little?"

A third hazard to avoid when writing questions is bias. Biased questions contain language or phrasing that is likely to influence or predetermine the answers received. Bias can be created in both obvious and subtle ways. The use of loaded terms such as "socialized medicine" or "reverse discrimination" is an obvious source of potential bias. Bias can also be created in more subtle ways. Consider this question: "Do you believe the free market will take care of all social problems, or do you feel that some government regulation is needed?" The question is inherently biased—only the most extreme free-market libertarian would agree with it. If the researcher *wants* results showing that only a small minority of respondents support free market economics, a question worded in this manner will work very well. A different approach to wording would be necessary if we really want to know what our respondents think about the issue. In general, any question that offers the respondent a choice between an extreme alternative ("all social problems will be solved") and a moderate one ("some regulation is needed") will prompt most respondents to select the moderate answer.

Sometimes it is necessary to introduce a question with background information so that the respondent will understand it. However, even when the question itself is worded carefully, introductory background material can be a source of bias. Consider this illustration:

> Since there are so many dangers associated with the operation of nuclear power plants and the disposal of waste from them, and since the world's supply of the uranium needed to fuel these plants will be exhausted in about thirty years anyway, some people argue that it is foolish to invest so much in developing nuclear power when we could be devoting resources to the development of safe and inexhaustible energy sources like solar, wind, and methane. Do you agree that our nation should sharply curtail its investment in nuclear energy?[1]

It is important that the questionnaire be as brief as possible, particularly in the case of surveys directed at the mass public. Longer questionnaires lead to lower response rates and an increase in the number of incomplete responses. Further, there will also usually be significant differences between respondents and nonrespondents in such cases, since it is likely that those who take the time to complete a lengthy questionnaire will have an unusual degree of interest in the subject. If so, the results will not be representative of the whole population.

Finally, a respondent's answer is normally useful only if he or she knows something about the subject. People are often reluctant to acknowledge a lack of information, however, and will, therefore, guess at an answer even when they do not know anything about the subject involved. **Filter questions** can be used to determine if the respondent is in fact acquainted with the matter under study. Suppose, for example, we wish to survey public opinion concerning recent Supreme Court decisions on abortion rights. If we were, for whatever reason, primarily interested in a sample of informed individuals, we could include several items at the beginning of the questionnaire designed to test the potential respondent's knowledge of the subject. Respondents whose answers suggested they were not well informed could be omitted from the data analysis. In this fashion, we could protect our analysis against the confounding effects of "guesses" offered by poorly informed respondents.

Cross-Sectional and Longitudinal Surveys

Most survey research involves the collection of data at a single point in time. Surveys of this type can tell us much about the characteristics, attitudes, and other important features of the population involved, but only at one point in time. Such a survey is, therefore, referred to as a **cross-sectional survey**. It gives us a view of a cross-section of the population as of the date of the survey.

The U.S. Census is perhaps the most familiar example of a cross-sectional

---

1. This example is taken from Manheim and Rich (1991), p. 137.

survey. Such surveys are very good sources of descriptive information. They may also be very helpful for purposes of exploratory analysis in that cross-sectional data often suggest useful hypotheses and ideas for additional research.

Cross-sectional surveys can also shed light on causal relationships. For example, we may want to determine if people's income levels affect the likelihood of their voting in a national election. A cross-sectional study that collected information about the income levels and voting behavior of a representative sample of eligible voters could help us to investigate this question. If, as a result of that survey, we found that a greater proportion of those with high incomes than those with low incomes were regular voters, this would certainly represent useful evidence that income does have an impact on voting behavior.

Cross-sectional surveys are not always ideal for such analysis, however. In many causal relationships, the cause occurs long before the effect. A cross-sectional study measures both at the same moment in time. Perhaps the attainment of a high income level while in one's twenties creates a long lasting predisposition to vote, while no such tendency appears among those who attain a high income at a later point in life. If so, it would be difficult to detect this relationship via a cross-sectional survey.

A **longitudinal survey** is designed to deal with such problems. There are three common varieties—trend, cohort, and panel.

A **trend survey** is that involves different samples independently drawn from the same general population in question (such as residents of Kansas or French women) at different times. Such surveys are useful for studying changes over time in the population from which the samples are taken. The weekly polls of potential voters that have become a fixture during American presidential campaigns are examples of trend studies.

A **cohort survey** is similar to a trend survey but focuses on specific groups of people who share particular statistical or demographic characteristics. For example, we might be interested in the behavior, attitudes, and achievements of individuals who received a college degree in 1965. If so, and if we wished to follow this group over time, we might proceed by surveying separate samples drawn independently from this category of individuals at five-year intervals, say in 1965, 1970, 1975, and so on. This would make it possible for us to identify and measure the relationship, if any, between events and other potential influences occurring at one point in time and their effects observed at later periods. Of course, we would be studying *different individuals* at each time period. Each of our samples would, however, be representative of the *same specific population*, in this case 1965 college graduates.

The primary difference between trend and cohort studies, therefore, lies in their populations. The size and makeup of the general populations studied in trend surveys can change markedly over time as new individuals and subpopulations enter the picture. By contrast, the specific populations targeted in cohort studies are normally altered only by attrition. As with our group of 1965 college graduates, such a population can only lose members. It can never gain them and, thus, cannot increase in size over time.

Because they make use of different samples, the results of trend and cohort studies may be subject to varying interpretations. Consider the controversy during the 1988 presidential campaign over the economic effects of President Reagan's policies. Economic data from trend studies indicated that the proportion of Americans belonging to the middle class had diminished between 1981 and 1988. Democrats claimed this reflected the downward mobility of many formerly middle-class, industrial workers whose factories had closed during the Reagan years and who had subsequently been unable to find comparable employment. Many of these workers, the Democrats asserted, had been forced to take low-paying jobs and had, as a result, lost their middle-class status. In contrast, Reagan supporters argued that the shrinkage in the size of the middle class simply reflected an increase in the number of citizens who were becoming rich as a result of Reagan's policies.

Which, if either, of these interpretations was correct could not be determined on the basis of trend data, from which it was clear only that there had been a reduction in the middle-class segment of the population. Actually, both the upper and lower classes grew to some extent during the Reagan years, while the middle class shrank in size. (The exact numbers depend on how the income groups are defined.) Perhaps the lower class grew because of high birthrates among the poor, a point made by Reagan supporters. Or perhaps, as Democrats argued, it grew as a result of downward mobility that afflicted middle-class citizens as a result of Reagan policies. Any of these interpretations would be consistent with the trend data.

A cohort survey could have provided additional information. This would have required studying individuals from one or more specific cohorts, those whose income level ranged from $18,000 to $23,000 in 1979, for example. By conducting a series of surveys involving samples independently drawn from this same cohort at various points in time, we could have determined more precisely what happened to this cohort (those who were middle-class in 1979) during the Reagan administration.

Even more precise information can be gathered by a **panel survey.** Panel studies are longitudinal studies in which a single sample of the population is drawn and studied at different points in time. The *same* individuals are interviewed again and again. (In cohort studies, we interview different samples of the same population at different times.) Because they track specific individuals over time, panel studies allow us to identify and measure changes in the behavior, attitude, or fortunes of a specific group of individuals. In the above example, a panel study could have helped us determine what happened between 1981 and 1988 to individuals who belonged to the middle class at the beginning of 1979.

Thus, panel and cohort surveys provide a great deal of helpful information not available through trend studies. Both, however, are more costly and difficult to conduct. Cohort surveys involve multiple surveys of a number of samples (each drawn at the different times) from the target population. Panel studies require that we maintain contact with our panel for a period of time that may extend for several years or more.

Of course, cohort and panel surveys each have their own advantages and disadvantages, factors that must be considered when designing research. Cohort studies may be affected by the fact that the composition of a cohort can change over time, thus affecting our results. Our cohort of 1965 college graduates, for example, will grow smaller, as its members die or move to other countries. While no new members can ever be added to the cohort (since by definition no 1965 degrees will ever be awarded after 1965), the people that leave the cohort over time may be politically different in some important sense from those that remain. If so, our repeated measurements may detect changes that simply reflect the changing composition of the cohort, leading us to infer incorrectly that social forces or influences have altered the attitudes or behavior of the cohort itself.

A panel study avoids this problem because the same individuals are studied. Yet, this advantage of panel analysis creates a potential problem. When we ask people the same or similar questions repeatedly, they may become sensitized to the questions or the subject matter. They may be conscious of giving answers that represent a change from a previous position, and they may be alerted to think more about the issue than persons not in the panel by virtue of repeated exposure to the questions. This is a threat to the "external validity" of our research, as discussed in chapter 2. Our panel subjects' heightened sensitivity to the questions in the surveys makes it difficult to generalize from their responses. Deciding whether to use cohort or panel analysis requires a thorough understanding of the problem being researched so that the significance of these factors can be assessed.

Of course, in all longitudinal analysis—even trend studies—great care must be exercised to ensure that our measurements are consistent. If we measure our variables in different ways at different times, we may lose the ability to determine whether any trends detected reflect real changes or are simply the result of the use of different measuring sticks.

Controversy over this very problem, the use of different questions to tap the same variables over time, was at the heart of one of the most acrimonious disputes in modern political research. In their 1976 book, *The Changing American Voter*, Norman Nie and his co-authors claimed to have discovered evidence that the American electorate had become much more ideological during the 1970s (Nie et al. 1976). Their findings were in stark contrast to those of one of the most famous works in modern political science, Angus Campbell et al.'s *The American Voter* (1960), which had held that most Americans were very unsystematic and nonideological in their political views. Nie's claims were subsequently disputed by a team of authors headed by George Bishop

(1978), who argued that the changes reported in *The Changing American Voter* were almost entirely attributable to the fact that the survey questions used to obtain public opinion data were changed in 1968. The issue is one that continues to provoke controversy in American political science.

The excerpts that follow illustrate the use of surveys in political research. The first, by Stanley Feldman and John Zaller, explores the idea that Americans form their attitudes on social welfare issues by applying basic ethical principles. The second excerpt, by James Gibson, explores attitudinal changes in the Russian public that may help to explain that country's prospects for a stable democratic order.

——————————— Excerpt 7 ———————————

Feldman and Zaller began their research with the idea that analysis of responses to simple, multiple-choice survey questions inherently obscures the extent to which Americans base their issue positions on fundamental principles. They claim that traditional survey analysis creates the impression that Americans adopt issue positions haphazardly, easily changing their attitudes in response to immediate events, candidate personality, or other factors. Feldman and Zaller suspected that, by exploring more extended survey responses, they could find evidence that Americans form their issue positions on a more abstract, principled basis.

Feldman and Zaller argue that American conservatism and liberalism can both be traced to the distinctive American political culture. An interesting implication of this idea is that contemporary liberals will suffer more "value conflict" in their political attitudes than conservatives. The authors contend that the political culture contains firm support for limited government and individualism and that liberals generally support these concepts nearly as much as conservatives do. Support for active government policies in social welfare therefore causes problems for liberals that do not afflict conservatives.

Feldman and Zaller explore these ideas by analyzing data from a 1987 National Election Studies (NES) pilot study that contained open-ended probes. The probes were added to two standard sets of NES questions; items pertaining to whether or not citizens should be guaranteed jobs and a basic standard of living, and items pertaining to increased government spending. They refer to the survey as a "two-wave panel design" because the respondents were interviewed twice, in May and again in June. However, unlike the typical panel study, the authors were not interested in changes in responses over time. For our purposes, therefore, this would not be considered a genuine panel study, but a cross-sectional survey for which responses were gathered over a two-month period.

The Political Culture of Ambivalence: Ideological Responses to the Welfare State

Stanley Feldman, *State University of New York at Stony Brook*

John Zaller, *University of California, Los Angeles*

American Journal of Political Science 36, no. 1 (February 1992): 268–307. Copyright © 1992 by the University of Wisconsin Press. Reprinted with permission.

Writing just after the crest of the postwar liberalism symbolized by the Great Society, Free and Cantril (1968) observed an apparent contradiction in the political beliefs of many Americans. A large proportion of the public enthusiastically supported the specific federal programs that constitute the modern American welfare state. However, a similarly large number of people also endorsed a series of strong statements that condemned big government and praised economic individualism. Free and Cantril described this as a "schizoid combination of operational liberalism with ideological conservatism" (1968, 37). While in practice people accept the role of the federal government in maintaining social welfare, "the abstract ideas they tend to hold about the nature and functioning of our socioeconomic system still seem to stem more from the underlying assumptions of a laissez-faire philosophy than from the operating assumptions of the New Deal, the Fair Deal, the New Frontier, or the Great Society" (1968, 30).

Other observers of U.S. society have detected similar sorts of conflicts but see them as an enduring feature of U.S. political ideology rather than a short-term failure to adapt to changing circumstances. This conflict is usually seen as a clash between two major elements of the political culture: achievement and equality (Lipset 1979), capitalism and democracy (McClosky and Zaller 1984), or freedom and equality (Rokeach 1973). Rather than making an ideologically clean choice between these competing values, people tend to accept both of them, emphasizing one over the other in specific situations, but never wholly rejecting either.

These claims about American values are important because they purport to describe a fundamental property of public opinion—one that, it is asserted, greatly affects the course of public policy in the United States. For example, Free and Cantril argue that Americans need to adapt their ideological convictions to the changing role of government in order to "implement their political desires in a more intelligent, direct, and consistent manner" (1968, 181). But such claims are highly problematic in that they presume a level of ideological awareness of the public that is, by many accounts, unrealistic. In fact, it has become almost a commonplace in the political behavior literature that Americans are ideologically innocent.[1] One can readily imagine, therefore, that many of the people who endorse welfare state programs while proclaiming allegiance to laissez-faire ideals are completely unaware of any tension between them. What analysts such as Free and Cantril call value "schizophrenia" may be just another instance of ideology-free thought.

Our article is an attempt to resolve this difficulty. Contrary to the evidence of "ideological innocence," we argue that Americans do, for the most part, understand the philosophical underpinnings of the policies they endorse, and that, much more often than the belief systems literature would lead one to expect, Americans make use of cultural values and principles in explicating and justifying their political preferences. Further, we show that, exactly as the Free and Cantril analysis would suggest, it is liberals rather than conservatives who are most beset by value conflict over social welfare because they are the ones who must somehow reconcile activist government with traditional principles of economic individualism and laissez-faire.

This paper thus has two separate but closely related aims. The first is to confirm the oft-made claim that popular support for the welfare state in the United States must continually struggle with the values of nineteenth-century liberalism. What is novel about our confirmation is that it is the first to be based on systematic coding of data obtained from open-ended probes of a large, nationally representative sample. This gives us an evidentiary base for our claims that is significantly stronger than that which has been available to previous researchers in this area. The second aim of the paper is to clarify and propose a resolution to the Converse-Lane controversy over political ideology. We shall not dispute Converse's claim that most people are relatively nonideological in that they normally fail to organize tightly their symbolic concerns in accord with liberalism or conservatism. In fact, our data will help show why this is true, at least for social welfare issues. But in a more revisionist vein, we shall show that Americans do understand and use cultural values and principles in evaluating and articulating many of their political preferences. These two claims do not contradict each other; rather they reflect a long-standing feature of the political culture.

The Prevalence of Ideology in the United States

In Converse's (1964) analysis of mass belief systems, the central idea is that of constraint, namely, the capacity of one political idea to control or "constrain" another. Thus, if people both embrace a general principle, such as economic individualism, and derive specific policies from this value, their more specific ideas are constrained by ideological principle. If, on the other hand, people hold general values that are manifestly inconsistent with most of their concrete policy preferences, the preferences are said to be unconstrained by ideological principle. Converse's conclusion, of course, was that most individuals have unconstrained belief systems in the sense that their attitudes are not organized by the left-right continuum or any other sort of dimensional continuum. Inconsistency in policy preferences and political beliefs is thus a characteristic of a lack of ideological structure.

Several researchers have examined other types of evidence and have come to an entirely different conclusion. In her in-depth interviews with 28 adults from New Haven, Hochschild (1981) describes in detail the "ambivalence" that emerges from her subjects' attempts to apply traditional norms of economic differentiation to modern problems of social welfare. Many of her respondents seemed at least somewhat aware of the underlying conflicts, although "they find it easier to live with, and to try to ignore, even distressing normative tensions than to undertake the enormous effort needed to resolve them" (1981, 258). Similarly, Reinarman's (1987) interviews with six public sector and six private sector workers are full of statements that alternately reflect belief in the free market and individualism, recognition that the system is not completely open and that people need assistance, and criticisms of the bureaucratization and performance of the federal government. In both of these studies, conflict and ambivalence is interpreted not as confusion, inconsistency, or lack of sophistication but as a problem of reconciling the multiple values, beliefs, and principles simultaneously present in the political culture.

Value conflict and ambivalence of this sort are not easily identified with the types of fixed choice questions typically used in mass survey instruments. And worse, when they are identified, they may easily be taken as evidence of lack of constraint—and hence lack of concern for abstract principles. Yet, as both Hochschild and Reinarman show, it is dangerous to equate lack of consistency with lack of understanding of the principles that underlie policy preferences (see also Lane 1973).

The first step toward untangling these issues is to specify as clearly as possible the relationship between the content and structure of the political culture and the individual-level organization of political preferences and beliefs.

By political culture we mean a set of values that are widely endorsed by politicians, educators, and other opinion leaders and that animate the principal political institutions of a society. In the United States, these values include freedom, equality, individualism, democracy, capitalism, and several others. This distinctive constellation of values originated in radical British politics, diffused to North America in the colonial period, inspired the organizers of the American Revolution (Baylin 1967), and diffused widely enough by the 1830s to be clearly observable at the mass level by the time of Tocqueville's visit to the United States. More recent survey-based studies confirm that most Americans continue to embrace the core values of this political culture (Devine 1972; Lipset 1979; McClosky and Zaller 1984).

Yet many analysts contend that U.S. political culture embodies a substantial amount of unresolved value conflict, especially between freedom and equality (Lipset 1979; McClosky and Zaller 1984). How do people respond to this conflict?

Even the most cursory examination of U.S. politics reveals that many of the elite sources of political culture, especially partisan politicians, are more enthusiastic about some aspects of the culture than others. Thus, some tend to favor freedom, especially individual economic freedom, over other values, especially equality and popular sovereignty. These people are widely considered, and usually consider themselves, to be conservatives. Others manifest the reverse preference ordering and are considered liberals. These recognized liberal and conservative opinion leaders, by the policies they favor and the pronouncements they make, effectively create a set of ideological conventions for organizing conflict among the values of the political culture. Members of the public who attend closely to politics become aware of these organizing conventions and tend to internalize the one that is most congenial to their own value predispositions. People who, on the other hand, devote little attention to politics remain relatively innocent of liberal-conservative ideology.[2]

Ideology and culture are thus closely related. In fact, liberal-conservative ideology may be considered a response to conflicts within the culture. Faced with tension between achievement and equality (Lipset 1979), between laissez-faire principles and pressures for a welfare state (Free and Cantril 1968), between freedom and equality (Rokeach 1973), or between capitalism and democracy (McClosky and Zaller 1984), conservatives tend to opt for the former value set and liberals for the latter. As McClosky and Zaller write, "Such ideological conflict as exists in America is confined within a broad framework of almost universal public support for the basic values of capitalism and democracy. . . . [But when] asked to decide between preserving a laissez-faire economy and enacting measures that promise greater social and economic equality, conservatives emphasize capitalistic values while liberals emphasize democratic values. Although both liberals and conservatives accept the basic values of the two traditions, each group emphasizes those parts of the [political culture] most compatible with its own philosophical disposition" (1984, 233). In sum, nearly all Americans have absorbed the principal elements of their political culture, and as Hochschild in particular has shown, they are highly sensitive to its characteristic fault lines. Yet they are relatively nonideological in that most do not reconcile these tensions in ways that would lead to the development of consistent liberal or conservative ideologies. These two conclusions—which, we believe, help clarify the Lane-Converse controversy—constitute our presuppositions as we enter this study.

The Intersection of Political Culture, Ideology, and the Welfare State

Weak though ideological conflict may be in the United States, it obviously remains an important influence. A principal purpose of this study is to show

how liberalism and conservatism relate to the values of the larger political culture. Inasmuch as democratic and egalitarian traditions are present in the political culture alongside individualism and limited government, both conservatives and liberals are forced to deal with inherent tensions: conservatives cannot easily dismiss equality and democracy as core values in U.S. society nor can liberals ignore the values of individualism and limited government.[3] Nonetheless, policy disputes over the welfare state raise value conflicts that are far more troubling to liberals than to conservatives. Conservatives can, after all, readily justify antisocial welfare attitudes by appeals to the values of individualism and limited government. And if pressed that these values leave too little room for equality and democracy, conservatives can reply that they are strong proponents of equality—but equality of opportunity rather than of outcomes. Indeed, it has been argued that Americans (especially conservatives) attach so much importance to equality of opportunity precisely because it appears to offer an unassailable formula for reconciling economic individualism with egalitarianism (Potter 1954; Verba and Orren 1985).

The solution for supporters of the welfare state is not so simple. Direct appeals to equality in justification of a more active commitment to assisting the poor run up against the values of limited government and a free market economy. And to the extent that the welfare state requires some redistribution of income, counterclaims will be generated that this infringes on individual liberty and places limits on the extent to which individual effort is rewarded (see Verba and Orren 1985). Perhaps even more critically, it may not be possible to develop a more positive conception of equality in a political environment in which the language of debate is dominated by liberal individualism (Hartz 1955; Wills 1971).

In view of these difficulties in finding ideological justification for their preferences, supporters of the welfare state have historically tended to fall back on pragmatic and ad hoc justifications. Clearly this was the case with the most important American welfare reformer of the century, Franklin D. Roosevelt, who, in seeking support for his New Deal policies, prided himself on the claim that he was just looking for ideas that would work. Other major liberal figures of the recent past, notably John Kennedy and Lyndon Johnson, were likewise renowned for their pragmatic searches for down-to-earth solutions. We thus anticipate that, in attempting to reconcile their support for social welfare measures with a national political tradition that is in many ways inhospitable to such measures, social welfare liberals will tend to point to particular programs that they consider especially important and useful, rather than to invoke overarching ideological principles.

The claim that liberals are more susceptible than conservatives to value conflict over social welfare policy receives support from two very different sets of studies. Rokeach (1973) has argued that an individual's political ideology can be recovered from the relative rankings of the values of freedom and equality. In the U.S. case, conservatives rank freedom very highly but place somewhat less emphasis on equality. Liberals, on the other hand, also rank freedom highly but insist that equality is at least as important. They are confronted therefore with the problem of balancing two *equally important* values. For this and other reasons, Tetlock (1984, 1985, 1986) argues that liberals will be more prone to value conflict than conservatives and that this will be reflected in the greater complexity of liberal arguments—complexity defined as "guidelines or criteria for coping with the tension between the desired and undesired effects of a policy" or "rules that clarify why 'reasonable people' might take different stands on a policy issue" (Tetlock 1986, 820). He finds support for this hypothesis across a number of groups.

These arguments generate several additional hypotheses that we wish to test. First, we anticipate that social welfare liberals will exhibit more value conflict over social welfare policy than will conservatives. Second, supporters of social welfare should be more likely than opponents to use concrete references to programs and social groups to defend their policy preferences. Conversely, we expect social welfare conservatives to be more likely to justify their preferences by appeals to values, especially individualism. Finally, we also want to investigate the substantive basis of support for social welfare policy. If arguments about the classical liberal basis of the political culture and the belief in equality of opportunity are correct, how is the social welfare policy defended by its supporters?

Studying Ideological Conflict and Ambivalence

When questions such as these have been empirically studied, the methodological vehicle generally has been in-depth interviews with a relative handful of purposefully selected respondents (see, e.g., Lane 1962; Sennett and Cobb 1972; Lamb 1974; Hochschild 1981; Reinarman 1987). These studies have the advantage of providing a wealth of information about the underlying beliefs (and reasoning processes) that people use in evaluating policy options. Their use of open-ended methodology, in combination with the great amount of time devoted to each respondent, produces a detailed picture of the respondent's belief system not easily obtained from fixed-choice survey questions. And consensual aspects of beliefs and values can be explored, since the purpose of these studies is typically not to analyze covariances across subjects.

Despite their valuable contributions, there are serious limitations to what can be learned from in-depth interview methods. One derives from the difficulty of generalizing from small, nonrepresentative samples. How typical are the opinions of 15 people from "Eastport" or a similar number from the West Coast? Although the authors of these studies resist overgeneralizing from their samples, it remains highly desirable to know whether the results they report can be generalized to the public as a whole. Another shortcoming is that it is extremely difficult in samples of 15 or 30 people to detect even large individual differences in response patterns. Hochschild (1981), for example, emphasizes the absence of ideological cleavage among her respondents. But with only 28 respondents and no standard measures, how can she be certain of this? Questions also can be raised about the degree to which the active participation of the investigator influences the respondents' answers to the questions and probes. Would these people seem as "sophisticated" as they do without a probing researcher? A related problem arises in the selection of cases for analysis. In writing up their results, researchers seem to gravitate toward individuals who have more interesting things to say. The result is that the reader's impressions may be disproportionately influenced by the remarks of a handful of unusually articulate or colorful respondents. Finally, the conclusions from these in-depth interviews have accumulated with little connection to the bulk of the research in public opinion that uses mass survey methodology. This has unfortunately created two almost independent literatures that are often seen as producing different conclusions about ideology and political conceptualization.

In light of these problems, a secondary goal of this paper is to explore the utility of new types of open-ended questions on mass survey samples. We want to see whether focused, open-ended probes, in combination with systematic coding of all responses given, can be used to explore the sorts of questions typically addressed with in-depth interviews. This would provide an additional methodological vehicle for studying questions related to political ideology and political reasoning, one that would combine advantages of both survey research and depth interviews.

Data and Methods

The data for this analysis are drawn from the 1987 National Election Studies pilot study. The pilot study was based on reinterviews with a random sample of 450 people originally interviewed as part of the 1986 National Election Study. The pilot study was a two-wave panel design with respondents first interviewed in May and then again in June. For experimental purposes the survey was split into two random half samples.

The responses used in this study were produced by open-ended probes added to a pair of standard NES policy questions: (1) guaranteed jobs and standard of living and (2) increased government spending versus cuts in services.[4] Two forms of the open-ended probes were used. For half the respondents (form A) the issue questions were asked in the normal way but were immediately followed by these open-ended questions:

> Still thinking about the question you just answered, I'd like you to tell me what ideas came to mind as you were answering that question. Exactly what things went through your mind?
>> Are there any (other) reasons that you favor [the option just selected]?
>> Do you see any problems with [the option just selected]?

For the other half of the sample (form B), interviewers read the policy items in the standard way, but without pausing for the respondent to answer, they asked the respondent to "stop and think" about the question. For the jobs and standard of living question, the exact probes were

> Before telling me how you feel about this, could you tell me what kinds of things come to mind when you think about government making sure that every person has a good standard of living? (Any others?)
>
> Now, what comes to mind when you think about letting each person get ahead on their own? (Any others?)

These open-ended probes were designed to elicit the thoughts that respondents had as they went about answering the two social welfare questions.[5] Our hope was that these probes would reveal how respondents frame issues, what values or other considerations were especially important to them, and what degree of ambivalence (if any) they experienced. In form A the intent was to have people answer the survey question as they normally would and then immediately find out what they were thinking about as they did so.[6] In the second form, respondents were asked first to think about each component part of the question *before* giving their position on the issue.

All responses to these probes were recorded by the interviewers and then coded according to an elaborate coding scheme. The substance of each response was coded along with the direction of the statement (i.e., whether it favored a given side of the issue), indications of affect, and degree of elaboration.[7] The coders were unaware of our intent to study the active use of values and principles by the U.S. public. The substantive codes involved more than 150 discrete categories. For ease of presentation and interpretation, those categories have been combined into two coding schemes. The first combines all the initial codes to yield 15 master categories plus a residual code. The second focuses more closely on just the major political values. The Appendix contains a detailed description of the substantive comments that are included in each category.

To control for variations in "talkativeness," the coding schemes reflect whether an individual made any comment that falls within each substantive category. Thus, multiple comments in any one category or elaborations on a single theme are not counted as separate comments. (Each category is coded as a 0–1 dummy variable.) To maximize the number of respondents we have to work with, the two half samples have been combined. A detailed check of the distributions of responses produced by the two different probes showed a very high degree of similarity.[8] The substance of the comments made seems not to have been affected by the form of the open-ended probe. Finally, we have combined the two waves of responses to each policy question. Since the two issue questions were asked in both waves, the results we shall present come from each respondent having two distinct opportunities to talk about these issues.

These data are rich in information about the considerations that people used to respond to these two survey questions, but they are also difficult to manipulate statistically. There is a trade-off between preserving the informational value of the 150 codes and each respondent's opportunities for multiple responses, and the presentation of simple summary statistics. Since this is an initial exploration of the use of open-ended questions to explore popular understandings of public policy preferences, we have chosen to present the data in relatively unprocessed form. This will give the reader an opportunity to examine the patterns of responses in close to their natural state. A few summary statistics will be presented, but the bulk of the data presentation will involve analysis of frequency distributions for the open-ended responses.

The Nature of Beliefs About Social Welfare Policy

Table 1 shows the distribution of responses across the 15 master categories for the two policy questions. For each question the distributions are shown separately for those who gave two prosocial welfare, two antisocial welfare, or mixed responses to the policy questions across the two waves of the pilot study.[9] For convenience we will often refer to the prosocial welfare position as "liberal" and the antisocial welfare position as "conservative." *The ideological labels do not necessarily imply any broader understanding of an ideological continuum or extension to ideological views outside the social welfare domain.* Before examining the differences among these three groups, it is useful to get a general feel for the comments our respondents gave to these series of open-ended probes.

The first thing to note is the widespread and active use of abstract terminology. Looking first at the services and spending item, we find that 53% of respondents made at least one remark that either invoked a value such as individualism, humanitarianism, or limited government or made an argument at a comparable level of abstraction.[10] Overall, one out of every 10 of the individual comments from the probes of the spending/services question referred to an abstract value or principle. The remainder referred mainly to specific programs or problems that were especially important to the respondent. These results are all the more impressive in that they derive from a question that is fairly concrete and does not explicitly raise these value concerns.

Turning now to the item on job guarantees and living standards, we again find that a high proportion of respondents invoked some value or principle. The largest number of these responses refer to individualism. Altogether, about three out of four people invoke this value in some way. Some references were little more than repetitions of the question ("Well, I think people *should* get ahead on their own if they can"), but usually people provided their own renditions of the concept of individualism. NES policy precludes us from providing verbatim transcriptions of any individual's remarks. However, we can convey the flavor of these remarks by quoting from the code book to the pilot study some of the most commonly invoked codes referring to individualism:[11]

> Code 140. Individuals should *make it on their own;* people must make use of the opportunities they have; people should be responsible for themselves; people should just work harder; people have the right to work as much or little as they want; they control their own fate.

> Code 141. *Dependency;* living off handouts is bad; welfare makes people dependent; "if it's too easy to get welfare, no one would work anymore"; people become lazy or lose self-respect if they are on welfare; "the more you give, the more they want."

> Code 142. People who don't/won't work *don't deserve help;* people who are poor deserve to be poor; "if you can't make it in America, you have only yourself to blame"; anyone who really tries can make it.

There are certain common themes across these two social welfare questions: specific mentions of federal programs and groups affected; taxes, budget problems, and general antigovernment feelings; and values of individualism and compassion for the disadvantaged. However, the job guarantee item produces many more comments that invoke values and principles than does the services item. In fact, 95% of respondents made use of at least one value or general concept in discussing their thoughts on this issue. Moreover, 61% of all of the responses to the open-ended questions invoked a value or principle. This is all the more impressive since the responses in most of these categories are unaffected by the respondents' levels of political information.[12]

These findings should remove whatever doubt may exist that the results obtained from Lane-style in-depth interviews depend on either the particular samples chosen or the probing interview technique used by the investigators. When the subject of discussion is the substance of government welfare policy rather than presidential politics, Americans are, by our survey-based evidence, quite able to make active use of values and principles in articulating their views. The values they invoke are not the partisan values of liberalism and conservatism but the common cultural values of America's liberal tradition.

Prosocial and Antisocial Welfare Arguments

We have hypothesized that social welfare liberals would experience more conflict in discussing welfare policy because they are the ones who must reconcile their policy preferences with the pronounced individualistic and antigovernment emphasis of the political culture. A closer reexamination of Table 1 provides initial confirmation of that expectation.

Looking first at the services/spending issue, we find that those opposed to increasing government programs draw upon three highly consistent concerns: taxes and budgets, opposition to big government (laissez-faire and bureau-

Table 1

Distribution of Responses by Policy Preferences (in percentages)

	Spending/services			Jobs/standard of living		
	Anti-welfare	Mixed	Pro-welfare	Anti-welfare	Mixed	Pro-welfare
1. Personal comments	5.9	9.5	13.5	7.3	7.7	9.7
2. Politics	13.7	4.7	2.3**	1.5	1.8	3.2
3. Specific group references	21.6	31.4	46.6**	8.8	14.8	19.4
4. Specific program comments	86.3	91.7	96.2	40.9	40.2	69.4**
5. Sophisticated program comments	21.6	17.8	16.5	.7	2.4	6.5*
6. National conditions	7.8	8.3	8.3	8.8	19.5	24.2**
7. Anti-American	9.8	0.0	0.0**	16.8	6.5	1.6**
8. Taxes/budget	56.9	38.5	35.3**	9.5	7.7	14.5
9. Positive government role	2.0	2.4	7.5	16.8	33.7	43.5**
10. Antigovernment orientation	58.8	32.0	22.6**	58.4	39.1	37.1**
11. Individualism	35.3	21.3	13.5**	95.6	72.8	50.0**
12. Equality of treatment	0.0	0.0	0.0	8.0	5.9	3.2
13. Qualified assistance	9.8	7.7	10.5	21.2	24.9	33.9*
14. Lack of opportunity	0.0	1.2	2.3	10.2	7.1	22.6**
15. Fairness/equality/assistance	7.8	16.9	25.6**	22.6	24.9	33.9*
16. Other abstract comments	1.9	8.1	1.5	.7	10.1	9.7**
N =	51	169	133	137	169	62

Note: Frequencies total to more than 100% due to multiple responses to each question.

*differences across groups significant at .05 level; **differences across groups significant at .01 level.

cracy), and individualism. In contrast, the comments of social welfare liberals are characterized by positive responses to particular government programs and feelings of sympathy for affected groups but also by concern about taxes and the size of government. In fact, 35% of social welfare liberals mentioned tax and budget issues, and 22% made some antigovernment statement. It is also notable that scarcely any advocates of more government services advocated a positive role for government or a more egalitarian society. Thus, few supporters of more government services were able to offer a consistent ideological justification for their positions, and many indicated awareness of negative consequences of government spending. Antisocial welfare people are much more consistent in their rejection of greater services—complaining about tax and budget problems, specific programs, and big government, on the one hand, and invoking the values of economic individualism, on the other. Though, at the same time, many do cite one or more government programs of which they approve and show some sympathy for needy groups.

Responses to the jobs and living standards question provide further support for our argument. Those on the conservative side of this issue are virtually unanimous in their use of individualistic arguments, citing such things as the value of hard work and the sufficiency of equal opportunity, and problems of fairness and dependency. Almost 60% of them also complain about the general role of government. At the same time, only a small handful of those opposed to government guarantees admit that some people are disadvantaged and need assistance and that the government has some role in providing social welfare services.

Supporters of guaranteed jobs and living standards show substantially more evidence of sympathy for the disadvantaged, but much of it is qualified: their basic posture is that people should get ahead on their own but those who cannot do so should receive assistance. They are also likely to make references to particular programs or to the poor state of the national economy. A little over 40% of them made a favorable reference to the positive role of the federal government, but more made either a negative reference to the role of government or a positive reference to individualism. Thus, while those opposed to government guarantees indicated some ambivalence in their qualified admission that some people are disadvantaged, supporters of the welfare state were deeply conflicted. When they spoke in purely abstract or principled terms, they were more unfavorable than favorable toward social welfare, even though they had endorsed the social welfare position on both waves of the survey.

People who support guaranteed jobs and living standards defend their positions with two main types of arguments. The first type is an endorsement of specific programs or indication that certain people need assistance. The second type of argument is more abstract. Although less widespread than the conservatives' use of individualism and antigovernment arguments, this argument centers on the contention that there is not full equality of opportunity along with support for government activity to intervene when people need assistance. Thus, while opposition to social welfare stems in part from a commitment to equal opportunity, support for social welfare is often justified by beliefs that significant barriers to equal opportunity exist (see Kluegel and Smith 1986).

Conclusions and Implications

Ideological Responses to the Welfare State

The data we have examined show clearly that most Americans can draw with apparent ease upon several elements of the U.S. political tradition in justifying their social welfare preferences. The elements of the tradition most commonly invoked were suspicion of big government, humanitarianism, the Protestant ethic, and above all, economic individualism. The fact that references to these values emerged spontaneously while discussing policy questions is evidence that they have real meaning to the people who invoked them. This conclusion corroborates the position of Lane, Hochschild, and others who contend that ordinary people view the world through the prism of a distinctive cultural bias—the ideology of classical liberalism. This set of ideas, according to many scholars, virtually defines the political culture and has, by our data, diffused thoroughly in the population. At the same time, however, our findings also confirm Converse's claim that most Americans are nonideological, where the term ideological refers to the use of the liberal-conservative continuum to organize one's political attitudes. We found some evidence of consistent left-right ideological structuring of justifications for welfare state policy preferences and some tendency for more politically aware persons (particularly among conservatives) to become more consistent. But these tendencies are rather modest.

Our results offer strong support to studies, especially that of Hochschild, that have identified ambivalence as a fundamental feature of political belief systems. Most people are internally conflicted about exactly what kind of welfare system they want. Even those who take consistently pro- or consistently antiwelfare positions often cite reasons for the opposite point of view. The reason for this, we believe, is that ordinary people are both regularly exposed to arguments that extol individualism and decry big government and also to political rhetoric that urges sympathy for the poor and state action to ameliorate existing social ills. Sensitivity to such arguments obviously does not make ideological consistency, in the liberal-conservative sense, more likely. Indeed, the more people attend to these contradictory messages, the more difficult it may be to maintain a consistent ideological liberal-conservative position. Seen this way, ideological consistency requires not just attention to politics and political debate but a rejection of some elements of the political culture in favor of others.

Ambivalence and inconsistency are not found with equal frequency in all segments of the population. Social welfare conservatives exhibit relatively less value conflict. Many of them do, to be sure, admit that people sometimes need government help but the ability of conservatives to appeal to a wide range of individualistic and antigovernment values keeps their sympathy for the needy within definite and comfortable bounds. Conflict does emerge for opponents of social welfare when they think about specific government programs and their beneficiaries. Thus, the more welfare conservatives think about welfare policy in abstract terms, the better they can feel.

Ambivalence with respect to social welfare policy is more pronounced among welfare liberals. They must reconcile their humanitarian impulses with the conservative principles of individualism and limited government. Many find this difficult to do. They end up acknowledging the values of economic individualism even as they try to justify their liberal preferences.

That the U.S. political tradition is inhospitable to the welfare state is scarcely news at this point. Many prominent analysts, as noted earlier, have viewed this as a fundamental feature of this nation's political culture. What is surprising is the extent to which the elements of this inhospitality are internalized even in the minds of people who most strongly support welfare state policies.

There are alternative ways to interpret our findings on liberal ambivalence that ought to be noted. One possibility is that our analysis is time bound. Our results showing that social welfare liberals have higher levels of value conflict than welfare conservatives may reflect the current defensive position of liberalism in the United States rather than any inherent differences between liberal and conservative reactions to the welfare state. More generally, since our data come from a single snapshot of attitudes in the summer of 1987, analysis of these data cannot, by itself, establish that liberals are always more conflicted over social welfare policy than conservatives. However, there is a great deal of other evidence that our data have captured a long-standing and largely constant feature of opinion in the United States. Hartz (1955), writing in the mid-1950s, discussed the lack of an ideological justification for the welfare state in its formative years. Free and Cantril (1968), reporting on survey data collected in 1965 (the height of enthusiasm for the welfare state in this country), vividly showed that contrast between opposition to the philosophical underpinnings of the welfare state and high levels of support for specific programs. Hochschild's (1981) in-depth interviews from the mid-1970s explored in detail the ambivalence that emerges when Americans are asked to think about social welfare. (See also Rokeach 1973; Reinarman 1987.)

Our results are thus consistent with observations of Americans' attitudes over the past several decades. Our hypotheses—derived from an examination of the literature on U.S. political culture—also led us to expect the patterns of conflict and ambivalence found in these data. Our conclusions are thus supported by a substantial body of empirical analyses and theoretical discussions of U.S. politics and society in addition to the data presented here.

A second alternative interpretation focuses on our theoretical framework. Aaron Wildavsky (1987a, 1987b) has recently proposed a typology of political cultures, one which he designates as egalitarian culture. Egalitarians, he argues, are levelers who tend to like social welfare measures because they make citizens more equal, but who dislike the government that undertakes these measures because it is hierarchically structured. Hence, they end up praising and attacking the welfare state simultaneously.

Thus, whereas we attribute liberal ambivalence to conflict within the political culture, Wildavsky attributes it to conflicts within an ideology. Which explanation is correct cannot be determined with the data presently available.[13] But either way the main conclusion remains that social welfare liberals are more deeply conflicted over this issue and that they can express their ambivalence in relatively abstract and principled terms.

It is important to recognize that liberals may not be more internally conflicted than conservatives on all issues. In other issue domains, it may turn out that conservatives are the ones who must reconcile competing cultural values. (See Tetlock 1986 for evidence on this point.) Civil liberties may be a case in point. Efforts to justify limiting freedom of expression come into conflict with the libertarian tradition in this country (see McClosky and Zaller 1984). Here, civil libertarians may be better able to bring their position into line with the basic principles of the political culture, and those who wish to limit freedom of expression may be the ones who experience ambivalence most deeply and who must offer pragmatic or nonprincipled reasons to justify their preferences.

There are clearly some ways around the ambivalence and conflict we have described. One partial solution evident in our data is the tendency of supporters of social welfare to draw upon more concrete justifications for their positions while opponents of social welfare depend much more on abstract values and principles. This tends to diminish the total impact of the most serious conflicts for each group. A second solution is the ability of people to shape general values to particular political positions. So, while opponents of social welfare programs extol the value of hard work, welfare state supporters argue for greater government activism so that all individuals will have a chance to work. Similarly, while the antigovernment attitudes of social welfare conservatives often take the form of principled commitment to limited government and the ideal of laissez-faire, liberals emphasize instead the problems of bureaucracy and the practical limits to what government can accomplish— emphases that leave open the possibility that government can sometimes play a positive role in promoting social welfare. It is perhaps an indication of the power of cultural values that they can be simultaneously accepted overwhelmingly by the public and interpreted in various ways congenial to peoples' partisan political beliefs.

The Measurement of Complex Attitudes

As we have seen, the pilot study data suggest that many people do not possess a single attitude toward the welfare state. Rather, they seem to possess a range of only partially consistent reactions to it. Complex attitudes of this type are, we believe, best captured by a combination of open-ended and closed-ended interview techniques, as we have attempted in this paper. Studies that rely exclusively on closed-ended questions can, as Free and Cantril (1968), in particular, have shown, reach substantive conclusions similar to our own, but they cannot tap the underlying structure of these attitudes as well as studies that employ a more diverse measurement strategy. Since, moreover, public attitudes toward the welfare state are probably not uniquely complex, it seems likely that studies of other types of attitudes can also profit from a mixed measurement strategy.

Although the open-ended probes used in this study have not produced the wealth of information of a Robert Lane-type interview, they have, with the aid of a suitably elaborate coding scheme, generated quite a lot of information—much more, certainly, than can standard closed-ended questions alone. A major advantage of our approach is that such information is available for a representative cross-section of the public, thereby eliminating the concerns about generalizability that arise in depth studies. The large increase in the number of cases available in our approach also makes it possible to detect and analyze relationships among types of beliefs. Finally, our use of strictly standardized probes to elicit responses and professional coders to tally the results help to allay the concern, always present with data from depth interviews, that investigators may have inadvertently prejudiced their findings either by injecting their own attitudes into the interview process or by giving disproportionate weight to some kinds of individuals or some kinds of comments.

This is not to say that open-ended survey techniques should replace depth interviews. Depth interviews have proven immensely useful in generating insights about the nature of public opinion and will surely continue to do so. But the techniques employed here should prove a useful supplement to the older method.

Justifying the Welfare State

Writing at a time when the progressive accomplishments of the New Deal still seemed fragile, Hartz (1955) argued that the justification for the welfare state in the United States rested mainly on pragmatic concerns: its proponents emphasized the need for government action to solve a wide range of practical problems, but shied away from linking their programs to a European-style ideology of positive government and egalitarian democracy.

More than 30 years after Hartz, we find that supporters of the welfare state still lack a clear *ideological* justification for their positions. Many welfare liberals expressed serious misgivings about the welfare state. Moreover, even the people most friendly toward welfare state policies exhibited very little support for greater equality of outcomes, social responsibility for guaranteeing everyone the material necessities for a decent life, or individual entitlement to such necessities. Although the effect of many social welfare policies is to move society a bit closer to equality, supporters of those policies do not seem able to mobilize egalitarian arguments in their behalf. In fact, our analysis was unable to solve a key puzzle: even people who scored high on a closed-ended egalitarianism scale made few or no references to egalitarianism in the open-ended remarks. How are we to account for this?

It is of course possible that such egalitarian justifications do exist but that our questions could not elicit them. Even so, given the ease with which people could draw upon other cultural values, the inability to articulate egalitarian principles is significant. We can suggest two alternative explanations. It is possible that the people who do have egalitarian values (as indicated by their responses to the closed-ended questions) are unable to articulate those principles because of the strength of economic individualism in the United States and the absence of clear egalitarian rhetoric.[14] It is also possible that it is the egalitarianism scale that is at fault. Positive responses to these questions may reflect such other sentiments as humanitarianism or social benevolence. In this case the open-ended data are telling the correct story. Humanitarian sentiments are widespread; egalitarian principles are rare.

Our data suggest, therefore, that support for welfare state policies derives from sympathy and humanitarianism, not egalitarian principles.[15] That sympathy exists in the context of support for an individualistic system. Advocates of social welfare programs thus acknowledge that people should work hard and government should have limited powers but when people fail or have their opportunities limited they should receive some measure of help. Programs to assist the disadvantaged are defended by a combination of the perception of the lack of equal opportunity, sympathy for the disadvantaged, and support for specific programs. Our analysis is thus in accord with a major conclusion of the Verba and Orren study of elites: "American leaders, even the most egalitarian ones, [similarly] opt for measures to increase equality that are consistent with the norm of opportunity" (1985, 257).

The power of this largely pragmatic justification for social welfare should not be underestimated. As Ladd and Lipset (1980) have argued, despite the increasingly conservative tone of recent political debate, public support for most government welfare programs remains high. And after two full terms in office, Ronald Reagan had remarkably little success in dismantling the welfare state. However, as our data have shown, the values of the political culture severely limit the development of a more encompassing ideological justification for the welfare state. Under these circumstances it is perhaps not surprising that liberalism was seen as losing support among the public as the economic pie began to expand less rapidly in the 1970s (Medcalf and Dolbeare 1985). Forced to defend their positions in the aftermath of high inflation and economic stagnation, many liberals have been accused of giving up on the principles of a liberal social welfare state. And while it would be naive to assert any simple connection between public opinion and government policy, it is interesting to note that in comparison to other Western democracies the United States ranks relatively low in the extent of the welfare state and the distribution of wealth in society (Verba and Orren 1985; Smith 1987) as well as in *popular* support for the principles of the welfare state (Smith 1987).

Opponents of the welfare state are better served by the political culture. Conservatives stand ready to cite traditional beliefs in individualism and limited government to provide a consistent basis for their critiques of the growth of the welfare state. These critiques are not easily dismissed by a majority of the public even as they stand behind many of the specific programs that continue to form the basis of domestic policy.

Appendix

I. Construction of the 15 master codes from the open-ended responses. The original coding scheme for the open-ended probes was reduced to the smallest number of categories that did not require combining substantively inconsistent comments. Most of the description provided for each category is drawn directly from the instructions used by the coders. The full set of codes included in each category (from the pilot study code book) is available from the authors upon request.

1. *Personal comments.* All statements with an explicit self-frame of reference. For example: R's taxes are too high; R is not prejudiced; R makes it on own; R once got help; R's personal experience with a specific program or friend or relative's experience.

2. *Politics.* Statements that reflect concern with political context. For example: political conflict would block implementation of R's preferences; politicians would never give the people what they want on this; the lobbyists wouldn't like it; it would really shake up a lot of people.

3. *Specific group references.* Comments that reflect concern with the problems or needs of particular groups. For example: elderly (senior citizens); women as group; working/single mothers; poor people; working people; business people, industrialists.

4. *Specific program comments.* All simple statements (positive or negative) about particular government programs. For example: child care; defense; jobs or job training; small business assistance; social security; unemployment benefits; welfare.

5. *Sophisticated program references.* Comments that discuss programs at a fairly general or abstract level. For example: references to "New Deal"-type programs; focus on how programs work; complaints about waste or inefficiency in specific programs or areas.

6. *National conditions.* Comments about the state of the country or consequences for national conditions if policies are changed. For example: economic conditions of country (high unemployment, poor business conditions, competition from abroad); natural resource problems; program would help the whole country by spurring the economy; crime would increase/decrease.

7. *Anti-American.* Reference to foreign or un-American ideology; idea is like socialism or communism; goes against the American way; it's against capitalism.

8. *Taxes/budgets.* Government is spending too much; problem of unbalanced budget; complaints about overall tax burden; society can't afford what it will cost; high taxes hurt the economy.

9. *Positive government role.* All statements that assert some sort of role for the government in providing social welfare benefits. For example: the government is responsible for making sure that citizens have a chance to get

ahead; government responsibility for taking care of its citizens; government responsibility for handling a problem; optimism or conviction that we could do it if we really wanted to.

10. *Antigovernment orientation.* All comments critical of the role of government in social welfare policy or of the performance of the government. For example: concept of limited government; government is not responsible for citizens' welfare; government has gotten too big; government bureaucracy or red tape; wastefulness of government; inherent limits to what anyone can accomplish; problem should be handled by private sector or by market forces.

11. *Individualism.* All positive statements referring to the work ethic, equal opportunity, or fairness. For example: individuals should make it on their own; people should be responsible for themselves; welfare makes people dependent; people who are poor deserve to be poor; some people are lazy; references to pride and self-esteem from work; equality of opportunity is important and does exist; unfair to those who work if some people don't have to work.

12. *Equal treatment.* Equal rights for individuals; no one should have special privileges; all groups should be treated the same.

13. *Qualified assistance.* People should make it on their own, but some may need help; any comment indicating that *R* feels it is important both that individuals help themselves and that government provide aid; helping the people who need it without giving too much help to those who don't.

14. *Lack of opportunity.* Equality of opportunity is important but does not exist; common people don't have a fair chance; government should create more opportunity; some people work hard and still don't get ahead.

15. *Fairness/equality/assistance.* All statements supporting assistance to the needy regardless of the justification given. For example: people need the help; some people can't make it on their own; we should help our own before spending money on foreign aid or foreign wars; social responsibility, duty, or obligation to care for the needy; individuals are entitled to have enough to live decently; economic equality; wealth should be spread around more.

II. Construction of the elaborated categories for individualism, humanitarianism, and antigovernment orientations.

1. *Total individualism.* Sum of categories 11, 12, 13, and 14.

a. *Equality of opportunity.* Equality of opportunity does exist; everyone gets the same chance at the start of the race, but you expect some to finish ahead of others.

b. *Fairness.* Unfair to those who work if some people don't have to work; welfare cheats; many people are on welfare who don't deserve to be.

c. *Work/effort.* Individuals should make it on their own; people who don't work don't deserve help; some people are lazy.

d. *Value of work.* Inherent positive value of work and achievement; it is good for people to work.

e. *Dependency.* Living off handouts is bad; welfare makes people dependent; people on welfare should be required to do useful work in exchange for support.

f. *Competitiveness.* It would erode competitiveness of the economic system; survival of the fittest.

g. *Qualified help.* People should make it on their own, but some may need help; people should try to get ahead on their own, but government should help when necessary; problem is helping the people who need it without giving too much help to those who don't.

h. *Equal treatment.* Equal rights for individuals; no one should have special privileges; all groups should be treated the same.

i. *Lack of equal opportunity.* Equality of opportunity is important but does not exist; common people don't have a fair chance; government should create more opportunity; some people work hard and still don't get ahead.

2. *Total humanitarianism.* Sum of categories 13, 14, and 15.

a. *Equal outcomes.* Economic equality; wealth should be spread around more.

b. *Social responsibility.* Social responsibility, duty, or obligation to care for the needy; society, or individuals in society, have obligation to take care of those who need help.

c. *Individual entitlement.* Individuals are entitled to have enough to live decently; people have a right to have enough to eat.

d. *People need help.* People need the help; some people can't make it on their own; we should help our own.

e. *Qualified help.* People should make it on their own but some may need help; people should try to get ahead on their own, but government should help when necessary; problem is helping the people who need it without giving too much help to those who don't.

f. *Lack of equal opportunity.* Equality of opportunity is important but does not exist; common people don't have a fair chance; government should create more opportunity; some people work hard and still don't get ahead.

3. *Total antigovernment.* Sum of categories 8 and 10.

a. *Limited government/laissez-faire.* Concept of limited government; government is not responsible for citizens' welfare; government trying to do too much; government has gotten too big; private charities and churches should take care of the needy rather than the government.

b. *Bureaucracy.* Government bureaucracy or red tape; government is inefficient; wastefulness of government.

c. *Limits.* Inherent limits to what anyone can accomplish; impossibility of planning large-scale social change.

d. *Taxes/budget.* Government is spending too much; problems of unbalanced budget; complaints about overall tax burden; society can't afford what it would cost; taxes are too high; high taxes hurt the economy.

III. Egalitarianism questions:

1. One of the big problems in this country is that we don't give everyone an equal chance.

2. If people were treated more equally in this country we would have many fewer problems.

3. It would be better for everyone if the distribution of wealth in this country were more equal.

4. We have gone too far in pushing equal rights in this country.

5. This country would be better off if we worried less about how equal people are.

6. All in all, I think economic differences in this country are justified.

Notes

1. See Kinder and Sears (1985) for a recent review of the evidence.

2. There have been a number of discussions of the individual-level roots of ideology and ideological conflict. Space prevents us from discussing this literature in any depth. Hypotheses have pointed variously to orientations toward change and group evaluations (Conover and Feldman 1981), feelings of sympathy and humanitarianism (Conover 1988), priorities attached to the values of freedom and equality (Rokeach 1973), and orientations toward social order, social change, and social benevolence (McClosky and Zaller 1984). These individual-level predispositions may then orient people toward one or the other of the packages of cultural values: liberalism or conservatism.

3. Individualism and egalitarianism are extremely broad concepts that are variously defined (and ill-defined) in U.S. political culture and political ideology literatures. We focus on *economic individualism:* the commitment to merit as the basis for the distribution of rewards in society and the belief that people ought to work hard. Egalitarianism has a number of dimensions that must be distinguished: equality of opportunity—each person should have the same initial chance of succeeding; formal or legal equality—all people should be treated equally; and equality of rewards. In the last case the desire need not be for complete equality but may involve a limited range of wealth, a floor on income, or an income limit (Verba and Orren 1985; Hochschild 1981).

4. The wordings of the two policy questions are as follows. *Spending/services:* Some people think the government should provide fewer services, even in areas such as health and education, in order to reduce spending. Other people feel it is important for the government to provide many more services even if it means an increase in spending. Which is closer to the way you feel or haven't you thought much about this? *Jobs and standard of living:* Some people feel the government in Washington should see to it that every person has a job and a good standard of living. Others think the government should let each person get ahead on their own. Which is closer to the way you feel or haven't you thought much about this? A third question—government assistance to blacks—was also probed in the pilot study, but the responses to this question have not been used in this paper. Although the patterns of responses to this question mirror those of the spending/services and jobs questions, many of the comments on government assistance to blacks referred directly to blacks (i.e., discrimination against them or their opportunity to get ahead) or to attributes of blacks. One entirely new category of responses is thus created (negative attitudes toward blacks), and many of the other responses that reflect the same general categories used for the two social welfare questions are intertwined with race. Using a common coding scheme runs the risk of confounding these general categories with race. The alternative strategy of creating a new set of categories for comments that involve references to race would make the presentation and analysis exceedingly long and messy.

5. These two questions were chosen, in part, because they have been the primary NES social welfare issue items for the last decade (the history of the guaranteed jobs items goes

back to the 1950s). This, of course, does not ensure that they do an adequate job of representing Americans' attitudes on social welfare policy. As a check on this, these two questions were factor analyzed along with other questions on domestic spending priorities and general attitudes toward economic equality and redistribution. A clear first factor emerged from the analysis with the two NES issue questions loading strongly on that factor.

6. This is based on work done by Ericsson and Simon (1984) that shows that people are able to report the thoughts they had while completing a task if they are asked immediately after they have completed the task.

7. The coding scheme was developed by the authors in consultation with Steve Pinney of the coding section of the Institute for Social Research at the University of Michigan. The actual coding was carried out by experienced coders of the ISR staff and subject to frequent cross-checking by Pinney.

8. Differences between the two forms are evident in the *process* by which people answered the questions (see Zaller and Feldman 1988). For the present purposes, there appear to be few differences in the substance of the dimensions people thought about. The most significant difference between the two forms is that there are substantially more missing cases for the retrospective form than for the stop and think form. Those people who offered no opinion on the issue question were dropped from all of the following analysis.

9. As can be seen in Table 1, a large number of people gave different responses to the social welfare questions across the two waves of the pilot study. This is consistent with all other studies that have looked at response stability in issue preferences. The major explanations for this temporal instability are that it either reflects nonattitudes or high levels of random measurement error. A third interpretation is that this response instability is a result of conflicting or ambivalent considerations (Zaller and Feldman 1988). The evidence to be presented here will offer some support for the latter view.

10. We used a very conservative definition of abstract remarks. This includes responses in categories 9 through 14 as well as those comments in category 15 that refer to some value or principle (not just references that people need help). If the definition of abstract remarks were expanded to include categories 5, 7, and 8 as well, the proportion of respondents making at least one abstract comment rises to 75%. We are using abstract and concrete here to refer to the nature of the *terms* used in the responses. We think it is important to distinguish between use of a general principle (like all people should get ahead on their own) and reference to a specific condition or government program. This distinction does not necessarily imply that the *reasoning* processes underlying these responses parallel the same abstract and concrete patterns. Indeed, it is possible that concrete responses can be given by someone reasoning abstractly while abstract comments may be given by someone who is thinking about the world in a very simple manner.

11. The italicized phrase is the central theme; the supplemental language was loosely adapted from the transcripts (to avoid things that particular respondents might have said) in order to indicate to the coders the kinds of remarks that would justify use of the code.

12. These two policy questions clearly differ in the extent to which they appeal to "prime" values and principles. The spending/services question is very concrete. On the other hand, the guaranteed jobs question explicitly mentions letting people get ahead on their own. It is perhaps not surprising to find more references to values and principles in responses to the second question. There are several things to keep in mind, however. First, despite the lack of priming by the question, there are a large number of responses to the spending/services question that refer to values and principles. If a concrete question like this defines the lower limit to the number of such responses, it is still substantial. Second, we are much more interested in how those on opposing sides of each issue defend their positions than on comparisons of numbers of responses across issues. Although the levels may vary, our analysis shows many common patterns in the responses to each question. Finally, some may be concerned that responses to the guaranteed jobs question are biased because the conservative position more clearly evokes value concerns than the liberal position. While we cannot completely dismiss this concern, it is important to note that those opposed to greater government spending are also much more likely to raise individualistic arguments than those in favor despite the lack of any explicit primes in that question.

13. It should be noted, however, that there is little evidence in our data that supporters of

social welfare programs are strong egalitarians who wish to impose a more equal distribution of resources in U.S. society.

14. It is important to distinguish here between equality of opportunity and formal equality, on the one hand, and egalitarianism as a principle for evaluating the distribution of resources in society. The first two are, according to virtually all political analysts, part of the political culture; the third has lacked articulate supporters (see Verba and Orren 1985).

15. Since respondents were not asked to explain their open-ended comments, our methodology does not permit us to examine the origins of the principles that people use to justify their positions on social welfare policy. We therefore cannot investigate the basis for the expressions of sympathy and humanitarianism that appear most frequently among those supportive of social welfare. Discussions of the origins of altruistic sentiments have suggested that such factors as personality, socialization, and social background may explain individual differences (for a summary, see Conover 1988). Alternatively, sympathy and humanitarianism may derive from Judeo-Christian ethics (Bellah et al. 1985; Reichley 1985; Wald 1987). If so, Judeo-Christian ethics could provide a principled basis of support for social welfare more comparable to the role of individualism and antigovernment orientations in opposition to welfare.

References

Baylin, Bernard. 1967. *The Ideological Origins of the American Revolution.* Cambridge: Harvard University Press.

Bellah, Robert N., Richard Madsen, William M. Sullivan, Ann Swindler, and Steven M. Tipton. 1985. *Habits of the Heart.* Berkeley: University of California Press.

Campbell, Angus, Philip E. Converse, Warren E. Miller, and Donald E. Stokes. 1960. *The American Voter.* New York: Wiley.

Conover, Pamela Johnston. 1988. "So Who Cares? Sympathy and Politics." Presented at the annual meeting of the Midwest Political Science Association, Chicago.

Converse, Philip E. 1964. "The Nature of Belief Systems in Mass Publics." In *Ideology and Discontent,* ed. David Apter. New York: Free Press.

Devine, Donald J. 1972. *The Political Culture of the United States.* Boston: Little, Brown.

Ericsson, K. Anders, and Herbert A. Simon. 1984. *Protocol Analysis.* Cambridge: MIT Press.

Feldman, Stanley. 1988. "Structure and Consistency in Public Opinion." *American Journal of Political Science* 32:416–40.

Free, Lloyd A., and Hadley Cantril. 1968. *The Political Beliefs of Americans: A Study of Public Opinion.* New York: Simon and Shuster.

Hartz, Louis. 1955. *The Liberal Tradition in America.* New York: Harcourt Brace Jovanovich.

Hochschild, Jennifer L. 1981. *What's Fair? American Beliefs about Distributive Justice.* Cambridge: Harvard University Press.

Huntington, Samuel P. 1981. *American Politics: The Promise of Disharmony.* Cambridge: Harvard University Press.

Kinder, Donald R. 1983. "Diversity and Complexity in American Public Opinion." In *Political Science: The State of the Discipline,* ed. Ada Finifter. Washington, DC: American Political Science Association.

Kinder, Donald R., and Lynn M. Sanders. 1987. "Pluralistic Foundations of American Opinion on Race." Presented at the annual meeting of the American Political Science Association, Chicago.

Kinder, Donald R., and David Sears. 1985. "Political Behavior." In *The Handbook of Social Psychology,* 3d ed., ed. Gardner Lindzey and Eliot Aronson. Reading, MA: Addison-Wesley.

Kluegel, James R., and Eliot R. Smith. 1986. *Beliefs About Inequality.* New York: Aldine De Gruyter.

Ladd, Everett Caril, and Seymour Martin Lipset. 1980. "Public Opinion and Public Policy." In *The United States in the 1980's,* ed. Peter Duignan and Alvin Rabushka. Stanford: Hoover Institution.

Lamb, Karl A. 1974. *As Orange Goes.* New York: Norton.

Lane, Robert E. 1962. *Political Ideology.* New York: Free Press.

————. 1973. "Patterns of Political Belief." In *Handbook of Political Psychology,* ed. Jeanne Knutson. San Francisco: Jossey-Bass.

Lipset, Seymour Martin. 1979. *The First New Nation.* New York: Norton.

McClosky, Herbert, and John Zaller. 1984. *The American Ethos.* Cambridge: Harvard University Press.

Medcalf, Linda J., and Kenneth M. Dolbeare. 1985. *Neopolitics: American Political Ideas in the 1980's.* New York: Random House.

Potter, David M. 1954. *People of Plenty.* Chicago: University of Chicago Press.

Reichley, A. James. 1985. *Religion in American Public Life.* Washington, DC: Brookings Institution.

Reinarman, Craig. 1987. *American States of Mind.* New Haven: Yale University Press.

Rokeach, Milton. 1973. *The Nature of Human Values.* New York: Free Press.

Sennett, Richard, and Jonathan Cobb. 1972. *The Hidden Injuries of Class.* New York: Random House.

Smith, Tom W. 1987. "The Welfare State in Cross-National Perspective." *Public Opinion Quarterly* 51:404–21.

Tetlock, Philip E. 1984. "Cognitive Style and Political Belief Systems in the British House of Commons." *Journal of Personality and Social Psychology* 46:365–75.

————. 1986. "A Value Pluralism Model of Ideological Reasoning." *Journal of Personality and Social Psychology* 50:819–27.

Tetlock, Philip E., Jane Bernzweig, and Jack L. Gallant. 1985. "Supreme Court Decision Making: Cognitive Style as a Predictor of Ideological Consistency of Voting." *Journal of Personality and Social Psychology* 48:1227–39.

Verba, Sidney, and Gary R. Orren. 1985. *Equality in America.* Cambridge: Harvard University Press.

Wald, Kenneth D. 1987. *Religion and Politics in the United States.* New York: St. Martin's Press.

Wildavsky, Aaron, 1987a. "Choosing Preferences by Constructing Institutions: A Cultural Theory of Preference Formation." *American Political Science Review* 81:3–22.

————. 1987b. "The Media's 'American Equalitarians.'" *Public Interest* 88:94–104.

Wills, Gary. 1971. *Nixon Agonistes.* New York: Knopf.

Zaller, John. 1986. "Pretesting Information Items on the 1985 NES Pilot Study." Report to the Board of Overseers for the National Election Studies.

Zaller, John, and Stanley Feldman. 1987. "Frames of Reference and the Survey Response." Presented at the annual meeting of the American Political Science Association, Chicago.

Discussion Questions

1. What would be the advantages and disadvantages of using a face-to-face survey for this research? What problems of representativeness would have been created or obviated by using such a survey?

2. The authors reported the language used to "probe" for the background principles behind the respondents' issue positions. What kinds of problems could this language have produced? Do you think the wording colored the findings? Why or why not?

3. What was the basis for the authors' conclusion that liberals are more affected by value conflict than conservatives? Do you find their conclusion convincing?

4. The authors' interpretations of the responses in Table 1 were critical for their conclusions. In particular, the authors had to determine which

kinds of responses were "abstract principles" and which were not. Do you think the authors made fair judgments about this?

5. This study was made possible by use of a National Election Study survey. Consider how you would design a survey of students at your university to confirm Feldman and Zaller's findings. What kind of survey instrument would be appropriate? Explain how you would deal with the problems of representativeness, question wording, and sample size.

Commentary

Feldman and Zaller conclude that Americans are able to identify principles that guide the development of their issue positions. These principles, rooted in the political culture, create more problems for liberals, essentially because the U.S. political tradition is "inhospitable" to the welfare state. These interesting conclusions may help explain why welfare policy continues to be such a heated and confusing topic in American political life.

Their findings were made possible by the analysis of survey questions that included "probes" for more extensive responses. According to the authors, more conventional questionnaire items would have left the basic principles behind Americans' issue positions obscure. Feldman and Zaller's design allowed them to determine how often people referred to abstract concepts in explaining their positions. As Table 1 indicates, a large proportion of the respondents referred to "individualism, humanitarianism, or limited government" in accounting for their positions on welfare policy.

Closer examination of Table 1 reveals that, especially for liberals, values are often in conflict. Looking at the "spending/services" half of the table, "liberals" are the 133 respondents in the "prowelfare" column. The authors note that a large percentage of these respondents were concerned about taxes (35.3 percent), and that nearly a fourth (22.6 percent) stated antigovernment sentiments. Thus, considerable ambivalence exists at the level of principle among these prowelfare respondents, leading the authors to conclude that "few supporters of more government services were able to offer a consistent ideological justification for their positions."

On a more technical note, the authors reported the "significance" levels for the findings in Table 1. Following our discussion of sampling in chapter 8, the table entries marked with a single asterisk indicate a difference across the three groups (antiwelfare, or "conservatives"; mixed; and prowelfare, or "liberals") on those items that would have been produced by a chance selection of subjects only 5 percent of the time. Those marked with double asterisks indicate differences that could have been produced by a chance selection of subjects only 1 percent of the time. For any of the marked entries, therefore, the authors can confidently claim that the differences between conservatives and liberals in the sample actually reflect differences between conservatives and liberals in the population.

Feldman and Zaller's study is a thought-provoking effort to explore the basis of American attitudes with respect to a major issue of continuing public debate. Their study helps us to understand why welfare is a deeply divisive political issue. Their analysis also shows why simpler forms of surveys may produce misleading results.

Excerpt 8

The future of democracy in Russia is one of the most important and perplexing problems that contemporary leaders face. Although Russia has enormous economic difficulties (in some ways, Russia is best considered a developing nation), it has a large population and a substantial number of nuclear weapons. The collapse of communism has removed state-sponsored totalitarianism, but it has not produced stable democracy, at least not yet.

To many political scientists, it is well established that democracy requires more than a set of laws, institutions, and a voting system. It also requires a culture in which citizens substantially trust other citizens and accept the basic principles of tolerance for opposing views. One of the most famous classics in comparative politics, a book entitled *The Civic Culture*, was an effort to determine the cultural foundations of stable democracy and to determine which countries actually have them (Almond and Verba 1963). Russian citizens lived for many decades in a country in which the government firmly repressed freedom of expression while it systematically made citizens suspicious of dissenters. Perhaps the political culture that developed under these conditions is simply not supportive of democracy.

James Gibson's study uses survey analysis to determine whether or not the attitudes and behavior of Russian citizens are consistent with what he calls a "civil society," a necessary condition for stable democratic government. He used a panel study of Russian citizens, gathering information on the basic state of contemporary Russian political culture and on recent changes. His conclusions are somewhat more optimistic than those of many other observers who have analyzed conditions in modern Russia.

Social Networks, Civil Society, and the Prospects for Consolidating Russia's Democratic Transition

James L. Gibson, *Washington University in St. Louis*

American Journal of Political Science 45, no. 1 (January 2001): 51–69. Copyright © 2001 by the University of Wisconsin Press. Reprinted with permission.

Few who study Russian political culture are optimistic about the development of a strong civil society in that country (e.g., Roeder 1999). In addition to the debilitating burden of hundreds of years of authoritarianism, contemporary Russia is said to lack two crucial elements of a civil society—interpersonal trust and a broad array of nonstate voluntary organizations. For instance, Rose (1998, 11) found that 80 to 90 percent of Russians do not belong to any voluntary associations.[1] My national survey in 1996 revealed that only 31 percent of Russians believe that most people can be trusted (with another 19 percent being uncertain whether most can be trusted). In 1998, the figures were roughly the same (31 percent and 11 percent, respectively).[2] Thus, many take contemporary data such as these as a confirmation of the view that Russian political culture is inhospitable to democratization. Too distrustful to form groups to promote their self and collective interests, Russians today continue their ancient tradition of extreme atomization, selfishness, and anomie (see Crawford and Lijphart 1995).

Atomization, Social Networks, and Democracy

One important social impediment to democratic consolidation in Russia is that the legacy of totalitarianism may reassert itself. For instance, Bernard (1996) argues that one of the primary objectives of Stalinism was precisely the destruction of civil society so that potential threats to monocratic rule could be exterminated. Stalinism "destroyed all self-organized forms of intermediate public organization and replaced them with transmission belt organizations whose purpose was to monitor society, mobilize it behind the leadership's program, and convey orders from the top downward" (1996, 314). According to some, this legacy persists in contemporary political cultures and is manifested in learned helplessness, receptivity to paternalism, and a confrontational attitude toward conflict (Bernard 1996, 323).

Totalitarianism undermines civil society through the atomization of individual citizens. For instance, Bahry and Silver argued that totalitarian states "atomize society so that people become isolated and mistrustful of one another and hence unable to concert their efforts in organized political activity"

(1987, 1065; see also Kornhauser 1959). Under a system of totalitarian atomization: "Society itself thereby becomes an instrument of coercion: the memory of mass terror, the elimination of autonomous intermediary groups between state and individual, and the continued reliance on informers breed an atmosphere of social intimidation that undermines any collective activity not officially sanctioned by the state" (Bahry and Silver 1987, 1069). Moore, writing before the end of Stalinism, asserted:

> The regime deliberately seeks to sow suspicion among the population, which to a marked extent results in the breakup of friendship groupings, in the work situation and elsewhere, and the isolation of the individual. . . . Terror ultimately destroys the network of stable expectations concerning what other people will do that lie at the core of any set of organized human relationships. (Moore 1954, 158, 176)

Thus, one form of "un-civil" society is that which is characterized by social atomization: the absence altogether of social networks (see also Kumar 1993). In such a society, every individual is disconnected from every other.

A second type of "un-civil" society has entirely different characteristics— it is a society made up of strong, but *closed* social networks. Granovetter refers to these as "strong ties," defining the "strength" of a tie as a "combination of the amount of time, the emotional intensity, the intimacy (mutual confiding), and the reciprocal services which characterize the tie" (1973, 1361). The family or the clan is an exemplar of a network characterized by strong ties. Such networks tend to be internally homogeneous and cohesive,[3] thereby inhibiting interactions with those outside the network and resulting in the atomization of small groups, if not individuals (see also Banfield 1958).

Neither social atomization nor "strong ties" is conducive to the development of a civil society. "Weak ties," by contrast, facilitate civil society. "Weak ties" characterize social networks that are not based primarily on family relationships and "are more likely to link members of *different* small groups than are strong ones, which tend to be concentrated within particular groups" (Granovetter 1973, 1376, emphasis in the original). Social interaction, especially outside the narrow confines of one's family, contributes to the development of broader, less selfish, and more socially engaged attitudes (as long ago argued by Alexis de Tocqueville).[4] For instance, Mondak and Gearing assert: "Although some forms of political participation can occur despite the absence of social interaction, it is difficult to overstate the pivotal role civic engagement plays in mass politics. People who do not interact with one another may fail to develop an appreciation for any form of communal good, and thus they may be limited in their capacity to see politics in terms of general rather than purely personal interests. Talk—actual face-to-face discussion about politics and society—is an essential ingredient for the emergence of an effective citizenry" (1998, 616). Or as Putnam put it: "Dense but segregated horizontal networks sustain cooperation *within* each group, but networks of civic engagement that cut across social cleavages nourish wider cooperation" (1993, 175), which of course facilitates democratic governance. Thus, civil society profits from social networks characterized by relatively weak and hence permeable boundaries; such networks facilitate cooperation among citizens.

In polities attempting democratic transitions, weak ties are especially effective at transmitting novel information about unfamiliar political institutions.[5] In such societies, citizens are actively trying to learn the new "rules of the political game," and learning from fellow citizens is a crucial element of this process (see Meyer 1994). New ideas spread with difficulty in a perfectly atomized society and find impediments to crossing strong ties. "Whatever is to be diffused can reach a larger number of people, and traverse greater social distance . . . when passed through weak ties rather than strong" (Granovetter 1973, 1366).[6] Thus, a reasonable hypothesis is that *those embedded in social networks characterized by weak ties are most likely to adopt the emergent values of a new regime, and, in this instance, to endorse democratic institutions and processes.*

Of course, weak ties are capable of diffusing any type of information, not just information favoring democracy. *Novel information,* of every sort, is the type of information most effectively transmitted across weak ties. It is possible, therefore, that weak ties might also facilitate the dissemination of information undermining democratic governance. Indeed, in stable democracies, weak ties may well contribute *nothing* to social learning about democratic institutions and processes, since the information is readily available to all. The effect of weak ties in promoting democratic values is most likely greatest in transitional regimes, where citizens have little experience with democratic governance, and where democratic institutions and processes are not well understood or discussed.

Social networks, to the extent they are heterogeneous and politically relevant, also contribute to democratic values through the simple process of political discourse. Lake and Huckfeldt claim that ". . . social relations are primarily responsible for the communication and transmittal of political information and expertise among and between groups and individuals" (1998, 581). Mondak and Gearing (1998) make a similar argument (though their empirical results do not support the theory).[7] Mutz (1999) concludes that "cross-cutting exposure" (by which she means political discussions with non-like-minded network members) contributes substantially to the development of democratic values in the American mass public. Thus, "weak" social networks that are politically relevant may contribute to the development of democratic values through processes of diffusion *and* through practice at democratic discussion.

Soviet scholars have long recognized the importance of networks such as the ones I consider here.[8] So-called "kitchen circles"—"groups of friends who met in the kitchens of their apartments and led endless conversations about the meaning of creation, art, and politics" (Greenfeld 1992, 23)—have long been an integral part of Russian political culture and politics.[9] Further, more systematic research on Soviet political culture has recognized the importance of word-of-mouth communications among citizens. As Remington asserts: "The Soviet case is intriguing . . . because, despite a modern, elaborate media system, which is used regularly (i.e., daily or several times a week) by fully 80 percent of the population, studies show that strikingly high proportions of the population—as many as half or more—also regularly obtain information from informal social contacts such as neighbors, relatives, and co-workers" (1981, 804). This is in sharp contrast to the United States, where "only a very small proportion cite conversation with other people as one of the sources from which they obtain most of their news" (Remington 1981, 806).

Thus, in this article, I am especially interested in the following attributes of social networks:

- The *size* of social networks: how extensive they are.
- Network *politicization:* the degree to which the network members engage in political discussions.
- The *"strength"* of the ties among network members: the degree to which ties cross social groups.

These network attributes provide some purchase on the possibility of developing a strong civil society. Though I cannot claim that large, politicized, and "weak" social networks are a *sufficient* condition for an effective civil society, they are most likely *necessary* for the consolidation of democratic transitions.

Research Design

This analysis is based primarily upon a panel study of the Russian mass public, initiated in 1996, continued in 1998, and completed in 2000. The overall focus of the survey was on attitudes toward democratic institutions and processes. In the first wave, face-to-face interviews were completed between May 8 and June 13, 1996, with the overwhelming majority (90 percent) of the interviews being conducted in May (the period of the run-up to the first round of voting in the Russian presidential election). Noninstitutionalized residents of Russia 16 years old and older were eligible to be interviewed. The sample is representative of the entire territory of Russia, and was drawn from thirty-eight Primary Sampling Units (PSUs). At least forty-two interviews were conducted in each PSU; no more than seventy interviews were conducted in a single PSU, except for the Moscow and St. Petersburg PSUs (128 and 112 interviews, respectively).

Interviews were attempted with 2,442 respondents, with a resulting response rate of 84 percent.[10] Approximately 15 percent of the interviews were verified (face-to-face) by our field supervisors. Up to eight call-backs were used. Individual respondents were selected using the Kish selection method (Kish 1965, 398–401), and consequently the data are weighted to reflect the size of the household.[11] Local interviewers were used, but they were trained by project personnel traveling from Moscow. The average length of the interview was 87 minutes (standard deviation = 31 minutes, median = 85 minutes), with a range from 25 to 255 minutes. As is common in surveys in Russia and elsewhere, women were slightly overrepresented in the sample (58 percent female in the sample versus 55 percent in the population).[12]

The second wave of the panel was fielded in April, 1998.[13] The response rate was 82.7 percent. No contact could be made with 13.0 percent of the first-wave respondents, the interview could not be completed with another 0.6 percent, and 3.7 percent of the first-wave respondents refused to be reinterviewed. By far, the most common reason for failing to complete the second interview was inability to contact the respondent (75.1 percent), and the most common reason for this inability was that the respondent had moved to another place. Contact was made with another portion of the first-wave respondents, but the interview could not be completed for a variety of reasons (accounting for 3.4 percent of the nonresponse—e.g., the respondent was sick or drunk). In 21.6 percent of nonresponses, the subject refused to be interviewed, usually without much substantive explanation. Even by the most permissive coding standards, only ten first-wave respondents refused to be reinterviewed out of some sort of fear of political or criminal reprisals. Generally, this second-wave response rate is quite high by comparative standards.[14]

I have employed a variety of statistical tests to determine whether the 1996 and 1998 samples differ. Specifically, I conducted significance tests on many of the responses in the 1996 survey to determine whether 1998 respondents differed from 1998 nonrespondents. Particularly interesting are the results from two sets of questions measuring the propensity to engage in self censorship and perceptions of whether the Russian government represses dissent. In not a single instance do the 1998 respondents and nonrespondents differ significantly (indeed, none of the differences even approaches statistical significance). Thus, the 1998 sample is no less willing to express its political views than the 1996 sample, adding considerably to my confidence in the representativeness of the 1998 sample.

For very limited purposes, I take advantage of a survey we conducted in the entire former Soviet Union in 1992 (see, for example, Gibson 1997). This survey included a representative subsample of Russia. The methodology of that survey in virtually every respect duplicates the methodology of my 1996–1998 panel, even to the point of using the same survey team in Russia. In addition, I make use of a seven-country survey I conducted in 1995.[15] Representative samples of the mass public were interviewed face-to-face in Bulgaria, Hungary, Poland, Russia, France, and Spain, and by telephone in the United States. Noninstitutionalized residents of each country 18 years old and older were eligible to be interviewed.

The Structure of Social Networks

Borrowing from the (U.S.) General Social Survey, we began our discussion of social networks with the following question:

> From time to time, most people discuss important matters with other people. Who are the people with whom you discuss such matters? Just tell me *only* their first names or initials. IF LESS THAN 3 NAMES MENTIONED, PROBE: Anyone else? ONLY RECORD FIRST 3 NAMES.

Table 1 reports data on the number of network members identified (a network attribute typically known as "network size").[16]

The Russian respondents in 1996 claimed fairly extensive social networks. The average number of network members identified was 2 (out of a possible maximum of 3), and 43.4 percent were capable of naming an entire complement of network alters. Only a very small proportion of Russians was unable to name any network members.

Compared to social networks in our seven-country survey, the number of network members mentioned by the Russians in 1996 is about average.[17] The Russian mean of 1.99 is about the same as France (2.02), is considerably higher than the United States (1.80), but lower than Hungary (2.27). The figure is also higher than the results from the comparable (but smaller) survey in Russia in 1995 ($0 = 1.79$).[18] These data yield little evidence of a distinctive legacy of social atomization in Russia, at least in terms of isolating Russians from each other.[19]

Table 1 also reports results from a survey we conducted in Russia in 1992. These data provide some purchase on the question of how social networks may have changed in Russia over the course of the 1990s. In 1992, most Russians (60.8 percent) named three network members, and the average number of alters named is the highest of any of the countries. The decline in the number of network alters identified in 1996 is substantial and no doubt reflects the diminishing necessity of social networks in the economic domain (e.g., the ready availability of goods), as well as the increasing strains on ordinary Russians to make a decent living (see Greenfeld 1992).[20]

No clear East-West differences exist in the size of the social networks. Indeed, Hungary has the largest percentage of people with extensive networks, while Russia (1995) and the U.S. have the smallest percentages.[21] The figures in Bulgaria, France, Poland, and Spain are very similar. Ironically, one of the most democratic countries in the group (the United States) has one of the lowest percentage of respondents with large networks, while perhaps the least democratic country (Bulgaria) has a considerably higher percentage. Thus, there seems to be little direct relationship between democracy and social networks.

But are these networks politically relevant? We also asked the respondents to describe the extent of political discussions with each of their network members. Their responses are also reported in Table 1.

Considerable variability exists in the extent of political discussions within these social networks.[22] In Poland, Hungary, and Bulgaria, such discussions occur with remarkable frequency. The Americans are below average in the frequency of discussing politics, are quite similar to the Spanish, and in every instance their mean score is higher than the French. In general, these social networks are important centers of political discussions in most of these countries. Cross-national differences in network politicization are greater than are such differences in network density (as indicated by the eta coefficients in Table 1).

Russia in 1995 differs considerably from the other countries, with between one-fourth and one-third of the respondents claiming *never* to discuss politics with their network members. Russian social networks are by far the least politicized of the countries in the 1995 surveys. The differences between Russia and Bulgaria (to focus on another Slavic country undergoing difficult change) are stark indeed.

By 1996, however, Russian social networks were extremely politicized, with the Russians scoring the largest mean level of political discussion of any of the countries (except the Russians in 1992). Consider first political discussions with the first-named network member. In Russia, political conversations are very common, with nearly 80 percent of the respondents talking about politics at least weekly (data not shown).[23] Political discussions with the other network members are also quite common. In Russia in 1996, 38.1 percent of the respondents claimed to have political discussions nearly daily, as compared to 18.1 percent of the respondents in our 1995 survey in the United States. Russian networks obviously carry considerable political content. It appears that the 1995 Russian data may have been heavily affected by political alienation and disgust during the particular period of the survey (surrounding the parliamentary elections of 1995) and may well represent a short-term aberration.[24]

The key issue here is of course Russia, and especially how to understand the 1995 survey. Many interpretations of the Russian data are possible. But the data are not incompatible with the view that the parliamentary elections resulted in a temporary decrease in political discussions among Russians, perhaps as a result of political alienation and fatigue connected with the specific election. Note as well that the mean frequency of discussion reported in Table 1 is in part a function of the smaller network sizes reported by Russians in 1995.

The final attribute of networks—whether they are based on "strong" or "weak" ties—is more difficult to measure. Following Granovetter (1973) and Huckfeldt et al. (1995), I assume that strong ties are present when networks are composed of members of the same family, and that weak ties characterize relationships across family boundaries. This assumption is based on the belief that, at least among those naming a family member as a part of the social network, within-family relationships are stronger. Thus, the number of

Table 1

Attributes of Social Networks

The size of social networks

Country	Percentage		Number of members identified[a]		
	No network members	Three network members	Mean	Std. dev.	N
Russia, 1995	19.8	39.1	1.79	1.16	772
United States	10.4	31.6	1.80	1.00	810
Russia, 1996	12.9	43.4	1.99	1.06	2,059
France	19.9	55.0	2.02	1.22	762
Poland	16.1	54.9	2.08	1.15	824
Spain	13.2	55.0	2.13	1.10	775
Bulgaria	13.1	56.1	2.13	1.11	1,180
Hungary	9.8	61.4	2.27	1.04	777
Russia, 1992	7.6	60.8	2.33	.97	2,536

The politicization of social networks—talking politics

Country	Percentage discussing politics (1st network alter)		Frequency of discussions (All network alters)[b]		
	Never	Daily	Mean	Std. dev.	N
Russia, 1995	34.5	8.4	2.36	1.32	611
United States	5.7	18.1	4.34	1.20	723
Russia, 1996	6.0	38.1	4.84	1.16	1,783
France	12.0	14.3	3.97	1.36	610
Poland	5.5	27.3	4.50	1.19	686
Spain	8.2	27.4	4.38	1.35	662
Bulgaria	11.1	33.8	4.41	1.49	1,013
Hungary	9.0	33.0	4.45	1.39	701
Russia, 1992	3.1	48.1	5.04	.95	2,334

The prevalence of "weak" network ties

Country	Percentage		Number of weak ties[c]		
	No weak ties	All weak ties	Mean	Std. dev.	N
Russia, 1995	44.7	8.8	.89	.98	772
United States	49.6	4.7	.73	.87	810
Russia, 1996	39.5	9.6	1.01	1.00	2,059
France	42.5	11.8	1.03	1.06	762
Poland	51.3	10.1	.86	1.04	824
Spain	38.8	12.4	1.08	1.05	775
Bulgaria	46.7	10.7	.92	1.03	1,203
Hungary	52.5	6.5	.77	.95	786
Russia, 1992	24.5	17.7	1.39	1.04	2,536

Network political capacity

Country	Mean	Std. dev.	N
Russia, 1995	3.37	2.37	772
United States	3.83	2.34	810
France	4.39	2.86	762
Poland	4.50	2.77	824
Bulgaria	4.54	2.77	1,203
Russia, 1996	4.59	2.67	2,059
Hungary	4.71	2.54	786
Spain	4.76	2.77	775
Russia, 1992	5.66	2.59	2,536

$^a\eta = .16, p < .000.$
$^b\eta = .47, p < .000.$
$^c\eta = .21, p < .000.$
The capacity index ranges from 0 to 9, with high scores indicating greater network capacity.

nonfamily network members can be used as an indicator of the prevalence of "weak" ties. Table 1 also reports these data.

A large percentage of people rely exclusively upon family members for their social networks ("no weak ties"). The percentage naming no nonfamily network members ranges from 24.5 percent in Russia (1992) and 38.8 percent in Spain to 52.5 percent in Hungary.[25] Much smaller percentages draw *all* of the network members from nonfamily sources. According to the mean scores, "weak" ties are most common in Russia (1992 and 1996), Spain, and France, and are least prevalent in Hungary. The American respondents score roughly at the mean of the seven countries. Yet, cross-national differences are relatively small in comparison to within-country differences. Once more, a simple "legacies of Communism" explanation is insufficient to account for these data. Weak ties are relatively common in France, but so too are they in Bulgaria. It appears from these data that social networks bear few scars from the era of Communist domination in Russia and Central and Eastern Europe.

A summary indicator of the potential for political effectiveness of each network tie would be useful for the hypothesis testing that follows. To construct such a measure, I scored each tie according to its strength and degree of politicization (and, of course, its existence). Summing across the three network ties yields an index of the *political capacity of the respondent's social network*.[26] Capacity is the ability of the social network to transmit political information and to provide experience at politics through political discussions. Networks with high capacity are broad (including many members), are politicized (in the sense of talking about politics being common), and are "weak" (network ties transcend family boundaries). The index varies from 0 (social isolates, without any network partners) to 9 (all three network alters are weak ties, and the network is highly politicized). According to this measure (see Table 1), social networks should be most effective at facilitating social learning in Spain and Hungary and least effective in Russia (1995) and the United States. The Russians in the 1992 survey stand out as distinctive. This capacity measure is moderately related to level of education, interest in politics, and (self-proclaimed) opinion leadership in each of the countries. It is not, however, associated with the respondent's gender.

This cross-national analysis reveals that Russians have extensive social networks that are highly politicized and that often transcend family units. Though such networks are also found in some parts of the West (e.g., Spain), Russian social networks (at least in 1996) are distinctly different than such networks in the United States. In terms of political capacity, it appears that Russian networks have considerable potential for shaping political values.

Social Networks and Political Trust

To what degree are Russian social networks characterized by trust?[27] The 1996 Russians were asked to report their level of trust of each network member. The mean scores on the five-point response set indicate moderately high levels of trust in each of the network alters. Over 43 percent of the Russians assert that they trust the first network member at the highest level, and the mean level of trust is above 4.0. Trust in the next two network members is lower, but if we treat the two highest points on the scale as indicative of a relatively high level of trust, over 60 percent of the Russian respondents trust each network member considerably. Even though Russians have high levels of weak ties, trust in the network partners is common.

Social Networks and Ideological Agreement

The respondents were also asked to indicate the degree to which they agreed politically with each of the network members. Again, their responses were collected on a five-point scale.

Fairly high levels of ideological agreement also characterize Russian social networks, although there is clearly less agreement than trust in these social networks. Most Russians do not assert that their networks partners agree completely with them, but strong disagreement is quite rare.[28] Thus, Russian social networks are relatively large, quite politicized, and the interrelationships are characterized by a great deal of trust and a moderate degree of ideological agreement.

Summary

Russian social networks may well have emerged primarily as a response to the repressive state. Unable to organize publicly, Russians may have substituted private social networks for formal organizations (see Booth and Richard 1998). But Russians are not atomized, and as a consequence, Russian social networks have a variety of characteristics that may allow them to serve as important building blocks for the development of a vibrant civil society. In addition to carrying considerable political content, these networks are characterized by a relatively high degree of trust. Because the networks are not closed (strong), they link Russians together to an extent not often recognized by most analysts.

Interpersonal Trust

Many theories of civil society assume that interpersonal trust is essential to successful democratic governance. Mishler and Rose describe the conventional wisdom when they assert: "Trust is necessary [to the establishment of civil society] so that individuals may participate voluntarily in collective institutions, whether in political institutions, such as political parties, or in economic and social institutions, such as labor unions, business associations, and churches" (1997, 419). Further: "'Generalized social trust' (trust in people in general), trust in government and public officials, tolerance, and optimism are all seen, in many versions of the argument, as integral components of social capital directly linked to its beneficial impact on participation and civic engagement and democracy in general" (Foley and Edwards 1998, 13). As a consequence, there has been a tidal wave of research recently on interpersonal trust in a wide variety of contexts (e.g., Fukuyama 1995; Braithwaite and Levi 1998; Norris 1999). Several scholars argue that, at least at the macro level, interpersonal trust and effective democratic governance are intimately interconnected (e.g. Putnam 1993; Inglehart 1990, 1997; Muller and Seligson 1994), even if there is debate about the causal structure of trust (e.g., Brehm and Rahn 1997).

How trustful are Russians? The conventional measure of interpersonal trust asks whether "most people can be trusted" or whether one "can't be too cautious when dealing with people." Table 2 [3 in original] reports the responses of the Russians in my surveys, as well as the responses from a variety of surveys compiled as part of the World Values Survey.[29] The World Values Surveys were conducted in the early 1990s.

Russians in 1998 expressed more distrust than trust—59.0 percent said one cannot be too cautious, while only 30.5 percent claimed that other Russians can be trusted. These figures at first glance seem to indicate low levels of trust. But in comparison to the countries in the World Values Survey, Russians are *not* particularly distrustful. The percentage of Russians responding that one cannot be too cautious is lower, for instance, than the percentage in Spain, France, and Portugal (focusing on Western European countries) and is dramatically lower than [that in] most countries in Eastern and Central Europe. Indeed, if we take sampling error into account, the Russian data are not that different from the British data. This is a remarkable finding in light of the political, social, and economic turmoil in contemporary Russia.

Table 2

Cross-National Differences in Interpersonal Trust

Country	Percentages				
	Cautious	Uncertain	Trust	Total	Weighted N
Sweden	30.6	9.8	59.6	100.0	1,047
Switzerland	34.9	38.6	26.5	100.0	1,358
Norway	34.9	0.0	65.1	100.0	1,156
Finland	35.6	4.5	59.9	100.0	584
China	39.6	.7	59.7	100.0	1,323
Denmark	40.8	3.6	55.6	100.0	154
Netherlands	43.1	4.5	52.4	100.0	521
Canada	46.0	3.2	50.7	100.0	1,727
Russia, 1992	47.9	14.9	37.1	100.0	2,529
United States	48.6	2.8	48.6	100.0	2,004
West Germany	51.3	17.4	31.2	100.0	3,059
Ireland	52.3	.7	47.0	100.0	179
Japan	52.5	9.9	37.6	100.0	2,224
Iceland	54.1	4.0	41.9	100.0	700
Great Britain	54.6	3.3	42.1	100.0	2,805
Northern Ireland	55.4	1.7	42.9	100.0	79
Russia, 1996	58.2	6.2	35.6	100.0	2,094
Russia, 1998	59.0	10.5	30.5	100.0	1,719
India	59.7	9.2	31.2	100.0	2,511
Italy	60.2	4.3	35.5	100.0	2,280
Austria	60.8	10.9	28.4	100.0	1,460
Mexico	60.8	8.6	30.6	100.0	1,515
Belgium	61.6	7.8	30.6	100.0	307
Spain	62.2	6.0	31.8	100.0	2,059
Moscow	64.4	2.8	32.9	100.0	1,010
East Germany	65.4	12.0	22.5	100.0	1,328
Poland	65.5	0.0	34.5	100.0	852
South Korea	65.8	0.0	34.2	100.0	1,229
Bulgaria	66.0	5.2	28.8	100.0	1,031
Lithuania	69.2	0.0	30.8	100.0	1,000
South Africa	71.7	0.0	28.3	100.0	1,622
Nigeria	71.9	6.7	21.4	100.0	460
Czech-Slovak	72.2	0.0	27.8	100.0	1,394
France	72.4	6.3	21.4	100.0	2,806
Estonia	72.4	0.0	27.6	100.0	1,008
Hungary	73.1	3.0	23.8	100.0	998
Argentina	73.6	4.1	22.4	100.0	1,002
Byelorus	73.6	1.3	25.1	100.0	1,010
Chile	75.1	2.8	22.1	100.0	1,500
Portugal	76.2	3.0	20.8	100.0	477
Slovenia	77.7	6.0	16.3	100.0	1,034
Latvia	81.0	0.0	19.0	100.0	903
Romania	82.4	1.8	15.8	100.0	1,103
Turkey	88.9	1.3	9.9	100.0	1,025
Brazil	92.5	.9	6.6	100.0	1,747

Note: The source of the data for most countries is the World Values Survey, conducted in the early 1990s. The countries are ranked on the percentage asserting one cannot be too cautious in dealing with people. [Most surveys were for whole countries, but one was for city of Moscow alone.]

Notes

1. This estimate discounts union membership, including only those union members "who trust local union leaders to represent their interests" ([Rose] 1998, 11, footnote 4; see also page 27, which seems to provide some contradictory evidence).

2. Mishler and Rose (1999) report that Russians are the least trustful of any Central and Eastern Europeans. However, this conclusion is undermined slightly by the fact that the metric for the responses to the question differed in Russia.

3. McLeod et al. (1999, 746) note that social networks composed mainly of close family members, relatives, and friends tend to be "relatively homogeneous in background and attitudes and provide material and spiritual support. Conversely, political discussion networks whose purpose is exchanging and sharing information are more likely to be heterogeneous." See also Huckfeldt et al. (1995).

4. This is also one of the concerns of the vast literature on "particularized contacting" as a form of political participation. For instance, Mondak and Gearing argue that the source of information is related to its content: "In a fully atomized society, citizens could acquire information exclusively from impersonal sources such as national broadcast media, and then assess that information purely from the perspective of narrow self interest" (1998, 628–629).

5. Most analysts see novel political information and values as originating outside the borders of the formerly dictatorial systems (e.g., Gibson, Duch, and Tedin 1992). Processes of diffusion appear to have been crucial in providing citizens alternative models of political organization. For an excellent analysis of how the diffusion of political values brought about the demise of East Germany, see Rohrschneider (1999).

6. Of course, once information penetrates a group characterized by "strong" ties, it diffuses throughout the network quite readily. But since "weak" ties are more permeable, novel information is more readily accessible, and therefore Granovetter and I contend that "weak" ties are more conductive to social learning in transitional regimes.

7. A portion of the findings of Mondak and Gearing on atomization within Cluj-Napoca, Romania, surely has to do with the deep ethnic divisions that characterize that research site.

8. See, for example, Ledeneva (1998) on *blat* networks. "*Blat* is the use of personal networks and informal contacts to obtain goods and services in short supply and to find a way around formal procedures" (1998, 1). However, she does not consider *blat* networks to be exactly the same as social networks (1998, 104). For instance: "*blat* networks include not only immediate contacts but also people whom one knows only indirectly by recommendation" (1998, 117). It is highly unlikely that the latter sort of relationship would be included in the responses to our social network questions. She also distinguishes between "horizontal" and "vertical" *blat* networks, defining the former as "composed of people of similar status, known as 'people of the circle' (*svoi lyudi*)" (1998, 121), and the latter as "composed of people of different social strata interested in each other's connections and linked by kin, personal contacts or, most often, intermediaries known as 'useful people' (*nuzhnye lyudi*)" (1998, 121). The social networks on which I focus are much more likely to be horizontal networks.

9. For an interesting anthropological study of the nature and content of the discussions held within Russian social networks see Ries 1997. She observes (1997, 21) that: "The Soviet state was, of course, a critical agent in the continuous sacralization of private talk, since only in these quiet communicative exchanges [like those in the kitchen] did most people feel free to communicate honestly and openly; however, it would greatly oversimplify the dynamic relationship between local cultural worlds and the vast state apparatus to say that private talk was valued only because it provided a space of freedom from the state's vigilance."

10. Of the 383 interviews not completed, about half (8.1 percent of the total) were instances in which we were unable to make contact with the respondent, and the other half (7.6 percent of the total) were refusals.

11. The weight adjusts for unequal household sizes, while maintaining the actual number of respondents.

12. This is according to the Russian Federation State Committee on Statistics (1994, 26–27). Despite overrepresenting women, I have not weighted the data for this factor, in part because *so-called* "post-stratification" requires the not entirely tenable assumption that people who are available to be interviewed are similar in all important respects to people who are not available to be interviewed.

13. Over 92 percent of the interviews were conducted in April. The remainder was distributed as follows: March—three interviews; May—eighty-four interviews; and June—forty-eight interviews.

14. For instance, the highly influential *Political Action* panel reported response rates ranging from 65 percent in The Netherlands to 40 percent in West Germany (Jennings, van Deth, et al. 1989, Table A.1, 376). Gibson (1996) reports analysis of Russian and Ukrainian panel data based on a response rate of 52 percent, and Gibson and Caldeira (1998) analyze panel data with a rate of between 30 percent and 76 percent across the countries of the European Union.

15. The Russian survey was conducted over the period from November 1995 through January 1996, and the U.S. survey was conducted in 1995 and 1996 as well. Since such small percentages of the respondents were interviewed in 1996, I refer to these surveys as generally having been conducted in 1995.

16. Social networks have a variety of characteristics, and a technical language describing these has emerged. In general, I follow the conventions outlined in Knoke (1990, see the appendix, 235–240). Network size is "the number of people cited as important discussion partners in response to the sociometric name generator . . ." (Burt 1987, 82).

17. Caution should be exercised in all cross-national comparison of survey results (and indeed with within-country comparisons of survey data collected over fairly long periods of time). Survey practices differ within different countries and survey firms (see, for example, footnote 29, below), even though we specifically sought to control such practices in the seven-country study. Further, we cannot be certain that the respondents in different countries are equally forthcoming in their willingness to identify their network alters (although the correlations between trust in people in general and the number of network members named are quite weak in the two surveys for which both variables are available—Russia 1992 and Russia 1996). These cross-national findings must therefore be treated with caution.

18. This difference is, of course, statistically significant, although note that the relationship between the year of the survey and network size is quite small ($\eta = .08$).

19. Furthermore, those who asserted that there are no people with whom they discuss important matters were queried about the sort of political discussions they have with various types of people. Despite their initial answers to the name generator, these people are far from apolitical. The percentages who claim to discuss politics with various types of people are: friends—52.2 percent; neighbors—29.0 percent; family members—54.2 percent; coworkers—37.9 percent. Thus, these people are clearly not political isolates.

20. It is possible that the function of social networks is evolving in Russia. For instance, as Ledeneva notes, "connections in the socialist economy were predominantly 'value oriented' (rhetoric of friendship, requests for others), while now they are driven by considerations of self-interest and mutual profit" (1998, 200). Further, she claims: "Nowadays personal contact is still a necessary but no longer also a sufficient condition for getting things done" (1998, 200). One of her respondents described the change in the information-providing role of networks as follows: "It used to be information about what, where and how things could be obtained. Now it is information about money, business, laws and regulations, tax evasion, etc." (1998, 209). Finally, she concludes: "The informal networks, networks of interests and networks of control, ensuring trust and reduction of risks are in fact indispensable in today's Russia" (1998, 211).

21. I should acknowledge that my U.S. survey reveals fewer network alters than found in several other studies. I have no ready explanation for this finding. Note, however, that the sample size is relatively small, telephone interviewing was used, and that we asked for fewer network alters than some other studies. The percentages of respondents naming no network members do not differ greatly across various surveys (e.g., Mutz 1999 reports a percentage of 8), but the number able to name a full complement of alters does vary.

22. The frequency of political discussion with each network alter was measured with the following question: "How often do you discuss political questions with [EACH OF THE NETWORK MEMBERS]." The possible responses were: 1. Practically every day, 2. At least once a week, 3. At least once a month, 4. Once a year, 5. Less than once a year, and 6. Never.

23. In 1992, fully 82.2 percent of the respondents spoke about politics with the first network member at least weekly.

24. To what degree are these cross-national differences a simple function of differences in

the proximity of the survey to an election? Based on the limited analysis possible with so few cases, my conclusion is that cross-national effects of the election cycle are small. Consider France, which had a presidential election while the survey was in the field. Yet France had one of the lowest levels of network politicization. Conversely, consider Spain, which has a relatively high level of network politicization. The survey was done in March/April 1995; the closest election was the parliamentary election of March 1996, nearly a year away. The conclusion I draw here (based on the proximity of the survey to an election in all of the countries) is that national differences are more important than differences based on the electoral cycle.

25. These figures include people in the denominator who were not able to name a full complement of network members.

26. The index was created from three smaller indices characterizing the capacity of each network relationship. Each dyad was scored first on the existence of a relationship (0 or 3), then for the degree of politicization of the relationship (normalized, 0 through 1.0), and finally for whether the relationship was "weak" or not (0 through 3). Each of these indices ranges from zero (no relationship) to 3 (weak relationship, very frequent political discussions). Thus, in effect, the political capacity of each existing relationship is a weighted function of its politicization and weakness.

27. Comparable cross-national data are unavailable for both network trust and ideological agreement.

28. In keeping with the relatively high degree of politicization of Russian social networks, only very small percentages of the respondents are unable to characterize the level of political agreement with each network member.

29. Caution must be exercised in interpreting this table since the data were collected under a variety of national circumstances. Perhaps most important is how readily survey agencies accept "don't know" responses. In our surveys, we are entirely willing to accept such a response. But given the infrequency of "don't know" responses in many of the World Value Surveys, it seems unlikely that "don't know" was as easily accepted in all of the countries.

References

Arato, Andrew, and Jean Cohen. 1992. *Civil Society and Democratic Theory.* Cambridge, Mass.: MIT Press.

Bahry, Donna. 1993. "Society Transformed? Rethinking the Social Roots of Perestroika." *Slavic Review* 52:512–554.

Bahry, Donna, and Brian D. Silver. 1987. "Intimidation and the Symbolic Uses of Terror in the USSR." *American Political Science Review* 81:1065–1098.

Bahry, Donna, Cynthia Boaz, and Stacy Burnett Gordon. 1997. "Tolerance, Transition, and Support for Civil Liberties in Russia." *Comparative Political Studies* 30:484–510.

Banfield, Edward C. 1958. *The Moral Basis of a Backward Society.* Glencoe, Ill.: Free Press.

Bernhard, Michael. 1996. "Civil Society after the First Transition: Dilemmas of Post-communist Democratization in Poland and Beyond." *Communist and Post-Communist Studies* 29:309–330.

Booth, John A., and Patricia Bayer Richard. 1998. "Civil Society and Political Context in Central America." *American Behavioral Scientist* 42:33–46.

Braithwaite, Valerie, and Margaret Levi, eds. 1998. *Trust and Governance.* New York: Russell Sage Foundation.

Brehm, John, and Wendy Rahn. 1997. "Individual-Level Evidence for the Causes and Consequences of Social Capital." *American Journal of Political Science* 41:999–1023.

Burt, Ronald S. 1987. "A Note on the General Social Survey's Ersatz Network Density Item." *Social Networks* 9:75–85.

Crawford, Beverly, and Arend Lijphart. 1995. "Explaining Political and Economic Change in Post-Communist Eastern Europe: Old Legacies, New Institutions, Hegemonic Norms, and International Pressures." *Comparative Political Studies* 28:171–199.

Ekiert, Grzegorz. 1991. "Democratization Processes in East Central Europe: A Theoretical Reconsideration." *British Journal of Political Science* 21:285–313.

Foley, Michael W., and Bob Edwards. 1998. "Beyond Tocqueville: Civil Society and Social Capital in Comparative Perspective." *American Behavioral Scientist* 42:5–20.

Fukuyama, Francis. 1995. *Trust: The Social Virtues and the Creation of Prosperity.* New York: Free Press.

Gibson, James L. 1995. "The Resilience of Mass Support for Democratic Institutions and Processes in the Nascent Russian and Ukrainian Democracies." In *Political Culture and Civil Society in Russia and the New States of Eurasia,* ed. Vladimir Tismaneanu. Armonk, N.Y.: M.E. Sharpe.

Gibson, James L. 1996. "Political and Economic Markets: Changes in the Connections Between Attitudes Toward Political Democracy and a Market Economy Within the Mass Culture of Russia and Ukraine." *Journal of Politics* 58:954–984.

Gibson, James L. 1997. "Mass Opposition to the Soviet Putsch of August 1991: Collective Action, Rational Choice, and Democratic Values in the Former Soviet Union." *American Political Science Review* 91:671–684.

Gibson, James L., and Gregory A. Caldeira. 1998. "Changes in the Legitimacy of the European Court of Justice: A Post-Maastricht Analysis." *British Journal of Political Science* 28:63–91.

Gibson, James L., and Raymond M. Duch. 1993. "Political Intolerance in the USSR: The Distribution and Etiology of Mass Opinion." *Comparative Political Studies* 26:286–329.

Gibson, James L., Raymond M. Duch, and Kent L. Tedin. 1992. "Democratic Values and the Transformation of the Soviet Union." *Journal of Politics* 54:329–371.

Granovetter, Mark S. 1973. "The Strength of Weak Ties." *American Journal of Sociology* 78:1360–1380.

Greenfeld, Liah. 1992. "Kitchen Debate." *The New Republic* 207:22–25.

Huckfeldt, Robert, Paul Allen Beck, Russell J. Dalton, and Jeffrey Levine. 1995. "Political Environments, Cohesive Social Groups, and the Communication of Public Opinion." *American Journal of Political Science* 39:1025–1054.

Inglehart, Ronald. 1990. *Culture Shift in Advanced Industrial Society.* Princeton: Princeton University Press.

Inglehart, Ronald. 1997. *Modernization and Postmodernization: Cultural, Economic, and Political Change in 43 Societies.* Princeton: Princeton University Press.

Jennings, M. Kent, Jan W. van Deth, et al. 1989. *Continuities in Political Action: A Longitudinal Study of Political Orientations in Three Western Democracies.* Berlin: Walter de Gruyter.

Kish, Leslie. 1965. *Survey Sampling.* New York: John Wiley & Sons.

Knoke, David. 1990. *Political Networks: The Structural Perspective.* New York: Cambridge University Press.

Kornhauser, William. 1959. *The Politics of Mass Society.* New York: The Free Press of Glencoe.

Kubik, Jan. 1994. *The Power of Symbols Against the Symbols of Power: The Rise of Solidarity and the Fall of State Socialism in Poland.* University Park: Pennsylvania State University Press.

Kumar, Krishan. 1993. "Civil Society: An Inquiry Into the Usefulness of an Historical Term." *The British Journal of Sociology* 44:375–395.

Lake, Ronald La Due, and Robert Huckfeldt. 1998. "Social Capital, Social Networks, and Political Participation." *Political Psychology* 19:567–584.

Ledeneva, Alena V. 1998. *Russia's Economy of Favours: Blat, Networking and Informal Exchange.* New York: Cambridge University Press.

McLeod, Jack M., Dietram A. Scheufele, Patricia Moy, Edward M. Horowitz, R. Lance Holbert, Weiwu Zhang, Stephen Zubric, and Jessica Zubric. 1999. "Understanding Deliberation: The Effects of Discussion Networks on Participation in a Public Forum." *Communications Research* 26:743–774.

Meyer, Gordon W. 1994. "Social Information Processing and Social Networks: A Test of Social Influence Mechanisms." *Human Relations* 47:1013–1047.

Mishler, William, and Richard Rose. 1999. "What Are the Origins of Political Threat? Testing Institutional and Cultural Theories in Post-Communist Societies." Unpublished manuscript. University of Arizona.

Mishler, William, and Richard Rose. 1997. "Trust, Distrust and Skepticism: Popular Evaluations of Civil and Political Institutions in Post-Communist Societies." *Journal of Politics* 59:418–451.

Mondak, Jeffery J., and Adam F. Gearing. 1998. "Civic Engagement in a Post-Communist State." *Political Psychology* 19:615–637.

Moore, Barrington, Jr. 1954. *Terror and Progress in the USSR: Some Sources of Change and Stability in the Soviet Dictatorship.* Cambridge: Harvard University Press.

Muller, Edward N., and Mitchell A. Seligson. 1994. "Civic Culture and Democracy: The Question of Causal Relationships." *American Political Science Review* 88:635–652.

Mutz, Diana. 1999. "Cross-Cutting Social Networks: Testing Democratic Theory in Practice." Presented at the Annual Meeting of the Midwest Political Science Association.

Nelson, Daniel N. 1996. "Civil Society Endangered." *Social Research* 63:345–368.

Norris, Pippa. 1999. *Critical Citizens: Global Support for Democratic Government.* New York: Oxford University Press.

Ost, David. 1990. *Solidarity and the Politics of Anti-Politics: Opposition and Reform in Poland Since 1968.* Philadelphia: Temple University Press.

Putnam, Robert D. (with Robert Leonardi and Raffaella Y. Nanetti). 1993. *Making Democracy Work: Civic Traditions in Modern Italy.* Princeton: Princeton University Press.

Remington, Thomas. 1981. "The Mass Media and Public Communication in the USSR." *Journal of Politics* 43:803–817.

Ries, Nancy. 1997. *Russian Talk: Culture and Conversation during Perestroika.* Ithaca, N.Y.: Cornell University Press.

Roeder, Philip G. 1999. "The Revolution of 1989: Post-communism and the Social Sciences." *Slavic Review* 58:743–755.

Rohrschneider, Robert. 1999. *Learning Democracy: Democratic and Economic Values in Unified Germany.* New York: Oxford University Press.

Rose, Richard. 1998. "Getting Things Done in an Anti-Modern Society: Social Capital Networks in Russia." *Studies in Public Policy,* #304, Glasgow, Scotland: Centre for the Study of Public Policy, University of Strathclyde.

Russian Federation State Committee on Statistics. 1994. *The Demographic Yearbook of the Russian Federation 1993.* Moscow.

Stokes, Gale. 1993. *The Walls Came Tumbling Down: The Collapse of Communism in Eastern Europe.* New York: Oxford University Press.

Tismaneanu, Vladimir, ed. 1995. *Political Culture and Civil Society in Russia and the New States of Eurasia.* Armonk, N.Y.: M.E. Sharpe.

Weigle, Marcia A., and Jim Butterfield. 1992. "Civil Society in Reforming Communist Regimes: The Logic of Emergence." *Comparative Politics* 25:1–24.

Yamagishi, Toshio, and Midori Yamagishi. 1994. "Trust and Commitment in the United States and Japan." *Motivation and Emotion* 18:129–166.

Discussion Questions

1. What steps did Gibson take to ensure that his sample was representative of the broader population?

2. Why did Gibson use a "probe" in the question regarding how many persons each respondent reported discussing important issues with? Is it likely that the probe ("Anyone else?") added to the accuracy of the results?

3. What was the benefit of using a panel study for this research project? Were there any potential problems in using such an approach?

4. Why was it useful for Gibson to compare the Russian results to those for other countries?

Commentary

Gibson's study gives us a fascinating look at Russian culture, suggesting that Russians have developed extensive social networks in which they discuss political issues with great frequency. The fact that Gibson's study includes comparisons with other countries, including the United States, enables us to see the results for Russia in perspective. Given Russia's totalitarian past, many readers were surprised to see that Russians have more extensive social networks and discuss politics more than Americans do.

Several features of the research design employed here were important in making this such a persuasive study. Unlike many studies, this one received substantial federal funding to enable the author to plan and execute an ambitious design for collecting survey data. Gibson notes that interviews were completed in thirty-eight "Primary Sampling Units" that were drawn from all parts of Russia. Thus, the results cannot be seen as representing only the attitudes and behavior of, for example, residents of one or two large cities. The response rate was also quite impressive. Typically, the Gibson study succeeded in getting responses from over 80 percent of its subjects, a high figure for this kind of research.

Note also that this was, in part, a panel study, in which the same persons were contacted for repeat interviews at different times. One of the problems of panel studies, as noted above, is that respondents may be affected by the repeated experience of the questions and the subject they address. Researchers must make judgments about whether this problem is significant; Gibson was confident that, given the nature of the questions in this survey, this was not likely to be a problem.

The author took great care to ensure that the execution of the survey by the interviewers was careful and consistent. For example, when asking respondents about the number of people with whom they discuss important matters, the interviewers were given specific instructions to ask "Anyone else?" only if the respondent initially indicated fewer than three names. Interviewers also only asked for the first names or initials of the persons, in order to minimize the respondents' concerns for privacy.

The Gibson study illustrates the importance of careful questionnaire construction, extensive data collection efforts, and the benefits of appropriate comparisons to make survey results important and convincing. The study enabled him to look at change across time, even addressing the possibility that a low point in respondents' reports of social networking may have been a temporary reaction to a dispiriting parliamentary election. Overall, the study's conclusion that "Russians have extensive social networks that are highly politicized and that often transcend family units" is interesting and important. As we struggle to determine the future of this struggling country, Gibson's results will be important for years to come.

6 Indexing

Political research involves some concepts that are relatively easy to measure. Concepts such as a nation's per capita income, votes cast for a presidential candidate, and a respondent's racial or ethnic identity can all be measured in a relatively straightforward manner (assuming one has the data). However, many important political concepts, such as a person's ideology, the extent to which a state is innovative, or a nation's political culture, represent difficult challenges to our skills in designing operational definitions.

Broad Concepts, Specific Data

It is usually difficult to devise measures for broad concepts, but the broadest concepts are often the most important. Frequently, researchers are interested in a broad concept for which the relevant available data are of a highly specific nature. For example, the late Jack Walker wanted to measure "state innovativeness," a very broad concept relating to the extent to which states are among the first or last to adopt laws that virtually all states have adopted at some time (Walker 1969). The empirical information that has bearing on this concept is of a highly specific nature: the years in which each state adopted each of several hundred widely adopted laws. Thus, the available and relevant data are of a highly detailed nature (e.g., Wisconsin adopted insurance regulations in 1912, Alabama adopted a state highway system in 1928, etc.), but no one would accept data on these individual specific items as "indicators of a state's innovativeness." Clearly, a state could be among the first to adopt laws on insurance regulations and still be very slow to adopt laws on hundreds of other subjects, and thus we would be very unwise to take one of these specific pieces of information as a measure of the concept at hand.

Walker thus created an **index** to measure his concept of state innovativeness. An index is a single indicator created by combining two or more specific indicators. The actual method by which the various indicators are combined varies. An index constructed by adding other indicators is known as an

additive index. Similarly, a **multiplicative index** is created by multiplying the scores of several indicators, and a **weighted index** assigns different weights to one or more of the indicators from which the index is constructed.[1]

Walker constructed his index of state innovation by listing a large number of laws that virtually all the states passed, along with the year in which the first state adopted each of them. Then he gave each state a score on each law by determining how many years passed between the first adoption of the law and its adoption by the state in question. Each state thus received a score for dozens of laws. He then added the scores on the individual laws together, producing an overall indicator of a state's innovativeness. If a particular state adopted most of these laws within a year or two of the year in which the first state adopted it, that state would receive a very high score. In very noninnovative states, many decades passed between the first adoption of a law and the year in which they adopted them. Walker realized that the only way he could produce an indicator of the concept, given the fact that the available information pertained to the dates of adoption of highly specific individual state laws, would be to combine the information into an index. Information about a single law would be a useless indicator, but combined in index form, the information provided a valid picture of the extent to which a state was *generally* "ahead of the pack" or *generally* a "laggard" in adopting new laws and policies.

Herbert McClosky's 1958 study, "Conservatism and Personality," is another classic (and controversial) illustration of indexing (McClosky 1958). McClosky was interested in whether conservatives could be distinguished from nonconservatives in terms of psychological traits. Many studies attempt to explain differences in individual attitudes in terms of socio-economic or demographic factors such as income, education, ethnicity, and occupation. McClosky, however, believed there was an important link between political conservatism and the psychological makeup of conservatives.

Studying this idea empirically required finding a meaningful way to measure conservatism. McClosky felt it would be inappropriate simply to ask people whether they were conservative. Some people are not sure what the term means, and many of those who have an idea define it in quite different ways. He began, therefore, by constructing a list of forty-three statements that, he argued, collectively captured the essential nature of conservatism. His conservatism index was derived simply by counting the statements— "You can usually depend more on a man if he owns property than if he does not." . . . "I prefer the practical man anytime to the man of ideas"—with which a given respondent agreed.

McClosky used an index because simple, direct measurement of the complete concept—conservatism—was considered impractical and because the available data captured only parts of it. A respondent's answer to any one of

---

1. This discussion is adapted from Manheim and Rich (1991), pp. 198–199. See also O'Sullivan and Rassel (1989), pp. 250–273.

McClosky's forty-three statements, while interesting, could not be interpreted as a valid indicator of his or her conservatism. Taken together, however, the respondent's complete set of responses provided a meaningful measure of his or her conservatism.

Indexes, then, are ideal for research problems in which it is impossible to measure the entire concept via any single indicator. In such cases, the solution is often to combine a series of indicators into a single, comprehensive measure that provides us with a single score.

Types of Indexes

An additive index is perhaps the most commonly employed type of index in political research. In constructing an additive index, each subject's scores on each of the individual items are simply summed to obtain a single score. This procedure is appropriate when the available data (or indicators) represent different measures of the same variable, and we have no particular reason to believe any one of these measures is more or less important than any of the others. Thus, to create a measure of the "political information level" for each of several countries, we could create an index made up of several indicators: the number of newspaper subscriptions per 100,000 people, the number of telephones per 100,000 people, the number of radios or televisions per 100,000 people, and so on. For a country with a highly informed population, these indicators would produce scores of, say, 70,000, 98,000, and 99,000, which we could add together to get an index score of 267,000. A less politically informed country would produce lower index scores. The rationale for using an additive index of this kind is that each element of the index may be incomplete on its own. If we used only the first element, newspaper subscriptions per 100,000 population, we would be giving low scores to countries whose citizens may be quite informed, but get their political information from the broadcast media. Using the newspaper indicator alone would produce a misleading score for such a country. An index of all three indicators is more likely to capture the "political information level" concept.

Other types of indexes are appropriate for other situations. Sometimes, however, the available indicators represent aspects of a phenomenon that are related to the concept at hand, yet different in kind, making it inappropriate to add scores together. For example, assume that we want to measure the severity of riots. Two aspects of riot severity are the number of people involved and the number of hours that the riot lasts. We cannot add 2,750 people to 3½ hours to get a meaningful index score. However, we could argue that the severity of a riot is a matter of how these two elements interact. We could then *multiply* the number of rioters by the hours of duration, producing a measure of "demonstrator hours" for each riot (see Manheim and Rich 1991). The logic behind such a construction would be that, with a given number of rioters, a two-hour riot is twice as severe as a one-hour riot, and that, when comparing riots that last the same amount of time, the severity corresponds to the number of participants. Neither indicator captures riot severity alone, but they only work together as parts of a multiplicative index.

If we have reason to believe one or more of our indicators is more or less important than the others, we will want to create a weighted index. Returning to the example above of a "political information level" index, if we feel that newspaper subscriptions are twice as important as radio ownership in terms of the amount of political information they convey, we could use weighting to adjust the index scores. We would then multiply by two each country's number of newspaper subscriptions per 100,000 people before adding it to the number of radio and televisions per 100,000 people. The final index scores would thus be more sensitive to each country's number of newspaper subscriptions, as our theoretical understanding would suggest.

One Index for Each Concept (Dimension)

Whatever the type of index, the concept it measures must itself be **unidimensional** if our index is to be a valid indicator. A **multidimensional** concept consists of several separate sub-concepts that vary in a divergent manner and thus cannot be measured reliably with a single index. For example, consider how a researcher would construct an index of conservatism. Perhaps we would begin by listing several dozen statements that we have heard from politicians and thinkers normally considered conservative. Some of these statements would emphasize social or moral concerns, such as those expressed by William Bennett or George Will. These statements would include positions on abortion, prayer in school, and the dangers of "gangsta rap," for example. We would also have statements from conservatives emphasizing economic issues, including people such as Walter Williams and Milton Friedman, focusing on reducing the size of government and the burden of taxes and business regulation. We would need to decide, given the rather different themes expressed by the "social conservatives" and the "libertarian conservatives," whether or not a single phenomenon called "conservatism" actually exists.[2]

The reason we would need to consider this problem is that, if there are really two separate dimensions, "social conservatism" and "libertarian conservatism," *a single index made up of items drawn from both of these strands of conservative thought would be misleading.* Consider what would happen if we constructed an index of, say, fifty items, twenty-five reflecting "social conservatism" and twenty-five reflecting "libertarian conservatism." We then apply the measure by giving the set of statements to two people, asking both of them to indicate their agreement or disagreement with each of the fifty

---

2. These terms are intended not to refer to any standard meanings developed by political theorists specializing in the study of ideology, but simply to convey a widely recognized distinction among contemporary political thinkers.

statements. The first person is a firm social conservative, indicating agreement on all the statements about social conservatism, but her utter opposition to libertarian ideas leads her to indicate disagreement with nearly all of the twenty-five statements reflecting libertarian conservatism. The second person is essentially nonideological, approving of half of the social conservatism statements and half of the libertarian statements. Both persons would get the same score on our index, producing a very misleading conclusion that they are roughly identical with respect to their conservatism. The measure would produce a very inaccurate comparison of these two individuals.

The solution is to have an index for each identifiable dimension. An index of social conservatism would contain many items, but all of them should relate to that dimension, and not libertarian ideas. Similarly, an index of libertarianism should not be confounded by including statements derived from social conservatism. An index is ultimately a measuring instrument, and, as such, it must, as we discussed in chapter 2, be both valid and reliable. An index made up of items from two or more identifiable dimensions will certainly not give us a valid way of comparing cases.

—————————— Excerpt 9 ——————————

The American states vary with respect to how competitive the two major parties are in their elections. Political scientists have long been intrigued by the possibility that differences among the states in this respect could make a difference in the policies they adopt, the rate at which their citizens participate in politics, and many other factors. States in which one party is almost always sure to win may be less likely to produce progressive policies than states in which nearly every election is closely contested, for example. Perhaps elected leaders in states in which the opposition party is never a threat have less of an incentive to produce results, knowing that they are going to win re-election anyway. It is also arguable that states with hotly contested elections generate more voter turnout. The point is that there are many reasons to suppose that differences exist among states with respect to how competitive their parties are, but doing empirical research on the subject requires that we have a good measure.

The simplest, and probably the most obvious way to measure state party competition would be to look at the closeness of the last statewide race for governor. States in which one of the two parties won easily would be considered "low" in party competition, while states where the election was very close would be considered "high." This measure would be better than nothing, but we would realize that results in a given gubernatorial race could be affected by such things as a particular governor's personal appeal, scandals, and other factors not relevant to the overall competitiveness of the two parties in a given state. An alternative would be to look at the proportion of seats won by each party in the state legislature. We would probably also want to gather information over some specified period of time, so that we would not base our measure on a single election that may have been, for any number of reasons, unusual.

Holbrook and Van Dunk noted that, for many years, the most widely used approach to measuring state party competition was the "folded Ranney index" (Ranney 1976). This index is based on the proportion of seats won by the Democrats in both houses of the state legislature, the percentage of votes won by the Democratic candidate in gubernatorial election, and the proportion of time that the executive and legislative branches were controlled by the Democrats. Ranney averaged each of these factors over a specified period. Each of these items ranged from 0, indicating, for example, that the Democrats had not won any seats in the legislature or any votes in the gubernatorial election or that they had never controlled the executive branch during the period studied, to 1, indicating complete Democratic control. Ranney simply averaged these items into one index, and the averages would therefore also range from 0 to 1.

Ranney's index is a good example of a basic, unweighted, additive index. Several items were simply added together, and then averaged, to get each state's score on the index. In its basic form, the index was basically an indicator of the strength of the Democratic party, with high scores indicating that a state had a strong Democratic party and low scores indicating a weak Democratic party. The states with the greatest amount of party competition were thus those with the middle scores. To make the index show a range from low to high party competition, the scores were "folded" by subtracting .5 from every score (which then produced a range of scores from –0.5 to +0.5). Then, the absolute value of each score (i.e., disregarding the minus sign) was subtracted from 1 to get the "folded" Ranney index score. States in which the winning party rarely faces much competition should receive a "low" score regardless of whether it is the Democratic or Republican party that dominates the state's political scene. After subtracting .5 from each state's score, those at the ends (–0.5 and +0.5) are the states in which one party dominates. The "folding" step tells us that, after disregarding the minus sign, the states with the low scores will be those at the extremes, while the states in the middle of the original range will get the high score.

Although the Ranney index is helpful and has been used extensively, Holbrook and Van Dunk were convinced that it was not the best measure possible. For some purposes, they felt that an index focusing on the actual votes, not simply on which party won a given seat (or governorship), would produce a better picture of how competitive the parties are in each state. Their measure represents an important alternative to Ranney's well-known measure.

Electoral Competition in the American States

Thomas M. Holbrook and Emily Van Dunk, *University of Wisconsin, Milwaukee*

American Political Science Review 87, no. 4 (December 1993): 955–962. Copyright

Introduction

Electoral competition in the American states has generated more debate and research than perhaps any other concept in the field of American state politics. The interest in competition began with the regional studies of Key (1949) and Lockard (1959) and has expanded to dozens of articles attempting to link competition to policy outcomes, voter turnout, and other political phenomena. Much of the literature focuses on the influence of competition on policy outcomes. The guiding hypothesis for many studies has been that competitive political systems will display a tendency to produce more liberal policies than will noncompetitive political systems, a hypothesis derived from Key's 1949 *Southern Politics in State and Nation* (but see Uslaner 1978).

Though the theoretical underpinnings of this hypothesis are not always clearly articulated, we see the connection between political competition and liberal public policies as resting upon two interconnected assumptions. First, elected officials in competitive areas will be highly responsive to constituency needs, due to the risk of electoral defeat. Second, due to higher overall levels of voter participation in competitive environments, lower socioeconomic class interests will constitute a greater share of the electorate in competitive states than in noncompetitive states.[1] Therefore, in striving to represent the interests of their constituents, elected officials in competitive states will provide benefits to lower socioeconomic interests to a greater degree—and will display a greater propensity to support liberal policies (policies for the havenots, according to Key 1949)—than will elected officials in noncompetitive states, all else held constant.

While the empirical evidence is somewhat mixed, most studies indicate that competitive political systems do produce more liberal policy outcomes, though the effects are sometimes small when compared to socioeconomic variables (Dawson and Robinson 1963; Dye 1966, 1968, 1984; Holbrook and Percy 1992; Lewis-Beck 1977; Lowery 1987; Cnudde and McCrone 1969; Marquette and Hinckley 1981; Meier 1991; Plotnick and Winters 1985; Tompkins 1975; Walker 1969).

Another, less developed but related branch of research suggests that competitive environments generate higher rates of voter turnout. The logic underlying this relationship can be based either on individual-level incentives or on the incentives and behavior of candidates and political parties. First, close elections are likely to generate more interest and information, thereby reducing certain costs associated with voting. Close elections also provide a strong incentive for the candidates and parties to organize and mobilize the electorate (Powell 1986). Most empirical studies have supported the relationship between competition and turnout (Dye 1966; Milbrath 1971; Patterson and Caldeira 1983; Wolfinger and Rosenstone 1980), although there is some evidence to the contrary (Gray 1976).

The literature cited is only a sampling of the vast scholarship that has been generated on competition in the states. A number of indicators of competition have been developed and used over the past three decades (Broh and Levine 1978; Dawson and Robinson 1963; Golembiewski 1958; Ranney 1976; Zody and Luttbeg 1968). Perhaps the most commonly used indicator is the folded Ranney index (Ranney 1976). While the Ranney index has been subjected to considerable analysis (Barrilleaux 1986; King 1988; Patterson and Caldeira 1984; Tucker 1982), it—or variations on it—stands as the most widely used indicator of political competition in the states. We offer an alternative indicator of competition, one based on district-level outcomes in state legislative elections.

We shall discuss and compare the Ranney index and the alternative measures, then assess both measures in terms of face and empirical validity and briefly consider indicator reliability. Finally, we discuss the implications of the findings.

Ranney Index

The Ranney index is used as an indicator of the degree of two-party competition in the states. This index was developed in Ranney's (1976) "Parties in State Politics," originally published in 1965, and continues to be updated by Bibby and his colleagues (1990). The original index is actually a measure of the strength of the Democratic party in state government. The Ranney index takes into account the proportion of seats won in the state House and Senate elections, the Democratic percentage in the gubernatorial election, and the percentage of the time the governorship and state legislature were controlled by the Democratic party. These factors are averaged together over a specified period of time, yielding a measure that ranges from 0 (complete Republican domination) to 1 (complete Democratic domination). The midpoint, of course, indicates evenly divided control, or (in the words of those who use the index) *perfect competition.* The utility of this scale as a measure of party competition is realized by folding the scale so the two noncompetitive extremes are brought together at the low end and the midpoint becomes the high point.[2] The resulting index ranges from .5 (no competition) to 1 (perfect competition).

The folded Ranney index has itself been the subject of a significant amount of analysis. One branch of research has focused on the sources of competition. Patterson and Caldeira (1984) found that competition (measured with the Ranney index) is greatest in large, diverse states with strong party organizations. Barrilleaux (1986) is critical of Patterson and Caldeira's cross-sectional approach and examines change in the Ranney index during the 1970s. Although there are some similarities, many of Barrilleaux's findings sharply contradict those of Patterson and Caldeira.

Another branch of research addresses potential problems with the Ranney index. Tucker (1982) suggests that one problem with the Ranney index is that it is averaged over periods of time that are too long to generate a stable indicator. King (1988) identifies the gubernatorial election component as a distinct dimension that does not fit well with the state legislative components. Both Tucker and King recognize some problems with the folded index but are still supportive of its use and suggest only minor modifications. Stonecash (1987) is much less generous, finding fault not only with the Ranney index but with any aggregate cross-state index of party competition generally.

District-Level Competition

The measure of electoral competition offered here is based on district-level state legislative election results from 1982 to 1986.[3] Though rarely used, district-level competition has been examined before. Tidmarch, Lonergan, and Sciortino (1986) produced several measures of district-level competition in the states from 1970 to 1978. Unfortunately, their work was virtually ignored by others in terms of providing data for an alternative measure of competition in the states. Garand (1991) examined marginality in state legislative elections in 16 states from 1968 to 1986. Weber, Tucker, and Brace (1991) also examined the phenomenon of vanishing marginals in the lower houses of 20 state legislatures. To date, however, there has been no effort to produce a single, district-based measure of electoral competition in the states as an alternative to the Ranney index.

Like the Ranney index, the district-level measure is based on several components. First, we use the percentage of the popular vote won by the winning candidate. Second, we use the winning candidate's margin of victory. These first two components are not necessarily redundant. It is not uncommon in state legislative races to have more than two candidates in a race. Because of this, the winning candidate may have a relatively low vote percentage and still have a wide margin of victory over the second-place candidate. Third, we consider whether or not the seat is "safe." Though there is some disagreement on this matter, we follow the example of Tidmarch, Lonergan, and Sciortino and adopt a winning percentage of 55% or more as a safe seat. Finally, we consider whether the race was contested or not.

Any one of these components could serve as an indicator of district-level competition. We feel, however, that the best indicator is one that takes into account as much information as possible. Therefore, each of the several components is averaged across districts and combined into a single index value for each state from 1982 to 1986.[4] Complete absence of competition is indicated by a score of 0 on the district-level measure. This would be a case where all candidates are unopposed. As the scale increases from 0, it indicates greater competition. A score of 100, however, is theoretically impossible as long as someone wins the contests.

Table 1 presents the values for both the district-level measure and the Ranney index.[5] The states are ordered according to their value on the district-level measure. For both indicators, higher values represent more competition. Generally speaking, there is some overlap between the two indices, suggesting both that southern states tend to be the least competitive and that midwestern states tend to be the most competitive. There is significant disagreement, also. For instance, Delaware—which is tied on the Ranney index with North Dakota as the most competitive state—ranks only twenty-sixth in terms of district-level competition.

The relationship between the two indices is further depicted in the scatterplot in Figure 1. Note that there is considerable variation in district-level competition among those states ranked as the most competitive on the Ranney index. Also, many of the states with the highest district-level competition fall near the middle of the Ranney index. The correlation between the two indices (.68) is moderately strong but not particularly impressive if they are thought to be measuring the same concept.

The differences between these two measures of competition are of no small consequence. Both measures allege to be indicators of electoral competition in the states.

Validity

Whenever attempting to measure a concept indirectly through indicators, the crucial question is whether the indicators are valid representations of the concept. The validity of the Ranney index and the district-level indicator is assessed. First, we examine the indicators in terms of face validity.

Face Validity

The issue addressed by face validity is whether, on the face of it, an indicator appears to be a valid representation of the concept. Of the two indicators used here, the strongest case for face validity can be made for the district-level indicator. Our reasoning is quite simple. The Ranney index is based largely on aggregate party strength in government, not on actual election results. The only part of the Ranney index that takes into account any individual election results is the gubernatorial election component. Recall that King (1988) found

Figure 1 **Plot of Competition Indicators**

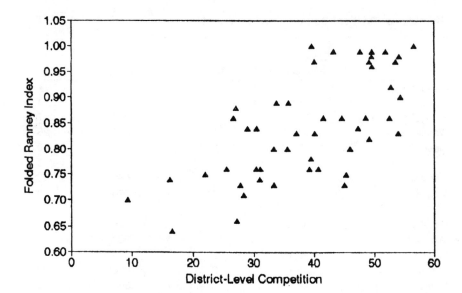

this component to be empirically distinct from the state legislative component. This is not surprising since one component is based on election results and the other is not. Even though the Ranney index does include the gubernatorial election component, it may not be prudent to accept this as an indicator of the degree of competition in the political environment. Given that only one gubernatorial election is held every four years in most states, it is possible that the results of this election may not represent the true degree of competition in the state. This leaves the Ranney index otherwise void of actual election results. In short, the Ranney index is really a measure of party control of state government, not the competitiveness of state elections.

The district-level indicator does not have the same problem. In fact, the district-level indicator is based entirely on actual outcomes in state legislative districts. Given how the indicator is computed, it is difficult to imagine a more direct measure of electoral competition in the states.

Reliability

Having examined the validity of the two indicators of electoral competition, we now turn to the final stage of the analysis: judging the reliability of the indicators. The issue of reliability concerns whether the indicator produces consistent results over repeated measurements. If, over repeated measurements, similar results are given, the indicator is said to be a stable, or reliable measure. The particular reliability test we selected is the Spearman-Brown prophecy formula, which is based on the split-halves reliability test (Car-

Table 1

Measures of Political Competition in the States

State	District-level competition	Rank	Folded Ranney	Rank
North Dakota	56.58	1	1.000	1
Oregon	54.25	2	.900	14
Nebraska	54.06	3	.980	7
Washington	53.94	4	.830	26
Alaska	53.46	5	.970	9
Connecticut	52.81	6	.920	13
Minnesota	52.44	7	.860	18
New Jersey	51.81	8	.990	3
Ohio	49.61	9	.960	12
Nevada	49.60	10	.990	3
Michigan	49.58	11	.980	7
Vermont	49.16	12	.970	9
Wisconsin	49.13	13	.820	29
Iowa	48.55	14	.860	18
New York	47.68	15	.990	3
California	47.29	16	.840	23
Maine	45.90	17	.800	30
Utah	45.29	18	.750	39
West Virginia	44.97	19	.730	43
Indiana	44.59	20	.860	18
Montana	43.34	21	.990	3
Illinois	41.61	22	.860	18
Virginia	40.71	23	.760	34
Pennsylvania	40.19	24	.970	9
Colorado	40.18	25	.830	26
Delaware	39.66	26	1.000	1
Rhode Island	39.49	27	.780	33
South Dakota	39.19	28	.760	34
New Mexico	37.10	29	.830	26
Kansas	35.81	30	.890	15
Idaho	35.60	31	.800	30
Arizona	33.90	32	.890	15
North Carolina	33.42	33	.800	30
Hawaii	33.40	34	.730	43
Florida	31.13	35	.760	34
Maryland	31.00	36	.740	41
Wyoming	30.46	37	.840	23
Massachusetts	30.39	38	.760	34
New Hampshire	29.01	39	.840	23
South Carolina	28.32	40	.710	46
Kentucky	27.81	41	.730	43
Alabama	27.27	42	.660	49
Missouri	27.12	43	.880	17

Tennessee	26.72	44	.860	18
Oklahoma	25.49	45	.760	34
Texas	21.96	46	.750	39
Mississippi	16.48	47	.640	50
Georgia	16.19	48	.740	41
Arkansas	9.26	49	.700	47
Louisiana	—	—	.690	48

Note: States are listed in order of competitiveness on the district-level indicator (most competitive to least competitive). The district-level indicator is based on district-level state-legislative election outcomes from 1982–1986, with high values indicating high levels of competition. The Ranney index is based on party control of the state legislature and the governorship from 1981–1988 (Bibby et al., 1990), with high values indicating high levels of competition.

mines and Zeller 1979, 411). In order to conduct the reliability test, it is necessary to measure both indicators at two different points in time. The measurements for the Ranney index were taken from 1974 to 1980 and 1981 to 1988 (Bibby et al. 1990). The measurements for the district-level indicator are taken from 1972 to 1976 and 1982 to 1986.[6]

The reliability estimates for the Ranney index (.77) and the district-level indicator (.94) suggest that both indicators are fairly stable but that the district-level indicator exhibits considerably more stability than the Ranney index. What this means is that competitive states in one time period will be more likely to show up as competitive in another time period on the district-level measures than on the Ranney index. Although electoral competition is subject to change, we expect such changes to be slow in nature. Therefore, we expect to see little change in the indicators.

Conclusion

Electoral competition plays a central role in American state politics. Besides the importance of competition to studies of policy, participation, and other political phenomena, it is important on purely normative grounds. Simply put, in the absence of competition, accountability suffers. Given its centrality in state politics, it is vitally important that quantitative studies be based on valid, accurate indicators of competition. The findings of such studies are, in large part, only as good as the indicators they use.

We undertook the task of comparing two measures of competition in the states—the Ranney index and a district-level indicator—in terms of both validity and reliability. On every front, the district-level indicator proved to be both empirically and intuitively superior to the Ranney index. The primary problem with the Ranney index is that it is based largely on aggregate party balance in state government, not on election results. Aggregate party balance is an important concept and clearly has implications for public policy, but it is not the same as competition, at least not the type of competition that is relevant to the individual legislator.

The consequences of relying on the Ranney index or on other indicators derived in the same manner may be quite severe. The evidence in Table 1 shows that the interpretation of the impact of competition on public policy is quite different when using the Ranney index than when using the district-level indicator. In the case of the Ranney index, we could conclude that competition was of little relevance to either public policy or voter turnout. With the district-level indicator we concluded just the opposite, that electoral competition was significantly related to both policy outputs and voter turnout. This raises the possibility that the mixed results of previous studies of the impact of competition on policy may have resulted, in part, from erroneous measurement of competition.

Clearly, the results of empirical research are greatly affected by how we attempt to operationalize complex concepts. We offer the district-level indicator as an alternative measure of electoral competition that we believe has strong face and empirical validity.

Notes

1. Hill and Leighly (1992) have developed a measure of class bias in state electorates that gauges the difference in turnout between upper- and lower-income groups in the states (high values indicate upper-class bias). This measure of class bias is negatively related ($r = -.45$) with the indicator of electoral competition developed herein, supporting the assumption that lower-class interests are better represented in the electorate in competitive states than in non-competitive states.

2. The formula for the folded scale is $1 - \text{ABS (Ranney} - .5)$.

3. The data used to construct this index are provided by the Inter-University Consortium for Political and Social Research (ICPSR). Specifically, the data are taken from *State Legislative Election Returns in the United States, 1968–1986* and were collected by the ICPSR.

4. The formula for statewide values of the district-level measure is

100 – (average % vote for winners + average margin of victory +
% uncontested seats + % safe seats)/4).

The components of the index are taken from the legislative districts and averaged or percentaged for the entire state. Cronbach's alpha for the index is .89. Returns for Louisiana general elections were not available for the time period used in this analysis.

Due to the difficulty in calculating these components for multimember free-for-all (MMFFA) districts, the district-level measure of competition excludes these districts. One potential problem with this exclusion is that the MMFFA districts could experience significantly different levels of competition than other districts in the same state. Were this the case, the measure presented here would not be a fair representation of the competitive environment in states with a significant number of MMFFA districts. To test this possibility, we created a measure of competition for MMFFA districts based on the number of candidates per position. We then correlated this measure of competition with the level of competition in non-MMFFA districts (using the district-level measure already described) for all states that use MMFFA districts (Arizona, Indiana, Maryland, New Hampshire, New Jersey, North Carolina, North Dakota, South Dakota, Vermont, West Virginia, and Wyoming). The correlation between these two measures is .87, indicating that competition in non-MMFFA districts reflects the level of competition in MMFFA districts in states that use both types of districts.

5. The Ranney index values used here are from 1981 to 1988 (Bibby et al. 1990).

6. Vermont is excluded from the earlier period due to missing data.

References

Albritton, Robert. 1990. "Social Services: Welfare and Health." In *Politics in the American States,* 5th ed., edited by Virginia Gray, Herbert Jacob and Robert Albritton, 411–446. Glenview, IL: Scott, Foresman.

Barrilleaux, Charles J. 1986. "A Dynamic Model of Partisan Competition in the American States." *American Journal of Political Science,* 30:822–840.

Bibby, John, Cornelius Cotter, James Gibson, and Robert Huckshorn. 1990. "Parties in State Politics." In *Politics in the American States,* 5th ed., edited by Virginia Gray, Herbert Jacob and Robert Albritton, 85–112. Glenview, IL: Scott, Foresman.

Broh, C. Anthony, and Mark S. Levine. 1978. "Patterns of Party Competition." *American Politics Quarterly,* 6:357–384.

Carmines, Edward G., and Richard A. Zeller. 1979. *Reliability and Validity Assessment.* Beverly Hills and London: Sage Publications.

Cnudde, Charles F., and Donald J. McCrone. 1969. "Party Competition and Welfare Policies in the American States." *American Political Science Review,* 63:858–866.

Colby, David C., and David G. Baker. 1988. "State Policy Responses to the AIDS Epidemic." *Publius,* 18:113–130.

Dawson, Richard E., and James A. Robinson. 1963. "Interparty Competition, Economic Variables, and Welfare Politics in the American States." *Journal of Politics,* 25:265–289.

Dye, Thomas R. 1966. *Politics, Economics, and Public Policy in the American States.* Chicago: Rand McNally & Co.

Dye, Thomas R. 1968. "The Independent Effect of Party Competition on Policy." *State Politics.* Belmont, CA: Wadsworth Publishing Co.

Dye, Thomas R. 1984. "Party and Policy in the States." *The Journal of Politics,* 1097–1116.

Fenno, Richard. 1978. *Home Style: House Members in Their Districts.* Boston: Little, Brown.

Garand, James. 1985. "Partisan Change and Shifting Expenditure Priorities in the American States." *American Politics Quarterly,* 13:355–392.

Garand, James. 1991. "Electoral Marginality in State Legislative Elections, 1968–86." *Legislative Studies Quarterly,* 16:7–28.

Golembiewski, R.T. 1958. "A Taxonomic Approach to State Political Party Strength." *Western Political Quarterly,* 11:494–513.

Gray, Virginia. 1976. "A Note on Competition and Turnout in the American States." *Journal of Politics,* 38:153–158.

Hall, Bob, and Mary Lee Kerr. 1991. 1991–1992 *Green Index.* Washington, DC: Island Press.

Hansen, Susan B. 1990. "The Politics of State Taxing and Spending." *Politics in the American States,* 5th ed., edited by Virginia Gray, Herbert Jacob and Robert Albritton, 771–785. Glenview, IL: Scott, Foresman.

Hill, Kim Quaile, and Jan E. Leighley. 1992. "The Policy Consequences of Class Bias in State Electorates." *American Journal of Political Science,* 36:351–365.

Holbrook, Thomas M., and Stephen L. Percy. 1992. "Exploring Variations in State Laws Providing Protections for Persons With Disabilities." *Western Political Quarterly,* 35:201–220.

Key, V.O., Jr. 1949. *Southern Politics in State and Nation.* New York: Vintage.

King, James D. 1988. "Interparty Competition in the American States: An Examination of Index Components." *Western Political Quarterly,* 41:779–790.

Lewis-Beck, Michael. 1977. "The Relative Importance of Socioeconomic and Political Variables for Public Policy." *American Political Science Review,* 71:559–561.

Lockard, Duane. 1959. *New England State Politics.* Princeton: Princeton University Press.

Lowery, David. 1987. "The Distribution of Tax Burdens in the American States: The Determinants of Fiscal Incidence." *Western Political Quarterly,* 30:137–158.

Marquette, Jesse F., and Katherine A. Hinckley. 1981. "Competition, Control, and Spurious Covariation: A Longitudinal Analysis of State Spending." *American Journal of Political Science,* 25:362–375.

Meier, Kenneth J. 1991. "The Politics of Drug Abuse: Laws, Implementation, and Consequences." *Western Political Quarterly,* 34:41–69.

Meyer, Louis S. 1982. "Consumer Protection." In *The Book of the States, 1981–82,* 24:540–545. Lexington, KY: The Council of State Governments.

Milbrath, Lester. 1971. "Individuals and Government." In *Politics in the American States,* 2nd ed., edited by Herbert Jacob and Kenneth Vines. Boston: Little, Brown & Co.

Patterson, Samuel C., and Gregory Caldeira. 1983. "Getting Out the Vote: Participation in Gubernatorial Elections." *American Political Science Review,* 77:675–689.

Patterson, Samuel C., and Gregory Caldeira. 1984. "The Etiology of Partisan Competition." *American Political Science Review,* 78:691–707.

Plotnick, Robert D., and Richard F. Winters. 1985. "A Politico-economic Theory of Income Redistribution." *American Political Science Review,* 79:458–473.

Powell, G. Bingham, Jr. 1986. "American Voter Turnout in Comparative Perspective." *American Political Science Review,* 80:17–44.

Ranney, Austin. 1976. "Parties in State Politics." In *Politics in the American States,* 3rd ed., edited by Herbert Jacob and Kenneth Vines. Boston: Little, Brown & Co.

Stonecash, Jeffrey M. 1987. "Inter-Party Competition, Political Dialogue, and Public Policy: A Critical Review." *Policy Studies Journal,* 16:243–262.

Tidmarch, Charles M., Edward Lonergan and John Sciortino. 1986. "Interparty Competition in the U.S. States: Legislative Elections, 1970–1978." *Legislative Studies Quarterly,* 11:353–374.

Tompkins, Gary. 1975. "A Causal Model of State Welfare Expenditures." *Journal of Politics* 37:392–416.

Tucker, Harvey. 1982. "Inter-Party Competition in the American States: One More Time." *American Politics Quarterly,* 10:93–116.

Uslaner, Eric. 1978. "Comparative State Policy Formation, Interparty Competition and Malapportionment: A New Look at V.O. Key's Hypotheses." *Journal of Politics,* 40:409–432.

Weber, Ronald, Harvey Tucker, and Paul Brace. 1991. "Vanishing Marginals in State Legislative Elections." *Legislative Studies Quarterly,* 16:29–48.

Wright, Gerald, Robert Erikson, and John McIver. 1985. "Measuring State Partisanship and Ideology with Survey Data." *Journal of Politics* 47:469–489.

Zody, Richard, and Norman Luttbeg. 1968. "An Evaluation of Various Measures of State Party Competition." *Western Political Quarterly,* 21:723–24.

Discussion Questions

1. What does a measure of party competition based on election results tell us that the Ranney measure does not? Why could this be an important difference?

2. Is the Holbrook/Van Dunk index a weighted index?

3. The components of the Holbrook/Van Dunk index are drawn from the period from 1982 through 1986. What difference would it have made if the authors had drawn information from a longer period, such as 1970 through 1986? What difference would it have made if they had drawn the information from a single year?

4. The authors stated that their index is "based entirely on actual outcomes in state legislative districts," and that "it is difficult to imagine a more direct measure of electoral competition in the states." In what ways can we argue that the Ranney index is a less valid measure?

5. Reliability has to do with whether or not a given measure shows the same results when applied to different cases (or different periods). How did Holbrook and Van Dunk evaluate the reliability of their measure?

Commentary

Holbrook and Van Dunk were convinced that a genuine measure of state-to-state differences in party competition must be based on the vote totals in each district. The Ranney index focused entirely on which party won legislative or gubernatorial elections. The crucial difference is that Ranney's index disregarded the margin of victory, an important consideration in determining how competitive the two parties are in a given state. For certain purposes, Ranney's decision to focus simply on which party won each legislative seat or gubernatorial election is entirely defensible; a state in which one party wins 75 percent of the legislative seats clearly has less party competition than one in which the parties each receive close to half of the seats, regardless of the margins of victory in the various contests. But Holbrook and Van Dunk persuasively argued that a better measure should take more information into account, and their index did just that.

One of the most compelling parts of the excerpt was Table 1, showing the state scores and ranks on the Holbrook/Van Dunk index and the scores and ranks on the Ranney index. As they note, scores on the two indexes were positively correlated (+.68), indicating that states that received high scores on one index *tended* to have high scores on the other, but also indicating that the two measures were not identical. For example, Arizona and Kansas were both ranked fifteenth in the Ranney index, but thirty-second and thirtieth in the Holbrook/Van Dunk index. The two indexes were measuring somewhat different phenomena.

A key issue that must be addressed in using either the Ranney or the Holbrook/Van Dunk approach is the time period to be covered by the measure. It is possible to take data from a very long period, say twenty-five years or more, and it would also be possible to compute the measure on the basis of data from a single election year. The decision as to an appropriate length of time requires that we have a good grasp of the concept at hand. As Holbrook and Van Dunk explain, the purpose of the index is to measure how closely the two parties compete for the political support of the residents of each state, and party identification is one of the more enduring allegiances that Americans have. Since voters may stray from their parties in a given election (perhaps due to a scandal or important positive or negative factors about a candidate), using data from a single election could give a distorted picture of the actual levels of support for the two parties.

On the other hand, computing the index with data from a very long period would produce scores for each state that could be out of date. An index score for Texas, for example, drawn from data from 1970 through 1996, would include data from a period in which the Democratic party had great support in many legislative races and also data from the last few elections in which the Republicans have dominated much of the state. The score drawn from such a long period would probably indicate that Texas has very close party competition, since the measure would average periods of Democratic and Republican dominance. If we are interested in the current degree of party competition, we need to look at a shorter time period, but not so short as a single election.

Holbrook and Van Dunk's article illustrates that index construction, like virtually all measurement tasks in political research, requires a firm understanding of the concept and the available data. The Ranney index was a good place to start but, for many research goals, the index described here is a more useful way to measure the centrally important concept of state party competition.

7 Content Analysis

Documents have always been an important source of political data. Government papers, legal documents, and the writings of major public figures have long been of particular interest to political scientists. Especially in recent years, the content of material in newspapers and broadcast media has played an increasingly important role in contemporary politics.

Political scientists have made use of documentary materials to study political change, electoral campaigns, the leadership process, and a wide variety of other important subjects. Documents, unlike data on program expenditures, employment levels, or election results, can help reveal political motives. Often they provide a basis for seeing through official pronouncements to the underlying political realities.

However, unlike many forms of political data, the evidence contained in documents is not normally in quantitative form. Although speeches, transcripts of newscasts, and other kinds of documentary evidence may still be very useful, analysts normally have to make judgments about their content, judgments that are inevitably subjective. For some purposes, it is helpful to find ways of developing objective ways to generate quantitative data from documents. The process by which researchers convert the contents of documents into quantitative form is known as **content analysis**. By using modern content analysis methods, researchers are able to employ the power of statistical analysis in circumstances under which only subjective, journalistic impressions would otherwise be possible.

The specific procedures employed by content analysts vary in complexity and sophistication. Content analysis can be as straightforward as simply counting the number of speeches reported for each U.S. senator in the *Congressional Record* over a given period. It can also involve sophisticated quantitative analysis of attitudes, values, and positions as reflected in the written or spoken statements.

In addition to the basic steps characteristic of all political research—hypothesis construction, sampling, and so forth—content analysis involves two special procedures. First, the researcher must decide upon a unit of analysis.

In a content analysis of, say, newspaper stories, the story might be the basic unit of analysis. Alternatively, the unit of analysis might be the paragraph, sentence, or column-inch. The proper unit of analysis depends on the nature of the research problem. In a study of newspaper editorial support for incumbent candidates, the unit of analysis might be the editorial. Thus, our data would consist of one "score" for each editorial included in our sample. If each sentence is scored, then the sentence is the unit of analysis.

Second, the researcher must develop a set of coding rules. These rules provide the basis for translating text into data. Since they must apply consistently to a broad range of material, they must be developed with great care, and they must be stated precisely and clearly. The need to develop a coding scheme for data is, of course, a common feature of political research. Even such seemingly straightforward variables as personal income or age must often be categorized in accordance with coding rules for purposes of statistical analysis. (Thus, we might devise a scheme for coding personal income in which "low income" is under $7,000 per year; "medium income" is $7,000 to $25,000 per year, etc.) The distinguishing feature of content analysis, therefore, is not the existence of coding rules, but the application of such rules to verbal statements in textual form.

In the early 1970s, the American Security Council Education Foundation, a conservative advocacy group, conducted a classic example of content analysis. The foundation believed that network coverage of national security issues was severely unbalanced. Concluding that this violated the Federal Communication Commission's (FCC) fairness doctrine, which (until 1988) required balanced coverage of important public issues on radio and television, the foundation hoped to force a change in network behavior by filing a complaint with the FCC.

The foundation was already convinced that the evening news was unfair in its coverage of defense issues, but it needed some way of convincing the FCC, and, if the commission failed to act, some way of persuading the Court of Appeals that the FCC should have acted. The foundation employed content analysis to help make its case. Using videotapes of all *CBS Evening News* broadcasts during 1972, the foundation transcribed those portions that were relevant to "U.S. military and foreign affairs, Soviet Union military and foreign policy, China military and foreign policy, and Vietnam." Each sentence of each report was then isolated and individually coded or scored by members of the foundation in accordance with the following coding rules:

> Viewpoint A holds that the threat to U.S. security is more serious than perceived by the government or that the United States ought to increase its national security efforts;
>
> Viewpoint B holds that present government threat perception is essentially correct or U.S. military and foreign policy efforts are adequate; and

Viewpoint C holds that the threat to U.S. security is less serious than perceived by the government or that U.S. national security efforts should be decreased.

With these coding rules, the foundation obtained the following results: 3.54 percent of the CBS newscasters' sentences reflected Viewpoint A, 34.63 percent reflected Viewpoint B, and 61.83 percent reflected Viewpoint C. This, the foundation claimed, *proved* that CBS had violated the fairness doctrine. Neither the FCC nor the court agreed.[1]

While the court's decision was not based on a critique of the foundation's methodology, two methodological problems are apparent in this example. The first is that the foundation's coding rules were quite general, even vague, and left much room for subjective judgment. If the coding was done by a person already convinced that every other word from the CBS news anchor was an attack on the Pentagon, we could not be very confident of the accuracy of the results. And, even assuming a neutral coder, the categories require a great deal of interpretation. Consider the following sentence: "China announced today that it will send its foreign minister to a meeting in North Korea." Whether this is scored A, B, or C depends more on the coder's knowledge of China's relationship with North Korea, or perhaps U.S. relations with North Korea, than on the content of the sentence itself.

A second potential problem stems from the selection of sentences as the basic unit of analysis. The difficulty here is that it is possible, indeed likely, that at least some of the resulting scores were for remarks taken out of context. How, for example, is one to code an anti-Pentagon statement from a liberal member of Congress that is reported by the anchor? Perhaps the newscaster's story raised doubts about the politician's motives in criticizing the Defense Department. Yet, since the sentence was coded in isolation, the score would give us an inaccurate reading of the thrust of the newscast. Good content analysis requires that such problems be anticipated and handled with extreme care.

There are two particularly important precautions we can take to improve the validity of our content analysis data. The first is to make our coding rules as detailed as possible. Explicit, clear, and complete coding rules reduce the researcher's dependence on the objectivity of the coder. If, for example, the American Security Council Education Foundation's coding rules had stipulated that a sentence could be coded as Viewpoint C *only* when it took one of, say, a dozen or so specific forms—"North Korea reduced its defense budget," or "The Russians have stopped sending military assistance to the Iraqis"—it would have greatly enhanced the credibility of its final results by reducing the coder's leeway for interpretation.

---

1. See *American Security Council Education Foundation v. FCC*, 607 F2d 438 (1979). However, the foundation loss was not due to its use of content analysis. The case failed on the FCC's ruling that fairness doctrine complaints were only meaningful with respect to specific issues.

Typically, of course, it is impossible to specify our coding rules so completely that the coding process becomes entirely automatic or mechanical. Written or oral materials will inevitably present us with ambiguity and, thus, with the need to rely on the coder's judgment to a greater or lesser degree. Another useful measure we can employ to enhance the validity of our data, therefore, is the use of *multiple* coders.

In its simplest form, multiple coding can involve the use of a second coder to help identify ambiguous cases. Any case not scored identically by the two coders is then subjected to further analysis in an attempt to determine which, if either, of the scores assigned is correct. This process may in turn lead to other possible outcomes including the development of a more precise set of coding rules or the elimination of the case as uncodable.

In more elaborate designs, each case may be independently scored by a panel of coders and a final score determined by taking the average of the individual scores awarded by all the panel members. This approach also allows the researcher to determine which, if any, cases are so troublesome that they should be omitted from the analysis. If there is virtually no agreement among the coders with respect to a given case, the case contains confounding attributes (or perhaps the coding rules need further work).

We can be very confident about our measurements when several coders independently assign the same scores to a large proportion of the items they code. Studies using content analysis often calculate the **intercoder reliability** to evaluate the extent of agreement among coders. The specifics of this calculation depend on the nature of the project, but the basic idea is to indicate the percentage of the cases in which the coders agreed. A 96 percent intercoder reliability score would mean, for example, that the reader could be certain that the coding rules were clear and meaningful, because different coders assigned the same scores to nearly all the cases.

In comparison with other more direct methods of obtaining quantitative data, content analysis is relatively complex, time consuming, and costly. For some types of problems, however, it is the fastest and cheapest method of gathering data. Content analysis of official documents is much more manageable, for example, than traveling to China for candid interviews with members of the Communist party. Documents are plentiful and relatively easy to access, and coding schemes can be developed by virtually any researcher. Hence, content analysis can always produce data. Validity and reliability, the two basic goals of good operationalization, are the critical issues in evaluating the data produced by content analysis. When the data produced reflect valid and reliable measurement, content analysis can generate impressive results, as shown in the following excerpts.

—————————— Excerpt 10 ——————————

Many Americans are frequently divided about newspaper and television coverage of political campaigns and issues. On the one hand, there is strong support for the principle of the "freedom of the press," at least in the abstract. On the other hand, many citizens and analysts feel that the press should be "fair." As discussed previously, the FCC once enforced a "fairness doctrine" in licensing renewal proceedings, insisting that television and radio stations give equal time to all sides on controversial issues and in campaigns. The state of Florida took the idea further in the 1970s, passing a law requiring that the print media also follow principles of fairness in dealing with political life. The U.S. Supreme Court held the Florida law unconstitutional, concluding that it amounted to an impermissible restriction on freedom of the press.[2] A similar logic led the FCC to abandon the fairness doctrine in 1988. As more than one observer has noted, fairness in newspapers and broadcast media may be desirable, but it is not required by the Constitution.

Nevertheless, the extent to which newspapers and broadcasters are evenhanded in dealing with politics remains a heated empirical question. Most journalists working for influential newspapers and important broadcast networks admit to being Democrats, and Republicans and their supporters have frequently argued that "media bias" hampers their ability to get their messages across. Others argue that, even if most journalists support the Democratic party, they are primarily concerned with professional standards for their advancement, and this requires them to be generally balanced in their political reporting. Media bias remains an issue that generates a great deal of controversy.

Russell Dalton, Paul Beck, and Robert Huckfeldt designed an empirical study to address this problem. Their study involved the use of content analysis to assess the degree to which newspaper coverage of the 1992 presidential campaign tended to favor Bill Clinton or George Bush, and their results, while not tremendously surprising, provide empirical footing for the continuing debate.

As you read the excerpt, pay special attention to the authors' design regarding coding, the selection of the unit of analysis, and the way that they used the quantitative data produced by the content analysis.

---

2. See *Miami Herald Publishing Co. v. Tornillo,* 418 U.S. 241 (1974).

Partisan Cues and the Media: Information Flows in the 1992 Presidential Election

Russell J. Dalton, *University of California, Irvine*
Paul A. Beck, *The Ohio State University*
Robert Huckfeldt, *Indiana University*

American Political Science Review 92, no. 1 (March 1998): 111–126. Copyright © 1998 by the American Political Science Association. Reprinted with permission.

Most of what voters learn about the political process and contemporary events is mediated through a variety of institutional and individual information sources. Most people have not met their elected representatives, attended a government hearing, or read the legislative proposals under consideration by Congress. Nevertheless, people form impressions and evaluations of these actors and events through the information provided by intermediaries, such as the media, political organizations, and people with whom they discuss politics. The most regularly used information source, by virtually all accounts, is the mass media, especially television and the press.

The media's role as an intermediary is most evident at election time, when the media are the primary conduits for information on the campaign. Few voters attend a rally or have direct contact with the presidential candidates or their representatives. Instead, information presented in the media provides people with cues about the policy positions, qualities, and abilities of the candidates. The media also report on the progress of each campaign, including how the American public is reacting to the candidates and their messages. From this information, as well as other sources, the public forms its images of the candidates and its voting choices.

How does this learning process work? Some analysts posit that the media have a direct influence on the public by reinforcing partisan predispositions or persuading voters to support particular candidates (e.g., Bartels 1993; Noelle-Neumann 1984; Zaller 1996). The predominate position in the literature, however, is that the media affect what factors to consider in judging the candidates by the way they present the topics of the campaign (Iyengar 1991; Iyengar and Kinder 1987; Patterson 1993). The media thus shape how the public thinks about the candidates rather than influence candidate preferences per se. Despite widespread acceptance of the media's important role in disseminating political information, scholarship remains divided on the central questions about the nature and effect of this information.

Our research addresses the question of media influence from a methodological perspective different from the one that has dominated scholarly research in recent years. In a tradition largely neglected since the days of the Columbia studies of voting (Berelson et al. 1954; Lazarsfeld et al. 1948; but see Patterson 1980), this article examines the direct persuasive influence of the media. Our specific interest is whether the content of press reports affects partisan preferences at election time.

It is curious that media research has not focused on the press, where variation in media content is most likely to be found. Instead, most studies have concentrated on television coverage of campaigns. Opinion surveys routinely show that television is most often cited as a source of political information, and its visual power has drawn scholars to research this medium. Yet, television news coverage is less likely to show systematic partisan bias in election content because of its history of government regulation, its origins in an advertising rather than a partisan culture, and its need to address a national viewership. Since the three networks have developed a largely impartial orientation, television seems less likely to influence partisan preferences directly. One can argue that partisan cues are more likely to be found in newspapers because of their greater variety in ownership, differences in circulation bases, and earlier traditions of party-aligned reporting. Yet, studies of newspaper coverage of campaigns have not focused on variation in partisan content, and no comprehensive national study of newspaper coverage of a presidential election has ever been undertaken.

Our research represents the first national examination of how the print media actually presented a presidential campaign and how this information was perceived by voters and potentially influenced their preferences. We assembled a nationally representative collection of newspaper coverage of the 1992 presidential election. These data enable us to describe and analyze the political information that Americans received from their daily newspapers as well as the variation in coverage across the nation. With a parallel survey of the readers of these newspapers, we also assess how individuals perceived the political cues the press provided on the candidates and issues and whether this information influenced voting choices.[1]

Even more important, by examining the complete intermediation process for newspapers—from the content of the media to its effect on voters—we can test general theories of political learning and the nature of media influence. For instance, there is basic disagreement on the accuracy with which people perceive the political cues emanating from the media and on the factors that influence these perceptions (Neuman 1986; Zaller 1992). We can examine this linkage with our empirical evidence. In addition, the literature is unclear about how the information provided by the media is integrated into predispositions and thus influences political preferences. Our merger of objective media content and attitudinal data enables us to examine this complex process.

The findings of this study speak to several important questions in the current debate on the media's role in American electoral politics: the content of the press's coverage of presidential elections, the potential for media bias in election coverage, and the influence of newspapers on their readers. Because of the public's reliance on the media as an information source, the answers to these questions address an essential aspect of the democratic process: the role of the press as information provider.

Tracing Information Flows from the Press

Early communications scholars feared that the modern mass media would be a powerful instrument of partisan persuasion and propaganda. These concerns lessened with the first empirical studies of the media's influence in elections (Berelson et al. 1954; Lazarsfeld et al. 1948). The results gave rise to the so-called minimal effects view: The media do not appear to exert a major persuasive influence on partisan preferences (Klapper 1960). The contemporary view is that media influences are primarily the cognitive effects of agenda setting and framing how events and candidates are perceived (Iyengar and Kinder 1987; McLeod et al. 1994).

At the same time, other researchers have continued to explore the media's potential for persuasion. Robert Erikson (1976) found that a newspaper's editorial endorsement was significantly related to county-level voting patterns. John Robinson (1974) and Steven Coombs (1981) also documented a direct relationship between newspaper endorsements and the voting patterns of readers. Elisabeth Noelle-Neumann (1984) claimed that the media can have a strong influence on voting preferences when their message is clear and consistent. Larry Bartels (1993) showed that measurement error may significantly attenuate estimations of media effects, and he argued that the direct influence is much stronger than previously recognized. John Zaller (1996) provided new evidence that media content can affect policy preferences and political evaluations. In summary, there is evidence that media content can have a direct influence on public opinion and, specifically, voting preferences.

The First Stage

Our research traces the flow of political information from newspapers to the voter and then assesses the effect of this information on partisan choices. This requires that we examine the flow through several distinct stages.[2] The process begins with the information provided by the press. At this stage, we are concerned with clarity and direction of the political signals disseminated through the media. The strength of political cues in a newspaper's election reporting presumably affects the accuracy of their reception and ultimately their effect.

The nature of the information provided through the media also has fundamental implications for its potential persuasive effects. For example, Zaller (1992) and others (Noelle-Neumann 1973; Ross et al. 1976) argue that uniformly one-sided messages ("one message model") promote conformity to the message and are powerful sources of persuasion. Differentiated messages

(Zaller's "two message model") are cognitively more complex and force receivers to search for cues about which messages to believe. Thus, the nature of political messages provided by the press has important consequences for the direction and degree of the public's response. By examining the content of the press's coverage of election campaigns we can determine the initial characteristics of this information process.

Surprisingly, prior research has not produced systematic information on the degree to which American newspapers provide clear partisan cues and evaluative information to their readers. Several studies describe the coverage of the presidential candidates in the elite press and track these trends over time (e.g., Graber 1993, chapter 6; Stempel and Windhauser 1991), but they are limited in several respects. Most research focuses on only a few elite newspapers or local newspapers to lessen the burden of coding media content. Although the *New York Times* may consider that it publishes "all the news that's fit to print," it is read by only a small fraction of the American public. The typical voter reads a local newspaper with limited circulation, and these local papers may vary considerably in their partisan cues. Thus, to assess the information provided by the media, one needs to evaluate a sample of newspapers that represents the range of American media.

In addition, the coding of the information content of the press has not been fully satisfactory. Political communications research often relies on surrogates or partial measures of content. For instance, several analysts have used a newspaper's editorial endorsement as a measure of its partisan content (Coombs 1981; Erikson 1976; Robinson 1974); others have explicitly excluded editorial material (e.g., Stempel and Windhauser 1991). Studies of news content also have variously measured only headlines or articles appearing on the first page. Because of these different approaches, it is not surprising to find that prior research yields ambiguous conclusions about what partisan cues the press provides. Statistics on editorial endorsements show that fewer newspapers now explicitly endorse a presidential candidate (Stanley and Niemi 1994), and there is evidence of a general decrease of partisanship among the contemporary press (Rubin 1981). Conversely, others argue that the press has become more openly critical of politicians and has created unfavorable candidate images (Sabato 1991), although substantial empirical evidence of these effects has been lacking. Campaign organizations, often all of the parties and candidates, routinely claim that the media are projecting biased images of their candidate (see discussion in Patterson 1993, chapter 5). What is needed is a full and direct assessment of the partisan cues provided by the press so that we can generalize about the nature of election coverage.[3]

The Second Stage

The second step in the process of information flow involves readers' perceptions of the objective content of the media. How accurately do readers assess the partisan content of their daily newspapers? The primary source of reader perceptions should be the objective information provided by the media, but that is potentially diverse. There is an ebb and flow to election campaigns, so a single source may report positive news on a candidate one day and negative news the next. Even the same event is open to multiple interpretations, and these contrasting views may be expressed in a single article or separate reports. Furthermore, newspapers often print several different campaign articles in the same issue, and the partisan direction of each may vary. There is also variation between the news coverage of a campaign and what appears on the editorial pages. The interaction between news and editorial reporting may affect the clarity of the message the press conveys. We will explore how alternative sources of political cues, such as news coverage versus editorial content, shape a paper's partisan image among its readership.

Beyond the objective information, a reader's own characteristics may determine his or her perceptions of the media's message (Becker and Kosicki 1995). For example, research on information flows often shows that individuals project their predispositions onto information sources (or screen out opposing messages), unless the source provides an unavoidable message (Klapper 1960; McGuire 1985; Zaller 1992). Yet, research has found a much different process at work for media usage. Robert Vallone and his colleagues (1981) presented evidence of a "hostile media phenomenon" in the 1980 election; they found that most Americans evaluated media treatment of presidential candidates as fair and impartial, but when voters perceived bias in media coverage, they typically saw the source as opposing their preferred candidate (also see Beck 1991).

In addition, several different research approaches suggest that political sophistication or attentiveness may influence the accuracy of perceptions. For example, it is claimed (Neuman 1986; Zaller 1992) that political attention and political sophistication may increase the public's accuracy in perceiving political cues and thus enhance media effects. Research on political learning from the media seems to reinforce this point (Neuman et al. 1992, chapter 6). This literature suggests a potential interaction between political sophistication and the awareness of political cues. We will explore these possible interactions as part of the perceptual process.

The Third Stage

The last stage of the process involves the effect of media-based information on political choice. The literature stresses that individual characteristics interact with the message to determine media effects, but the nature of this interaction is disputed. For instance, there is a general belief that partisan predispositions condition media effects, but the nature of these influences is debatable (Schmitt-Beck 1996, 276). If we draw a parallel to the party contact literature, for example, then a hostile media may either mobilize or demobilize partisans. Do Democrats reading a paper that prefers Bush shift toward the Republican candidate, or does this news about the opposition motivate them to support Clinton even more? Either option is theoretically possible, but only empirical evidence can determine which is a more accurate description of reality.

Research also suggests that political sophistication may affect the nature of media influences, although the pattern of influence is debated. Scholars such as Zaller (1992) claim that while the politically sophisticated may be more attentive than others to political cues, their greater awareness may create a stock of political information that lessens the media's persuasive effects. Consequently, there are reasons to expect stronger media effects among the less sophisticated—if media cues are perceived in the first place. Conversely, uses and gratification theory suggests that highly interested individuals have a greater need for orientation, which facilitates their attentiveness and media influence (Weaver 1980). Both expectations are plausible, which led Philip Converse (1966) to suggest a curvilinear model of persuasive effects.

Summary

The media are a major source of political information for Americans, but the nature and influence of this information flow are unclear. The sheer number of newspapers and their history of partisanship create great potential for diversity in the message being sent to voters in different locales, but we do not yet know the clarity of the media's partisan content during a presidential election. Moreover, there are fundamental unanswered questions about how the information presented by the press is perceived by the public. How clearly do people perceive partisan cues that may emanate from the press, and what factors shape these perceptions? Finally, does the information gained through the media influence partisan choice? Research provides insights into selective parts of this process, but the whole process has not been examined in a nationally representative project. This may explain the contrasting claims that the media has strong or minimal influence.

Our goal is to examine the workings of the information process to help answer these questions. Yet, ours is also a limited goal. Newspapers are only one part of the media equation in modern campaigns. Most individuals, in fact, claim that television is their primary information source. If the media have a persuasive influence, however, then this should be most apparent for the press because of its partisan history and potential for variation, so this is the focus of our research.

Data Resources

Our study provides an unusual opportunity to look at the complete information flow from the press to the voters. The core of our analysis is the first nationally representative sample of newspaper coverage of a presidential election. We began by randomly selecting 40 counties to represent the American population. For each we then coded the major daily newspaper read by county residents for a sample of days during the 1992 presidential campaign. This produced a sample of newspapers representative of those read by a cross-section of the American public. Our research team analyzed the campaign coverage of these 46 newspapers between Labor Day and election day. We coded 6,537 items, including news coverage of the campaign, news analyses, opinion and editorial articles, political cartoons, and letters to the editor. We coded each for its location in the paper, presentation, and topics covered. More directly relevant to this research, we also coded each item for its overall evaluative content regarding the Bush, Clinton, and Perot campaigns.

This content analysis was done in conjunction with interviews of a nationally representative sample of people who lived in the counties served by these newspapers. A total of 1,318 telephone interviews were completed after the election. Among other questions, we asked respondents what newspaper they read, how attentive they were to political news, and whether they felt their daily newspaper leaned more toward one presidential candidate than another. Finally, we collaborated with a study of television coverage of the 1992 election, and we include some preliminary data from this project.[4]

The analytic strength of our research is based on the potential content variation across the newspapers in the sample. We expected to find significant variation since the range is from the recognized elite press (*New York Times*, *Washington Post*, and *Los Angeles Times*) to small town dailies (such as the *Paris News* in Paris, Texas) and includes newspapers with diverse political leanings. Given this range, we can determine whether readers can accurately perceive the political cues provided through the press and the factors that affect these perceptions. We also can examine whether election reporting influences voter choice and the factors affecting this calculus.

Press Coverage of the 1992 Presidential Campaign

One of the most debated aspects of the 1992 election was the role of the media in the campaign. At the Republican convention the criticisms of the media were almost as loud as the cheers for the party's nominee. Bush held up bumper stickers proclaiming "Annoy the Media: Re-elect George Bush," and there was a lively trade in T-shirts that read "Blame Me: I'm with the Media." Clinton's advisors similarly claimed that the media followed a double standard, focusing on the challenger while exempting Bush from the same kind of scrutiny. When the election was over, Perot's former press aide blamed the media for creating an unfairly negative image of his candidate. Indeed, the subtitle of the 1992 campaign might be "blame it on the media."

The 1992 campaign reflects the continuing debate on the role of the media in modern democracies. What cues does the press provide voters on the strengths and weaknesses of the contestants in an election? How much do they favor one candidate over another? What influence does this information have on electoral choices? The answers have basic implications for the nature of electoral politics and the quality of information upon which voters must decide.

One of our central concerns is whether the press presented a strong partisan message in coverage of the 1992 campaign. We assessed the overall evaluative content of each newspaper article by judging whether it created an image that would be positively or negatively viewed by the respective campaigns.[5] Coders scored each article on a seven-point scale (1 = extremely negative, 7 = extremely positive).[6] For example, a generally positive article on Bush's well-received economic policy speech in Detroit would receive a positive score; but if an article contrasted the speech with Bush's record on the economy and his prior vacillation on economic policy, the story might receive a negative score.

Clearly, there are many elements to election reporting, as discussed in other media analyses (e.g., Bennett 1995; Patterson 1993), and the media's influence may occur in subtle ways. Nevertheless, the overall evaluative content of articles taps a central political cue that the media provide on the election: who is presented positively and who is presented negatively. Like the partisan cues of friends or social reference groups, this aspect of media coverage provides voters with guidance on their electoral choice from a known and generally credible information source. Moreover, it is exactly this aspect of media content that underlies much of the research on media effects on voting preferences (e.g., Erikson 1976; Noelle-Neumann 1984) and occupies the harshest critics of the media.

We first focused on articles that reported news about the campaign.[7] We examined news reports or news analyses in which the campaign was a significant part of the story; this excluded editorials, op/ed pieces, letters to the editor, and other nonnews campaign reports. Table 1 displays the evaluative content of 1992 election coverage. Roughly one-third of all news articles presented a balanced view; that is, the evaluative content favoring one candidate was matched by negative news (or equivalent coverage of a rival campaign) in the same story. Relatively few (roughly one-tenth) news articles contained no evaluative content; these provided straight factual information on the campaign. Articles on the Perot campaign most often lacked clear political cues for the readers.

Most news articles contained at least some evaluative content, such as whether one campaign was doing well or another was faring poorly. In 1992 the imbalance in this reporting was clear: Newspaper coverage of the Bush campaign was predominately negative. Whereas 51% of all news articles conveyed a negative image, only 11% reflected positively on Bush's campaign. By comparison, 17% of news articles on the Clinton campaign were negative, while 43% had positive evaluative content. References to Perot were lacking from most articles until October, when he reentered the campaign. Among the stories on Perot with an evaluative content, the negative outnumbered the positive by three to two.

Journalists may strive for balance and objectivity in the reporting of partisan or election news, but the political cues of the press tend to be more apparent in editorial pages. The last vestige of an earlier tradition of many papers as party propagandists, editorial positions are an important part of a newspaper's political identity. Therefore, we also examined the evaluative content of editorial pages. The second panel of Table 1 presents the evaluative content of editorials and op/ed pieces that explicitly dealt with the 1992 presidential election. These data accentuate the patterns found in news reports. Both Bush and Clinton received more critical editorial treatment, but their relative ranking was similar to that for news stories. The one significant difference is that Perot was treated much more critically in the editorial statements than he was in news reports.

The third panel of Table 1 presents comparable data from television reports on the campaign, which contained less evaluative content than press reports. Roughly half of all television news reports gave balanced views of the candidates or lacked evaluative content, but the general treatment of the candidates was similar to that in the press.[8] Both media presented more favorable reports on the Clinton campaign and more critical reporting of the Bush campaign. Perot received intermediate coverage by both media, and both devoted much less attention to his candidacy. Marion Just and colleagues (1996, chapter 5) used a different method but found a similar overall ranking of the 1992 presidential candidates in their coding of tone in network news and a small set of local newspapers.

Why did the Bush campaign fare so poorly in the media (also see Just et al. 1996, chapter 5)? One explanation lies in campaign style. In a separate coding of actions on the campaign trail, we found that Bush pursued a predominately negative strategy: attacking his opponents, criticizing their politics, and belittling the opposition (e.g., his "Ozone Man" comments about Albert Gore).[9] When Bush was an actor in a story, he pursued such negative actions 33% of the time. In contrast, Clinton was more upbeat and optimistic, advocating new policies and stressing the positive. We found that candidate style was strongly correlated with the overall evaluative content of articles, even though these are conceptually separate aspects of media coverage and were independently coded. A negative approach often yielded a story with negative evaluative content, perhaps because controversy stirred up reaction, especially if journalists tried to balance negative comments with a rejoinder from the other campaign.[10] In short, Clinton ran a presidential-style campaign that benefitted his candidacy; Bush did not.

The Bush campaign further suffered because of its content. The economy was prominent among voters' concerns and campaign coverage (Dalton et al. 1995). Stories about the economy or federal budget showed the Clinton can-

Table 1

The Evaluative Content of Election Coverage

	News reports			Editorial reports			Television reports		
	Bush	Clinton	Perot	Bush	Clinton	Perot	Bush	Clinton	Perot
Extremely positive	0.1%	1.0%	0.1%	0.7%	0.7%	0.8%	0.0%	3.7%	0.7%
—	3.1	17.0	5.8	5.7	9.5	4.2	2.2	15.9	2.5
—	7.7	25.4	13.3	5.9	17.9	10.5	7.1	14.5	7.3
Balanced	31.0	32.5	38.8	21.0	29.1	24.9	24.5	27.8	17.8
—	32.3	11.8	20.5	33.0	23.3	27.0	28.9	10.7	13.1
—	17.7	4.5	9.3	26.2	13.1	24.9	15.0	4.0	10.9
Extremely negative	1.2	.4	.7	3.9	1.3	3.4	3.3	0.0	4.0
No evaluative content	6.8	7.5	11.6	3.6	5.1	4.4	19.0	23.4	43.6
Total	100%	100%	100%	100%	100%	100%	100%	100%	100%
Mean score	3.39	4.44	3.82	3.19	3.84	3.13	3.29	4.51	3.43
(*N* of articles)	(3,039)	(2,823)	(1,523)	(1,094)	(989)	(503)	(453)	(428)	(275)

Note: Table entries are coders' assessment of the evaluative content of articles/stories from the perspective of each campaign. News reports include only news articles and news analyses in which the campaign was a visible part of the story; editorial reports include editorials by the newspaper and op/ed columns presented in the editorial section in which the campaign was discussed; television reports include all stories in which the campaign was visible. Mean scores are based on the 1–7 scale. The dashed lines indicate intermediate values on the 7–point scale, which were not labeled on the coding guide.

didacy in a relatively positive light while the Bush campaign emerged from such stories with a negative image of trying to defend its economic policies or attack its critics—this area showed the largest lead for Clinton in the relative favorability of election coverage. Another important news topic was the campaign itself, and the Bush candidacy also suffered in this regard. Struggling to define an identity for the campaign, reversing strategy, and openly trying to unify the party's diverging factions, the Bush effort hardly could avoid presenting a negative view of itself in 1992. In contrast, the Democrats were, for a change, unified and well organized. Even in the areas that might be considered strengths of the Bush campaign, such as foreign policy and candidate characteristics, Clinton's coverage was more positive than Bush's. In short, the Bush campaign was never able to define an agenda that advantaged its candidate, as it had in 1988. As other media analysts have observed, turning the Bush campaign into a positive news story in 1992 would have required a large positive bias in reporting actual events (Pomper et al. 1993, Weisberg 1994).

We also considered whether the evaluative content of election reporting reflected overt partisan bias by the press. This is an admittedly difficult judgment to make. Negative or positive news is not necessarily an indicator of

Figure 1. **The Evaluative Content of Press News Articles About the 1992 Election**

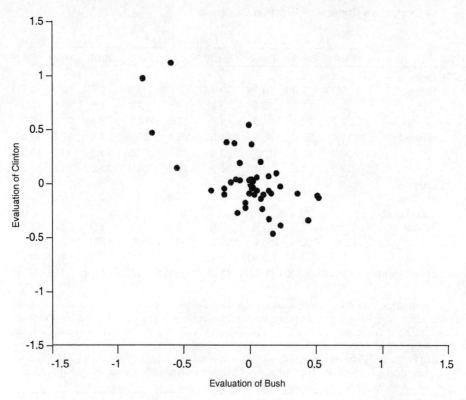

Note: Figure entries are mean scores on the 7-point evaluative measures, expressed as deviations from grand means (Bush mean = 3.41; Clinton mean = 4.45). $N = 46$.

media bias—it may reflect an accurate view of the relative performance of each campaign. To test for possible media bias, we separately coded the tone of coverage to see if journalists added their own evaluations to their reporting of the news.[11] They seldom did so. Almost two-thirds of all news articles were purely descriptive (61.2%); in another one-sixth (16.3%) the journalist had mixed observations about the news being reported. Barely one-sixth (17.3%) included evaluative comments from the reporter, and these were almost evenly balanced between comments that either reinforced or undermined the candidates' statements. Thus, the overall evaluative content of campaign news did not reflect the explicit comments of journalists.

In the end, however, we are primarily concerned with whether the press presented partisan cues in 1992, rather than the source of these cues. Although the press speaks in mixed messages and varied tones, there were significant partisan cues in newspaper coverage of the 1992 presidential campaign.

Notes

1. Another component of this project is the cross-national replication of the basic design by research teams in Germany (Max Kaase, Hans-Dieter Klingemann, Manfred Kuechler, and Franz Urban Pappi), Great Britain (John Curtice, Anthony Heath, and Roger Jowell), Japan (Hiroshi Akuto), and Spain (Richard Gunther, Bradley Richardson, and Jose Ramon Montero).

2. This is a simplified variant of McGuire's (1985) multistep process of information flow. We feel, however, that the three stages we examine constitute the core of the process and represent major empirical elements of media influence.

3. There are political cues and influences of the press beyond the direct partisan cues we examine here (see, e.g., Bennett 1995, Edelman 1988, Patterson 1993).

4. For additional information on the television analyses, see Semetko 1996.

5. We created three separate variables in coding the overall evaluative content of each article in terms of the Bush, Clinton, and Perot campaigns. The instructions for the Bush variable were as follows: "Code the overall content of the article *that involves Bush, Quayle, or the Bush/Quayle campaign* in terms of its favorability or unfavorability to the Bush campaign. Evaluate the article from the perspective of the Bush campaign and assess the content of the article from this perspective. In other words, would the Bush campaign like seeing this article in print? If an article only focuses on Clinton (or other actors), then do not evaluate the Bush/Republican bias. If both candidates/campaigns are mentioned in the same article, then treat these as separate coding judgments; that is, an article might be negative to both candidates, positive to both, or a mix." (This was followed by examples of coding.)

The evaluations were coded on a seven-point scale: 1 = extremely negative, 7 = extremely positive. If the article contained no information that would lead to an evaluation of the candidates or the parties, then it was coded as "no evaluative content" (8).

6. After the first weeks of coding, we conducted intercoder reliability checks. A set of articles was double-coded to assess the reliability of our media measures. The evaluative content measures displayed high levels of reliability for each campaign; unfortunately, the data used to calculate the specific reliability coefficients were lost in a computer malfunction.

7. Each article was coded for its general type. News articles were reports on specific events that had occurred during the previous 48 hours. News analyses went beyond reporting the specific events: often these were reviews of the candidate's position or of campaign strategies.

8. The newspaper and television content data were separately coded by research groups working at the University of California, Irvine, and the University of Michigan. Both groups used the same coding protocol and instructions.

9. The coding instructions were as follows: "This is a judgment of the actions(s) taken by the main actor. First, judge whether the actor is *taking a critical or an affirmative action*; then code the intensity of this action. Not all stories have actors who are taking actions with an evaluative dimension; thus, there are separate codes for balanced and neutral stories. To illustrate: if the essence of the article is 'Bush strongly supports a capital gains tax,' then this is an affirmative action. If the essence of the article is 'Clinton criticizes North American Free Trade Agreement,' this is a critical statement." These evaluations were coded on a seven-point scale (1 = extremely critical, 7 = extremely affirmative).

10. Although this evidence is indirect, it tends to undercut the arguments on the effectiveness of negative campaigning (Ansolabehere and Iyengar 1995); for additional empirical evidence challenging the negative campaigning thesis, see Brians and Wattenberg 1997.

11. This variable was derived from Semetko et al. 1991. It determines whether the journalist added identifiable material that was intended to reinforce or undermine the message of the primary actors in the article. The coding instructions were as follows: "Were there identifiable comments by the reporter that reinforced (or reflected positively on) the candidate's actions or deflated the message of the candidate (negative comments or diminishing comments), or is the reporter making simple descriptive comments or straight comments with no evaluation?"

References

Ansolabehere, Steven, and Shanto Iyengar. 1995. *Going Negative: How Attack Ads Shrink and Polarize the Electorate.* New York: Free Press.

Bagdikian, Ben. 1992. *The Media Monopoly*, 4th ed. Boston: Beacon Press.

Bartels, Lawrence. 1993. "Messages Received: The Political Impact of Media Exposure." *American Political Science Review* 87(June): 267–85.

Beck, Paul A. 1991. "Voters' Intermediation Environments in the 1988 Presidential Contest." *Public Opinion Quarterly* 55(Fall):371–94.

Beck, Paul A., Russell J. Dalton, and Robert Huckfeldt. 1995. *Cross-national Election Studies: United States Study, 1992* [computer file]. ICPSR version. Columbus, OH: Paul A. Beck, Ohio State University/Irvine, CA: Russell J. Dalton, University of California/Bloomington, IN: Robert Huckfeldt, Indiana University [producers], 1993. Ann Arbor, MI: Inter-university Consortium for Political and Social Research [distributor], 1995.

Becker, Lee, and Gerald Kosicki. 1995. "Understanding the Message-producer/Message-receiver Transaction." *Research in Political Sociology* 7:33–62.

Bennett, W. Lance. 1995. *News: The Politics of Illusion*, 3d ed. New York: Longman.

Berelson, Bernard, Paul Lazarsfeld, and William McPhee. 1954. *Voting*. Chicago: University of Chicago Press.

Biocca, Frank. 1988. "Opposing Conceptions of the Audience: The Active and Passive Hemispheres of Mass Communication Theory." In *Communication Yearbook*, ed. J. Anderson. Newbury Park, CA: Sage.

Brians, Craig, and Martin Wattenberg. 1997. "Negative Political Advertising: Mobilizing or Demobilizing?" University of California, Irvine. Typescript.

Chaffee, Steven D., and J. D. Schleuder. 1986. "Measurement and Effects of Attention to News Media." *Human Communication Research* 13(Fall):76–107.

Converse, Philip. 1966. "Information Flow and the Stability of Partisan Attitudes." In *Elections and the Political Order*, ed. A. Campbell et al. New York: Wiley.

Coombs, Steven. 1981. "Editorial Endorsements and Electoral Outcomes." In *More than News*, ed. Michael MacKuen and Steven Coombs. Beverly Hills, CA: Sage Publications.

Curtice, John, and Holli Semetko. 1994. "Does It Matter What the Papers Say?" In *Labour's Last Chance?* ed. Anthony Health, Roger Jowell, and John Curtice. Aldershot, VT: Dartmouth.

Dalton, Russell, Paul Beck, Robert Huckfeldt, and William Koetzle. 1995. "Agenda Setting in the 1992 Campaign: The Flow of Campaign Information." Presented at the annual meetings of the Midwest Political Science Association, Chicago, IL.

Donsbach, Wolfgang. 1990. "Wahrnehmung von redaktionellen Tendenzen durch Zeitungsleser," *Medienpsychologie* 2(Fall):275–301.

Edelman, Murray. 1988. *Constructing the Political Spectacle*. Chicago: University of Chicago Press.

Erikson, Robert. 1976. "The Influence of Newspaper Endorsements in Presidential Elections." *American Journal of Political Science* 20(May):207–34.

Graber, Doris. 1993. *Mass Media and American Politics*, 4th ed. Washington, DC: CQ Press.

Huckfeldt, Robert, Paul Beck, and Russell Dalton. 1995. "Political Environments, Cohesive Social Groups, and the Communication of Public Opinion." *American Journal of Political Science* 39(November):1025–54.

Iyengar, Shanto. 1991. *Is Anyone Responsible?* Chicago: University of Chicago Press.

Iyengar, Shanto, and Donald Kinder. 1987. *News that Matters*. Chicago: Chicago University Press.

Just, Marion, Ann Criegler, Dean Alger, and Timothy Cook. 1996. *Crosstalk: Citizens, Candidates, and the Media in a Presidential Campaign*. Chicago: University of Chicago Press.

Klapper, Joseph. 1960. *The Effects of Mass Communication*. Glencoe, IL: Free Press.

Lazarsfeld, Paul, Bernard Berelson, and Hazel Gaudet. 1948. *The People's Choice*. New York: Columbia University Press.

McGuire, William. 1985. "Attitudes and Attitude Change." In *The Handbook of Political Psychology*, ed. Elliot Aronson and Gardner Lindzey. Vol. 2, 3d ed. New York: Random House.

McLeod, Jack, Gerald Kosicki, and Douglas McLeod. 1994. "The Expanding Boundaries of Political Communication Effects." In *Media Effects*, ed. Jennings Bryant and Dolf Zillmann. Hillsdale, NJ: Lawrence Erlbaum.

Neuman, W. Russell. 1986. *The Paradox of Mass Politics*. Cambridge: Harvard University Press.

Neuman, W. Russell, Marion Just, and Ann Crigler. 1992. *Common Knowledge: News and the Construction of Political Meaning.* Chicago: University of Chicago Press.

Niemi, Richard. 1974. *How Family Members Perceive Each Other.* New Haven: Yale University Press.

Noelle-Neumann, Elisabeth. 1973. "Return to the Concept of Powerful Mass Media." *Studies of Broadcasting* 9(Spring):67–112.

Noelle-Neumann, Elisabeth. 1984. *The Spiral of Silence.* Chicago: University of Chicago Press.

Patterson, Thomas. 1980. *The Mass Media Election.* New York: Praeger.

Patterson, Thomas. 1993. *Out of Order.* New York: Knopf.

Pomper, Gerald, ed. 1993. *The Election of 1992.* Chatham, NJ: Chatham House.

Robinson, John. 1974. "Perceived Media Bias and the 1968 Vote." *Journalism Quarterly* 49(Summer):239–46.

Ross, Lee, Gunter Bierbrauer, and Susan Hoffman. 1976. "The Role of Attribution Processes in Conformity and Dissent." *American Psychologist* 31(February):148–57.

Rubin, Richard. 1981. *Press, Party and Presidency.* New York: Norton.

Sabato, Lawrence. 1991. *Feeding Frenzy.* New York: Free Press.

Schmitt-Beck, Ruediger. 1996. "Mass Media, the Electorate, and the Bandwagon: A Study of Communication Effects on Vote Choice in Germany." *International Journal of Public Opinion Research* 8(Fall):266–91.

Semetko, Holli. 1996. "The Importance of Issues in Election Campaigns." Presented at the annual meetings of the European Consortium for Political Research, Oslo, Norway.

Semetko, Holli, Jay Blumer, Michael Guveuitch, and David Weaver. 1991. *The Formation of Campaign Agendas.* Hillsdale, NJ: Lawrence Erlbaum.

Stanley, Harold, and Richard Niemi. 1994. *Vital Statistics on American Politics.* Washington, DC: CQ Press.

Stempel, Guido, and John Windhauser, eds. 1991. *The Media in the 1984 and 1988 Presidential Campaigns.* Westport, CT: Greenwood Press.

Vallone, Robert, Lee Ross, and Mark Lepper. 1981. "Perceptions of Media Bias in a Presidential Election." Stanford University. Typescript.

Vallone, Robert, Lee Ross, and Mark Lepper. 1985. "The Hostile Media Phenomenon: Biased Perception and Perceptions of Media Bias in Coverage of the Beirut Massacre." *Journal of Personality and Social Psychology* 49(September):577–88.

Weaver, David. 1980. "Audience Need for Orientation and Media Effects." *Communication Research* 7(July):361–76.

Weisberg, Herbert, ed. 1994. *Democracy's Feast.* Chatham, NJ: Chatham House.

Zaller, John. 1992. *The Nature and Origins of Mass Opinion.* New York: Cambridge University Press.

Zaller, John. 1996. "The Myth of Massive Media Impact Revived: New Support for a Discredited Idea." In *Political Persuasion and Attitude Change*, ed. Diane Mutz, Paul Sniderman, and Richard Brody. Ann Arbor: University of Michigan Press.

Discussion Questions

1. What was the unit of analysis in this study?

2. How did the authors code the newspaper stories to form quantitative data? Was their choice of a 7-point scale appropriate?

3. What steps did the authors take to ensure that the coding was reliable and valid?

4. Did the authors have a firm basis for concluding that the data they gathered was representative of the broad universe of newspaper coverage?

Commentary

The first task in a content analysis is the selection of a unit of analysis. Dalton, Beck, and Huckfeldt decided on newspaper articles or stories that focused on the 1992 presidential campaign. Taking stories from a wide array of newspapers across the country, they did not limit themselves to one or two newspapers. Thus, they were on firm ground when they claimed that their findings reflected the state of newspaper coverage in general regarding the 1992 campaign, in which George Bush was running against Bill Clinton and Ross Perot.

As in most content analysis studies that involve some evaluation of the "tone" or position taken in documents, some subjectivity characterized the coding in this study. Coders were asked to judge how positive or negative each story was in terms of its coverage of the respective candidates, giving each story a score of 1 to 7, with 7 indicating "extremely positive" and 1 indicating "extremely negative." Thus, the data consisted of several different kinds of reports for each candidate (news reports, editorial reports, and television reports), with scores indicating what proportion of reports in each category for each candidate was "very negative," "somewhat positive, "neutral," and so forth. Several thousand stories were coded for the study.

The authors explained how coding was sometimes ambiguous. In the case of a generally well-received speech by President Bush about economic policy, for example, a largely supportive story reporting the speech would be coded as positive, but it would be coded as negative "if the article contrasted the speech with Bush's record on the economy and his prior vacillation on economic policy." The point is that assigning a "positive" or "negative" score to a particular news story required that the coders knew something about recent economic policy; it was not enough for them to react simply to the words in the story being coded.

Of course, when this kind of judgment is involved, considerable risks regarding subjectivity emerge. Consequently, the authors used multiple coders and then checked to see if intercoder reliability was acceptable. (Normally, intercoder reliability is checked by confirming that there is a high correlation among the values assigned to the articles by the several coders.) If intercoder reliability turned out to be low, it would indicate that there was no consistent connection between the content of the articles and the different values assigned. In other words, low intercoder reliability would indicate that the coding was essentially random, and the data could not be used as a meaningful measure of the concept.

The authors found that the newspaper stories were consistently more favorable toward Bill Clinton than toward the other candidates. Some analysts have argued that, in 1992, Bill Clinton was "new" while the other candidates were familiar, making Clinton a more attractive news story. Other analysts argue that the results demonstrated partisan bias on the part of journalists. The authors here speculated that the more positive coverage of Clinton was a consequence of Bush's campaign tactics and the state of the economy. Whatever the actual cause, any scientifically grounded analysis of the politics of the media must begin with a valid and reliable method for measuring content, and this study achieved this purpose very well.

Science should not be limited to problems for which usable data happen to be conveniently available. Many important political research problems can be studied only through analysis of such soft sources as documents and newscasts. Content analysis, when properly designed and carried out, can extend the reach of systematic, empirical inquiry.

8 Sampling

Much political research involves testing hypotheses about large numbers of people, political activities, units of government, or policies. In such cases, it is usually impractical to collect data concerning the entire population or universe in which we are interested. The solution is to study a subset or **sample** of cases drawn from that population. Underlying this tactic is the assumption that we can learn something about the larger group in question by studying a sample of its members. Effective sampling enables us to do just this.

It is difficult to exaggerate the importance of sampling. If, for example, we are interested in measuring the attitudes of "American voters" on some particular policy or issue, it is not particularly helpful to proceed by questioning a set of persons who are, for one reason or another, easily accessible to us. Just any sample will not do. If we are to make accurate and meaningful inferences about the population involved, our sample must be representative of that population. If it is not, if it is different in some important way from the population, our results can be useless.

Perhaps the most infamous example of erroneous findings resulting from flawed sampling was a *Literary Digest* poll undertaken during the 1936 presidential campaign between the Democratic candidate, Franklin Roosevelt, and the Republic candidate, Alf Landon. Based on that poll, which reflected the opinions of more than one million potential voters, the *Digest* predicted a landslide victory for Landon. The actual outcome was a landslide victory for Roosevelt. Greatly embarrassed, the *Literary Digest* went out of business shortly thereafter.

This spectacular failure was a result of faulty sampling. In conducting its poll, the *Digest* contacted a sample of voters drawn from telephone directories and automobile registration lists. The flaw in this procedure lay in the fact that ownership of telephones and cars was far less common in 1936 than today. Cars and telephones were primarily owned by wealthier voters, who were also far more likely to be Republicans. In short, the *Digest*'s sample was not representative of the larger population. It did not, therefore, give the magazine useful information about the population.

Why and How Sampling Works: The Random Sample

The underlying principle on which all sampling techniques are based is that of the **simple random sample**. If our sample is truly random, every case in the population will have an equal chance of being selected for inclusion in our sample.

Observing this principle does not mean we can be absolutely certain that any given sample is representative of the population from which it is drawn. The sample will nearly always differ in some way from the population it is intended to represent; this difference is the **sampling error**. However, the use of random sampling allows us to calculate the **probability** that any characteristic or relationship we observe within the cases in that sample will also be found in the population. When we have genuinely random samples, we are able to draw inferences about the population by studying a sample. Further, while we can never be absolutely certain that any inferences we draw about a population by studying a sample are correct, we can adjust our sampling procedures to produce almost any desired level of confidence in our findings.

If we have a random sample, the size of the sample relative to the population is the most important factor in determining how confident we are of our sample's representativeness. Samples should be large enough to help us make confident inferences. How large is large enough depends on several factors: (a) the desired level of confidence, (b) the desired level of precision, and (c) the variability within the population.

In general, there is a direct relationship between sample size, on one hand, and the precision of our results and the confidence we have in them, on the other. The larger the sample, the more precise our results and the greater our confidence in any inferences we might draw about the population. Thus, if we desire to have a very high degree of confidence in the accuracy of our results, we will need a larger sample than would otherwise be the case.

At the same time, the sample should be small enough to make the research process efficient and timely. Larger samples use more resources and require more time for data collection and analysis, leading to delays or shortfalls that may threaten the study.

Thus, there are no automatic answers to the question of sample size. Rather, the appropriate sample size depends on the purpose of our research, for it is our purposes that determine the needed level of confidence. Sometimes we want to be able to make inferences about parts of the sample. If so, the sample will have to be large enough to ensure that a meaningful number of cases of each relevant type is included. If, for example, we are interested in comparing the opinions of black voters to those of white voters, our sample would have to be large enough to ensure that it contains a representative sub-sample of both groups.

Confidence Level and Confidence Interval

But what do we mean by confidence when discussing sampling procedures? This simple everyday term has two distinct aspects when discussing sampling. The first of these is the degree of confidence we wish to have that our findings—derived from studying our sample—do, in fact, apply to the intended population. This is known as the **confidence level**. Confidence levels are usually expressed in decimal form with the number involved representing the probability that our sample is representative of the larger population. Thus a confidence level of 0.95 means there is a 95 percent chance that the relationship or characteristic detected in our sample also exists in the population (and a 5 percent chance that it exists only in the sample, as a result of having randomly selected a sample that just happens to have this characteristic when the population does not).

There is another type of confidence involved in sampling, however, and that is the **confidence interval**. The confidence interval refers to the accuracy with which we can predict the value of a given variable in the population based on our observation of the sample. The confidence interval is usually expressed as a percentage. Thus a confidence interval of "3 percent" (read as plus or minus 3 percent), for example, would mean we are confident that (at some specified level) our sample measurements are within 3 percent of the figures for the actual population.

It is the researcher's task, then, to take into account the desired confidence level and confidence interval when determining the size of the sample to be drawn. It is important to note, however, that for any given sample there is an inverse relationship between the confidence level and confidence interval. That is to say, once we have selected a sample size adequate to yield the desired degree of confidence and precision, we must choose how to present our results. The choice is between (a) a narrower confidence interval with a lower confidence level or (b) a wider confidence interval with a higher confidence level. For example, we may be able to say: "We are 99 percent confident that 58 percent of the citizens in this state support the McCain-Feingold campaign finance reform bill, plus or minus 6 points," or "We are 95 percent confident that 58 percent of the citizens in this state support the McCain-Feingold campaign finance reform bill, plus or minus 4 points."

The rub here is that, in most cases, we would probably prefer both to minimize the confidence interval and maximize the confidence level. That is, we would prefer to have both precise estimates of population characteristics *and* a high degree of confidence that our results are representative of the target population. As a general rule, however, this is not possible. We can, of course, always choose to increase our sample size, since larger samples result in increases in both types of confidence. For a given sample size, however, confidence and precision are inversely related.

An example of the relationship between confidence intervals and confidence levels may be helpful. Suppose that we had sent questionnaires regarding future presidential candidates to 100 persons selected at random from the population of a rural county with 100,000 residents. Suppose too (for simplicity's sake) that all 100 people returned their questionnaires. When we tabulate the returned questionnaires, we find that 55 percent of these respondents indicated that their first choice for president is Hillary Clinton.

In trying to determine the level of her support in this county, how much should we rely on the fact that we found that 55 percent of those in our sample indicated support for Hillary Clinton? Would we be justified, on the basis of these 100 survey responses, in claiming that Hillary Clinton is supported by more than half of the voters in this county? Is there a way to determine whether the results of our little survey are representative of actual preferences among the larger number of voters who make up the population of this county?

If our sample is truly random, there certainly is. An experienced pollster would, in fact, be able to answer this question in words something like the following. "And so, based on our survey, we are 95 percent certain that between 45 percent and 64.9 percent of the voters in the county support Hillary Clinton." As an alternative, the same pollster might note that he or she is 99 percent certain that between 42.5 percent and 67.25 percent of the voters in the county are Hillary Clinton supporters. In short, given the fact that 55 percent of our random sample of 100 citizens stated support for her, our pollster would be able to estimate, with a specified level of confidence, the likely proportion of Hillary Clinton supporters in the county population within a given range, or confidence interval. Note too the inverse relationship between the confidence level and confidence interval in our pollster's predictions. As the former increases, from 95 percent to 99 percent, the latter becomes broader, or less precise. Such results are characteristic of inferences derived from sample data.

Standard Error

How is our pollster able to make such statements? The answer lies in his or her familiarity with the basic principles of sampling, which simply constitute a special application of probability theory, and most especially an understanding of the concept of **standard error**, a statistic that refers to the difference between the values we observe in our sample and those characteristic of the target population.

We can calculate the standard error from the following formula:[1]

---

1. The $1 - n/N$ term is essentially 1 when the population is large. It is normally omitted from the formula unless the population is small. To illustrate what is meant by large and small, $1 - n/N = 0.999$ in this example. (Since the sample size, or n, is 100, and the population size, or N, is 100,000, the arithmetic is 1 minus the quotient of $100 \div 100,000$.) Since 0.999 is close to 1, and since multiplying something by 1 leaves it unchanged, the term $1 - n/N$ can be omitted in this case, and, for that matter, in most political science research.

$$SE = \sqrt{\left(1 - \frac{n}{N}\right)\left(\frac{pq}{n-1}\right)} \qquad (1)$$

n is the sample size (100), N is the population size (100,000), p is the proportion of observed cases with the quality or characteristic in question (here, the proportion of Hillary Clinton supporters in the sample, or 0.55), and q is simply $1 - p$ (or 0.45). Inserting these numbers from our example into the formula, our pollster would quickly determine that the standard error (SE) for this particular case is 4.9 percent.

The arithmetic is as follows:

$$SE = \sqrt{\left(1 - \frac{100}{100,000}\right)\left(\frac{(0.55)(0.45)}{100-1}\right)} \qquad (2)$$
$$SE = 5\%$$

What does this mean, and how does this help us? The short answer to this question is that once we know the standard error, we can use it to calculate our confidence interval at any specified confidence level. Thus, assuming only that our sample is truly random, we can, once our results are in hand, calculate the standard error of those results and use that statistic to determine a confidence interval for any specified confidence level.

A complete explanation of how and why this is so requires a grasp of concepts such as standard distributions and the normal curve, not to mention a variety of technical details that lie beyond our purposes here. An intuitive explanation on the other hand may be helpful to many readers.

In terms of our example, we are certain that 55 percent of the people *in our sample* are Hillary Clinton supporters. What we want to know, however, is what this tells us about the proportion of citizens *in the whole county* who support her. Suppose, just for the purpose of discussion, that the real proportion of county voters who support Hillary Clinton is 52 percent. (We could never know this, of course, unless we contact every one of the county residents.) If 52 percent is the actual number of Hillary Clinton supporters, how likely is it that a random sample of 100 voters drawn from this population would contain *no* Clinton supporters? Clearly this is possible (we know that there are many thousands in the county who oppose her), but not terribly likely. Similarly, it is equally unlikely that we would draw a random sample of 100 voters from this population that consists *entirely* of Clinton supporters. It is, in short, highly unlikely that we would randomly select 100 persons, all of whom were either Clinton supporters or opponents, from a population in which slightly more than half of the members are actually supporters.

To put it another way, if dozens of researchers independently selected random samples of 100 persons each from this county, we would expect that very few of these samples drawn would profoundly under- or over-represent

Figure 8.1   **Distribution of Samples with Different Levels of Support for Hillary Clinton**

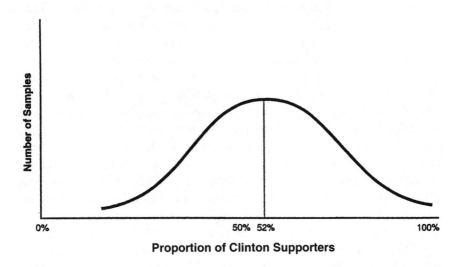

Proportion of Clinton Supporters

the actual proportion of Clinton supporters. Rather, the proportion of Clinton supporters in most of the samples we would draw—*assuming the samples involved are truly random*—would be fairly close to the actual proportion of Clinton supporters in the county population. If we were to draw an infinite number of random samples from this population and were then to graph the proportion of Clinton supporters contained in each of these samples, the resulting graph would take the form of a curve like that in Figure 8.1. (The horizontal axis indicates the proportion of Clinton supporters, and the vertical axis indicates how many samples with each proportion might be drawn.) This curve would be centered over the real proportion of Clinton supporters in the population.

The curve in Figure 8.1 is known as a **normal curve**. Its shape can be readily understood in terms of our example. What the shape of the curve shows us is that while it is *possible* to select a given sample containing an extremely unrepresentative proportion of Clinton supporters from our hypothetical county population, we are unlikely to draw very many such samples. In other words, the probability of our drawing a sample containing any given proportion of Clinton supporters increases as that proportion approaches the real proportion in the population. Thus, the largest single number of samples drawn would be those in which the proportion of Clinton supporters equals the real proportion. The second largest number would be those containing the next closest proportions (on either side of the real percentage); the third largest would be those containing the third closest, and so forth. This is entirely a matter of the laws of probability.

When graphed, the resulting shape, as we have noted, is a normal curve. Of course, it would be wasteful and expensive to draw dozens of 100-person samples. However, if our one sample is really random, we are able to say that *if we had drawn dozens of such random samples*, the proportion of Clinton supporters in the samples would form a normal curve. The normal curve has a convenient property that allows us to draw inferences about the population based on observation and measurement of our sample: 95 percent of the cases it represents (here the "cases" are our infinite number of separately selected 100-person samples) will lie within two standard errors of the mean (the real proportion of Clinton supporters in the county). Thus, having calculated our standard error as 4.9 percent, simple arithmetic enables us to emulate our pollster by saying, "We are 95 percent certain that the proportion of Clinton supporters in the *county* (the thing we actually care about) is between 45 percent and 64.8 percent" (i.e., 55 percent—*the pro-Clinton proportion found in our sample*—plus or minus two standard errors). Similarly, if we want still more confidence (and we are willing to give up some precision to get it), we can be 99 percent certain that the real proportion of Clinton supporters in the county is no further than approximately 2.5 times the standard error away from the sample figure of 55 percent (or, between 42.5 percent and 67.25 percent).

We can infer several other things about the impact of sample size on confidence levels and intervals by reexamining our formula. What happens, for example, as n (our sample size) increases? The answer, as a few quick calculations will confirm, is that as n increases, the standard error gets smaller—assuming all other factors remain the same. If we had responses from a random sample of 1,000, for example, our standard error would be only 1.6 percent. If so, and if we were to find that 55 percent of the citizens in this 1,000-person sample support Clinton, we could be 95 percent certain the proportion of Clinton supporters in the population is between 51.8 percent and 58.2 percent. In short, increasing our sample size would increase the accuracy of our result—by reducing the width of our confidence interval.

National political opinion polls usually report their results as having a "margin of error of three percentage points." This is, strictly speaking, incorrect. It has simply become conventional to use a confidence level of 95 percent, and it requires a sample size of only about 1,200 cases to produce a confidence interval of 3 percent with 95 percent certainty. A random sample of approximately 1,200 persons produces findings that are precise enough to be of practical usefulness while also being relatively inexpensive to implement, important considerations for polls that have to be taken daily or weekly during a national election campaign.

Further increases in sample size would have a similar but diminishing effect. If we increased our sample size to 10,000, for example, we would greatly increase our research costs (by a factor of roughly ten) in return for which we would reduce our standard error to 0.5 percent. Given this, it is unlikely we would find such an increase in our sample size cost effective. Increasing our costs by a factor of ten to obtain a one-point improvement in our standard error would probably not represent an attractive tradeoff. As always, however, our final decision would be determined by our purposes and, of course, by the resources available.

Alternatives to the Simple Random Sample

Although the random sample remains the ideal, there are alternatives that must serve in some research designs. This is fortunate, because opportunities to use a simple random sample are relatively rare in political research. An unbiased, complete list of the population may not be available, or such a list may not be available in a convenient form. Logistical or practical difficulties may intrude. For example, genuine random sampling prohibits the substitution of cases even if, as can easily occur, this results in a sample containing many individuals who are physically difficult to contact or live at great distances from one another.

For this reason, much research, especially survey research, involves the use of **cluster sampling** or, as it is sometimes known, **multistage random area sampling**. In cluster sampling, we first divide the population into a series of units, each of which contains more than one individual member of the population. Our sample is then drawn by first selecting the units to be sampled and then further breaking those units down into one or more levels of subunits until we reach a level at which the total number of subunits—each of which still contains more than one individual member of the population—roughly corresponds to our desired sample size. We then select one individual member from each of these subunits for inclusion in our sample.

Cluster sampling has several advantages. It enables us to concentrate our energies on a relatively few geographic areas of manageable size. Further, it allows some flexibility in the selection of the individual member to be included in the sample while preserving most of the statistical benefits of randomization. It is particularly useful in dealing with large, mobile populations and is commonly employed in survey research.

Stratified sampling is another useful alternative to the simple random sample. Stratified sampling is helpful when (a) we wish to study in detail a specific subgroup found in our target population, and (b) the size of that subgroup relative to the population is so small we cannot be sure a simple random sample of reasonable size will contain a useful number of subjects from the subgroup. In stratified sampling, we divide the population into several **strata** and then randomly select members from each stratum for our sample. In so doing, we are, in effect, drawing multiple random samples, one from each of the strata identified. This must be taken into account when evaluating our findings and stating our conclusions. Nonetheless, stratified sampling can, under the right circumstances, serve as an approximation of a simple random sample while ensuring our ability to obtain detailed information about a small subgroup within our general population.

————————————— Excerpt 11 —————————————

Public participation in our civic life is disappointingly low. Historians tell us that voting turnout during the first part of the twentieth century was quite high, often reaching 80 percent, despite the existence of pre-modern transportation systems and lower literacy rates. Turnout rates declined after the early 1960s, and now only around half of eligible voters bother to go to the polls during presidential elections. Other forms of participation also appear to be weak and intermittent.

Scholars from many fields have studied the problem, suggesting several different explanations. Some are convinced that the shift to "investigative journalism" by the print and broadcast media created great cynicism among the public. Others argue that the country has never recovered from the divisiveness of the Vietnam War, the Watergate scandals, and the violent struggles of the 1960s. Still others point to the apparent failure of many government initiatives to provide solutions to poverty and racism as reasons that people are "turned off" by politics.

Another possible factor is the rapid expansion of suburbanization. Millions of Americans began to flee urban residential neighborhoods shortly after World War II, when a tremendous growth in automobile ownership coincided with extensive highway construction. The trend has never abated, and now more Americans live in suburbs than in central cities. It is arguable that living in suburbs, with their reduced population density and their separation from urban political problems, leads many citizens to emphasize private interests over the political concerns that would otherwise motivate them to become involved in civic life.

It is clear that, in rough historical terms, the growth of suburbanization has coincided with the decline in civic involvement. This fact is enough for some critics of suburbia to conclude that suburbanization is, in fact, the *cause* of declining civic involvement. However, Professor J. Eric Oliver was convinced that the issue must be addressed through careful scientific research. His study was designed to compare civic involvement in cities and suburbs and therefore involved some important aspects of sampling.

City Size and Civic Involvement in Metropolitan America

J. Eric Oliver, *Princeton University*

American Political Science Review 94, no. 2 (June 2000): 361–373. Copyright © 2000 by the American Political Science Association. Reprinted with permission.

Since the time of Aristotle, political theorists have puzzled over a difficult question: What is the optimal size for a democratic polity? In the 1967 presidential address to the American Political Science Association, Robert A. Dahl (1967, 960) offered an answer: Most democracies are too big to allow citizens actively to determine the "vital aspects of their lives in common." Small polities, however, often lack the capacity to address meaningful political issues. The idealized unit, Dahl reasoned, must be able to achieve collective goals but avoid the "consummatory" participation of the modern nation-state. Since we seem "destined to live in cities," Dahl proposed dividing large metropolitan areas into federations of municipalities between 50,000 and 200,000 in size. These cities would be small enough to facilitate civic participation but large enough to generate meaningful political discourse.

Over the past fifty years, Dahl's vision has become a reality. Most Americans now live in small to medium-sized cities or "places" within large, densely populated metropolitan areas.[1] Since 1950, the proportion living in metropolitan areas has risen from 57% to 75%. Yet, proportionally fewer Americans reside in large cities: Less than 19% currently live in cities of more than 250,000, compared to 23% in 1950; 56% now live in metropolitan places smaller than 250,000, compared to 34% in 1950 (U.S. Bureau of the Census 1975, 1993). America has changed from a country bifurcated between isolated rural towns and big central cities to one that consists largely of small and medium-sized suburbs.

The civic consequences of this shift are unclear and the empirical research on the civic effects of city size is inconclusive. On the one hand, the migration to smaller, suburban places has coincided with a well-documented decline in such activities as voting and organizational membership (Putnam 1995; Teixeira 1992; Wattenberg 1996). This suggests that participation is lower in smaller, suburban places, a finding supported by Fischer (1976). On the other hand, several studies report that residents of smaller places are more likely to participate (Kasarda and Janowitz 1974; Nie, Powell, and Prewitt 1969; Verba and Nie 1972). Yet, all these works fail to provide definitive evidence: Fischer's estimates do not control for many important individual-level characteristics; Kasarda and Janowitz and Nie, Powell, and Prewitt compare only "urban" and "rural" places; and Verba and Nie's results, from a sample of only 120 cases, are not statistically significant. Moreover, all these studies use data more than 30 years old, and city size has not been analyzed in the participation research since then, which means that the effects of city size are unmeasured relative to the recent trends in suburbanization.

America's metropolitan expansion also calls into question many key assumptions about city size in classical democratic theory. For instance, does it have the same effect in a metropolitan setting of contiguous municipal boundaries, uninterrupted land development, and interdependent local economies? Does Dahl's ideal democratic city of 50,000 foster as much civic engagement if it is in the middle of greater Los Angeles or isolated on the Kansas plains? Previous work has not examined these important questions. To complicate matters, most suburban places are not like large cities in miniature but are highly differentiated in social composition and land usage, characteristics that also shape civic participation. Oliver (1999) finds that people in affluent suburbs participate less than people in heterogeneous, middle-income places and that the effects of city affluence are greater than population size. Indeed, population size may no longer be the most important civic characteristic of a city.

The size issue also remains enigmatic partly because of the absence of any general theory on the relationship between social environments and political participation. Most social theorists either ignore civic participation (Simmel [1905] 1969; Tonnies 1988; Weber [1905] 1958; Wirth [1938] 1969) or do not link their speculations to models of why people participate in civic processes (Dahl 1967; Dahl and Tufte 1973; Montesequieu [1748] 1991; Rousseau [1772] 1994). Indeed, latter-day democratic theorists offer mostly vague and contradictory expectations about how polity size directly shapes civic involvement. Theorists of participation, meanwhile, mostly focus on individual-level factors and rarely take social context into account (Olson 1965; Rosenstone and Hansen 1994; Verba, Scholzman, and Brady 1995; Wilson 1972). Despite Lewin's (1935) near-axiom that human behavior is a function of both individual and environmental characteristics, most studies of civic participation concentrate on models of isolated, rational actors or on hypotheses validated by individual-level survey data. To establish causal linkages between city size and participation, a theoretical bridge between studies of context and participation is needed.

This article explores the civic ramifications of city size, particularly in contemporary metropolitan and rural settings. I start by outlining a theory about the relationship between social environments and civic activity in the metropolis using a "civic voluntarism" model. Then, based on a data set constructed from the 1990 Citizen Participation Study (Verba et al. 1995) and the 1990 Census, I estimate four types of civic activity and find them all to be lower in larger places, a relationship that occurs irrespective of the metropolitan context. Large size depresses participation partly because residents are less likely to be mobilized and are less interested in local political life. These findings demonstrate the civic relevance of municipal boundaries in an era of metropolitan expansion: City boundaries define communities, and smaller places are civically richer. Before celebrating the civic virtues of sub-urbanization, however, other city-level characteristics need consideration. Tom Hayden notwithstanding, smaller cities are not simply more baloney; rather, they are distinct cuts of meat, some more civically palatable than others.

Civic Voluntarism and Social Contexts

Previous theories on the civic effects of city size are inconclusive partly be-cause they fail to explain which factors influence participation and how they may be shaped by the social environment. For example, Dahl and Tufte (1973) make a series of deductive inferences about civic participation in large and small democratic units. They reason that "smaller democracies provide more opportunity for citizens to participate . . . but, larger democracies provide citizens opportunities to participate in decisions . . . to control the most im-portant aspects of their situation" (p. 13). In their framework, a city's popula-tion does not affect the nature of the civic act: Casting a ballot or contacting a government official is essentially the same in sprawling Houston as in tiny Startzville. Rather, place size shapes participation indirectly by altering the opportunities for involvement. But Dahl and Tufte assume that smaller places provide more opportunities for participation and that availability stimulates involvement. These assumptions, however, are not based on any general theory or empirical tests. Dahl and Tufte do not demonstrate whether or how a polity's size changes the opportunities for participation, whether opportunities really do influence involvement, or what intervening characteristics may be operat-ing. Such criticisms hold equally for other theoretical speculations (e.g., Montesequieu [1748] 1991; Rousseau [1772] 1994; Weber [1905] 1958; Wirth [1938] 1969). To overcome these deficiencies, the individual determinants of participation must be identified, and hypotheses then must be formulated on whether they differ between large and small places.

What are the determinants of political participation? A voluminous litera-ture offers a wide range of theories (e.g., Olson 1965; Rosenstone and Hansen 1993; Teixeira 1992; Verba and Nie 1972; Wilson 1972; Wolfinger and Rosenstone 1980), but I use Verba, Schlozman, and Brady's (1995) "civic voluntarism" model. According to their framework, political participation is a function of individual resources, interest, and mobilization; people are more likely to participate if they have skills and knowledge, if they are more psy-chologically engaged, or if they are recruited by others. Although not ex-plored in the original formulation of the model, each factor varies with a person's social environment. Psychological engagement in community life is clearly determined by context: When people feel they have more in common with neighbors or have a greater sense of efficacy, interest in local affairs is greater (Fischer 1976). Political mobilization varies with patterns of social interaction: When people are more familiar with one another, they are more likely to talk about politics and recruit others for action (Huckfeldt and Sprague 1995). Context even shapes the influence of individual resources: When participation is more difficult, the relevance of individual knowledge and skills grows (Wolfinger and Rosenstone 1980). By examining variations in political resources, interest, and mobilization between small and large municipalities, the causal connection between city size and participation can be specified.

Previous research in this area has arrived at strikingly contradictory conclusions. On one side are those who argue that both psychological engagement and mobilization increase with a city's population. Dahl (1967) and Deutsch (1961) believe larger places have more compelling issues to attract citizen attention; Fischer (1995) and Suttles (1972) find that larger places host more subcultures that mobilize citizens; Milbrath and Goel (1982) claim that greater media attention to big city politics stimulates citizen interest; and Dahl and Tufte (1973) speculate that larger polities have a higher level of political competition that mobilizes citizens and makes their participation more efficacious.

On the other side are those who suggest that a large population is a detriment. Early classics of urban sociology (Simmel [1905] 1969; Tonnies 1988; Weber [1905] 1958; Wirth [1938] 1969) argue that the size, density, and heterogeneity of larger places dissolve the social and psychological bonds that exist between neighbors in small towns. Surrounded by more strangers and greater social uncertainty, urbanites putatively seek psychic refuge in their primary social relations, shy away from formalized social contact, or feel content as "bystanders" to the political process (Finifter 1970; Latane and Darley 1970; Nie, Powell, and Prewitt 1969; Reisman 1953; Verba and Nie 1972). In addition, people in larger places are less likely to know their neighbors, have mutual friends, and see acquaintances in public settings (Fischer 1982; Lofland 1973), which in turn may inhibit political mobilization (Huckfeldt and Sprague 1995). Finally, even though the act of participating may be the same in different cities, the costs of doing so may vary. Larger cities require a more complex bureaucracy, have greater spatial distance between city offices and citizens, and have elected officials who represent more people, all of which may increase the difficulty of participation and the importance of individual resources (Hansen, Palfrey, and Rosenthal 1987).

These issues are further complicated when one considers that most Americans do not live in isolated towns but within larger metropolitan areas. Most studies designate large cities as "urban" or "metropolitan" and small places as rural, but Dahl's speculations suggest that municipal boundaries are important in their own right for defining community and patterns of social interaction. Thus, when considering population size, the effects of living in a municipality must be distinguished from living in a large urbanized area.

On the one hand, if city boundaries are unimportant amid a surrounding urbanized population, then the effects of metropolitan areas should both replicate and overshadow the effects of city size; it should not matter whether people are partitioned by the invisible walls of a municipal border. The important contextual element, in this instance, is the number of people in a given geographic region, not simply the number within a particular municipal jurisdiction. The major contextual influence on civic involvement will be the size of the metropolitan area and not the particular city, and the largest differences in participation will occur between small rural places and large metropolitan regions.

On the other hand, if city boundaries are important for defining the character of local political engagement or patterns of social interaction, then the metropolitan environment should not alter the place-size effects. Differences in participation between people in large and small places should occur irrespective of the size of the surrounding metropolis because political engagement and mobilization arise primarily from the community as defined by the city boundaries. If this is true, then residents of small places in both rural and metropolitan settings should have equal levels of participation relative to their counterparts in large cities.

In sum, if larger places stimulate citizen interest and nourish a variety of subcultural social networks, then participation should increase with population size; if greater size produces alienation and social disconnection or makes involvement more costly, then participation should decline with population gains. But the effects of metropolitan contexts may hinge on the importance of city boundaries for defining social behavior and political attitudes. If the boundaries are important, then the size of the surrounding area will not alter the effects of city size; if the boundaries are less important, then metropolitan effects will supplant the relationship between city size and participation, and larger differences should exist between rural and metropolitan areas.

Data and Analysis

Most data on citizen activity are either aggregate (e.g., statistics on precinct or county voting) or individual (e.g., surveys), which greatly restricts contextual induction (Achen and Shively 1995). An appropriate test of the effect of contemporary metropolitan social contexts requires information not only about individuals and their context but also a sample from a wide variety of places. To meet these criteria, I constructed a data set from the 1990 American Citizen Participation Study (CPS) (Verba et al. 1995) and the 1990 Census (U.S. Bureau of the Census 1991). The CPS is a national, cross-sectional survey of the participatory activities of the American public; among the approximately 15,000 respondents in the screener set, 2,500 took part in in-depth follow-up interviews. For this analysis, I use data from the follow-up interview portion of the CPS. These respondents were drawn from more than 800 different places. In order to measure the effects of social context, the respondents' residence was identified, and data from the 1990 Census for the summary level of place (i.e., city) were matched for each case.[2] With this individual-ized census information for such a large nationwide sample, the relationship between measures of social context (e.g., population size, median income) and individual behavior can be estimated while controlling for individual-level determinants, such as education, income, and age.

After constructing an appropriate cross-level data set, I then had to decide which civic behaviors to examine. These range from voting to joining volun-tary organizations (Putnam 1993; Verba, Schlozman, and Brady 1995), and studying the relation of all to city size is impossible in a single article. More-over, not all civic activities are equally susceptible to contextual influences. For example, social context should influence turnout in local elections more than in national elections. To estimate the consequences of city size, civic behaviors should be local in orientation, politically directed, and foster the type of social bonds that form the basis of civil society (Putnam 1993).

I chose four variables that best meet these criteria: *Contacting Locally Elected Officials*, *Attending Community Board Meetings*, *Attending Meetings of Voluntary Organizations*, and *Voting in Local Elections*. All these activities are not influenced by social context in exactly the same way, but all represent important aspects of locally oriented participation. Contacting officials and voting are the two most direct ways people communicate their preferences about local policies to local leaders. Attending the meetings of community boards and voluntary organizations, as Putnam (1995) argues, sustains the "norms and networks of reciprocity" upon which civil society is built.[3] Fur-thermore, participation in each of these activities should be sensitive to the incentives and opportunities discussed above. If all these acts are influenced by interest and mobilization, as Verba, Schlozman, and Brady (1995) suggest, then the effects of city size should be consistent across all.

Findings

I start by comparing average rates of participation in all four civic activities across five categories of city size (less than 5,000; 5,000 to 50,000; 50,000 to 250,000; 250,000 to one million; and more than one million); residents of metropolitan and rural areas are separated in the first two categories.[4] The participation measures are based on self-reports. Contacting officials and at-tending meetings are scored dichotomously (1 if the respondent had engaged in the activity in the past year, 0 otherwise); voting in local elections is mea-sured on a five-point scale (1 = never, to 5 = always).

With the exception of voting in local elections, the average rate of partici-pation in all types of civic activity tends to decline in larger places, although this effect is primarily limited to residents of metropolitan areas. As depicted in Figure 1, 40% of residents of metropolitan places of less than 5,000 report contacting local officials, compared to 30% in places between 5,000 and 50,000 and 25% in places of more than one million. Meeting attendance is 13 per-

Figure 1 **Average Rate of Participation in Four Local Civic Activities by City Size for Rural and Metropolitan Areas**

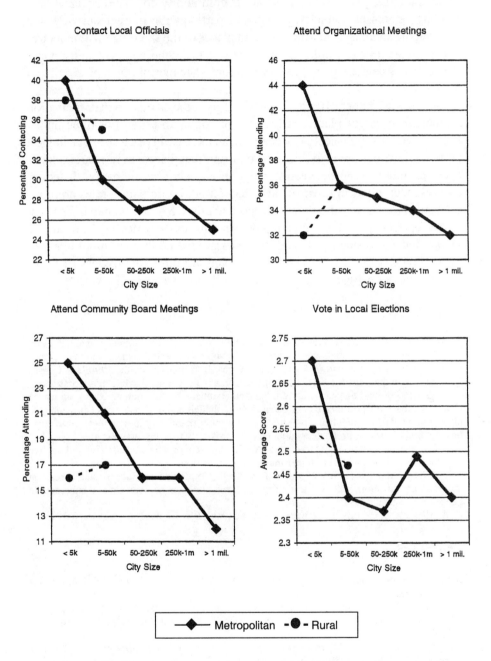

centage points lower in the largest than in the smallest places for community boards, and 12 percentage points lower for voluntary organizations. The average local voting score declines by .2 points between metropolitan places of less than 5,000 and those between 50,000 and 250,000 but then levels off.

Among residents of rural towns, contacting and voting rates decline between small and larger places, but attendance at community board or organizational meetings increases. On average, rates of participation in civic activities are lower in the smallest rural towns than in places of the same size within metropolitan areas. For example, the average rate of attending community board meetings is 9 percentage points lower in rural than metropolitan places of less than 5,000.

On the whole, these figures support the hypothesis that civic participation diminishes in larger places, at least in metropolitan areas. For three out of four indicators, steady decline occurs with an increase in place size. The highest participation rates are in the smallest metropolitan places. In rural areas, however, the relationship between population and civic participation differs in two respects. First, in towns of less than 5,000, participation rates are typically much lower in rural than metropolitan areas. Second, unlike the pattern in metropolitan areas, participation does not necessarily decline as rural size grows. Indeed, residents of rural places larger than 5,000 are more likely to attend board and organization meetings and are only slightly less likely to vote or contact officials than are rural dwellers in very small towns.

Notes

1. By "place" or city, I refer to all incorporated municipalities, although generally city refers to larger municipalities and place refers to smaller ones. Rural is measured as residence in any county that is not part of a metropolitan area. Borrowing from the 1990 U.S. Census (U.S. Bureau of the Census 1991), a metropolitan area is any county that contains a central city of at least 50,000 and the surrounding urbanized counties, that is, counties identified by the Census to have large portions of contiguous areas with high population density. Consequently, places of up to 50,000 population (the first two categories of city size used in this analysis) can be classified as rural or urban depending on their proximity to a metropolitan area.

2. Thirteen percent of the interviewees ($N = 2,500$) were omitted because they did not live in identifiable municipalities or under municipal jurisdictions.

3. Given Putnam's (1995) speculations about the importance of face-to-face contact in voluntary organizations, I chose meeting attendance rather than membership as the measure to gauge local "social capital."

4. All analyses for this article were conducted with *SPSS for Windows*, version 8.0.

References

Achen, Christopher, and W. Phillips Shively. 1993. *Cross-Level Inference.* Chicago: University of Chicago Press.
Berry, Brian. 1972. "Latent Structure of the American Urban System." In *City Classification Handbook: Methods of Applications*, ed. Brian Berry and Katherine Smith. New York: Wiley-Interscience.
Berry, Jeffrey M., Kent E. Portney, and Ken Thomson. 1993. *The Rebirth of Urban Democracy.* Washington, DC: Brookings Institution.
Bott, Elizabeth. 1971. *Family and Social Networks.* New York: Free Press.
Dahl, Robert. 1967. "The City in the Future of Democracy." *American Political Science Review* 61 (December): 953–70.
Dahl, Robert, and Edward Tufte. 1973. *Size and Democracy.* Palo Alto, CA: Stanford University Press.

Deutsch, Karl. 1961. "Social Mobilization and Political Development." *American Political Science Review* 55 (September): 493–514.

Finifter, Ada. 1970. "Dimensions of Political Alienation." *American Political Science Review* 64 (June): 389–410.

Finifter, Ada, and Paul R. Abramson. 1975. "City Size and Feelings of Political Competence." *Public Opinion Quarterly* 39 (Summer): 189–98.

Fischer, Claude. 1976. "The City and Political Psychology." *American Political Science Review* 69 (September): 559–71.

Fischer, Claude. 1982. *To Dwell Among Friends: Personal Networks in Town and City.* Chicago: University of Chicago Press.

Fischer, Claude. 1995. "The Subcultural Theory of Urbanism: A Twentieth-Year Assessment." *American Journal of Sociology* 101 (November): 543–77.

Hansen, Steven, Thomas Palfrey, and Howard Rosenthal. 1987. "The Downsian Model of Electoral Participation: Formal Theory and Empirical Analysis of the Constituency Size Effect." *Public Choice* 52 (Spring): 15–33.

Huckfeldt, Robert, and John Sprague. 1995. *Citizens, Politics, and Social Communication: Information and Influence in an Election Campaign.* New York: Cambridge University Press.

Kasarda, John D., and Morris Janowitz. 1974. "Community Attachment in Mass Society." *American Sociological Review* 39 (August): 328–39.

Latane, Bibb, and John Darley. 1970. *The Unresponsive Bystander: Why Doesn't He Help?* Englewood Cliffs, NJ: Prentice Hall.

Lewin, Kurt. 1935. *Principles of Topological Psychology.* New York: McGraw-Hill.

Lofland, Lyn. 1973. *A World of Strangers: Order and Action in Urban Public Space.* New York: Basic Books.

Massey, Douglas, and Nancy Denton. 1993. *American Apartheid: Segregation and the Making of the Underclass.* Cambridge, MA: Harvard University Press.

Milbrath, Lester, and M. L. Goel. 1982. *Political Participation.* Washington, DC: University Press of America.

Montesquieu, Charles. [1748] 1991. *The Spirit of Laws.* Littleton, CO: F.B. Rothman.

Nie, Norman, G. Bingham Powell, Jr., and Kenneth Prewitt. 1969. "Social Structure and Political Participation: Developmental Relationships." *American Political Science Review* 63 (June): 361–78.

Oliver, J. Eric. 1999. "The Effects of Metropolitan Economic Segregation on Local Civic Involvement." *American Journal of Political Science* 43 (January): 186–212.

Olson, Mancur. 1965. *The Logic of Collective Action.* Cambridge, MA: Harvard University Press.

Peterson, Paul. 1981. *City Limits.* Chicago: University of Chicago Press.

Putnam, Robert. 1993. *Making Democracy Work: Civic Traditions in Modern Italy.* Princeton, NJ: Princeton University Press.

Putnam, Robert. 1995. "Tuning In, Tuning Out: The Strange Disappearance of Social Capital in America." *PS: Political Science & Politics* 28 (June): 664–83.

Reisman, David. 1953. *The Lonely Crowd: A Study of the Changing American Character.* Garden City, NY: Doubleday.

Rosenstone, Steven, and John Mark Hansen. 1994. *Mobilization, Participation, and Democracy in America.* New York: Macmillan.

Rousseau, Jean-Jacques. [1772] 1994. *Discourse on Political Economy and the Social Contract.* New York: Oxford University Press.

Schneider, Mark. 1987. "Income Homogeneity and the Size of Suburban Government." *Journal of Politics* 49 (March): 36–53.

Simmel, George. [1905] 1969. "The Great City and Cultural Life." In *Classic Essays on the Culture of Cities,* ed. Richard Sennett. New York: Appleton-Century-Crofts. Pp. 26–42.

Suttles, Gerald. 1972. *The Social Construction of Communities.* Chicago: University of Chicago Press.

Teixiera, Ruy. 1992. *The Disappearing American Voter.* Washington, DC: Brookings Institution.

Tiebout, Charles. 1956. "A Pure Theory of Local Expenditures." *Journal of Political Economy* 64 (October): 416–24.

Tonnies, Ferdinand. 1988. *Community and Society.* New York: Transaction.
U.S. Bureau of the Census. 1975. *Historical Statistics of the United States, Colonial Times to 1970* (Bicentennial Edition), Part 2. Washington, DC: Government Printing Office.
U.S. Bureau of the Census. 1991. *1990 Census of Population and Housing: Summary Tape File 3 (AL - WY).* Washington, DC: U.S. Bureau of the Census.
U.S. Bureau of the Census. 1993. *Statistical Abstract of the United States: 1993* (113th ed.). Washington, DC: Government Printing Office.
Verba, Sidney, and Norman Nie. 1972. *Participation in America.* Chicago: University of Chicago Press.
Verba, Sidney, Kay Schlozman, and Henry Brady. 1995. *Voice and Equality.* Cambridge, MA: . Harvard University Press.
Verba, Sidney, Kay Schlozman, Henry Brady, and Norman Nie. 1995. *American Citizen Participation Study, 1990* [computer file] (Study #6635), ICPSR version. Chicago: University of Chicago, National Opinion Research Center (NORC) [producer], 1995. Ann Arbor, MI: Inter-University Consortium for Political and Social Research [distributor], 1995.
Weber, Max. [1905] 1958. *The City.* Glencoe, IL: Free Press.
Wattenberg, Martin. 1996. *The Decline of American Political Parties.* Cambridge, MA: Harvard University Press.
Wilson, James Q. 1972. *Political Organizations.* New York: Basic Books.
Wirth, Louis. [1938] 1969. "Urbanism as a Way of Life." In *Classic Essays on the Culture of Cities,* ed. Richard Sennett. New York: Appleton-Century-Crofts. Pp. 67–83.
Wolfinger, Raymond E., and Steven J. Rosenstone. 1980. *Who Votes?* New Haven, CT: Yale University Press.

Discussion Questions

1. Perhaps the most obvious way to generate samples for Oliver's research question would be to take random samples of people from cities, suburbs, and rural areas, and then to ask them questions about their political activity. Why did he choose the data generated by the 1990 Citizen Participation Study (CPS)?
2. Oliver notes that the CPS involved a set of 2,500 in-depth interviews with a selected group of the 15,000 initially surveyed. Is it accurate to say that the 2,500 persons interviewed in depth were a random sample of the population? What could make these persons different and therefore unrepresentative of the population at large?
3. What steps should be taken to insure that the persons interviewed were not, as a group, unrepresentative of the larger population?

Commentary

Oliver's research findings were striking in their consistency. Using four different measures of civic participation, he showed that participation in politics substantially declines as city size increases. Apparently, a smaller proportion of citizens living in large municipalities actually participate in politics, regardless of whether one measures participation in terms of voting in local elections, attending community board meetings, or contacting local officials.

Each of these kinds of participation is more common in smaller cities than in large ones.

Of course, this does not demonstrate that a great deal of political activity does not occur in large cities. The somewhat smaller number of politically active citizens in large cities still produce a great deal of political energy, and the gravity and scope of policy concerns in big cities make their efforts extremely important. Oliver's measures simply indicated the percentages of people in different municipalities that reported engaging in these activities; if a large proportion of citizens in one municipality "attended community board meetings" to express their views about a local library expansion, that fact helped to generate the findings in Figure 8.1, even if a somewhat smaller proportion of citizens in a nearby large city attended such meetings to discuss the redesign of a large freeway project.

The sample he used was drawn by the scholars who developed the CPS in 1990. It is noteworthy that this study involved an unusually large random sample of 15,000 persons. As discussed at the beginning of this chapter, results from a sample of 1,200 persons will have an acceptable confidence interval at a 95 percent confidence level, but the CPS gathered information from more than ten times as many people. Why go to this much trouble and expense?

The answer has to do with the researchers' interest in doing in-depth interviews with a subsample of the respondents. They wanted this group to be large enough to enable them to gather data on a wide range of specific factors such as religious affiliation, occupation, marital status, and many other things that could not be covered well in the brief surveys used for the larger group. If they had started with only 1,200 or so, they would probably have only gotten cooperation from a few hundred for the in-depth interviews. Selecting the respondents for the intensive interviews from a list of 15,000 also permitted the use of stratified sampling, so that the subsample would be sure to include a large number of several kinds of cases.

However, it is obvious that many people will not voluntarily agree to participate in in-depth interviews. Some people are reluctant to cooperate because they distrust strangers or fear for their privacy, or because they simply do not want to spend the time. It is certainly possible that the 2,500 persons who agreed to these in-depth interviews were different from those who refused and that the differences were relevant to the study. Perhaps the persons refusing to participate were especially opposed to political activity, and the same aversion to dealing with strangers made them unlikely to be active in civic affairs. Any conclusions drawn about political activity from the interviews with the persons who did agree to be interviewed would therefore be suspect.

Oliver, and the scholars who designed and carried out the CPS, obviously recognized this problem. The best use of the data is therefore in the study's *comparison* of participation activities across people in municipalities of different sizes. In other words, the study may tend to overstate the degree of political activity in all areas, since persons agreeing to the in-depth interviews could be persons who happened to be especially open to social interaction and involvement. However, the author assumes that this tendency of the sample to be biased toward active citizens was roughly consistent in all jurisdictions, and, thus, it is still possible to make use of the fact that the rates of participation varied in different areas. The differences were, as Figure 8.1 showed, substantial and striking regardless of which measure was used. It is the differences, not the absolute levels of activity, that are relevant to the hypothesis.

Oliver's study forces the critics of suburbia to reconsider some of their views. Rather than a mass of self-centered people focused on their lawns, country clubs, and private schools, the data show that there is a great deal of civic involvement in the smaller municipalities in metropolitan areas. As often happens, popular stereotypes are refuted by empirical research. The second half of Oliver's study addresses the possibility that other variables are important in sorting out the effect of city size on civic involvement, and we will revisit his study in chapter 12.

9   Rational Choice Analysis

The approach to political study known as "rational choice" is perhaps the most controversial of all approaches to the discipline. Its most basic element is the use of economic concepts and assumptions to derive theories of political behavior, particularly the assumption that all persons, in both private and public settings, make choices that maximize their wealth, power, security, or "utility." Economists have used this idea to great advantage in generating models of supply and demand behavior, and many political scientists believe that it can help to generate constructive questions about politics as well.

It is important to recognize that the rational choice approach is *not* an alternative to scientific research and that such theorizing does *not* make empirical data analysis unnecessary. All basic assumptions and perspectives about human behavior, including those drawn from psychology, sociology, or even biology, contribute to scientific progress only when they suggest testable hypotheses for empirical inquiry. When sociologists begin a research project on community organizations with the assumption that humans have a basic drive to interact with others, their assumption may suggest hypotheses regarding the growth of such organizations. Similarly, rational choice studies begin with the economist's assumption that people usually make wealth-enhancing decisions, an assumption that also suggests certain testable hypotheses. In both cases, any hypotheses suggested must be tested in order to produce real scientific advances.

Rational choice theorizing has prompted a huge body of work in political philosophy, to be sure, but it has also led to hypotheses regarding voting, interest group formation, the behavior of candidates and potential candidates for public office, the growth of public bureaucracy, and many other subjects. It is because of its impact in stimulating important hypotheses about politics that a chapter in this volume is devoted to rational choice.

The rational choice approach traces its lineage to several important books. One of the first was Kenneth Arrow's *Social Choice and Individual Values*, published in 1951. A decade later, James M. Buchanan and Gordon Tullock published *The Calculus of Consent*, which stated explicitly that "the representative or average individual acts on the basis of the same over-all value scale when he participates in market activity and in political activity" (Buchanan and Tullock 1962, p. 20). Both of these works were read primarily by a small group of specialists and thus had a rather narrow impact. However, in 1965 Mancur Olson's *The Logic of Collective Action* directly attacked one of the most widely accepted ideas in modern political science—the notion that interest groups naturally form where large numbers of citizens share important interests. The impact was enormous, making rational choice analysis tremendously controversial in the discipline. His insight is an excellent example of how an idea, with testable political science implications, can be derived from simple economic assumptions.

Olson's Rational Choice Milestone

The crucial element in Olson's approach is his distinction between the interests of an *organization* and those of its *individual members*. Before Olson, most political scientists assumed these interests to be identical. If several individuals share an interest in lower property taxes, for example, one would expect them eventually to band together in a collective effort to lobby for lower taxes. If workers at an auto plant agree that they should receive higher wages, they will act collectively to achieve their shared objective. According to this traditional view, virtually all interests shared by more than a few persons will be represented by active political organizations. This leads to an important implication: *The array of political organizations active in society at any given time will be roughly representative of society's needs and demands.* Thus, we have the basis for the idea of "pluralism," the often optimistic assumption adopted by most 1950s-era political scientists. Pluralists argued that the political interests of virtually all important groups in society are well represented by a balanced and ever changing set of diverse political organizations that compete in their efforts to influence public policy.

Olson thus cut to the heart of the pluralists' ideas when he stated that "rational, self-interested individuals will not act to achieve their common or group interests" (p. 2). How does he reach such an astonishing conclusion? Before participating in a group effort, according to Olson, the rational person will ask two related questions:

1. Will I receive my share of the group objective even if I do not contribute to the effort?
2. Will my contribution to the effort have a meaningful impact on the group's chances of achieving its objectives?

When the interest being sought involves a collective good, the answer to the first question is "yes." A **collective good**—sometimes called a public good—

such as national defense, clean air, or a lower crime rate, is shared by every-one who is in the relevant category of persons regardless of whether he or she has assisted with, or even agreed to, an effort to obtain it. For example, all persons who enjoy recreation in wilderness areas in public lands receive the benefits of wilderness preservation programs whether or not they contribute to the Sierra Club's lobbying efforts to get such programs enacted. In con-trast, a private good, such as a new sports car or a compact disc, is something a person can be excluded from enjoying if he or she does not purchase it.

The answer to the second question is usually "no," especially when the number of potential group members is large. Although it may be discourag-ing or even selfish to think this way, it is a fact that a single contribution to a major collective good (e.g., public broadcasting) will almost certainly have zero impact on whether or not the good is obtained. Because the noncontributor gets the same benefits as the contributor, and because a single contribution is very unlikely to make any difference in making the collective good a reality, argued Olson, rational individuals will not join in efforts to achieve a political goal they share with others, even when the goal is very important to them. It is far better, under such circumstances, to enjoy a "free ride" and consume the collective good as a result of the efforts of others. And, if the group effort to secure the good fails, at least one will have avoided wasting the contribution. Since all potential group members are likely to feel the same way, most po-tential interest groups never form.

Of course, some do. Olson pointed out, however, that his theory did not imply that groups cannot form, only that they cannot form through the *volun-tary efforts of persons driven by their concern for a group interest or public good*. Effective political organizations form either by devising some means of forcing potential members to join or by offering material rewards that are received only by contributors. The collective good being sought is not enough to generate memberships.

Consider the important example of labor unions. Pre-rational choice political scientists argued that unions form when a group of workers in a particular industry or firm see that a collective good (higher wages, better health insur-ance, safer working conditions) could be obtained by organizing. Traditional political scientists would expect the union to form, more or less automatically, because the deal is so attractive: for dues of perhaps $500 per year, the union would use its influence to obtain a wage hike of $3,000 per worker per year.

Olson stated that this is not the way it works. The rational worker realizes that he or she will receive the raise whether or not he or she contributes dues, and further, that contributing or withholding a single $500 dues payment would be unlikely to affect the union's chances of success in its organizing and negoti-ating efforts. Because each worker reasons in this way, the union cannot be formed simply by relying on the behavioral impact of the workers' shared interests.

The dispute between the rational choice and the traditional approaches sug-gests a testable hypothesis. If the rational choice approach is correct, we may hypothesize that unions relying on voluntary union dues (i.e., situations in which the workers have the choice of keeping the money for themselves or contributing it for dues) will not flourish, and that those that have the power to require workers to contribute, by forcing them to have a current union card and by forced payroll deductions, will succeed. The traditional approach would predict that unions relying on forced dues payments will not have significantly better success than those relying on voluntary dues payments, because it assumes that workers are motivated by the promise of collective benefits to make union-supporting decisions. Since the "carrot" of collective benefits is an enticement to contribute regardless of whether the union has the "stick" of compulsory dues payments, this approach would predict that the two kinds of unions would have relatively equal chances of success.

An empirical test of these hypotheses would require that we devise some way of measuring "union success" and compulsory dues payment systems. We would also have to select cases for analysis carefully, in order to have a representative sample of unions. However, it is unlikely that such a study will be attempted because the issue is not in doubt among people with any experience in observing labor unions. Only unions with compulsory dues arrangements succeed in obtaining substantial dues payments from a large proportion of workers. Although this observation clearly confirms the rational choice prediction, it would be helpful to confirm it through a genuine and systematic empirical study.

Beyond the case of labor unions, the most important implication of Olson's idea is that groups of people who do not have the ability to force members to contribute to collective goals will not form effective organizations proportional in size and strength to their numbers. Thus, the poor, consumers, and taxpayers are not nearly as well represented by effective political organizations as are unionized workers, licensed professionals, and other groups who are able to force their members and potential members to contribute. Following this logic, optimistic pluralist views (i.e., that all important political interests in society will be represented by proportionately influential political organizations) should be replaced by a more critical conclusion: *Political and economic conflict in society will become increasingly heated and unbalanced as the interests that can overcome, through whatever means, the barriers to organization gain disproportionate political influence* (see Olson 1982).

Olson's idea led to hundreds of scholarly journal articles and books in political science, economics, sociology, and other fields. Beyond the particulars of his work, the core idea he advanced provides a striking example of both the power and the controversy associated with the rational choice approach.

Controversies in Rational Choice

In 1994, two Yale political scientists published a provocative book entitled *Pathologies of Rational Choice Theory* (Green and Shapiro 1994). They began by noting that rational choice–based articles had become increasingly predominant in the major journals of the discipline, approaching 40 percent of the content of the *American Political Science Review*, for example, and that it had "recast much of the intellectual landscape in the discipline of political science" (p. 3). However, in their view, the rapid expansion of rational choice works in political science has been a generally unfortunate development.

Some of the arguments Green and Shapiro use against rational choice apply to poor research projects employing all kinds of approaches. They claim that many rational choice studies select biased data and ignore alternative explanations for their findings, an all too common failing in the published work in all social sciences. However, perhaps their most important criticism is that rational choice studies frequently fail to construct verifiable hypotheses. Green and Shapiro claim that, due to the almost religious attachment that rational choice scholars have to the theoretical underpinnings of their research, "theories are elaborated and modified in order to save their universal character" and "discordant facts are often either ignored or circumvented." Rather than rejecting a hypothesis when the facts tend to disprove it, rational choice analysts simply rework their theories and assert that they are still true despite the facts (p. 6). Due to these and other "pathologies," Green and Shapiro conclude that the rational choice approach "has yet to deliver on its promise to advance the empirical study of politics" (p. 7).

In response to this important volume, another political scientist from Yale edited *The Rational Choice Controversy* two years later (Friedman 1996). This collection of essays includes arguments on both sides of the issue. Some accepted the critical tone of Green and Shapiro; others went much farther. One article argued that rational choice theory is a socially destructive idea that is harmful to teach, because it may lead students to become selfish and unsupportive of civic values (pp. 25–36). However, many others (including Morris Fiorina, the author of the excerpt in this chapter) argued that rational choice analysis has produced some very real achievements and that Green and Shapiro's standard—that research must demonstrate clear empirical conclusions about political questions—has not been met by very many examples of research, regardless of whether a rational choice approach is part of the analysis.

Perhaps the problem with rational choice analysis is that, compared to other approaches to political science, rational choice enjoys a highly coherent theoretical foundation. Scholars who are drawn to this foundation may accept it uncritically, even claiming that the ideas they derive from the implications of economic assumptions need not be tested. It may also be true that, in an effort to advance their theories, they may construct biased research designs and retreat to "post-hoc rationalizations" to rescue their theories from inconvenient facts. Adherents of Marxist theory have been criticized along the same lines for generations, perhaps because, like rational choice theorists, Marxist thinkers are working within a field that has a similarly coherent set of ideas.

Most political scientists study research questions that do not relate directly to such elaborate and seductive theoretical foundations, and thus they are not as frequently tempted to reject data uncritically or to "save" hypotheses when facts refute them.

Nevertheless, rational choice analysis will continue to be a major part of political science research for the foreseeable future. Its adherents may oversell their predictions, and they may be tempted to accept hypotheses prematurely, but there is no denying that some important ideas have come out of this approach. As in all parts of the discipline, the best rational choice research begins with the construction of verifiable hypotheses and tests them with valid, reliable, and representative data. The excerpt below is a good example of constructive research in this field.

———————— Excerpt 12 ————————

Morris Fiorina is one of the most active and highly regarded contemporary American political scientists. A hallmark of his work is the application of empirical data to test ideas drawn from rational choice assumptions about political behavior. He is probably best known for *Congress: Keystone of the Washington Establishment* (1989, first published in 1977), which led to a rather unflattering impression of members of the U.S. Congress. Fiorina argued that the tremendous electoral advantage that incumbent members of Congress enjoy over challengers is due to the fact that they are able to manipulate the vast Washington bureaucracy to get votes from their constituents. Incumbents and challengers are on a level playing field when it comes to issues. If different positions on issues determined electoral success, we would expect that challengers would do roughly as well as incumbents because both will try to advocate popular issue positions, and there is no reason to suspect that incumbents will be consistently better than challengers at doing this. However, if generating agency favors and cutting bureaucratic "red tape" are the keys to winning elections, incumbents have a great advantage because incumbents are in a better position to influence the workings of the bureaucracy.

One of the most compelling elements of Fiorina's research in this area is his finding that the strength of the incumbency advantage has increased over time as the size and scope of the federal bureaucracy has grown. His work draws from the rational choice approach in that it begins with the assumption that members of Congress pursue their self-interest in deciding how to spend their valuable time (in his view, by increasing the time devoted to constituent service and decreasing the time devoted to dealing with major controversial issues). His book led to arresting implications, suggesting that members of Congress actually want administrative agencies to fail so that vote-hungry representatives will be able to curry favor back home by "fixing things" in Washington.

In the following 1994 article, Fiorina again begins with a basic rational choice assumption: Candidates and potential candidates for seats in state legislatures should be expected to make decisions about their careers, and about the attractiveness of running for legislative office, on the basis of what these decisions will mean for their financial and professional self-interests. Although Fiorina understands that every legislator and potential legislative candidate is a unique individual, he argues that some important overall trends may be affected by the different financial impacts that holding legislative office has on different kinds of people.

In particular, he argues that Republicans are generally more reluctant than Democrats to give up rewarding professional careers to serve in full-time legislatures. During earlier decades, when most state legislatures met on a part-time basis, however, Republicans enjoyed an advantage because they were more likely than Democrats to have careers (e.g., being partners in law firms) that enabled them to be temporarily absent. The emergence of "professionalized" state legislatures turned this advantage into a disadvantage, as many Republicans were unwilling to sacrifice professional careers in order to serve.

As you read the following excerpt, note how Fiorina begins with the rational choice assumption regarding the self-interested motivations of potential candidates. Having considered the possibility that this factor could produce a change in the partisan composition of state legislatures, he then devised an empirical test.

Divided Government in the American States: A Byproduct of Legislative Professionalism?

Morris P. Fiorina, *Harvard University*

American Political Science Review 88, no. 2 (June 1994): 304–316. Copyright © 1994 by the American Political Science Association. Reprinted with permission.

I shall focus on *one* aspect of the growth of divided government in the American states—the decline of Republican fortunes in legislative elections—and *one* contributing factor to this decline, namely, the development of legislative professionalism, or (as some might prefer to call it) careerism. Briefly, the analyses that follow are consistent with the argument that all other things being equal, professionalized legislatures are relatively more attractive to Democrats than to Republicans. Thus, postwar good government reforms that encouraged the professionalization of state legislatures had the unintended consequence of undercutting the Republican party in that arena.[1] Moreover, given that state legislatures are the traditional "farm teams" for Congress, the decline in Republican state legislative fortunes should naturally lead to some decline in their congressional fortunes as well.

Party Fortunes in State Legislative Elections

The decline in unified state government largely reflects a decline in unified *Republican* state government, which in turn largely reflects a decline in Republican *legislatures* (Fiorina 1992, chap. 3). Since World War II, there has been considerable variability but no partisan trend in gubernatorial elections. Legislative elections are another matter, however. Even while spotting the Democrats a 15-state lead in the southern and border states, in 1946 and 1952, the Republicans captured an absolute majority of state legislatures (Figure 1 [2 in original]). Their fortunes have slipped dramatically, however, and following the 1990 and 1992 elections, only five states had Republican legislatures. The impact of adverse national circumstances is clear (the 1958 and 1974 recessions, the Goldwater debacle), but it is also clear that such adverse shocks are embedded within a long-term secular decline. Note that the Republican collapse in state legislatures had taken place by the mid-1970s (Figure 1). Over the more recent period spanned by the State Legislative Elections Project (1968–86), there is little variation in the number of Democratic state legislators.

Interestingly, although there are several excellent studies of state legislative elections, none of them have addressed the Republican decline. Analyzing elections in 41 states between 1944 and 1984, Campbell (1986) finds that popular presidential candidates help state legislative candidates of their parties and that the longer the presidential coattails, the larger the subsequent off-year loss. Because Campbell's dependent variable is *change* in legislative seats, however, the steady decline in Republican strength does not stand out. Chubb (1988) examines Democratic lower-house success in nonsouthern legislatures over the period 1940–82, finding that state election results are significantly influenced by the coattails of candidates for higher offices, by national economic conditions, and by turnout surge and decline. He does not comment on the declining percentage of Republican legislators, though the decline is statistically incorporated in a lagged variable measuring the percentage of lower-house Democrats in the preceding legislature. Similarly, Simon, Ostrom, and Marra (1991) find that control of legislative chambers between 1950 and 1988 depends on such short-term factors as the president's standing in the polls and dramatic political events and such longer-term factors as the national party balance and the departure of the state outcome from its long-run equilibrium. Again, these authors do not comment on the Republican decline, though it is incorporated in the long-run equilibrium. Thus comprehensive statistical analyses establish that legislative outcomes in the states reflect both long-term party competition and short-term political events and conditions, but these analyses incorporate the Republican legislative decline statistically without calling attention to it or providing any substantive explanation for it. The analyses reported herein build on these earlier efforts but keep the Republican decline front and center.

As a starting point, let us take a closer look at party control in the state legislatures. As usual, the South is special. The Republicans have *never* won control of a southern or border legislative chamber in the postwar period: all of the action in Figure 1 occurs outside these regions. Thus, I omit the 15 southern and border states from consideration, along with Alaska, Hawaii, Minnesota, and Nebraska.[2] Controlling for short-term variation in the national political climate (measured by interelection change in Gallup approval ratings appropriately signed for the party of the president), the time trend of Republican control in the remaining 31 nonsouthern states is given in Table 1, column 1.

Since World War II, the Republicans have lost legislatures in the non-South at a rate of almost 2% per election. The passage of time is not an explanation, of course, but a context in which true explanatory variables operate. Elsewhere I have suggested that legislative professionalization works in favor of Democrats (Fiorina 1992). Substituting an extremely crude indicator of professionalization (the simple percentage of states whose legislatures meet annually) for the time trend in Table 1, we get column 2. For every 3% increase in states holding annual legislative sessions, the Republicans lost control of approximately 1% of the state legislatures. The trend in annual sessions

Table 1

Correlates of Republican Control of State Legislatures: Non-South, 1946–1990

Independent variables	Models		
	1	2	3
Constant	60.53	55.93	60.55
	(15.25)	(15.13)	(15.71)
Presidential approval change	−.59	−.58	−.59
	(.21)	(.22)	(.22)
Time trend	−1.74	—	−1.69
	(.57)		(1.61)
Annual sessions	—	−.36	−.01
		(.13)	.36
Republican control (t − 1)	.08	.17	.08
	(.19)	(.18)	(.20)
Corrected R^2	.55	.52	.52

Note: Figures are ordinary least squares estimates N = 22. Time trend: 1946 = 1, 1948 = 2, . . . , 1990 = 23.

tracks the time trend very closely (the simple correlation between the two variables is .95), and when both are included in the equation (column 3), multicollinearity deprives both of significance.

Of course, there are numerous other time series that trend upward (or downward) over this 23-election period. Any of these might perform just as well statistically as the trend in annual legislative sessions. I shall develop the argument that legislative professionalization enhances the electoral prospects of Democratic candidates, then present the evidence.

Opportunity Costs and Legislative Careers

In the early postwar years, most state legislatures were part-time, minimally supported institutions whose members were poorly compensated. Most were constitutionally limited to sitting every other year. Legislative scholars commonly label such bodies *amateur,* because under these conditions turnover is high, and service is an avocation, not a profession. Some state legislatures still fit this description. The Wyoming legislature, for example, is permitted to meet for 20 days during even years and 40 days during odd years. Members receive $75-per-day salary with a $60 per diem, for a total biennial compensation of less than $7,000. Other perks are minimal. Upper- and lower-chamber turnover rates are similar—about 30% per election in the early 1980s (Niemi and Winsky 1987, tbl. 1).

New York offers a striking contrast. It is a good example of what legislative scholars refer to as a *professional* legislature. In session annually from January through June and again for a period in the Fall, with almost 20 staff per legislator, each member receives a $57,500 annual salary and $75 per diem, as well as travel allowances. Moreover, two-thirds of the assembly and the entire senate receive so-called "lulus," that is, "in lieu of" payments for holding various party and committee leadership posts (Fowler and McClure 1989, 84–89, 96). Assembly turnover in the early 1980s was about 20% per election, with senate turnover under 15%. *Voluntary* turnover was less than 10% (p. 90).

In the early postwar years, most state legislatures fell on the amateur end of the continuum. But over the years, especially during the 1960s, many legislatures have become more professionalized (Kurtz 1991). In particular, legislative service has increasingly become a full-time occupation. Bazar reports that as of 1986, between 11% and 20% of legislators nationwide were full-time and that in some areas (e.g., the middle Atlantic states), over half were professional legislators (1987, 2). My hypothesis is that this development advantages Democratic candidates relative to Republicans. The hypothesis is a logical implication of several propositions previously noted by students of state politics.

First, legislative service does not make equivalent demands on people from different walks of life. Discussing Arkansas (an amateur legislature), Blair comments: "A realtor or banker or lawyer, the owner of a furniture store or car dealership, may have the time flexibility and financial security to adjust his or her schedule to a regular session of two months or more, increasingly frequent special sessions, and countless committee meetings and constituent obligations in between. The realtor's or lawyer's secretary, a bank teller, the furniture and car salespersons who must be at work if they are to receive an income, simply cannot serve" (1988, 164).

Second, if legislative service has an asymmetric impact on people from different occupational and income strata, we should expect *changes* in the conditions of legislative service to change the relative attractiveness of service for different categories of people. That is what Rosenthal reports:

> Minnesota is an example of a state in which marked change in the composition of the legislature has taken place. Lawyers, independent business owners, and farmers have left. Their places have been taken by young people, many of whom see the legislature as an entry level position for a career in politics. But as noticeable as anything else, the contemporary Minnesota legislature has more full-time members. . . . The neighboring state of Wisconsin has moved in the same direction, with younger members and fewer who work part time at the job. There is only a single farmer left in the senate. . . . Legislators themselves are not united on the benefits of professionalization: . . . in California the entire fabric of the process has changed. "The way it used to be, we only had men of means, of experience," a senior senator remarked. "Now we have full-time legislators." (1981, 58)

Finally, we have the common observation that the two parties are based in different socioeconomic strata. Arguing that the Republicans had an advantage in an era of part-time politicians, Key observed:

> Outside the South, the Republican group has . . . a far larger reservoir of persons with leadership skills on which to draw. Well-connected lawyers, businessmen with time and money to devote to politics, and perhaps to a lesser extent, persons with skill in professional politics gravitate in greater degree to the Republican party than to the Democratic. By the secondary network of economic relations within their own group—legal retainers, insurance commissions, real estate transactions, and the like—the business community within the Republican party can sustain a class whose time and energies may be dedicated principally to the practice of politics. . . . The Democratic Party, on the other hand, enjoys the handicaps in recruiting leadership created by its position as a party devoted in principle to mass causes. (1956, 256–57)

Now, as then, the parties have discernibly different socioeconomic bases. As mass surveys monotonously demonstrate, the Republicans have a higher-income, higher-status popular base than the Democrats, especially when the profit sector is distinguished. And elite surveys find that Republican elites come relatively more from the profit sector, Democrats from the public and other nonprofit sectors.[3]

Consider a simplified model based on the preceding propositions. Within a state, two parties compete for public office. Within each party is a pool consisting of all potential candidates, that is, those possessing the minimal qualifications deemed appropriate for service. The parties' candidate pools differ in their occupational and income characteristics. The Republicans are a higher-income, more private-sector party; their potential candidates are independent professionals, proprietors and farmers, and the independently wealthy (as well as their spouses, given that such families are better able to afford domestic substitutes). The Democrats are a lower-income, more public-sector party. Their potential candidates are union officials, teachers, and other public- and non-profit-sector employees. Given such differences, variations in the degree of legislative professionalism are likely to affect the decisions of those in the respective candidate pools.

Those in the Republican pool are advantaged where the legislature is on the amateur end of the continuum. They are more likely to have the career and financial flexibility to absent themselves from their principal occupations for one to three months a year. Some of their responsibilities can be moved to evenings and weekends or delegated to associates, relatives, or employees. Indeed, for lawyers in private practice, the contacts made in political life raise the value of their outside hours.[4] In contrast, salary and wage earners in the Democratic pool forgo their incomes when they take leave for legislative service—if leave is even feasible. Even if ambition levels are comparable, Republican candidates are more able to pursue their ambitions.

With a professional legislature, the logic reverses. If legislative service is a full-time occupation, legislators must sacrifice outside careers for legislative office. Those who have lucrative private-sector careers will tend to exit legislative service—or never enter—rather than abandon those careers. In contrast, for potential Democratic candidates, legislative service now becomes an attractive alternative career, probably better compensated and more highly regarded than their present careers. Again, even if ambition levels are equal between the respective candidate pools, Democratic candidates are now in a better position to act on their ambitions.

In sum, in amateur legislative settings the critical question is, "Who has the flexibility *to combine* legislative service and an outside career?" In professional legislative settings, the critical question is, "Who is willing *to sacrifice* an outside career for legislative service?" If the career patterns of Democrats and Republicans are as just posited, then, ceteris paribus, the answer to the first question is, "More likely, Republicans," and the answer to the second is, "More likely, Democrats."

Several aspects of the argument deserve additional comment. First, the argument says nothing about net *turnover* in legislatures. There is a substantial literature on that subject, of course. Reformers have supported professionalization partly as a remedy for excessively high turnover, and some research finds that correlates of professionalism (e.g., longer session length and higher compensation) do reduce turnover (Calvert 1979; Rosenthal 1974). The argument made here, however, is that increasing session length and compensation have a differential partisan impact, advantaging Democrats relative to Republicans.

Second, the argument is a *selection* argument. Institutional change (professionalization) has altered the mix of incentives facing legislative candidates so that prospective Republican candidates find legislative service relatively less attractive than in the past, while prospective Democrats find it relatively more attractive.[5] Increasingly, the former select out, and the latter select in. This logic resembles that of Ehrenhalt (1991), though the two arguments have different principal emphases. Noting that Democrats (including those of the most liberal persuasion) sometimes dominate local councils and state legislatures in seemingly conservative locales, Ehrenhalt hypothesizes a difference in party attitudes toward government. Democrats generally believe in government, like to use government to improve society, and consequently enjoy government service; Republicans, in contrast, are skeptical of government capacity, dislike government, and consequently find service much less rewarding. This too is a selection argument. The two arguments are not at all inconsistent. Indeed, they are quite complementary, and Ehrenhalt takes note of the greater career commitment evidenced by Democrats. But I have said nothing about psychological or ideological benefits and costs, only the more tangible costs and benefits of legislative service. Full-time service imposes higher opportunity costs on Republicans, and generous compensation raises the direct benefits of service for Democrats. If the logic of my argument is operative, party fortunes will respond to measures of *tangible* benefits and costs. Ehrenhalt's argument, in contrast, could be valid even in the absence of such relationships.[6]

A third point is that my argument is easy to caricature. I am not claiming that candidates for office look at nothing but the prospective wages and hours, with Republicans being discouraged by longer hours, and Democrats encouraged by higher wages. I am suggesting merely that such considerations affect career choices. On the margins, some qualified Democrats—however public-spirited—will find the sacrifices of service in an amateur legislature too great to bear. Similarly, some qualified Republicans—however public-spirited—will find the sacrifices of service in a professional legislature too great to bear. Such marginal decisions affect the respective candidate pools and, indirectly, the composition of the legislature.

One objection to the foregoing argument is that correlations between occupation, income, and partisanship, while significant, are far from perfect. The objection is well taken, but the empirical question is not the absolute strength of the correlations but whether they are strong enough to contribute to the explanation for the Republican legislative decline. That question can only be answered by looking at the evidence. From past research, we know that candidates' decisions vary systematically with measureable characteristics of the offices they hold, the offices they seek, their attitudes toward risk, and such features of the electoral context as party competitiveness and national forces (Black 1972; Jacobson and Kernell 1981; Rohde 1979; Schlesinger 1966, esp. chaps. 2, 3). This research simply expands the list of factors known to affect candidate decisions.[7]

Consider the experiences of two states. Figure 2 [3 in original] shows Ohio's interesting postwar history. Prior to 1972, the Republicans won the lower house in every year except 1958. But in the 1972 elections, *with George McGovern heading the ticket,* the Democratic percentage jumped 13 points, and they have been continuously in the majority since then. Did anything obvious happen around the time of this sharp change in partisan fortunes? Yes: at least two developments may be relevant. First, the 1970s reapportionment was carried out by a reapportionment board that had a three-to-two Democratic majority. Perhaps they were extraordinarily clever and produced a massive, lasting Democratic gerrymander.[8] Alternatively, Ohio voters approved a constitutional amendment providing for annual sessions. From a total of 315 days in the 1967 biennial session, the Ohio legislature moved to 717 in the 1971–72 annual sessions.[9] Coincidentally, between the 1968 and 1972 elections, the Democrats scored a 23% seat gain.[10] Simple regressions analogous to those reported earlier in Table 1 indicate that the increased session lengths account for more than half of the Democratic gain.

California (Figure 3 [4 in original]) provides a different illustration. Republican hegemony came to an end earlier than in Ohio—in the election of 1958. Since then, Republicans have attained majority status only in 1968. Since California has had annual sessions throughout the postwar period, that variable has no explanatory relevance. While days-in-session has been trending steadily upward, a simple regression analysis analogous to those in Table 1 shows little indication that length of session is related to the improvement in Democratic fortunes. But the third professionalism variable—real com-

Figure 1   **Unified Legislatures**

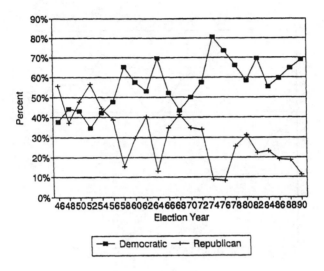

Figure 2   **The Case of Ohio**

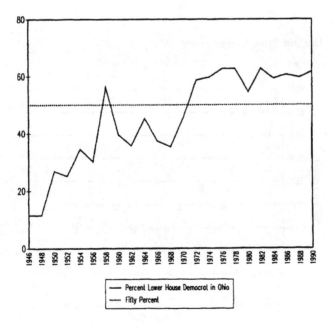

Figure 3 **The Case of California**

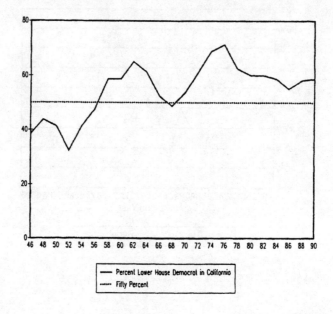

Figure 4 **Unified State Government**

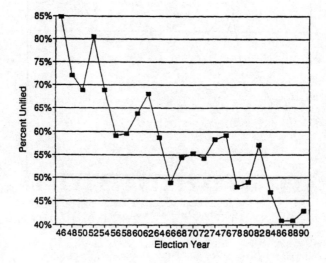

pensation—bears a significant relationship to Democratic success. Each $10,000 (biennial) increase in real legislative compensation is associated with a 1% increase in Democratic legislators. Thus, the observed $80,000 increase in real compensation in postwar California directly contributes to a 9% improvement in Democratic fortunes.[11]

Notes

1. Karl Kurtz (personal communication) has suggested that I differentiate *professionalization* from a *Professionalization* reform movement. The former refers to ongoing developments (however caused) that make state legislatures more like the Congress, whereas the latter refers specifically to good-government reform efforts, especially those of the 1960s.

2. Nebraska has nonpartisan legislative elections, Minnesota was nonpartisan before 1972, and Alaska and Hawaii had their first elections as states (1958 and 1959, respectively) after a significant part of the action in Figure 4 [1 in original] had already occurred.

3. On the well-known socioeconomic differences in the mass bases of the parties, see Miller and Traugott (1989, tbls. 2.4, 2.8, 2.18). On differences in party elites (convention delegates) see, e.g., Stanley and Niemi 1990, tbl. 4–10). More recently, Black and Black report that 45% of the delegates to the 1992 Democratic convention were employed by government in some capacity (1992, 5). (Unfortunately, they do not report a figure for Republicans, but it is undoubtedly lower.) I have been somewhat surprised by the scarcity of comprehensive data on occupational characteristics of party elites. In one case, for example, excellent data exist but are not reported separately by party (Bazar 1987).

4. Keefe and Ogul observe that for lawyers, "political involvement may well bring an unearned increment by attracting, through publicity and social visibility, new clients and higher fees" (1993, 140). Interestingly, Bazar reports a sharp drop in the number of lawyer legislators between 1976 and 1986, citing "the time requirements of legislative office," stringent disclosure laws, and the legalization of advertising as contributing factors (1987, 3).

5. There is nothing novel about this argument. Classic references include Aristotle, who took note of the claim that the Athenian law courts deteriorated after pay for service attracted a more "common" kind of men (Fritz 1964, 97–98), and J. S. Mill, who opposed parliamentary compensation on grounds that it would discourage successful professionals and attract "adventurers of a low class" (Acton 1972, 311). Indeed, the standard argument in favor of decent legislative compensation is that in its absence, legislative service is the privilege of the rich, who presumably are not representative of the entire polity.

6. There is an obvious synthesis of the two arguments: Desiring full-time careers in government, Democrats work to professionalize state and local offices.

7. Francis (1993) has shown that representatives in high-paying state legislatures are significantly more likely than those in low-paying legislatures to wait for open seats rather than challenge incumbent senators. This finding suggests too that career decisions do depend on mundane wages and hours considerations.

8. The aggregate statewide vote for lower House Democrats jumped from 46% in 1968 to 54% in 1970 and fell slightly to 53% in 1972. The 1972 gain in seats with no gain in votes over 1970 is consistent with the gerrymandering hypothesis. The 7% jump in votes between 1968 and 1972 (even while McGovern was drawing little more than a third of the statewide vote) is consistent with an improvement (decline) in the quality of Democratic (Republican) candidates.

9. As far as I can determine, the legislature had been "fudging" somewhat by recessing at the end of the odd-year session and meeting for a time in the even years. In the intervening 1969–70 legislature, they sat for 414 days by extending the session into the even year.

10. Interestingly, a contemporary observer (Asher 1978) speculated that these developments would have unintended consequences. Asher cautioned that professionalization in Ohio would lead to insulation of incumbents, as was apparently occurring in the U.S. House of Representatives.

11. Lest some prejudiced readers dismiss this finding as a reflection of the stereotypical materialism of Californians, I point out that the analogous regression estimated for Wisconsin, purported to be one of our more altruistic states, yields a coefficient (.022) precisely *twice* as strong as California's.

References

Acton, H.B., ed. 1972. *John Stuart Mill, Utilitarianism, "On Liberty," and "Considerations on Representative Government."* London: Dent & Sons.

Asher, Herbert B. 1978. "The Unintended Consequences of Legislative Professionalism." Presented at the annual meeting of the American Political Science Association, New York.

Bazar, Beth. 1987. *State Legislator's Occupations: A Decade of Change.* Denver: National Conference of State Legislatures.

Black, Gordon. 1972. "A Theory of Political Ambition: Career Choices and the Role of Structural Incentives." *American Political Science Review* 66:144–59.

Black, Gordon S., and Benjamin D. Black. 1992. "Americans Want and Need a New Political Party." *Public Perspective* 4:3–6.

Blair, Diana D. 1988. *Arkansas Politics and Government.* Lincoln: University of Nebraska Press.

Calvert, Jerry. 1979. "Revolving Doors: Volunteerism in U.S. State Legislatures." *State Government* 52:174–81.

Campbell, James E. 1986. "Presidential Coattails and Midterm Losses in State Legislative Elections." *American Political Science Review* 80:45–63.

Campbell, James E. 1993. *The Presidential Pulse of Congressional Elections.* Lexington: University of Kentucky Press.

Chubb, John E. 1988. "Institutions, the Economy, and the Dynamics of State Elections." *American Political Science Review* 82:133–54.

Ehrenhalt, Alan. 1991. *The United States of Ambition: Politicians, Power, and the Pursuit of Office.* New York: Random House.

Fiorina, Morris P. 1992. *Divided Government.* New York: Macmillan.

Fowler, Linda L., and Robert D. McClure. 1989. *Political Ambition.* New Haven: Yale University Press.

Francis, Wayne L. 1993. "House to Senate Career Movement in the U.S. States: The Significance of Selectivity." *Legislative Studies Quarterly* 3:309–20.

Fritz, Kurt von. 1964. *Aristotle's Constitution of Athens and Related Texts.* New York: Hafner.

Jacobson, Gary C., and Samuel Kernell. 1981. *Strategy and Choice in Congressional Elections.* New Haven: Yale University Press.

Keefe, William J., and Morris S. Ogul. 1993. *The American Legislative Process.* 8th ed. Englewood Cliffs: Prentice Hall.

Key, V.O., Jr. 1956. *American State Politics: An Introduction.* New York: Knopf.

Kurtz, Karl T. 1991. *Understanding the Diversity of State Legislatures: The Red, White, and Blue Legislatures.* Denver: National Conference of State Legislatures.

Miller, Warren E., and Santa Traugott. 1989. *American National Election Studies Data Sourcebook: 1952–1986.* Cambridge: Harvard University Press.

Niemi, Richard G., and Laura R. Winsky. 1987. "Membership Turnover in U.S. State Legislatures: Trends and Effects of Districting." *Legislative Studies Quarterly* 12:115–24.

Rohde, David W. 1979. "Risk Bearing and Progressive Ambition: The Case of Members of the United States House of Representatives." *American Journal of Political Science* 23:1–26.

Rosenthal, Alan. 1974. "Turnover in State Legislatures." *American Journal of Political Science* 18:609–16.

Rosenthal, Alan. 1981. *Legislative Life.* New York: Harper & Row.

Schlesinger, Joseph A. 1966. *Ambition and Politics: Political Careers in the United States.* Chicago: Rand McNally.

Simon, Dennis. 1989. "Presidents, Governors, and Electoral Accountability." *Journal of Politics* 51:286–304.

Simon, Dennis M., Charles W. Ostrom, Jr., and Robin F. Marra. 1991. "The President, Refer-

endum Voting, and Subnational Elections in the United States." *American Political Science Review* 85:1177–92.
Stanley, Harold W., and Richard G. Niemi. 1990. *Vital Statistics on American Politics*. 2d ed. Washington, DC: CQ Press.

Discussion Questions

1. Is Fiorina's assumption about the motivations of potential candidates for state legislative elections accurate? How accurate should it be in order to serve as the basis for a testable hypothesis?
2. How did rational choice theory contribute to Fiorina's research project? Did the fact that he approached the subject in this way help him with his research?
3. Some people find that rational choice assumptions are degrading and send socially destructive messages. React to this idea in the context of Fiorina's article.
4. Can you think of alternative approaches to explaining the pattern Fiorina identified (declining success for Republicans in state legislatures) that do not incorporate the factor of candidates' self-interest?

Commentary

Fiorina's argument is remarkably convincing. He began with the assumption that potential candidates should be expected to make rational choices about their self-interest, particularly in terms of financial and professional considerations. His theorizing simply applied this assumption to develop an expectation regarding how the move to "professionalize" state legislatures would have *different impacts* on the two major parties. In getting from his basic assumption to his hypothesis, Fiorina had to incorporate some important information about what "professionalization" involves (i.e., an increase in the number of days that legislators have to serve each year) and a critical generalization about candidates from the two parties (i.e., that Republicans generally have more lucrative careers than Democrats).

Some rational choice theorists stop at this point. After generating a plausible argument tied to their rational choice assumptions, they often consider the matter settled, especially if it is possible to point to a few individual examples that are consistent with the overall claim. However, Fiorina has long recognized the need to take his research to the next step, providing an empirical test of the hypotheses that emerge from his theorizing. Perhaps the strongest part of his article is the fact that he is able to show that the fall in Republican successes in state legislatures occurred at the same time that these legislatures adopted work schedules that increasingly required legislators to sacrifice their existing professional careers.

It is perhaps ironic that, in the fall election following the publication of his article, Republican fortunes at all levels of government experienced a significant upsurge. This may have been a reaction to the early years of the Clinton administration, which involved some rather rocky moments for the Democrats. Undoubtedly, many other factors were involved as well, including a growing anti-incumbency mood that worked for the Republicans, and a continuing shift among Southern voters to the Republican party. In any case, it is important to note that Fiorina's argument simply identifies a factor—advancing state legislative professionalization—that works against Republican fortunes at the state level. Other factors can overwhelm its influence in any given year.

Another point well illustrated by Fiorina's study is that generalizations, even flawed ones, may be used in a constructive way. Many readers were stunned by Fiorina's assertion that "Democrats, on average, have less lucrative career opportunities than Republicans." Anyone can instantly think of examples of wealthy, professionally successful Democrats. However, if we are interested in an aggregate trend, data about generalized characteristics can be appropriately used. Individual exceptions may be interesting, but they are not relevant to the comparison being drawn at the aggregate level.

Fiorina's study of the changing partisan composition of state legislatures shows how a rational choice approach can suggest a line of inquiry that may not have been considered in its absence. Political scientists have written about the phenomenon of state legislative professionalization for many years, investigating the impact of this factor on state policy-making, state innovativeness, and other issues. However, the idea that this development, which most observers assumed would be politically neutral, would have a *partisan* impact is a notion that springs most directly from a rational choice perspective. By focusing attention on the personal self-interest of potential candidates, a researcher was prompted to consider an important hypothesis that may have otherwise gone unexplored.

10 Univariate Analysis:
Statistics of a Single Variable

While many political research problems involve relationships between two or more variables, a surprising amount can often be learned from analysis of a single variable. Such familiar statistics as the president's current approval rating, the unemployment rate, and current median household income are, after all, single variable measures. Simple statistics of this type are often referred to as descriptive statistics because their primary purpose is to help us understand a subject (nation, government, campaign, citizenry) in somewhat greater detail, often by describing the way that some aspect of the subject changes over time. These measures are **univariate** (one variable) statistics. Analysis that employs univariate statistics is, therefore, univariate analysis.

One of the simplest ways in which to analyze the behavior of a single variable is to prepare a **frequency distribution**, which is essentially a list or summary of the number of cases that have a specified value. Most frequency distributions are designed to show us how many cases fall into each of several categories (denoting a range of values) constructed by the researcher. Thus, in analyzing the household income of survey respondents, the researcher is likely to report this information in terms of the number or proportion whose income falls into categories such as $100,000 and above, $60,000–100,000, etc. A frequency distribution that employs well-chosen categories will provide the reader with much useful information, including a strong indication of the extent to which the variable involved does, in fact, assume different values among different cases. This information can be immediately useful and can also guide subsequent research design. If, for instance, the frequency distribution reveals very little variation on the part of the variable involved, this would alert us to the probable futility of including this variable in further analyses involving the use of more advanced analytic tools such as multiple regression (see chapter 12).

Frequency distributions are of considerable value in political research. They are, however, often more helpful to the researcher than to the reader in that they take up a considerable amount of space when printed and must be examined carefully and at some length in order to be fully understood. There are, however, several simple types of single variable statistics that are commonly used to summarize the characteristics of any given frequency distribution.

Central Tendency and Dispersion

These summary statistics are generally of two types: measures of **central tendency** and measures of **dispersion**. Measures of central tendency provide us with the typical or average score for the set of cases studied considered as a group. Measures of dispersion tell us the extent to which the scores differ among the cases involved. The three most commonly used measures of central tendency are the **median**, the **mean**, and the **mode**. The most commonly used measure of dispersion is the **standard deviation**.

Measures of central tendency essentially tell us which score on the variable in question is the most representative of all the cases. For example, when we say the average income of Connecticut households is $24,000, we are simply saying that this is the *typical* figure. The most common measure of central tendency for data on household income is the median, or the value in the middle of the frequency distribution; half of the cases studied are higher, and half are lower on that variable. The mode is simply the most often encountered value or score. The mean is found by adding all the values for all the subjects or cases with respect to a given variable and then dividing the total by the number of cases. It is often called an average. The median and mean are by far the most frequently encountered measures of central tendency.

Measures of dispersion tell us about the extent of variation (with respect to the variable in question) among our cases or subjects. This is important because two sets of cases with identical means, medians, or modes may differ significantly in other important respects. Consider two different groups of 100 persons each. In the first group, every one of the 100 people has an annual income of $30,000. In the second group, forty people have salaries of $10,000, forty others earned $50,000, and the rest $30,000. Although the mean income for both groups is $30,000, the two groups are very different. There is a much wider range of income among the persons in the second group.

The standard deviation is the most commonly used measure of dispersion. Among its many useful properties, as discussed in chapter 8, is its ability to tell us the distance from the mean we must go to find (approximately) two-thirds of our cases. That is, the standard deviation tells us how closely our cases are grouped around the mean.[1] As with most other statistical measures, this use of the standard deviation is appropriate only under certain conditions. The data involved must be interval or ratio level and the scores normally

---

1. For a fuller discussion, see chapter 8 in this volume. See also Manheim and Rich (1991), chapter 17.

distributed. Fortunately, these conditions are often met in political research, and political scientists thus make extensive use of the standard deviation.

Taken together, measures of central tendency and dispersion for a given variable can tell us a great deal about a set of cases. Once calculated for one group of subjects, they can be compared to those for some reference group (or to those for the same group at another time). Theory construction often begins by analyzing the distribution of scores on a single variable.

—————————— Excerpt 13 ——————————

Fred Greenstein's study is a convincing demonstration of the power of simple single variable statistics. Employing such measures, he refined our understanding of children's views of political leaders and thereby identified promising areas for future research, some of which are still being explored over twenty-five years after his study was originally published. As Greenstein pointed out, conventional wisdom at the time of his study held that children simply have an idealized view of their nation's leader as benevolent. To investigate this question, he undertook an exploratory, cross-national study of children in three different countries, including a comparative look at the attitudes of black and white children in the United States.

Greenstein points out that understanding pre-adult attitudes can be very helpful in analyzing cross-national differences in political systems. The ideas we develop about politics when we are very young typically persist as we become more informed and experienced adults. His findings, therefore, are considerably more significant than might be apparent at first glance, and they have been widely discussed.

The following excerpt reports on a large number of variables. Nonetheless, the author's findings are based on univariate analysis, and the statistical procedures used are quite basic. As you read the excerpt, ask yourself if Greenstein's study succeeds in generating information that advances our understanding of the topic and that might be exploited in future research.

The Benevolent Leader Revisited:
Children's Images of Political Leaders
in Three Democracies

Fred I. Greenstein, *Princeton University*

American Political Science Review 69 (December 1975): 1371–1398. Copyright ©
1975 by the American Political Science Association. Reprinted with permission.

Political Culture and Socialization in Britain, France and the United States

The following widely held or implied assumptions are what might be called
the textbook theory of politics and society in the three nations with which this
study is concerned:

1. Britain and the United States are "stable democracies."
2. France is an "unstable democracy" marked by widespread distrust of
    political leaders and internal cleavage.
3. Britain and the United States differ substantially in social structure
    and political psychology. Britons traditionally accept the legitimacy of
    political authority, whereas Americans are ambivalent, though not
    wholly negative, toward their leaders.
4. Thus, the United States exhibits an uneasy compromise between French-
    and British-like properties. Indeed, if the United States were organized
    in the centralized fashion permitted by British social structure and val-
    ues, unstable, French-style outcomes would result.
5. American politics are more centrifugal than British politics, partly be-
    cause of the greater social heterogeneity of the U.S., and particularly
    the greater number of potentially antagonistic groups. The single most
    enduring element of this politically explosive social heterogeneity re-
    sults from the heritage of slavery. The presence of "two nations" in the
    United States has been a fundamental source of political conflict from
    the framing of the Constitution through the 1970s, by which time
    American blacks had become increasingly alienated and racially proud.
    By the 1970s, blacks were direct protagonists in American politics,
    and not merely the objects of political conflict and machination.

These deliberately simplified textbook claims imply assumptions about
political socialization that would place white American children between
English and French children in their evaluations of political leaders, but would

predict that these aspects of political psychology do not take the same form among black and white American children. Blacks presumably would resemble the French in their distrust of their nation's leaders; whites would be more like the British children in their trust of leaders.

"The literature" speaks with many voices, however. Recent writings contain numerous observations and assertions that contradict the foregoing sketch, partly because of reassessment of the traditional assumptions. Here are some brief illustrations of how the conventional wisdom has altered with respect to the four comparison groups in this study and also the study of political socialization in general:

1. A principal debate in the recent literature on English political culture and socialization is whether the Bagehot-derived presumption that the "English common people" are "deferential" to higher authorities stands up empirically. Indeed, important questions have been raised about whether the very notion of deference has been adequately explicated in the literature.

2. The emphasis of Gallic negativism toward political authority in the textbook account of French political culture has a corollary in the notion that the French populace consists of highly politicized citizens, each of whom is deeply committed to his own preferences among the panoply of subtly nuanced French political ideologies. In contrast to the "Frenchman-as-ideologue," recent studies have found an exceptionally apolitical (possibly antipolitical) French electorate that provides few restraints on the impulses of the thin political stratum of the populace to view over what Freud called "the narcissism of small differences." Some interpretations of French politics also stress the putative "individualism" of the French, but other writings stress the importance of hierarchical, even autocratic, authority relations in French politics and society, more like the conventional stereotype of "the Germans" than of "the French." After all, runs the *mot*, "Charlemagne was also Karl der Grosse."[1]

3. The empirical studies of American adults conducted up to the early 1960s seem to suggest that the positive aspects of adult ambivalence toward leaders are considerably more consequential for political behavior than are negative attitudes such as generalized distrust for politicians. The early studies of American children show almost unequivocally positive references to the "benevolence" of political leaders. This early "benevolent leader literature" has since been referred to as an "irrelevant" characterization of a bygone era.[2] After all, this literature preceded the Vietnam protests, ghetto insurrections, increasing signs of deeper, ideological conflict and distrust of authorities in the adult population, protest activities by college and high school students during Johnson's final years in office, and, after the apparent calm of

Nixon's first term, Watergate and its aftermath. That certain of these trends even occurred raises important questions about the value of the benevolent-leader literature. As more than one commentator has noted, some of the same pre-adolescents who blithely idealized Eisenhower and Kennedy in the early studies may well have been the leaders of protest against "the system" a few years later.

In the second wave of mid- to late-1960s political socialization research, an important study of the highly distinctive, culturally and physically isolated population of poor whites in Appalachia was instructively titled "The *Male*volent Leader."[3] To some extent this title came to represent the expectation that in the post-Eisenhower, post–New Frontier-Great Society era, *all* segments of the pre-adult American population were likely to acquire political orientations lacking the idealized qualities reported in the research a decade earlier. Another study by Tolley in 1971 of the attitudes of grade-school children toward the Vietnam conflict reported many indications of children's actual or hypothetical willingness to criticize the President for fostering military conflict. Tolley, who summarized his findings under the heading "The Fallible Leader, 1971," noted that although his data were not comparable to the data of the early studies, he felt sure there had been a reduction in children's idealization of the American President.[4]

4. Substantial changes in the political consciousness and behavior of American blacks have occurred since the 1950s. Evidence exists that blacks at all age levels exhibit political negativism, distrust, and cynicism, but findings on this score are far from consistent, perhaps because race relations and "the black experience" in the United States, in spite of certain overriding uniformities, are highly variable from one context to another. In addition, black political orientations probably have a distinctive subcultural patterning, which needs to be characterized in its own terms and not merely as part of a continuum of French, American white, and English orientations.

5. One may also speculate about the adequacy *in general* of the empirical characterizations of pre-adult (and adult) political orientations toward leaders. Political scientists interested in political socialization have been relentlessly monistic in their use of paper-and-pencil surveys, especially fixed-choice questionnaires, in studying children. As a result, questions have been raised about the possible artifactuality of the early political socialization research. The same fixed-choice response can have different meanings to different respondents, and individuals whose attitudes are essentially the same sometimes choose different responses depending on how they perceive item wordings. Worse yet, a choice may be made more or less arbitrarily because it sounds right or because of the respondent's desire to cooperate. These dangers are increased when such techniques are applied to young children who may

not even recognize the terminology (e.g., the very word "government"), much less the rationale of an item such as the following from the Easton and Hess questionnaire: "What happens in the government will happen no matter what people do." When fixed-choice procedures are used cross-culturally, the possibility for misleading findings is multiplied, a point that emerges strongly from British critiques of an application of the Easton and Hess instrument to an English pre-adult population.

Even where open-ended approaches are used, problems of interpreting responses persist. In my New Haven study, the open-ended format made it possible to qualify or counter some interpretations suggested by the fixed-choice Easton and Hess study. The final data collection was less than ideal, however, because a paper-and-pencil procedure was used. Even if interviewing had been possible it would still have been difficult to elicit responses without suggesting or structuring them, and to interpret the resulting verbiage. These problems of interpretation exist especially in characterizing children's orientations as "benevolent." Children, or at least American children, are rather free with words like "help" in describing political leaders. But what do children mean when they say a leader is "a helper"? Are they exhibiting basic assumptions about the benevolence of leaders? Or are they merely mouthing a bit of conventional language? In either case, to what degree are their statements affective and evaluative, and to what degree are they cognitive?

One reason for suspecting the accuracy of political socialization findings that stress reasonably well-patterned pre-adult political orientations is that survey research on adults has reported remarkably low levels of information and attitudinal consistency. The conclusions of the literature on lack of patterning in adult orientations have since been softened both by events (the evident increase in attitudinal patterning as the "polarizing" political conflict of the 1960s proceeded), and by variant approaches to analyzing survey data on adults (e.g., approaches that emphasize the issues salient to an individual). Furthermore, it seems desirable to examine adult orientations in ways that do not force a respondent to answer questions about the issues currently concerning the active minority of the political leadership stratum. Since survey items often use *categories of discourse* that characterize "elite" rather than "mass" political thought and discussion, more "naturalistic" modes of eliciting political orientation might possibly show *greater* patterning in adult orientations than is presently reported, and *less,* or at any rate, different patterning in pre-adult orientations.

Methodological Premises and Procedures

Although the methodological problems just discussed might seem to point to a search for a philosopher's stone that would make possible "perfect" measurement of political orientations, a different strategy is called for: that of multiple indicators and, in particular, *multiple methods.* As Campbell and Fiske point out in a classic paper still insufficiently appreciated by political scientists, it is axiomatic that particular measurement approaches contain "biases." The most efficacious research strategy is to take advantage of, rather than seek to eliminate, these biases by employing compensating types of observational techniques, which produce instrument effects in varying but known directions. The findings elicited by different measurement techniques can be compared by a process analogous to triangulation[5] as it is used in surveying. The multimethod research procedure used in the present study enables us to examine the convergences and divergences among findings of four types: conventional fixed-choice items, open-ended questions, semi-projective story completions, and verbatim response quotations, but in this paper we draw selectively only on the latter three classes of data.

The open-ended items were designed to elicit children's perceptions of major roles and institutions in their political system. These questions were similar to those used, for example, in the University of Michigan Survey Research Center's election studies, but employed a more varied set of codes to analyze responses. The sequence of information items was somewhat unconventional because it was preceded by this statement:

> A new child comes to your school. He comes from another country. He says to you: "There are some things about [England, France, the United States] that I don't understand. Tell me what they are. . . ."

The "things" proved to be "the Queen," "the Prime Minister," "the President of the Republic," and other political roles and institutions.[6] The simple expedient of placing the child in a free-response circumstance sometimes elicited findings both contrary to and more accurate than those reported in previous research using fixed-choice items. For example, fixed-choice political socialization research points to great respect for the Supreme Court. Interviews show similar positive responses, but make clear that they are to the positively toned words "supreme" and "court," and do not reflect awareness of the activities of the institution.

The most distinctive methodological departure was the use of numerous questions in which our respondents were presented with carefully contrived, incomplete stories and asked to imagine the conclusions, after the manner of the familiar Thematic Apperception Test (TAT). The procedure is called *semi-*projective because it employs more culturally recognizable and less ambiguous stimuli than those used in orthodox projective tests, and the responses are analyzed in terms of surface psychocultural dispositions, such as cognitive and evaluative assumptions about political reality, rather than in terms of deep strata of the personality.

The data that follow are derived from thirty- to sixty-minute taped interviews with 297 ten- to fourteen-year-old children in four comparison groups of the following sizes: English, 80; French, 106; U.S. whites, 86; U.S. blacks,

25. The comparison groups are essentially evenly divided by sex. The interviews were conducted in geographically diverse schools, so far as was possible: Connecticut, Eastern Pennsylvania, and upstate New York in the United States; the Paris area and Provence in France; and London and East Anglia in Britain. To facilitate subgroup comparisons, the samples were deliberately stratified rather than seeking to follow population frequencies. Unfortunately, our resources did not permit a large number of black interviews in the United States, and consequently the black-white comparisons should be treated as provisional. By using a large number of schools and classrooms, and numerous interviewers for the English, French, and white American groups, possible measurement errors resulting from individual interviewer style and classroom climate were reduced. Black children were interviewed by a black, female interviewer.

The interviews conducted during the Watergate hearings were with white Connecticut children from the same schools where the previous Connecticut white interviews had taken place. A slightly truncated interview guide was used.

Although an attempt was made to match the groups by age, socioeconomic status, and community characteristics, some differences occurred. Analyses controlling for these factors made it clear that they were not responsible for the patterns in the tables to be presented. Sample size and space limitations preclude multivariate analysis in this presentation; instead marginals and verbatim content are extensively discussed and compared. I have abjured significance testing, which would give an aura of spurious precision to a richly complex but obviously exploratory body of data.

Children Explain Their Political Leaders and Institutions: Information, Images, and Affect

Tables 1 through 3 are based on the questions in which the respondent is asked to imagine a dialogue with a foreign child seeking information about respondent's country. Table 1 reports levels of information about the chief of state in each of the three nations and about the Prime Minister in Britain and France. To broaden the perspective on awareness of these five roles, information also is presented in Table 1 on awareness of the local member of the national legislature and the mayor, but for the remainder of this analysis, only the chief of state and prime ministerial roles will be discussed.

At present there is a scattered array of findings about levels of awareness of these roles on the part of children and adults in the three countries. At all age levels, the President is certainly the best-known American, and he is virtually the only public figure known to more than a small minority of children until late in adolescence. Although both children and adults in the United States, when confronted with the appropriately worded questionnaire item, can be induced to say that the Congress is "more important" to the nation than the President, the available evidence suggests that at all age levels the President is considerably more salient than that Congress and the individual members of Congress. A recent national study of children's awareness of their district congressman shows that by age thirteen only 11 percent can name that individual—indeed only about 40 per cent of young adults can. Awareness of local officials appears to vary from locality to locality in the United States. In my 1958 political socialization study, virtually all New Haven children by the fifth-grade level knew the name of that city's popular Mayor Richard C. Lee, whereas in the nearby community of East Haven only 40 per cent of a fifth-grade pretest sample were able to name the municipal chief executive.

Comparably detailed documentation does not appear to be available for either British or French adults and children. Roig and Billon-Grand do, however, provide evidence of the wide general awareness of the President of the Republic among French children,[7] and Greenstein, Herman, Stradling, and Zureik report data that provide some sense of how English children perceive the Queen and the Prime Minister.[8]

Virtually all the children professed to have *heard* of the four British and French and three American political roles in their respective countries. Professions of knowledge are easy, however. They may reflect reluctance to admit ignorance; they may result from confusion ("Congress" for "Chamber of Commerce," for example); or they may be a mere recognition that the term *sounds* familiar. A more accurate assessment of the children's level of information can be found in Table 1, row 2, which indicates the frequency with which children were able to supply the names of role incumbents in response to an open-ended question. Because the French children were polled during the interval between de Gaulle's resignation and Pompidou's election, as well as during the early Pompidou period when there had been little time to absorb the President's name, we combined the figures for awareness of the present incumbent and awareness of the previous incumbent. Well over 90 per cent of the children in each nation were able to name their head of state. The somewhat lower incidence of awareness of the Queen's name in England reflects no lack of familiarity with the royal role, but instead a tendency to perceive "the Queen" rather than "Elizabeth II" as the designation of the Monarch.

This impression of uniformly high levels of political awareness quickly vanishes as one looks further into Table 1. Whereas almost every English child is able to name Harold Wilson, only about half the French children are able to name the Premier. An increase in the prominence of the Premier as a figure to whom French *adults* orient themselves as the politics of the Fifth Republic evolved has been argued by Jean-Luc Parodi on the basis of time-series survey data, but at the pre-adult level the Premier appears to be at best a shadowy presence.

In all three countries, the legislative representative from the child's district is consistently less well known than any heads of state or prime ministers; only a quarter of the English, French, and U.S. white children and a mere 5 per cent of the U.S. black children were able to name their legislator.

The pattern of awareness of local executives strikingly suggests the importance of the mayoral role or its equivalent in the three political systems, a finding consistent with Roberta Sigel's observation that, in spite of the considerable affective component in early political learning and children's general inattention to government and politics, detailed, reasonably accurate cognitive learning about political roles and institutions *does* occur. French children, brought up in a political system with intensely localistic traditions in which *maire* and *mairie* are familiar fixtures, exhibit more information about the mayor and his job than do the children in the other two countries. The French lead the other comparison groups in local awareness substantially, whereas on the other leadership roles the differences among the French and the English and American are in the opposite direction. Seventy-one per cent of the French respondents and roughly half of the American respondents were able to name their mayors, but only one-tenth of the English respondents would name the largely ceremonial and decorative mayors of their cities.

The Cognitive Content of Political Imagery

We can usefully begin to look beneath the surface of the information-level distinctions in Table 1 by submitting role descriptions to an analysis of cognitive content. Table 2 presents twelve of the most substantively interesting image categories used in coding the political leadership roles, including only categories applicable to most or all of the roles and institutions. The categories evolved from repeated perusal of the open-ended data and, where appropriate, from the code used to classify the open-ended responses in my 1958 study. The image categories do not exhaust the themes that can be extracted from the open-ended data, but they do represent some of the most salient surface aspects of the children's descriptions of their national leadership roles and institutions.

I begin with an extended examination of the first category listed in Table 2—the seemingly workaday theme that the leader "rules, governs, or commands." This category is consistently used for the head of state, but rarely for the prime ministers, even in Britain, where the ceremonial leader (the Queen) rather than the effective leader (the Prime Minister) receives most references to ruling.

In view of the extensive literature on the dilemma of achieving equivalent meanings in cross-cultural measurement, it is striking to note the national variation in linguistic usage and connotation when children refer to general governance. The imagery used by the American children suggests a leader who is an important person with a high degree of control over his political system. In some responses the President appears as the only important decision maker in the political system. Other children describe the constitutional checks and balances. In neither case do the responses of these children in 1969–70 suggest that the executive power of the leader is peremptory, fright-

Table 1

Levels of Political Awareness[a] (percentages)

Response	England				France				U.S. whites			U.S. blacks		
	Queen	Prime minister	Legis-lator	Mayor	Presi-dent	Premier	Legis-lator	Mayor	Presi-dent	Legis-lator	Mayor	Presi-dent	Legis-lator	Mayor
Claims to have heard of role	100	100	98	100	100	100	93	100	100	99	100	100	100	96
Can name role incumbent	91	96	25	10	68	50	24	71	100	27	49	96	5	40
Can name previous incumbent	3	0	0	0	31	2	2	2	0		4	0		0
Mean number of images	3.3	3.0	1.9 (1.4)[b]	2.0	2.7	1.5	1.5 (.81)[b]	2.0	3.1	1.7	1.7	2.7	1.6 (1.3)[b]	1.8
Respondents with 0 images	0	10	20	14	0	0	50	2	0	10	17	0	36	12

(Braces in the original indicate combined percentages: England Queen 94, Prime minister 96; France President 99, Premier 52, Legislator/Mayor 73; U.S. whites President 100, Mayor 53; U.S. blacks President 96.)

[a]Row 1 is based on the following number of cases: 80 English, 106 French, 86 U.S. whites, 25 U.S. blacks, except that 1 English child was not asked about the mayor, 3 French children were not asked about the Premier, 12 French children were not asked about the legislator, and 2 U.S. black children were not asked about the legislator. In row 2 the following number of respondents were excluded: head of state—England 2, France 2, France 3; legislator—England 2, France 13, U.S. whites 9, U.S. blacks 4; mayor—England 7, France 7, U.S. whites 1. Mean number of images (rows 3 and 4) is computed from fourteen image categories that were common to all or most of the roles and institutions. Twelve of these categories are shown in Table 2. The image scores, like the image-mentioned percentages in Table 2, are based only on those respondents who were asked about the role or institution and showed awareness of it. The number of cases on which rows 3 and 4 are based is the same as the number for each role and institution in Table 3.

[b]Mean number of images for legislature.

ening, or authoritarian, nor that he has absolute control. American children often say the President is "in charge," but quickly add that he cannot engage in extreme arbitrary behavior, for instance, capriciously ordering capital punishment. My impression is that when they add this qualification, they have in mind an implicit notion that at least in some other nations, leaders do have such power. The American respondents say, for example, that the President "governs," is the "ruler of the country," "leads the country," is "the leader of the people," "heads the U.S.," "runs the United States," "runs the government," is the "chief executive," and, in one instance (without the connotations it would have to a lexicographer or a student of city political machines), is "the big boss."

Relatively few English children use the governance category in describing the Prime Minister, but many do in connection with the Queen. Their considerable use of verbs and nouns associated with monarchy is not surprising. Again, any connotation of sternness or oppressiveness in the wielding of power is notably absent. The Queen is described as "ruler of our country," "ruler of England and other nations that are in the Commonwealth," "ruler of Great Britain"; she "governs all of England," "rules over the people," "rules over the land," is "the reigning monarch," and "sovereign." As the foregoing quotations suggest, a substantial proportion of pre-adolescent English children think of their Queen as considerably more than a figurehead. Recent surveys of English school children make it clear that the English child first becomes aware of the political system through the monarch, who is perceived as the *effective* and not just the *formal* leader of the country.

Turning to France, we find a much sterner quality in the linguistic usages of the overwhelming (86 per cent) majority of children who made statements describing de Gaulle or Pompidou in terms of governance. There is not a single reference to the Premier in these terms. This finding, combined with the low level of awareness of the Premier evident in Table 1, makes it clear that Fifth Republic children focus their attention to national executive leadership entirely on the President. Both the great prevalence of governance imagery in the descriptions of the President of the Republic and the specific connotations of many descriptions fit into a larger pattern of findings consistent with the notion that in France authorities are viewed in sternly hierarchical terms.

Given de Gaulle's distinctive leadership style, it is remarkable that virtually no children refer to the personal qualities of the President, nor was de Gaulle's preoccupation with international statesmanship apparent beyond the 14 per cent who mentioned an international role—a percentage that does not vary between de Gaulle and Pompidou. De Gaulle's interest in *grandeur* and civil dignity did not lead to much emphasis on ceremonial aspects of the presidency. Instead, there is the single constellation of "rules-governs-commands" images. This stress on governance and absence of personalism is precisely what Percheron, who used a substantially different (word associa-

Table 2

Images of Political Roles and Institutions (percentages)

Image categories	England		France		U.S. whites	U.S. blacks
	Queen	Prime minister	President	Premier	President	President
Rules, governs, commands	62	24	86	0	64	42
Legislative, legal function	23	31	14	3	51	29
Makes decisions, solves problems	15	25	18	3	35	29
Communicative (makes speeches, etc.)	1	13	6	5	10	32
Economic role	8	28	12	3	8	12
Other domestic activity	13	17	11	8	15	20
International activities	9	13	14	4	44	40
Ceremonial activities	53	19	11	5	16	0
Symbolic representative of nation[a]	19	—	3	—	5	4
Trappings of office	35	16	3	1	9	8
Role with other government officials	35	69	33	87	18	12
Personal attributes	16	7	2	1	1	0
N[b]	(71–79)	(68–76)	(101–104)	(96–97)	(79–86)	(24–25)

[a] Not coded for the Prime Minister.

[b] Percentages based on those respondents familiar with the role, excluding those whose responses were coded as ambiguous.

Coding status: Intercoder percentage agreement ranges from 89% (row 3) to 98% (rows 5, 6, 7, 10, 11), averaging 95%. Intercoder agreement was also calculated by Scott's pi, which takes into account the random expected value of agreement given the number of coding categories. For an explanation of Scott's pi, see Ole R. Holsti, *Content Analysis in the Social Sciences and Humanities* (Reading, Mass.: Addison-Wesley, 1969), pp. 140–41. Pi values range from .66 (row 3) to .96 (row 11), averaging .83 (for the 60 cases double-coded).

tion) instrument, found in a 1969 study of children's images of the President of the Republic. Overall, the general "thinness" of imagery about these two French roles is more consistent with the apolitical than with the highly politicized conception of French political culture.

Turning directly to that widely studied phenomenon, American children's perceptions of their President, we note the frequent references to decision making and problem solving (35 per cent for whites, 29 per cent for blacks).

Although the American presidency is said to derive some of its political leverage from the fusion of the ceremonial with the political functions, white American children were no more likely to refer to ceremonial duties of the President than were British children to mention the Prime Minister in ceremonial contexts, and black children were less likely to make such references. Mr. Nixon's early "low profile" presidency, of course, came nowhere near the British monarchy as a stimulus for reference to ceremonial duties, nor does it elicit personal references to the President among our respondents.

Perception of the President's international role also warrants special mention. This function is rarely mentioned with respect to the other leaders, but is mentioned by two fifths of the American children. Indeed, there is even reason to believe that children (not to speak of adults) in other countries perceive the American President in this fashion.[9] One need not fall back on dated patriotic clichés like "leader of the Free World," to recognize the accuracy of this perception even before Mr. Nixon's peripatetic diplomacy in China and the Soviet Union enhanced his standing in the polls and insured his margin of electoral victory.

Clearly the American President circa 1970 occupies substantial cognitive space in pre-adult political orientations, but what of the affective matters dealt with in the benevolent leader literature?

Evaluative Aspects of Political Imagery

Even though we asked respondents simply to *describe* the leadership positions of their polity to the imaginary foreign child, their responses exhibit considerable affective content. In seeking to characterize the feelings underlying the statements children made to us, we must tread warily because much of the response content is ambiguous.

Table 3, which reports the frequency of positive, negative, affectively mixed, and neutral role descriptions for those respondents able to describe a role, brings us directly to whether the American benevolent-leader findings reported in the early 1960s are applicable to later and different populations, as well as to how accurate were the interpretations of the original Eisenhower-Kennedy Administration findings. The table presents data on the heads of state and the Prime Ministers of England and France, and the President of the United States.

Table 3 is the result of an extended sequence of codings designed to disentangle genuine expressions of affect from cognitive statements and vague conventional usages. Beginning with the criteria established in my 1958 study, coders were provided with a comprehensive set of indicators of positive and negative affect. Positive affect was described as follows:

> Respondent describes duties in a positive or benevolent way: "The leader takes care of the country," "helps people," "makes things better," "improves conditions," "looks

after us," "goes around to spread goodwill among the people," "most people look up to him or her," etc.

Negative affect included all negative or hostile references to the public figure or his duties, such as "hurts the country," "wastes time," and "does nothing but talk." Included in negative affect were criticisms of the current role-incumbent on partisan grounds even when it was evident that the child felt no animus toward the role itself. If the child indicated that the role was good but the individual holding it was not, or otherwise made both positive and negative statements, the "mixed" category was used. Neutral references included colorless and bland job descriptions.

This coding procedure produced striking patterns of cross-national and black-white American differences, but intercoder reliabilities were low, and some patterns of differences between roles within and between countries seemed inconsistent with our impressions from reading the interviews. For example, in the tabulation from the first coding, respondents were more positive toward the role of legislator than toward the President, whereas our impression from the interviews was that there was little cognizance of *or* affect toward the legislator. It turned out that "help" when used to describe a legislator often was an affectively neutral term, referring merely to the subordinate duties of an assistant. Even references to "helping the country" could not invariably be interpreted as evidence of positive affect, since it was not always certain that the term was more than a loose conventional usage.

A more differentiated set of criteria for distinguishing positive affect was therefore devised. (There had been little difficulty in securing agreement between the coders in the few role descriptions that conveyed negative connotations.) The differentiated code identifies the following subthemes that appear to evince positive affect: (1) *explicitly positive* evaluative statements that any reader would be hard pressed to interpret in non-affective terms; (2) statements not explicitly affective that describe the *importance or power* of the leader in an idealized way; (3) generalized references to *helping* (excluding the brief case-carrying variant); (4) references to unambiguously positive aspects of *role performance* (such as stopping wars or promoting economic prosperity); (5) references to the leader as a source of *moral guidance* or as a chooser of "right" policies; and (6) general statements about the importance of the leader, excluding any in which the word "important" seemed merely to be used mechanically as a synonym for "leader." After rereading the protocols several times, we added a seventh category, the variant of importance that stresses the *need to obey* the leader.

For each of the three countries, leadership role descriptions that fit any of the seven criteria are aggregated to produce the "positive-idealized" category of Table 3, which also reports the incidence of the differentiated positive affect subcategories. One of the principal findings summarized in Table 3 has already been alluded to: Given the open-ended stimulus of being asked to

Table 3

Levels of Affect and Idealization Vis-à-Vis Political Roles (percentages)

	England		France		U.S. whites	U.S. blacks
Response	Queen	Prime minister	President	Premier	President	President
Positive/idealized	47	28	30	3	55	32
Mixed	0	1	0	0	0	4
Negative	1	9	0	0	1	4
Neutral	51	62	69	97	43	60
Not ascertained	1	0	1	0	1	0
Total	100	100	100	100	100	100
N^a	(80)	(80)	(106)	(99)	(86)	(25)

Breakdown of responses coded as positive/idealized

Explicit positive affect	15.0	2.5	7.5	0.0	29.1	16.0
Other explicit idealization	3.8	0.0	2.8	0.0	2.3	4.0
"Helps"	8.8	2.5	2.8	0.0	2.3	4.0
Does good things	5.0	6.3	8.5	0.0	9.3	4.0
Says what's right	3.8	8.8	.9	1.0	1.2	0.0
"Important"	8.8	7.5	1.8	2.0	2.3	4.0
Must be obeyed	1.3	0.0	5.7	0.0	0.0	0.0
Subtotal	46.5	27.6	30.0	3.0	54.7	32.0
N^a	(38)	(22)	(32)	(3)	(47)	(8)

[a] Percentages based on those respondents familiar with role.

Coding status: Initial reliabilities were deemed inadequate. Intercoder discrepancies were resolved and coding criteria further specified by F.G., and all protocols were coded by F.G. and a second coder with resolution of discrepancies by discussion.

describe political leadership roles, very few of these end-of-the-1960s children spontaneously introduced negative assertions into their discourse. As we shall see in the analysis below of semi-projective story completions, the children were not *incapable* of making negative statements. Even the political information question produced *some* negative evaluations—by English children of the Prime Minister (these proved in every instance to be criticisms by middle-class children of Harold Wilson rather than of the prime ministerial role), and by black American children of the President. Although Percheron's word-association technique (used in 1969) and Roig and Billon-Grand's fixed-choice questions (used in 1962) did elicit negative pre-adult evaluations of the President of the Republic, none of the French respondents we interviewed made negative statements about their President.

Turning to positive evaluations and focusing only on the heads of state and Prime Ministers, we see that apart from the absence of evaluations of the perceptually bland French Premier, assertions falling into the positive-affect category were made by between 30 per cent and somewhat more than 50 per cent of those children in the four comparison groups who were familiar with the roles. The variations in level of positive affect complement the image content data already presented. In England the Queen is far more likely to be described in a positive light than is the Prime Minister; this difference is especially evident if the ratio of positive to negative evaluations is considered. In France, there is modest positive affect toward the President and, again consistent with Percheron's interpretations of French political orientations, there are more neutral references to the head of state by French children than by any of the other comparison groups.

Finally, to my surprise, the first-term Nixon-Administration counterparts of children in the Eisenhower-Kennedy Administration studies—namely the white American respondents—*were extraordinarily positive in their spontaneous descriptions of the President.* A reminder that the study was conducted in 1969–70 and not 1960 is provided by the finding that the American black children were only a little more than half as likely as the whites to refer to the President in positive terms, and somewhat more likely to make negative statements. Even the blacks, however, made more positive than negative assertions.

Notes

1. Relevant sources are reviewed in Fred I. Greenstein and Sidney Tarrow "The Study of French Political Socialization; Toward the Revocation of Paradox," *World Politics*, 22 (October, 1969), 95–137.

2. W. Lee Johnson, Jr., Letter to the Editor, *American Political Science Review*, 66 (December, 1972), 1317–1318.

3. Dean Jaros, Herbert Hirsch, Frederic J. Fleron, Jr., "The Malevolent Leader: Political Socialization in an American Subculture," *American Political Science Review*, 62 (June, 1968), 564–75.

4. Howard Tolley, Jr., *Children and War: Socialization to International Conflict* (New York: Teachers College Press, 1973), pp. 129–31. Recently, a "multifarious leader" has been introduced into the literature by a pair of investigators who compare black and white American children with a President-worshipping sample of Amish children. Dean Jaros and Kenneth L. Kolson, "The Multifarious Leader: Political Socialization of Amish, 'Yanks,' Blacks," in Richard G. Niemi and Associates, *The Politics of Future Citizens* (San Francisco: Jossey-Bass, 1974), pp. 41–62. For an exceptionally interesting study of the absence of conspicuous leadership figures in post-World War II Japanese political socialization, see Joseph A. Massey, "The Missing Leader: Japanese Youths' View of Political Authority," *American Political Science Review*, 69 (March, 1975), 31–48.

5. Donald T. Campbell and Donald W. Fiske, "Convergent and Discriminant Validation by Multitrait-Multimethod Matrix," *Psychological Bulletin*, 56 (March, 1959), 81–105. For a recent contribution to the literature perfecting the psychometrics of this approach, see Arne L. Kalleberg and James R. Kluegel, "Analysis of Multitrait-Multimethod Matrix: Some Limitations and an Alternative," *Journal of Applied Psychology*, 60 (February, 1975), 1–9. The term "triangulation" is first used in Eugene J. Webb, Donald T. Campbell, Richard D. Schwartz, and Lee Sechrest, *Unobtrusive Measures: Nonreactive Research in the Social Sciences* (Chicago: Rand McNally, 1961).

6. The verbatim response content makes clear that most children ignore the hypothetical foreign child and treat the item as a simple request for cognitive information. A few French children were explicitly suspicious of the foreign child and describe the precautions they would take in discussing politics with a stranger; a few English children cast themselves as tour guides, exhibiting Buckingham Palace to the young foreigner. In no case did the foreign child stimulus invoke nationalistic idealizations of domestic leaders or institutions. For a text of the interview schedule, see Greenstein and Tarrow, "Political Orientations of Children: The Use of a Semi-Projective Technique in Three Nations," pp. 535–49.

7. C. Roig and F. Billon-Grand, *La socialisation politique des enfants* (Paris: Cahiers de la fondation nationale des sciences politiques 163, Armand Colin, 1968). For a summary in English of the findings of Roig and Billon-Grand, see Greenstein and Tarrow, "The Study of French Political Socialization." On the orientations of French adults to de Gaulle and the French presidency as manifested in the General, see Institut français d'opinion publique, *Les français et de Gaulle* (Plon, 1971).

8. See Greenstein et al., "The Child's Conception of the Queen and the Prime Minister." On monarchy generally, see Paul Abramson and Ronald Inglehart, "The Development of Systemic Support in Four Western Democracies," *Comparative Political Studies*, 2 (January, 1969), 419–42.

9. In a small sample of sixth-grade Australian children studied by Connell in 1968, there was somewhat greater awareness of the President of the United States than of the Prime Minister of Australia! Connell, *The Child's Construction of Politics*, p. 125. For similar findings in a Canadian study, see Jon H. Pammett, "The Development of Political Orientations in Canadian School Children," *Canadian Journal of Political Science*, 4 (March, 1971), 132–41.

Discussion Questions

1. When Greenstein compares the frequency of certain responses from children in one country to those in another, is he still engaging in univariate statistical analysis?

2. A major purpose of Greenstein's study was to suggest paths for future study. Was he successful in this? Can you think of a hypothesis involving two or more variables that are suggested by Greenstein's data and findings?

3. Apparently, Greenstein felt that it was better to describe children's attitudes via simple single variable statistics than to attempt to test hypotheses about the possible *causes* of their attitudes. Presumably, factors such as income, education, and intelligence might plausibly have an effect on children's perception of their leaders. Was there any value in beginning research on these factors with Greenstein's approach?

4. Which of the following research problems would be better suited to a study using univariate analysis: (a) the effect of political culture on arms purchases, or (b) the effect of income on the voting turnout? Why? How would you go about designing a study using univariate analysis for the problem?

5. What types of hypotheses can be tested using univariate statistics of the type employed in the excerpt? Could we test hypotheses that involve a causal relationship between two variables? Why or why not?

Commentary

Greenstein made it clear at the outset that he was not interested in testing hypotheses. The purpose of his study was exploratory. For this reason, he chose to present his data in some detail, making extensive use of frequency distributions. One result of this is that it becomes possible for the reader to draw his or her own conclusions from Greenstein's data, perhaps challenging Greenstein's own interpretation in the process.

Of course, Greenstein's study involved other variables, particularly race and nation. He measured attitudes separately for each category of these other variables. If Greenstein had attempted to show a statistical relationship between some aspect of attitude toward the leader and race, his study would have involved bivariate analysis. The best way to see his study is as a series of univariate analyses.

This excerpt illustrates how rich and detailed frequency distributions can be, especially in comparison with presentations that rely on summary statistics. Consider Table 3. Here Greenstein in effect shows *all* of his raw numerical findings, leaving us to decide how to interpret them. Some points are obvious, of course; French children have very little interest in their premier, and black children in the United States have far less positive feelings about the president than white children.

Greenstein could have presented his data in less detailed form. He could, for example, have made greater use of measures of central tendency. Again consider Table 3. Here he might have scored positive responses as 3, mixed and neutral as 2, and negative as 1 (omitting entirely all "not ascertained" responses). He could then have computed mean scores for each category.[2] Had he done this for British children's perceptions of the Queen, he would have obtained an average or mean score of 2.44. (The arithmetic here would be simple: $(47)(3) + (51)(2) + (1)(1) = 244, \div 100 = 2.44$.) Calculating a similar score for other categories would have provided him with an interesting basis for comparison. French children were somewhat less positive about their president, for example, as indicated by the average score of 2.28 using this method.

The important point to be noted here, however, is that this approach would have entailed a *loss of information*. Perhaps it is important to know how many children had mixed responses and how many were neutral. If so, reporting only the means for each category would not be as informative. Greenstein reported the data in a manner appropriate for his purpose.

Note also Greenstein's great sensitivity to the basic problems of question construction in survey research. Greenstein took little for granted in inter-

---

2. This would require that the researcher consider the scores to be ratio or interval data for the purposes of this measure. Although often done, this is not precisely correct; it assumes that the difference between a score of one and a score of two is exactly the same as the difference between a score of two and a score of three.

preting answers. He noted, for example, that the initial responses of U.S. children suggested that they were as positive about legislators as they were about the president. Further inquiry revealed, however, that his respondents saw the legislators as being helpful in a very different way than the president, one that was more technical or subservient. Thus, the children in Greenstein's study clearly had a more idealized view of the president than of legislators, the apparent initial similarity of their responses on these two items notwithstanding. It is this kind of care and thoroughness that makes Greenstein's study sound and persuasive.

In short, Greenstein's study illustrates the value of the detail provided by a simple frequency distribution. Reading his article, we are able to see for ourselves both the extent of variation as well as the average scores for each group of cases. Often valuable in and of themselves, the insights provided by descriptive studies such as Greenstein's are often critical to the effective design of the subsequent, more sophisticated, research they make possible.

11 Bivariate Analysis:
Statistics of Two Variables

In the excerpt featured in the previous chapter, Greenstein's method of analysis essentially consisted of examining several frequency distributions for a single variable (measured in different ways). The results of such simple analysis can often be extremely helpful and interesting, especially in the early stages of theory-building.

More typically, however, we want to know about relationships among variables. We may speculate, for example, that Greenstein's finding about the differences between the perceptions of the U.S. president on the part of black and white children can be accounted for by a more general relationship between income and perceptions of the leader. Since African Americans, as a group, have lower incomes than other Americans, the existence of a strong relationship between income and perceptions of the leader could produce the results Greenstein reported. Perhaps it is not race, but poverty, that produces low opinions of the leader. A bivariate analysis could help to shed light on this possibility. To study it empirically, we would have to investigate the relationship between household income and children's attitudes about the president. Do children from wealthy families feel more positively about the president than children from poor families? Perhaps not. Only further research can tell us for sure.

Analysis of the relationship between two variables has a special name—**bivariate analysis**. Typically, we employ bivariate analysis when we want to know if two variables (or phenomena) are associated. As Manheim and Rich (1991) put it, "an **association** is said to exist between two variables when knowing the value of one for a given case improves the odds of our guessing correctly the corresponding value of the second" (p. 261). Accordingly, if we were to find an association between household income and children's feelings about the president, then ascertaining a household's income could improve our chances of guessing whether the children of that household had positive images of the president. Similarly, knowing whether the children involved had positive or negative images of the president could help us to guess whether the household was wealthy or poor. Of course, if there is no association, then knowing the value of one variable would be of no help in guessing the value of the other.

The two basic characteristics of any bivariate association are *direction* and *strength*. Bivariate associations can be positive or negative, strong or weak.

A *positive* association is one in which the values of the variables involved increase or decrease together. A *negative* association is one in which the values of the variables move systematically in opposite directions. Thus, if we find a positive association between household income and children's perceptions of the president, this means that as household income increases, so does the likelihood that the children involved will have positive feelings about the president. If so, we would expect children from wealthy households to be more likely to have positive feelings about the president than those from poor households.

But what if there were a negative association between household income and children's feelings about the president? Perhaps positive feelings about the president increase as household income decreases. If so, children from poorer households would be more likely to have positive attitudes about the president than children from wealthy families. Nonetheless, even though the direction of the association would have changed, we would still find that knowing the value of one variable would help us to guess the value of the other.

Some associations are stronger than others. Height and weight are quite strongly associated. While there are exceptions, most people who are especially tall are also heavier than average. The association is therefore very strong. Weaker associations simply have more exceptions. For example, wealthy voters in the United States are more likely to vote Republican; poor voters are more likely to vote Democratic. A positive association thus exists between wealth and a tendency to vote Republican. However, there are many relatively poor people who vote Republican and many relatively rich people who vote Democratic. Thus, the relationship is only moderately strong.

The magnitude or strength of bivariate associations is normally indicated by means of a **coefficient**. The value of most coefficients ranges from −1 (indicating a strong negative association), to 0 (indicating no association), to +1 (indicating a strong positive association). The closer the value of this coefficient is to 1 (regardless of direction), the stronger the association. Thus a coefficient of 0.9 indicates a strong positive association, and a coefficient of −0.9 indicates a strong negative association. A coefficient of 0.1, on the other hand, suggests a very weak (positive) association.

The appropriate measure for calculating a coefficient varies with the type of data. **Cramer's V** and **chi-square** (χ^2) are frequently used with nominal level data. **Goodman and Kruskal's gamma** (γ), **Kendall's tau** (τ), and **Spearman's rho** (ρ) are often used with ordinal level data (data that allows us to rank cases as greater or lesser in magnitude). When we have interval or ratio data (or are willing to treat our data as if they are measured at this level), **Pearson's r** and **regression analysis** are commonly employed.

In evaluating any bivariate association based on observations of sample data, we must also attempt to determine the likelihood that this association also occurs within the larger universe or population in which we are interested. Perhaps the cases included in our sample are ones that happen to have unusually high or low scores on both of our variables. If so, analysis of the sample data would reveal a strong positive association. This association, however, would not be an accurate reflection of reality but, rather, would result from our having had the bad luck to have selected an unusual set of cases when drawing our sample. In order to rule out this possibility, we employ **tests of statistical significance**, as discussed in chapter 8. An association that fails to attain statistical significance should not be regarded as describing the population in question even though it may be quite strong among the cases in the sample.

Thus, when analyzing bivariate relationships, the three most important factors to be considered are strength, direction, and statistical significance. It is important to remember, too, that establishing the existence of a bivariate association does not demonstrate causation. An apparent association between two variables may well be attributable to the influence of yet another variable or variables. Identifying the independent variable or variables responsible for causing change in our dependent variable under circumstances involving many potential variables is a complex process. We will discuss some of the more commonly employed methods for doing this in the next chapter.

———————— Excerpt 14 ————————

Shaw v. Reno was one of the most controversial Supreme Court cases of 1993.[1] At stake was the constitutionality of a plan submitted to the U.S. Justice Department regarding the way congressional districts were drawn in North Carolina. Following a directive from the Justice Department, the state of North Carolina had redrawn its congressional districts to ensure that African-American citizens would constitute a majority in two of the state's twelve districts. In order to accomplish this goal, one of the districts was drawn in a very unusual way so as to include several pockets of African-American citizens. The Supreme Court held the configuration of this district unconstitutional because it amounted to "racial gerrymandering." The controversy in *Shaw v. Reno* re-

---

1. *Shaw* v. *Reno*, 509 U.S. 630, 1993.

flects a much broader issue. Some activists and politicians argue that racial equality in the United States will not exist until more African Americans are elected to Congress. Others contend that the real need is to elect more people to Congress who will support bills that will help meet the needs of African Americans and other minority groups, regardless of the ethnicity of the persons elected.

It is perhaps ironic, but there are good reasons to believe that achieving the former goal (electing more African Americans to Congress) may come at the expense of the second goal (electing people to Congress who support policies favored by African Americans) if it is achieved by redrawing congressional district lines. The answer to this seeming contradiction is simple: When district lines are drawn in ways that create "majority-minority" districts (i.e., districts in which racial minorities constitute a majority), the *other* districts in the state have fewer minority voters in them. To the extent that the presence of minority voters in given congressional districts forces candidates for office to advocate and support policies that these voters favor, creating districts with *fewer* minority voters may remove this incentive. Thus, while concentrating minority voters in a few districts will certainly make it very likely that African-American candidates will win those districts' seats in Congress, it also may result in candidates being elected from other districts who are, as a group, less supportive of policies favored by minority voters.

Does the advantage of having some "safe" African-American seats in Congress outweigh the possible disadvantage of producing a Congress that also has more members with no incentive to represent the interests of minority voters? This is a fundamentally important question that has implications for race and politics in contemporary America, but it also raises issues regarding the basic nature of our system.

The following excerpt uses bivariate analysis to consider the relationship between two variables: (a) the proportion of African-American voters in each district, and (b) the extent to which the representative in Congress from each district supports policies favored by minority citizens.

Do Majority-Minority Districts Maximize Substantive Black Representation in Congress?

Charles Cameron, David Epstein, and
Sharyn O'Halloran, *Columbia University*

American Political Science Review 90, no. 4 (December 1996): 794–812. Copyright
© 1996 by the American Political Science Association. Reprinted with permission.

After the 1990 Census, the North Carolina state legislature drew up a reapportionment plan whereby only one district out of twelve had a majority of minority voters, that is, was a "majority-minority" district. This plan was then submitted to the Department of Justice under the preclearance procedures of Section 5 of the 1965 Voting Rights Act. Upon review, the Justice Department rejected the proposal, suggesting that the state construct a second such district to accommodate its 20% black population. North Carolina's second attempt did result in two majority black districts, the First and the Twelfth, but the latter was, to put it mildly, rather unusually shaped; it snaked along Interstate 85, occasionally ballooning out to capture pockets of black residents and, at times, remaining contiguous only at a single point. The Supreme Court reviewed the second redistricting plan in *Shaw* v. *Reno* and ruled that bizarrely shaped majority-minority districts may create unconstitutional racial gerrymanders.[1] Coming three weeks after the withdrawal of Lani Guinier's nomination to head the Civil Rights Division of the Justice Department, the *Shaw* decision intensified the debate over the role of majority-minority districts in promoting black representation in Congress.

The past quarter-century has seen the rise of what Guinier (1994) terms the "theory of black electoral success," according to which the advancement of minority interests can be measured by the number of minorities elected to public office. This goal has been achieved largely by the construction of concentrated minority voting districts, either through the decennial reapportionment or by switching from at-large voting to district-based systems in local elections. Proponents of these districts argue that, given polarized voting, minorities will remain underrepresented in the political process unless they have equal opportunity to elect the candidate of their choice. If this is true, and if minority voters generally elect minority candidates to represent them, then *descriptive representation*—increasing the number of minority officeholders—goes hand in hand with *substantive representation*—enacting legislation that furthers the interests to the minority community.

Yet, it is unclear that minority interests are always best served by the creation of concentrated minority districts. These dilute minority influence in surrounding areas, which may then elect representatives unsympathetic to minority concerns. If minority voters can influence their representative's actions without necessarily comprising a majority of the electorate, then majority-minority districts may increase the number of minority legislators but decrease the number of votes in support of minority legislation. That is, there may be a trade-off between descriptive and substantive representation. Thus, a basic question of constituency and governance remains unresolved: Do majority-minority districts maximize substantive black representation in Congress? Is it better for political minorities to wield a modest amount of influence in many districts or substantial influence in only a few?

The Debate on Majority-Minority Districts

Two distinct literatures discuss the effect of minority voting strength on a representative's responsiveness to minority interests. The first focuses on how an increase in the minority voting population translates into discernible policy gains. Its emphasis is on finding the appropriate functional relationship between the percentage of black voting-age population in a district and the legislator's roll-call voting behavior. The second literature concentrates on the effect of majority-minority districts in promoting descriptive and substantive representation of black interests. Although these literatures have sometimes been treated separately, we contend that answering the first question—how district composition translates into legislative behavior—is crucial in assessing the influence of majority-minority districts in promoting black interests. We review these literatures and then discuss how they can be integrated to give a broader perspective on the efficacy of majority-minority districts.

Minority Interests and Representation

In single-member district plurality-winner elections, what influence will electoral minorities have over the actions of their representative? A number of different answers have been advanced in the literature. If preferences within the electorate are polarized, with one group commanding a clear majority, then electoral minorities will have only a tenuous relation with their representative. If the majority is itself divided, then these minorities may have a good deal of influence over outcomes by trading their support in return for policy concessions. The first scenario corresponds to the situation of most blacks in southern politics since Reconstruction; the second reflects the position of blacks as key swing voters in national politics from the late 1950s to the mid-1960s.

We thus begin with two hypotheses about the relation between the percentage of black voters in a district and the behavior of their representative. The first, which we term *majoritarianism*, predicts that black voters in a district will have little influence on the voting behavior of their representative until they constitute a majority, at which point the representative's voting behavior takes a discrete jump toward minority-favored policies. The second, termed *influence districts,* posits a generally positive relation between the percentage of blacks and representation of black interests, as would most standard theories of interest group behavior.

Other possibilities have been mentioned in previous studies of race and representation. Historically, the most important of these was suggested by Key (1949) in his classic *Southern Politics.* Key notes that those counties with the highest proportion of blacks were the most likely to vote for Smith over Hoover in 1928 and to bolt the party in favor of Strom Thurmond's State's Rights ticket in 1948. He also suggests that members representing these same districts compiled relatively more conservative voting records. Thus, we might actually expect a *negative* relation between the percentage of blacks and support for minority legislation. The argument is that in a polarized district with a relatively large black population, minority issues become more salient. Representatives from these areas will feel pressured by conservative white constituents to prove that they have not been unduly influenced by black voters. We shall call this possibility the *polarization* hypothesis.[2]

A variant of Key's hypothesis comes from Keech (1968), who posits a *curvilinear,* or bimodal, relationship between the percentage of blacks and their representative's voting patterns. Keech asserts that the majority does not take much notice when the percentage of blacks in a district is fairly low, but once it reaches a critical level, say, 20–30%, the polarization effect takes over, and the representation of minority interests will be flat or actually decline until blacks comprise a majority of the voting population.

Finally, we consider the possibility of a *threshold* effect, that is, blacks will have no influence until they reach a minimum level of strength, after which a rising relationship to the representative's voting pattern is observed. Recent theoretical research (Epstein and O'Halloran 1995) derives this possibility from a multiple-principals model of representation. Indeed, McClain and Stewart (1995, 25) point to this possibility in their discussion of influence districts: "Surely there is a threshold of racial and ethnic minority representation necessary to have the interests of these groups represented at all."

These five theoretical models of minority representation are shown schematically in Figure 1. One purpose of our project, then, is to estimate the relation between minority voters and the representation of black interests in the modern Congress, to see which hypothesis, if any, best fits the data.

The overall efficacy of majority-minority districts in advancing black interests, therefore, remains unresolved. These districts certainly increase the number of minority candidates elected to office, that is, the descriptive representation of minorities.[3] But it is unclear that concentrated minority districts augment the substantive representation of minorities or the chance that legislation favored by the minority community will be enacted by Congress.

Figure 1   **Hypotheses Concerning the Relation Between Percentage of Black Voters and Representation Black Interests**

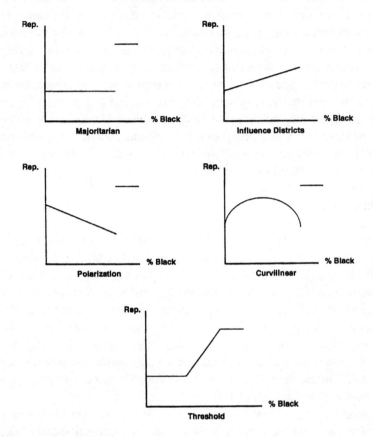

Majority-Minority Districts and the Representation of Minority Interests

We have reviewed two literatures, one relating the percentage of black voters in a district to their representative's voting behavior and the other debating the benefits of majority-minority districts. Although we have treated them separately, it is clear that they are intimately related. Assume, for instance, that the relationship between the percentage of blacks and support for legislation favorable to minorities is exactly linear, either increasing or decreasing. It then makes no difference how minorities are distributed throughout districts, as the average level of support will be the same in all cases.[4] If a minority group is underrepresented unless it comprises a majority in the jurisdiction, however, then the best way to ensure minority enfranchisement is to create as many majority-minority districts as possible. Finally, if partisan effects are the most significant feature in the political landscape, then reapportionment schemes which result in both minorities and Republicans being elected may decrease the overall average support for minority concerns.

Thus, in general, the representation relation and the optimal distribution of minority voters across districts are closely intertwined. To be more precise, an accurate measure of the former will allow us to calculate the configuration that gives minorities the greatest expected overall substantive representation. This may involve the construction of many concentrated minority districts, or few, or none. We investigate this question by first estimating the relationship between the percentage of black voters and legislators' representation scores. We then estimate the link between the black voting-age population and the probability of electing a black Democrat, nonblack Democrat, or a Republican to office in each of three geographic regions. Finally, we estimate the optimal apportionment of minority constituents in each region that maximizes substantive representation in Congress.

The Data

Table 1 [2 in original] describes the data used in the analysis. Legislators' support for minority issues is measured by the Leadership Conference on Civil Rights index (LCCR) for the 103rd Congress, which is compiled from votes cast on 14 bills considered important to minority interests. Since failure to vote lowers these scores, we have undertaken the standard procedure for attendance-correcting, eliminating from the total possible votes those measures on which a member did not actually cast a ballot. If a member was replaced through retirement or death, we calculated the average district support score.[5] The mean LCCR support score for all members was 59.6, ranging from a low of 7.7 to a high of 100.

Two comments are in order about our use of LCCR scores as a measure of minority representation. First, there is the issue mentioned above of descriptive as opposed to substantive representation. If descriptive representation is an overriding goal, then there can be no substitute for policies that favor the election of minorities to office, just as in the classic arguments for affirmative action. In practice, however, majority-minority districts have been neither sanctioned by the courts nor pursued by the Justice Department on the grounds of descriptive representation; the avowed goal has always been to increase the possibility that minorities can affect public policy by electing the candidate of their choice, regardless of race. There is also the "slippery-slope" argument that, once descriptive representation is acknowledged as a goal, it will be difficult to define exactly which groups should be afforded such an opportunity. Therefore, we investigate the effect of majority-minority districts on substantive representation and then examine the implications of the analysis for the number of minority candidates elected to office.

Second, the question arises as to whether the positions embodied in the LCCR votes are (1) merely liberal policies which are not actually helpful to the minority community and/or (2) not what the minority community actually wants, given a split in opinion between black elites and voters. Certain

Table 1

Data Sources, Descriptive Statistics, and Coding Rules

Variable	Description	Mean	Minimum	Maximum	Source
LCCR	Member's civil rights voting record	59.6	7.7	100	Leadership Conference on Civil Rights, Civil Rights Voting Record for the 103rd Congress
MODCQ	Support for measures in which more than 60% of black representatives voted alike	54.68	4.0	100	*Congressional Quarterly,* Key Votes of the 103rd Congress
Party	1 for Republicans; 0 otherwise	0.41	0	1	Barone and Ujifusa, *Almanac of American Politics, 1994*
Race	Race of member: 1 for black; 0 otherwise	8.7%	0	1	*Congressional Quarterly,* vol. 52, supplemental to issue no. 44, p. 10
BVAP	Percentage of blacks of voting age in the district	10.96%	0.099%	72.14%	1990 Census data
Cover	1 if district is covered under Section 5 of the VRA; 0 otherwise	28.7%	0	1	Bott, *Handbook of U.S. Election Laws and Practices,* pp. 249–51 and 257–62
South[a]	1 for southern states; 0 otherwise	31.3%	0	1	*Congressional Quarterly Almanac,* 1994
East[b]	1 for eastern states; 0 otherwise	21.0%	0	1	*Congressional Quarterly Almanac,* 1994

Note: LCCR = Leadership Conference on Civil Rights; CQ = *Congressional Quarterly,* BVAP = black voting-age population; Cover = judicial oversight under the Voting Rights Act.

[a]Alabama, Arkansas, Florida, Georgia, Kentucky, Louisiana, Mississippi, North Carolina, Oklahoma, South Carolina, Tennessee, Texas, and Virginia.

[b]Connecticut, Delaware, Maine, Maryland, Massachusetts, New Hampshire, New Jersey, New York, Pennsylvania, Rhode Island, Vermont, and West Virginia.

Figure 2   **Relation Between Black Voting Age Population and LCCR Voting Index Score**

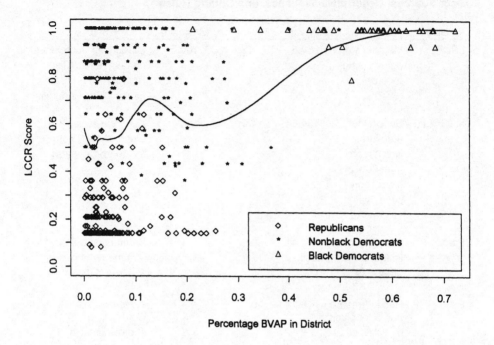

Percentage BVAP in District

commentators have argued, for instance, that liberal programs have failed to secure economic advancement for minorities and that alternative policies might better serve these populations. We do not pretend to answer the questions of whether the policy positions characterized by these votes are "correct" or whether each of these votes corresponds with the underlying preferences of the minority community. We do assert, however, that whatever the substantive opinions of the minority community, they are likely to be closer to the policy positions taken by legislators in districts with a substantial population of minority voters as opposed to districts with fewer minority constituents. The high correlation between LCCR scores and the MODCQ index, which is constructed from votes actually cast by black legislators, therefore suggests that LCCR scores are a reasonable measure of substantive minority interests.

The key independent variable in the analysis is the black voting-age population (BVAP) in each district as a proportion of total population. We also record each representative's region: South, East, and other. A number of studies have tried to capture additional subregional distinctions by including a Deep South variable. A better proxy for historic discrimination against minorities is to control for whether a district is covered under the preclearance procedures of the 1965 Voting Rights Act, as amended.[6] The variable *Cover* codes which districts are subject to judicial oversight of any changes to electoral systems or reapportionment plans. In our sample, 125 districts are covered, including 95 out of 137 districts in the South.

Finally, we have recorded the race and partisan affiliation of each member. The 103rd Congress had 38 black members, all but one of them Democrats. The partisan division for the Congress was 256 Democrats, 177 Republicans, and one Independent.[7]

We first determined the appropriate level of aggregation for our analysis. Figure 2 plots BVAP against LCCR scores for all members of the 103rd Congress. Included in the figure is an extremely flexible, highly data-sensitive regression line, a local regression or "loess" line.[8] The loess line indicates a generally rising pattern, with some evidence of bimodality at 20–30% BVAP. The figure also clearly identifies three distinct populations in the data: black Democrats, confined almost exclusively to the upper right quadrant of the figure; nonblack Democrats, located primarily in the upper left quadrant; and Republicans, located predominately in the lower left quadrant.

Notes

1. *Shaw* v. *Reno,* 113 S.Ct.2816 (1993). The decision remanded the case to the federal district court to review the reapportionment plan under strict scrutiny. The lower court eventually upheld the North Carolina district on the basis that it united urban interests as well as racial minorities, but the Supreme Court again ruled against the district in *Shaw* v. *Hunt* (1996).

2. Additional evidence of the polarization effect is demonstrated by Kernell (1973), who found that in Mississippi counties white voter turnout is highly correlated with the potential and actual black turnout. McDonald (1992, 81–2) provides additional examples of white backlash to minority mobilization.

3. See the essays in Davidson and Grofman (1994) for clear evidence that increased minority officeholding in the South is due almost entirely to the creation of majority black voting districts.

4. Assume the relation between representation and percentage of black voters is *Rep* = $a + b * (\%black)$. Consider a state with n districts and P_b percentage of black voters. Then, total representation will be equal to $na + b * P_b$ and average representation $(a + b * P_b)/n$, no matter how minority voters are divided among districts. This implies that linear methods for calculating representation will not be effective for devising optimal districting strategies.

5. Two districts changed partisan alignment in midsession. The roll calls from the first (Oklahoma 6th) were eliminated from the sample, although the election was used in calculating the electoral equations. In the second (Kentucky 2d), nine of the eleven votes were cast by Natcher (D) and only two were cast by Lewis (R). The district was coded as Democratic, and only those votes cast by Natcher were included in the analysis.

6. In 1975, the Voting Rights Act was amended to include language minorities (mostly Hispanic) as well as racial minorities.

7. Bernie Sanders (I-Vermont) is coded as a Democrat. The one black Republican in the 103rd Congress was Gary Franks, from Connecticut; his LCCR score of 0.21 was similar to that of other northeastern Republicans.

8. Loess fitting, which we employ below, has become a workhorse of modern nonlinear, nonparametric regression analysis. See Hardle (1990), Fox (1991), Chambers and Hastie (1993), and Venables and Ripley (1994); Cleveland (1993, 93–101) provides an accessible introduction to loess fitting, including an overview of the computational details.

References

Aranson, Peter, Melvin Hinch, and Peter Ordeshook. 1974. "Election Goals and Strategies: Equivalent and Non-equivalent Candidate Objectives." *American Political Science Review* 68 (March):135–52.

Barone, Michael, and Grant Ujifusa. 1993. *Almanac of American Politics, 1994.* Washington, DC: National Journal.

Black, Merle. 1978. "Racial Composition of Congressional Districts and Support for Federal Voting Rights in the American South." *Social Science Quarterly* 59 (December):435–50.

Bott, Alexander J. 1990. *Handbook of United States Election Laws and Practices.* New York: Greenwood Press.

Brace, Kimball, Bernard Grofman, and Lisa Handley. 1987. "Does Redistricting Aimed to Help Blacks Necessarily Help Republicans?" *Journal of Politics* 49 (February):167–85.

Browning, Rufus, Dale Rogers Marshall, and David Tabb. 1984. *Protest Is Not Enough: The Struggle of Blacks and Hispanics for Equality in Urban Politics.* Berkeley: University of California Press.

Bullock, Charles. 1981. "Congressional Voting and the Mobilization of a Black Electorate in the South." *Journal of Politics* 43 (August):662–82.

Cain, Bruce. 1992. "Voting Rights and Democratic Theory: Toward a Color-Blind Society." In *Controversies in Minority Voting,* ed. Bernard Grofman and Chandler Davidson. Washington, DC: Brookings Institution.

Chambers, John M., and Trevor J. Hastie, eds. 1993. *Statistical Models in* S. Chapman & Hall Computer Science Series. London: Chapman & Hall.

Cleveland, W.S. 1993. *Visualizing Data.* Summit, NJ: Hobart Press.

Combs, Michael W., John R. Hibbing, and Susan Welch. 1984. "Black Constituents and Congressional Roll Call Votes." *Western Political Quarterly* 37 (September):424–34.

Davidson, Chandler, ed. 1984. *Minority Vote Dilution.* Washington, DC: Howard University Press.

Davidson, Chandler. 1992. "The Voting Rights Act: A Brief History." In *Controversies in Minority Voting,* ed. Bernard Grofman and Chandler Davidson. Washington, DC: Brookings Institution.

Davidson, Chandler, and Bernard Grofman, eds. 1994. *Quiet Revolution in the South: The Impact of the Voting Rights Act of 1965.* Princeton, NJ: Princeton University Press.

Epstein, David, and Sharyn O'Halloran. 1995. "Interest Group Competition and Endogenous Coalition Formation." Manuscript, Columbia University.

Fox, John. 1991. *Regression Diagnostics.* Newberry Park, CA: Sage Publications.

Greene, William H. 1993. *Econometric Analysis.* New York: Macmillan.

Grofman, Bernard, and Chandler Davidson, eds. 1992. *Controversies in Minority Voting.* Washington, DC: Brookings Institution.

Grofman, Bernard, Robert Griffin, and Amihai Glazer. 1992. "The Effect of Black Population on Electing Democrats and Liberals to the House of Representatives." *Legislative Studies Quarterly* 17 (August):365–79.

Grofman, Bernard, Lisa Handley, and Richard Niemi. 1992. *Minority Representation and the Quest for Voting Equality.* New York: Cambridge University Press.

Guinier, Lani. 1994. *The Tyranny of the Majority: Fundamental Fairness in Representative Democracy.* New York: Free Press.

Hardle, Wolfgang. 1990. *Applied Non-Parametric Regression.* New York: Cambridge University Press.

Hausman, J., and D. McFadden. 1984. "A Specification Test for the Multinomial Logit Model." *Econometrica* 52 (September):1219–40.

Hill, Kevin. 1995. "Does the Creation of Majority Black Districts Aid Republicans?" *Journal of Politics* 57 (May):384–401.

Hinich, Melvin. 1977. "Equilibrium in Spatial Voting: The Median Voter Result Is an Artifact." *Journal of Economic Theory* 1 (December):208–19.

Keech, William R. 1968. *The Impact of Negro Voting.* Chicago: Rand McNally.

Kernell, Sam. 1973. "Comment: A Re-evaluation of Black Voting in Mississippi." *American Political Science Review* 67 (December):1307–18.

Key, V.O. 1949. *Southern Politics in State and Nation.* Knoxville: University of Tennessee Press.

Kousser, Morgan. 1993. "Beyond Gingles: Influence Districts and the Pragmatic Tradition in Voting Rights Law." *University of San Francisco Law Review* 27 (Spring):551–92.

Lublin, David. 1994. "Gerrymander for Justice? Racial Redistricting and Black and Latino Representation." Ph.D. diss., Harvard University.

McClain, Paula, and Joseph Stewart. 1995. "W(h)ither the Voting Rights Act after *Shaw* v. *Reno:* Advancing to the Past?" *PS* 28 (June):24–6.

McDonald, Laughlin. 1992. "The 1982 Amendments of Section 2 and Minority Representation." In *Controversies in Minority Voting,* ed. Bernard Grofman and Chandler Davidson. Washington, DC: Brookings Institution.

Overby, L. Marvin, and Kenneth Cosgrove. 1996. "Unintended Consequences? Racial Redistricting and the Representation of Minority Interests." *Journal of Politics* 58 (May):540–50.

Polsby, Daniel, and Robert Popper. 1993. "Ugly: An Inquiry into the Problem of Racial Gerrymandering under the Voting Rights Act." *Michigan Law Review* 92 (December):652–82.

Poole, Keith, and Howard Rosenthal. 1991. "Pattern of Congressional Voting." *American Journal of Political Science* 35 (February):49–67.

Press, William, Brian Flannery, Saul Teukolsky, and William Vettering. 1986. *Numerical Recipes.* Cambridge: Cambridge University Press.

Rice, John. 1988. *Mathematical Statistics and Data Analysis.* Pacific Grove, CA: Wadsworth.

Rousseeuw, Peter, and Annick Leroy. 1987. *Robust Regression and Outlier Detection.* New York: John Wiley and Sons.

Swain, Carol. 1993. *Black Faces, Black Interests: The Representation of African Americans in Congress.* Cambridge, MA: Harvard University Press.

Venables, W.N., and B.D. Ripley. 1994. *Modern Applied Statistics with S-Plus.* New York: Springer-Verlag.

Whitby, Kenny J. 1985. "Effects of the Interaction between Race and Urbanization on Votes of Southern Congressmen." *Legislative Studies Quarterly* 10 (November):505–17.

Whitby, Kenny J. 1987. "Measuring Congressional Responsiveness to the Policy Interests of Black Constituents." *Social Science Quarterly* 68 (June):367–77.

Yatrakis, K. 1981. *Electoral Demands and Political Benefits: Minority as Majority, A Case Study of Two Newark Elections 1970, 1974.* New York: Columbia University Press.

Discussion Questions

1. How did the authors measure the extent to which a member of Congress supports policies favored by racial minorities?
2. What is the independent variable? How was it measured?
3. Discuss the relationship depicted between the independent and dependent variables in Figure 2.
4. Figure 2 allows the reader to see the relationship between the independent and dependent variables for three kinds of representatives (Republicans, nonblack Democrats, and black Democrats). How would you interpret the relationship for each of the three groups?

Commentary

The authors went on to complete a rather complex multivariate analysis to help resolve the questions raised by the bivariate analysis. This initial inquiry showed how the support for minority-favored policies by each representative is affected by the percentage of black voters in their respective districts, producing some remarkable findings. As shown in Figure 2, African-American Democrats who support policies favored by minority citizens tend to be elected from districts in which African-American voters are in the majority. Supporters of what the Justice Department demanded be done to the congressional districts in North Carolina see these findings as confirmation for their argument.

However, the bivariate analysis also shows that, for other representatives in Congress, there is virtually no relationship between the proportion of African-American voters in a district and the positions taken by representatives in Congress from those districts.

These conclusions supported the authors' decision to move forward with a multivariate analysis designed to determine the gains and losses in support for minority-favored policies that can be attributed to the effort to create more "majority-minority" congressional districts. Their conclusion is striking: "Outside the South, substantive minority representation is best served by distributing black voters equally among all districts. In the South, the key is to maximize the number of districts with slightly less than a majority of black voters. . . . Overall, maximizing the number of minority representatives does not necessarily maximize minority representation. . . ." (p. 810).

Cameron, Epstein, and O'Halloran approached an extremely controversial issue with an imaginative research design. Although the completion of their study required them to use a multivariate analysis, their article shows that considering the relationship between two variables is often a good first step in addressing a complex problem.

12 Multivariate Analysis:
Statistics of More Than Two Variables

Virtually all important research problems in political science eventually involve sorting out complex relationships among a great many variables. To do this, we must often employ some form of **multivariate analysis**. By multivariate analysis we mean the study of relationships among more than two variables. An extensive range of techniques is available to use in multivariate analysis.[1] Our purpose here, however, is not to provide a comprehensive overview of this often highly technical subject but, rather, to illustrate its basic logic and its importance to political research.

An example may be useful in exploring the rationale for multivariate analysis. Suppose that in the course of a study of education policy in the American states we discover a positive association between two variables, the level of inter-party competition and the level of state spending on education. To put it another way, a bivariate analysis of our data reveals that states with high levels of inter-party competition spend heavily on education. Does this indicate a causal relationship? Are high levels of education expenditures the result of intense inter-party competition?

Some political scientists once thought so (e.g., see Key 1949.) They argued that effective inter-party competition promoted spending on education. In their view, elected officials in states with high levels of inter-party competition would be highly motivated to respond to public demands for increased spending in certain popular areas such as education. In states with weak inter-party competition, on the other hand, elected officials would be under less pressure to respond to such demands. Given the weakness of the opposing party, they were likely to be re-elected regardless. Thus, it was argued, the level of education expenditures in a state was largely caused by the level of inter-party competition in the state.

This argument, however, has a major weakness. It fails to take into account the possible effects of other variables, particularly the varying level of per capita income across the states. As it happens, the states with low levels of

---

1. See, for example, Tabachnick and Fidel (1983) and Bohrnstedt and Knoke (1988).

inter-party competition were found predominantly in the South, a region that had relatively low per capita income at that time. Since poorer states spend less money on education than wealthy states, some analysts suspected that a third variable, per capita income, was really responsible for much of the variation in state education spending. In this case, bivariate analysis provided an incomplete and somewhat misleading picture. For an accurate understanding of the underlying causal relationships, we must employ techniques that allow us to account for the influence of all relevant variables.

The missing ingredient in most bivariate analysis is **control**. An appropriately designed study of the relationship between inter-party competition and education spending would control for the effect of other variables such as per capita income. The notion of control is, in fact, basic to sound research design and, as you will recall from chapter 2, the key to successful experimentation. What an experimental research design provides is a way of ensuring that any observed changes in our dependent variable can confidently be attributed to changes in our independent variable. Experimentation, however, is often impossible in political research. This is why we must often engage in the quasi-experimental method of an "ex post facto" design, using multivariate analysis to approximate the logic of genuine experimental design. A large proportion of published political science studies consists of ex post facto designs.

One simple method for approaching the example with which we began this chapter would be to separate the American states into income groups such as high, medium, and low. Then, we would measure the association between the level of party competition and the level of education spending separately for each group of states. If you do this, you will find the relationship between inter-party competition and education spending is quite a bit weaker than it appears when all 50 states are treated as a single group. This method adds an element of control to bivariate analysis. However, this method quickly becomes very cumbersome and time consuming as the number of other variables for which we must control increases. Under these circumstances, we are much better off employing multivariate analysis.

Perhaps the most frequently encountered form of multivariate analysis is **multiple regression**. A full explanation of multiple regression lies beyond the scope of this book. Here we are concerned simply with its purposes and meaning in political research.[2] In brief, multiple regression is a statistical technique that enables us to calculate an estimate of the unique effect of each of several independent variables on the dependent variable. These estimates in turn make it possible to predict the value of the dependent variable for any given set of values for our independent variables.

Multiple regression involves three basic steps. The first is to identify all of

---

2. For a good introductory discussion of multiple regression, and a more complete explanation of the mathematics involved, see Manheim and Rich (1991).

the variables that our theory leads us to believe may have an effect on the dependent variable in question. The second is to construct an equation linking those variables. This is sometimes referred to as **modeling** or model specification, and it essentially states in equation form how we expect the independent variables to affect the dependent variable. The third is to gather and process data for the cases under study, determining how values on the independent variables are actually related to values on the dependent variable. Multiple regression analysis produces a series of coefficients that tell us the effect on the dependent variable of a change in each independent variable.

The multiple regression equation used to model the relationships among our variables will always take the general form:

$$\hat{Y} = a + b_1 X_1 + b_2 X_2 + b_n X_n$$

In this equation:

$\hat{Y}$ represents the estimate of the value of our dependent value (the ^ following the Y tells us this is an *estimated* value produced through knowledge of the values of the independent variables);

The first term on the right side of the equals sign, a, represents the average value of $\hat{Y}$ when the value of all of our independent variables equals zero (0);

Each of the Xs stands for a specific independent variable (X_1 = independent variable one, X_2 = independent variable two, and so on); and

Each of the bs stands for the average change in the dependent variable associated with a unit change in the associated independent variable *when the effects of all other independent variables are held constant*. Thus, b_1 = the unit change in $\hat{Y}$ when the values of all independent variables other than X_1 are held constant, b_2 = the unit change in $\hat{Y}$ when the values of all independent variables other than X_2 are held constant, and so forth. These are the *regression coefficients*.

A multiple regression equation with two independent variables would look like this:

$$\hat{Y} = a + b_1 X_1 + b_2 X_2$$

The equation states that changes in X_1 and in X_2 are associated with changes in Y, the dependent variable. It also tells us that the value of $\hat{Y}$ will equal a for cases in which the value of X_1 and X_2 are zero.

In interpreting a multiple regression equation, we will in most cases be primarily interested in the regression coefficients, or b_1 and b_2. The value of each coefficient can be positive, negative, or zero. Whatever that value, it tells us how many unit changes in the dependent variable are associated with a unit change in the respective independent variable. When the value of the regression coefficient is zero, this tells us there is no relationship between the independent variable involved and the dependent variable. If, on the other hand, the value of b_1 for example, were 1.8, we would read this to mean "as the value of X_1 increases by 1 unit, the value of the dependent variable $\hat{Y}$ increases by 1.8 units." Thus, if $\hat{Y}$ represents "annual salary in thousands of dollars," and X_1 represents "years of formal education," then a b_1 of 1.8 would mean that for every additional year of formal education, a person's annual income goes up (on average) $1,800.

When dealing with multiple regression coefficients, it is important to remember that their magnitude is affected by the units in which they and the dependent variable are measured. Depending on the units of measure involved, a regression coefficient can assume almost any value. For this reason, one must exercise caution in drawing inferences about the relative strength of the relationships involved from the absolute values of the coefficients in a multiple regression equation. This is particularly true when utterly different units of measure such as dollars, years, or percentages of legislative seats are being used. Under these circumstances, the value of the regression coefficient for X_1 may be 126.2 while the value of the coefficient for X_2 could be 0.76 even though the second variable is more strongly related to the dependent variable.

For this reason, we usually see **standardized regression coefficients** when reporting findings based on regression analysis. Standardized coefficients allow us to make straightforward inferences concerning the relative strength of the relationship between the dependent variable and each independent variable from the value of the regression coefficients.[3]

Since we are usually performing multiple regression analysis on a sample of the population, the coefficients only tell us the change in the dependent variable produced by a one-unit change in each of the independent variables *among the cases in the sample*. If there is no relationship among the variables in the population, it is still possible to select cases for our sample for which the variables are related. The possibility of sampling error, as discussed in chapter 8, thus affects multiple regression analysis just as it affects inferences about descriptive statistics. Consequently, most published studies reporting regression analysis also report the standard error for each regression coefficient. If the standard error is low enough, the researcher can be confident that the coefficient represents a relationship between that independent variable

---

3. Technically speaking, a standardized regression coefficient indicates the relationship between the independent and dependent variables in standard deviation units. In other words, a coefficient of 0.79 would indicate that as X increases by one standard deviation of X, Y increases by 0.79 standard deviations of Y.

and the dependent variable in the whole population, and not simply among the sample cases.[4]

Multiple regression analysis is a powerful but complex tool that must be used with some care and a thorough understanding of its basic assumptions.[5] It requires the use of interval or ratio level data, for example, and no, or very little, error in measurement of the variables involved. It requires too that *all* relevant independent variables be included. There must not, however, be a high level of correlation among the independent variables, a common hazard in social science research known as **multicollinearity**. A significant violation of any of these or several other rules may invalidate our results. Nonetheless, multiple regression remains a highly useful tool for much political research.

In the first excerpt in this chapter (a second selection from the article by J. Eric Oliver), the author employs multiple regression analysis to refine his earlier findings regarding the effect of city size on citizen participation.

———————— Excerpt 15 ————————

Excerpt 11 in chapter 8 was drawn from the first part of an article exploring a question regarding political participation by citizens in municipalities of different sizes. On the basis of an initial bivariate analysis, J. Eric Oliver showed that a smaller proportion of citizens in larger cities reported regularly engaging in political activity, as measured in four different ways. This result was, in itself, surprising and important, given the common impression of small town life in America.

However, determining that city size and political activity are inversely related did not resolve the question. As with most bivariate relationships, there is always a possibility that some other variable or variables were really responsible for the observed variations in participation, making the relationship between city size and participation spurious. A multivariate analysis was necessary to address this question.

It is well known that many factors affect the extent to which citizens participate in politics. Perhaps the most obvious factor is education: People with more education are more active in politics. If residents of large cities are, on average, less educated than residents of smaller municipalities, these differences in average education level could be responsible for the pattern shown

----

4. As a result of mathematics that we need not discuss here, regression coefficients that are at least twice as high as their standard errors are "significant" at the .05 level. In other words, when the standard error is half or less of the regression coefficient, there is only a 5 percent chance that the variables are unrelated in the population.

5. See chapter 18 of Manheim and Rich (1991) or Pedhazur (1982).

by the bivariate analysis. On the other hand, if we compare equally educated residents of larger and smaller cities and find the big city residents are less active in politics, we would be on much stronger ground in claiming that city size has a negative impact on political activity. Multivariate analysis allows us to shed light on this possibility. As we continue with a second excerpt from this fascinating study, Oliver discusses how he approached the problem of different levels of participation in American cities of different sizes.

City Size and Civic Involvement in Metropolitan America

J. Eric Oliver, *Princeton University*

American Political Science Review 94, no. 2 (June 2000): 361–373. Copyright © 2000 by the American Political Science Association. Reprinted with permission.

Part of the answer may lie in demographic differences rather than social context (Finifter and Abramson 1975), so demographic profiles are worth exploring in further detail. Table 1 lists average levels for *Years of School Completed*, *Age*, *Percent Homeowners*, and *Median Household Income* by place size for rural and metropolitan areas in the CPS/Census sample.[1] Compared to all residents of metropolitan areas, rural dwellers on average have completed almost one year less of school and live in places with a median annual household income almost $10,000 lower. As both an individual's education and city-level income are important determinants of civic participation (Oliver 1999; Verba, Schlozman, and Brady 1995), these lower resource levels may explain lower rural participation. Yet, rural residents are older and more likely to own a home, individual factors that correlate with higher participation rates. Furthermore, despite the steady decrease in civic participation within metropolitan areas, there are few demographic variations by size: Residents of small metropolitan places have, on average, levels of education, income, and age similar to those of people in large cities. The only demographic variance is that people in smaller places in metropolitan areas are more likely to be homeowners. Given at least some confounding demographic characteristics, multivariate equations are needed to isolate the specific effects of city size on participation.

Toward this end, I employed a logistic regression for the three dichotomous participation items and an ordinary least squares (OLS) regression for the voting scale. Each measure was regressed on several explanatory measures: *City Size* (measured in ten increments along a 0–1 scale); dummy variables for residence in *Rural* areas and *Small Metropolitan Areas* (less than one million), with residence in a metropolitan area of more than five million counted as the excluded category; an interaction term between city size and rural residence (city size × rural); individual characteristics associated with civic participation (Verba, Schlozman, and Brady 1995), such as *Education, Age, Income, Length of Residence, Marital Status, Homeownership,* race (*Black*), and sex (*Female*); and two other city-level social characteristics: affluence (*Median Household Income*) and racial composition (*Percentage Black*).[2] To control for regional effects, I included *South* as a dummy variable. The coefficients from the equations are presented in Table 2, and a full description of the variables is given in the Appendix.

Controlling for other individual and city-level characteristics does not alter generally the negative relationship between civic participation and city size. Comparing the predicted rates of participation between the smallest and largest places, the likelihood of contacting local officials drops by 16 percentage points, attending organizational meetings by 8 percentage points, attending community board meetings by 18 percentage points, and voting in local elections by .14 points on a five-point frequency scale (from an average score of 2.5 to 2.36).[3] The city size coefficients are statistically significant in all equations except the one predicting voting.

These findings have several points worth noting. First, the relative size of the coefficients demonstrates that city size is itself a powerful predictor of local civic activity. For example, the logistic coefficients in Table 2 for the three equations predicting nonelectoral participation are larger for city size than all other individual-level variables except for education, age, and income.[4] In other words, the differences in contacting officials or attending meetings between very small towns and the largest cities are greater than those between renters and homeowners, men and women, or married and single people.

Second, the predicted participation rate steadily declines as population increases. Alternative tests for a curvilinear relationship between city size and participation are generally negative.[5] The model predicts that, ceteris paribus, residents of a city such as Woodside, California (pop. 4,300), are 8% more likely to attend a local community board meeting than those in nearby Cupertino (pop. 41,000), who are 6% more likely to do so than people in neighboring San Jose (pop. 750,000). The effect of size is continuous: The larger a city becomes, the less likely are its citizens to participate in local affairs.

Finally, the effects of city size seem largely independent of the greater rural or metropolitan context. The coefficient for the interactive term in all four equations is small and not statistically significant. People in smaller rural places and in smaller suburban places are equally more likely to participate relative to people in large cities. In other words, the model predicts that compared to those in a city like Los Angeles, in a city the size of Santa Monica, California, residents are no less likely to participate in local civic activities than are people in rural and identically sized Sioux City, Iowa, even though Santa Monica is nestled within a metropolitan area that is 20 times as large.

On the whole, there are almost no differences in civic behavior according to either the size of the metropolitan area or whether the setting is rural. By itself, city size has no effect: None of the equations predict significant differences in participation between residents of small and large metropolitan areas. Moreover, controlling for size generally has little influence on the magnitude of the city size effect, as the predicted variations in participation by city population are roughly the same in the multivariate equations as they are in the cross-tabulations illustrated in Figure 1 [see Excerpt 11, p. 259]. The only civic activity that does vary between metropolitan and rural areas is attendance at community board meetings. Like the findings in Figure 1, people in rural places are less likely to attend community board meetings than people in metropolitan areas. But beyond this, rural dwellers living in similarly sized places are no less likely than people in metropolitan settings to undertake any other civic activity, such as contacting officials or voting in local elections. Most of the differences in participation rates between metropolitan and rural settings are the consequence of individual demographic characteristics.[6]

Appendix: Coding of the Variables

The data in this article come from two separate sources. The variables measuring participation, political interest, mobilization, and individual demographic variables come from the 1990 Citizen Participation Study (Verba et al., 1995). The contextual variables come from the 1990 Census of Population and Housing (U.S. Bureau of the Census 1991). The coding is described below.

Dependent Variables

These variables were coded with dichotomous, yes/no responses.

Contacting Local Officials

In the past 12 months . . . have you initiated any contacts with an elected official on the state or local level—a governor or mayor or a member of a city or town council—or someone on the staff of such an elected official?

Attending Community Board Meetings

Have you attended a meeting of (any official local governmental board or council that deals with community problems and issues, such as a town council, a school board, a zoning board, a planning board, or the like) in the past 12 months?

Attending Voluntary Organization Meetings

(Respondents identified a voluntary organization to which they belonged.) Here is a list of things that people sometimes have to do as part of the involvement with organizations. After I read each one, please tell me whether or not

Table 1

Average Education, Age, Home Ownership, and Median Household Income by Place Size for Rural and Metropolitan Areas

	Years of school completed	Age	Percentage home-owners	Med. household income	N
Rural place size					
Less than 5,000	12.4	44.9	72	$18,676	243
5,000 to 50,000	13.2	43.7	67	$19,990	292
Rural area average	12.8	44.2	69	$19,393	535
Metropolitan place size					
Less than 5,000	13.2	40.4	81	$28,527	152
5,000 to 50,000	13.6	41.1	72	$35,565	477
50,000 to 250,000	13.8	39.7	59	$28,719	492
250,000 to 1 million	13.9	40.6	53	$24,831	298
More than 1 million	13.7	39.8	42	$27,939	240
Metropolitan area average	13.7	40.3	61	$29,283	1,659

Sources: The multi-level data in these analyses are combined from two separate sources. The variables measuring individual participation and demographic characteristics (i.e., education, age, etc.) come from the 1990 Citizen Participation Study (Verba et al. 1995). For each respondent in the CPS, the place of residence was identified and indicators of city population size, median household income, percentage black, metropolitan area size, and rural residence were appended from the 1990 Census of Population and Housing (U.S. Bureau of the Census 1991).

you have engaged in that activity as part of your involvement with this organization. Have you (gone to a meeting)?

Mobilization

(A positive response to either of the following questions was scored as positive.) In the past 12 months, have you received any request directed to you personally asking you to contact a government official—asking you to write to or talk to a government official? and serve on community board or council?

The following variables were scored as indicated.

Voting

A five-point voting-in-local-elections scale was based on responses to the following question: In the past five years, how often have you voted in elections for local or city officials? (1 = never, 2 = rarely, 3 = sometimes, 4 = often, 5 = always).

Political Interest

(The political interest variables were drawn from two questions.) Thinking about your local community, how interested are you in local community poli-

Table 2

The Effects of City and Metropolitan Area Size on Local Civic Participation, with Controls for Individual and Contextual Population Characteristics

	Contact officials	Attend board meeting	Attend organization meeting	Vote local elections[a]
City-level variables				
City size	-0.712** (0.256)	-1.48** (0.036)	-0.424* (0.208)	-0.133 (0.134)
Med. household income	-0.588* (0.275)	-0.932* (0.009)	-1.04** (0.358)	-0.724** (0.004)
Percentage black	0.587 (0.349)	1.37** (0.414)	-0.530 (0.331)	0.309* (0.156)
Metropolitan area size[b]				
Small metro area	0.179 (0.145)	-0.245 (0.178)	-0.053 (0.142)	0.055 (0.179)
Rural	0.361 (0.263)	-0.761* (0.328)	-0.207 (0.260)	0.042 (0.141)
City size × rural	-0.440 (0.679)	1.59 (0.886)	-0.261 (0.683)	-0.528 (0.366)
Other variables				
Education	2.14** (0.232)	1.97** (0.291)	2.19** (0.226)	1.55** (0.117)
Income	0.816*** (0.052)	1.08** (0.261)	1.12** (0.201)	0.429** (0.109)
Age	0.652** (0.260)	0.528 (0.327)	0.538* (0.254)	2.23** (0.135)
Homeowner	0.357*** (0.132)	0.526** (0.174)	0.404** (0.126)	0.358*** (0.067)
Married	0.052 (0.115)	0.015 (0.146)	0.062 (0.111)	0.115 (0.059)
Black	-0.247 (0.157)	-0.456 (0.207)	0.269 (0.147)	0.055 (0.078)
Female	-0.239* (0.104)	-0.198 (0.124)	-0.090 (0.101)	0.038 (0.055)
Length of residence	0.182 (0.191)	0.343 (0.252)	0.241 (0.185)	0.217 (0.096)
South	-0.201 (0.126)	-0.308* (0.158)	-0.127 (0.121)	-0.172 (0.065)
Cox and Snell R^2	0.12	0.10	0.13	(r^2 0.28)
N	2,032	1,914	2,038	2,022

Source: See source note for Table 1.

** $p < .01$, * $p < .05$; standard errors are in parentheses.

[a]Coefficients from OLS regression.

[b]Excluded category is metropolitan area of more than one million.

tics and local community affairs? How interested in national politics and national affairs are you? (1 = not at all interested, 2 = slightly interested, 3 = somewhat interested, 4 = very interested).

Independent Variables

Education

The six categories were: less than 8 years of schooling, 8–12 years, high school diploma, some college, college degree, and advanced degree. The coding was from 0 (less than 8 years) to 1 (advanced degree).

Income

The eight categories were: less than $7,500 annually; $7,500 to $15,000; $15,000 to $25,000; $25,000 to $35,000; $35,000 to $50,000; $50,000 to $75,000; $75,000 to $125,000; more than $125,000. The coding was from 0 (less than $7,500) to 1 (more than $125,000).

Age

Recording from the original score of 18–92 years yielded a range from 0 (18 years old) to 1 (92 years old).

Length of Residence

0 = less than 2 years, 1 = 2 or more years.

South

0 = live outside South; 1 = live in Arkansas, Alabama, Florida, Georgia, Louisiana, Mississippi, North Carolina, South Carolina, Tennessee, Texas, or Virginia.

Contextual Variables

City Size

The ten categories were: less than 2,500; 2,500 to 5,000; 5,000 to 10,000; 10,000 to 25,000; 25,000 to 50,000; 50,000 to 100,000; 100,000 to 250,000; 250,000 to 500,000; 500,000 to one million; more than one million. Size was recorded on a 0–1 scale.

Median Household Income

Rounded and originally coded on a 50-point scale (0 = <$10,000; 1 = $11,000; ... 49 = more than $59,000), the recoding ranged from 0 (less than $10,000) to 1 (more than $59,000).

Percentage Black

Recoding from 0 to 97 yielded 0 (0% black) to 1 (97% black).

Rural

Residence in rural area = 1, in metropolitan area = 0.

Small Metropolitan Area

Metropolitan area with population of less than one million = 1, more than one million = 0.

Notes

1. The CPS measured individual income on an eight-point scale, so I used the measure for the median household income of the city from the 1990 Census as a measure of income differences by place size and metropolitan/rural context.

2. A multitude of social characteristics distinguish American places (Berry 1972), but racial and economic segregation is routinely identified as the most important by-product of suburbanization (Massey and Denton 1993; Schneider 1987). Therefore, in distinguishing among suburban places, I use measures of median household income and percentage black.

3. The aggregate marginal effect of city size on the probability of participating was calculated by first using the logistic coefficients to compute a predicted probability of participation (p) for each person in the sample: $p(x) = F(B_0 + B_1 + \ldots + B_n X_n)$. A second probability was calculated using the same equation except that for each respondent the lowest value of the city size scale (0) was substituted for the regular city size term. After recalculating both probabilities relative to the base of the natural logarithm, the difference between the two probabilities was then estimated for each respondent and the average scores were taken for each increment of the city size scale. For a full description of this procedure see Wolfinger and Rosenstone (1980, 123). Using this procedure, the logistic coefficient for city size in the equation predicting contacting (−.712) translates into a predicted average difference of 16 percentage points between residents of places with population of less than 2,500 and those in places with population of more than one million. For the OLS equation, the predicted effect of city size was derived by setting all other independent variables to their means and adding these to the constant term. This new average rate was then added to the value of the city size coefficient multiplied by the value of each increment along the city size scale.

4. Of course, because of the nonlinear character of the logistic regressions, the comparative magnitudes of the independent variables cannot be estimated perfectly from the coefficients. To calculate the relative effect of one coefficient compared to another, a probabilistic function for each variable, must first be estimated. For example, translating the coefficient for education (2.14) in the equation for contacting generates a predicted difference of 34 percentage points between those with only eight years of education versus those with an advanced degree. Nevertheless, comparing all the translated coefficients, the differences across city size are still larger than differences across any individual level variable except education, age, and income, just as the raw coefficients indicate. For example, the predicted differences in the rate of contacting officials across the city size scale (16 percentage points) is greater than that between renters and homeowners (6 percentage points) or men and women (5 percentage points).

5. For instance, when a squared term for city size is included in the equations, no large or statistically significant coefficients are generated. The relationship between city size and civic activity also can be found by breaking the size variable into nine dummies, with residence in a city of more than one million as the excluded category, and reestimating the equation. When

this was done, the coefficients for the dummy variables progressively dwindled as city size increased in all three equations in which size had a significant effect on civic involvement.

6. Other multivariate analyses demonstrate that, controlling for just city size, rural residents are less likely to attend organizational meetings and vote. When the variables measuring everything but education and income are included, people in rural areas continue to have a lower participation rate, although the differences are no longer statistically significant. Adding the education and income measures greatly attenuates the rural coefficients. This suggests that the lower levels of rural participation are due largely to socioeconomic differences. Interestingly, no matter what controls are added, rural dwellers are always more likely to contact local officials, although this difference is not statistically significant, and always less likely to attend community board meetings, a difference that is statistically significant.

References

Achen, Christopher, and W. Phillips Shively. 1993. *Cross-Level Inference.* Chicago: University of Chicago Press.

Berry, Brian. 1972. "Latent Structure of the American Urban System." In *City Classification Handbook: Methods of Applications,* ed. Brian Berry and Katherine Smith. New York: Wiley-Interscience.

Berry, Jeffrey M., Kent E. Portney, and Ken Thomson. 1993. *The Rebirth of Urban Democracy.* Washington, DC: Brookings Institution.

Bott, Elizabeth. 1971. *Family and Social Networks.* New York: Free Press.

Dahl, Robert. 1967. "The City in the Future of Democracy." *American Political Science Review* 61 (December): 953–70.

Dahl, Robert, and Edward Tufte. 1973. *Size and Democracy.* Palo Alto, CA: Stanford University Press.

Deutsch, Karl. 1961. "Social Mobilization and Political Development." *American Political Science Review* 55 (September):493–514.

Finifter, Ada. 1970. "Dimensions of Political Alienation." *American Political Science Review* 64 (June):389–410.

Finifter, Ada, and Paul R. Abramson. 1975. "City Size and Feelings of Political Competence." *Public Opinion Quarterly* 39 (Summer):189–98.

Fischer, Claude. 1976. "The City and Political Psychology." *American Political Science Review* 69 (September):559–71.

Fischer, Claude. 1982. *To Dwell Among Friends: Personal Networks in Town and City.* Chicago: University of Chicago Press.

Fischer, Claude. 1995. "The Subcultural Theory of Urbanism: A Twentieth-Year Assessment." *American Journal of Sociology* 101 (November):543–77.

Hansen, Steven, Thomas Palfrey, and Howard Rosenthal. 1987. "The Downsian Model of Electoral Participation: Formal Theory and Empirical Analysis of the Constituency Size Effect." *Public Choice* 52 (Spring):15–33.

Huckfeldt, Robert, and John Sprague. 1995. *Citizens, Politics, and Social Communication: Information and Influence in an Election Campaign.* New York: Cambridge University Press.

Kasarda, John D., and Morris Janowitz. 1974. "Community Attachment in Mass Society." *American Sociological Review* 39 (August):328–39.

Latane, Bibb, and John Darley. 1970. *The Unresponsive Bystander: Why Doesn't He Help?* Englewood Cliffs, NJ: Prentice-Hall.

Lewin, Kurt. 1935. *Principles of Topological Psychology.* New York: McGraw-Hill.

Lofland, Lyn. 1973. *A World of Strangers: Order and Action in Urban Public Space.* New York: Basic Books.

Massey, Douglas, and Nancy Denton. 1993. *American Apartheid: Segregation and the Making of the Underclass.* Cambridge, MA: Harvard University Press.

Milbrath, Lester, and M.L. Goel. 1982. *Political Participation.* Washington, DC: University Press of America.

Montesquieu, Charles. [1748] 1991. *The Spirit of Laws.* Littleton, CO: F.B. Rothman.

Nie, Norman, G. Bingham Powell, Jr., and Kenneth Prewitt. 1969. "Social Structure and Political Participation: Developmental Relationships." *American Political Science Review* 63 (June):361–78.

Oliver, J. Eric. 1999. "The Effects of Metropolitan Economic Segregation on Local Civic Involvement." *American Journal of Political Science* 43 (January):186–212.

Olson, Mancur. 1965. *The Logic of Collective Action.* Cambridge, MA: Harvard University Press.

Peterson, Paul. 1981. *City Limits.* Chicago: University of Chicago Press.

Putnam, Robert. 1993. *Making Democracy Work: Civic Traditions in Modern Italy.* Princeton, NJ: Princeton University Press.

Putnam, Robert. 1995. "Tuning In, Tuning Out: The Strange Disappearance of Social Capital in America." *PS: Political Science & Politics* 28 (June):664–83.

Reisman, David. 1953. *The Lonely Crowd: A Study of the Changing American Character.* Garden City, NY: Doubleday.

Rosenstone, Steven, and John Mark Hansen. 1994. *Mobilization, Participation, and Democracy in America.* New York: Macmillan.

Rousseau, Jean-Jacques. [1772] 1994. *Discourse on Political Economy and the Social Contract.* New York: Oxford University Press.

Schneider, Mark. 1987. "Income Homogeneity and the Size of Suburban Government." *Journal of Politics* 49 (March):36–53.

Simmel, George. [1905] 1969. "The Great City and Cultural Life." In *Classic Essays on the Culture of Cities,* ed. Richard Sennett. New York: Appleton-Century-Crofts. Pp. 26–42.

Suttles, Gerald. 1972. *The Social Construction of Communities.* Chicago: University of Chicago Press.

Teixiera, Ruy. 1992. *The Disappearing American Voter.* Washington, DC: Brookings Institution.

Tiebout, Charles. 1956. "A Pure Theory of Local Expenditures." *Journal of Political Economy* 64 (October):416–24.

Tonnies, Ferdinand. 1988. *Community and Society.* New York: Transaction.

U.S. Bureau of the Census. 1975. *Historical Statistics of the United States, Colonial Times to 1970* (Bicentennial Edition), Part 2. Washington, DC: Government Printing Office.

U.S. Bureau of the Census. 1991. 1990 Census of Population and Housing: Summary Tape File 3 (AL-WY). Washington, DC: U.S. Bureau of the Census.

U.S. Bureau of the Census. 1993. *Statistical Abstract of the United States: 1993* (113th ed.). Washington, DC: Government Printing Office.

Verba, Sidney, and Norman Nie. 1972. *Participation in America.* Chicago: University of Chicago Press.

Verba, Sidney, Kay Schlozman, and Henry Brady. 1995. *Voice and Equality.* Cambridge, MA: Harvard University Press.

Verba, Sidney, Kay Schlozman, Henry Brady, and Norman Nie. 1995. *American Citizen Participation Study, 1990* [computer file] (Study #6635), ICPSR version. Chicago: University of Chicago, National Opinion Research Center (NORC) [producer], 1995. Ann Arbor, MI: Inter-University Consortium for Political and Social Research [distributor], 1995.

Weber, Max. [1905] 1958. *The City.* Glencoe, IL: Free Press.

Wattenberg, Martin. 1996. *The Decline of American Political Parties.* Cambridge, MA: Harvard University Press.

Wilson, James Q. 1972. *Political Organizations.* New York: Basic Books.

Wirth, Louis. [1938] 1969. "Urbanism as a Way of Life." In *Classic Essays on the Culture of Cities,* ed. Richard Sennett. New York: Appleton-Century-Crofts. Pp. 67–83.

Wolfinger, Raymond E., and Steven J. Rosenstone. 1980. *Who Votes?* New Haven, CT: Yale University Press.

Discussion Questions

1. If Oliver had not employed multivariate analysis, what difference would it have made for the persuasiveness of his overall conclusions?

2. Oliver said that "controlling for other individual and city-level characteristics does not alter generally the negative relationship between civic
participation and city size." What does this mean?
3. An alternative, and very different, method of investigating the effect
of city size on political activity would be to conduct a survey of residents in cities of different sizes, asking them what factors lead them to
engage in political activity and which factors lead them to refrain from
it. Which approach, Oliver's or this survey method, would produce the
most useful results? What are the strengths and weaknesses of each?
4. What does it mean when Oliver indicates that several of the coefficients are "significant" at the .05 level?

Commentary

Multivariate analysis is primarily designed to determine whether or not an
observed relationship is spurious. By considering the effect on the dependent
variable of several independent variables at once, we are able to determine
the influence of one variable while "controlling" for the others. As stated
above, this means that we are essentially asking: For citizens with a given
level of education, what is the effect of the size of the cities in which they live
on their degree of political activity? Whenever there are other variables that
may explain variation in our dependent variable, multivariate analysis becomes essential.

In Table 1, Oliver listed four factors that he thought could affect a citizen's
degree of political activity (other than the size of the city the citizen lives in).
He listed educational attainment, age, whether or not the city in which the
person lives has a high percentage of homeowners, and median household
income of the person's city. Each of these factors can logically be thought to
affect one's propensity for engaging in political activity.

As discussed above in chapter 2, it is important to recognize that the quality of a given multivariate study is dependent on the completeness of the
analyst's list of possible explanatory variables. In a true experiment with control and experimental groups, the researcher does not have to be aware of the
possible factors that could affect the dependent variable because the experimental design ensures that, whatever variables *could* affect the dependent
variable, they will *equally* affect the control and experimental subjects. Any
differences between the two groups with respect to the dependent variable
therefore *must* be caused by the fact that one of the groups was exposed to the
independent variable and one was not. However, in the quasi-experimental
approach using multivariate statistical techniques, the researcher must be confident that he or she has included all possible variables that could affect the
dependent variable. We do not control for variables that are not included.

This is why Oliver includes so many variables in Table 2. A few of these
variables, education, income, and age, for example, are obviously candidates

for inclusion in the analysis. However, in a study of the effect of city size on participation, we might not immediately think of gender, homeownership, or region as relevant variables. Oliver made an effort to ensure that all even remotely arguable influences on participation were included, thus improving the strength of his conclusions.

Table 2 reports the results of the initial part of Oliver's multivariate analysis. Educational attainment apparently does have a positive effect on political activity, as does living in a municipality with a high income and high home ownership. However, city size remains a strong negative influence on political activity, even when controlling for the effects of these other variables.

Note that the coefficients in Table 2 include indications of their "significance." Strictly speaking, where the coefficients are marked with double and single asterisks, we can be 99 percent and 95 percent certain, respectively, that these relationships are found in the larger population; they are not found in Oliver's sample as a consequence of his having selected unrepresentative cases that happened to show those relationships. The stronger the relationship found for the cases in the sample, the greater is the likelihood that there is a corresponding relationship for the cases in the population, all other things being equal.

Virtually nothing in political science is mono-causal; the phenomena we study are far too complex to find that single causes explain them. Thus, multivariate analysis is needed both to address the possibility that an apparent relationship is spurious, and also to gauge the relative weight of several factors that, together, influence a dependent variable.

─────────────── Excerpt 16 ───────────────

Major elections in America create opportunities for people to discuss public issues and to learn about solutions and alternatives. Most of us pay considerable attention to the campaign speeches, conventions, and even paid political advertisements in an effort to decide which candidate should be elected. The issues involved have to do with foreign and domestic policy problems, difficult questions about moral values, and, quite often, the integrity of candidates.

However, recent research suggests that most of the subjects discussed in electoral campaigns have little to do with the outcome. According to many analysts, the state of the economy all but determines whether an incumbent or a challenger will win an election to a major office. Moreover, it often appears that it is not the overall, long-term prospects for the economy that are important; the *immediate* economic conditions are all that matter. Some people wonder whether, in light of these conclusions, campaigns matter at all. If people simply vote for incumbents when economic conditions are good, and for challengers when they are not, perhaps all the discussions and analysis that take place during campaigns are irrelevant and meaningless.

Diana Mutz suspected that the impact of economic conditions was probably more complex than the new conventional wisdom suggests. She began her study with the idea that citizens are able to distinguish between their personal economic situations and the economic condition of the nation (or state). She also felt that stories about the economy in newspapers would influence voters' perceptions of how well the economy was going. In short, an accurate and comprehensive analysis of the effect of economic conditions on elections would have to take these factors into account.

Mutz designed a multivariate analysis to test a general model of "the origins and effects of economic perceptions." She obtained data through two surveys of Indiana residents in 1987. The surveys contained questions regarding support for the incumbent governor and the incumbent president. They also contained questions about the respondent's personal economic experience, the frequency with which the respondent discussed economic problems with others, the respondent's exposure to mass media coverage of economic problems, and the respondent's perception of unemployment in both personal and national terms. (The actual wording of the questions is included in Appendix B.)

For Mutz, the primary question is whether people evaluate candidates on the basis of their own economic situations, "voting their pocketbooks," or on the basis of their assessments of the economic condition of the larger political community, the "sociotropic" explanation. Also, if media influences are important, the effect of the economy on elections may not be as simple as previously thought. Mutz's study thus has implications for students of both elections and mass communications and for campaign strategists.

Mass Media and the Depoliticization of Personal Experience

Diana C. Mutz, *University of Wisconsin-Madison*

American Journal of Political Science 36, no. 2 (May 1992): 483–508. Copyright © 1992 by the University of Wisconsin Press. Reprinted with permission.

Early studies of economic influences on voting simply assumed that people voted their pocketbooks: When national economic conditions worsened, more citizens experienced economic problems in their own lives, and these people logically voted against the incumbent party. When empirical findings at the individual level failed to support this explanation, research shifted from a focus on personal economic experiences to an emphasis on "sociotropic" judgments; that is, individuals' retrospective assessments of economic change at the collective level (see, e.g., Kinder and Kiewiet 1979, 1981; Scholozman and Verba 1979; Kinder 1981; Kiewiet 1983).

Perceptions of collective economic change at the national level have proved to be fairly consistent predictors of individual political preferences in U.S. congressional and presidential elections. However, studies have revealed little about the origins of these perceptions. By examining multiple sources of information, this study demonstrates the contribution of personal experiences and mediated information sources to perceptions of economic change at state and national levels.

Past neglect of mediated information sources as influences on economic perceptions is altogether understandable; the relative importance of other sources of information seemed superfluous compared to the immediate, tangible impacts that economic change had on people's everyday lives. But the general failure of the pocketbook voting hypothesis brought the understanding of communication influences to the forefront of research on economic influences on voting (see, e.g., Conover, Feldman, and Knight 1986; Kinder and Kiewiet 1981; Weatherford 1983a). Kiewiet (1983), for example, suggested that the information about economic conditions that informs sociotropic judgments must come from television or newspapers, or indirectly from mass media through a "two-step flow" of other people's reports of what they have heard from mass media. In short, the difference between the pocketbook and sociotropic hypotheses became construed as a controversy over the kind of economic information posited to have the most influence on economic judgments and ultimately, on political behavior as well (Kiewiet 1983).

Despite assertions about the importance of mass media in informing sociotropic perceptions, a substantial body of empirical findings suggests this is unlikely. Past research indicates that economic issues are precisely the type least likely to be influenced by mass media, presumably because of the immediacy and accessibility of personal experiences with economic problems as rival sources of information. In studies of agenda setting, for example, findings are often substantial when dealing with nondomestic issues, since most people must depend exclusively on news media for their information about international affairs. But such effects are weak to nonexistent for obtrusive issues that enter into people's personal life-space on a regular basis (e.g., McCombs and Shaw 1972; Zucker 1978). Personal experiences in particular are considered "superior" information sources that will override any mass or interpersonal communication influences. (For a review of this literature, see Chaffee and Mutz 1988.)

Moreover, the influence process suggested by Kiewiet and others would have to be a directional effect of positive or negative news presentations. There has been little research on effects from directional media content, perhaps owing to early disappointments (e.g., Lazarsfeld, Berelson, and Gaudet 1944). Instead, most research that documents media influence has focused on effects that result from the mere presence or absence of issue coverage, regardless of direction (e.g., Iyengar and Kinder 1987; MacKuen and Coombs 1981; Weaver et al. 1981). Studies of effects stemming from the nature of the content itself have been far less successful. The well-worn dictum that media tell people what to think about, rather than what to think, has remained intact with few exceptions.[1]

This study has two major goals. First, it aims to resolve the apparent contradiction between assumptions about the importance of media in forming sociotropic perceptions, and empirical evidence that suggests such influence is unlikely at best. Understanding the sources of these collective judgments is important because the accountability of political leaders centers on the accuracy of these perceptions; unlike personal experiences, collective economic perceptions may vary independently of the real world effects of economic policies. Second, this study furthers research on the politicization of personal experiences by demonstrating for whom and under what conditions personal experiences are politicized. Mass media are found to play an important role in determining the extent to which pocketbook or sociotropic concerns shape political evaluations.

This study also furthers an understanding of the processes that underlie the formation of retrospective judgments by demonstrating how the process of impression formation may be fundamentally different when evaluating state as opposed to national economic conditions. Findings suggest that the case against personal experiences as predictors of political preferences may be overstated as a result of reliance on national-level data.

Study Design: The Origins and Effects of Retrospective Economic Perceptions

To illustrate the theoretical development that underlies this study, Figures 1 through 4 take the reader through a progression of stages in the study of economic influences on voting, leading up to a general model that incorporates the information sources that influence economic perceptions. Survey evidence then documents these information sources' effects on people's perceptions of their own employment-related concerns and on their perceptions of state and national unemployment conditions.

The Pocketbook and Sociotropic Models

Figure 1 shows the relationship that so many scholars have looked for but seldom found, the influence of personal experiences with economic problems on evaluations of an incumbent. The broken line in Figure 1 suggests a weak relationship, if any, in keeping with the many studies that have reached weak or null conclusions.

In response to the failure of the pocketbook model, the sociotropic model provided an individual-level explanation for the aggregate-level findings. Thus, Figure 2 shifts the emphasis from personal experiences to collective judgments about economic conditions at the social level.

Following Kinder and Kiewiet's work, economic variables generally have been designated as either personal, "pocketbook" variables or collective, "sociotropic" variables referring to collective assessments of national economic conditions (Eulau and Lewis-Beck 1985). But structuring this theoretical puzzle as a choice among dichotomous alternatives ignores a wide range of intermediate referents between self and nation. One such option, group-level economic interests, has received limited attention thus far (see, e.g., Conover 1985; Kinder, Rosenstone, and Hansen 1983). Other possibilities, such as the state or local community context, also hold the potential for influence but have generated little research to date. Although some studies have addressed questions of economic influence in elections other than presidential and congressional ones, the measures of economic conditions have almost always been at the national level, with a few exceptions (see, e.g., Piereson 1977; cf. Klorman 1978; Pollard 1978). There is an unfortunate lack of research that matches local or state election outcomes with the economic context of their corresponding geopolitical units.

Nonetheless, Chubb (1988) suggests that the greater economic responsibility being taken on by states in recent years makes the relationship between voting and economic change especially likely to hold at the state level. Economic activities aside, general parallels between governors and presidents also recommend the likelihood of this relationship. As Schlesinger (1966) notes, executive, as opposed to legislative, incumbents are held most accountable for government activity during their term of office. Issues in general are also more important in high-information executive contests than in low-information legislative elections, for which voters fall back on such cues as party identification (Hinckley, Hofstetter, and Kessel 1974). On the other hand, the relatively low salience of state, as opposed to local or national, politics may prevent citizens from holding governors accountable for state economic conditions. As Jennings and Zeigler (1970, 524) note, "In a sense the states are caught between the immediacy of the local [political] system and the glamour and importance of the national and international systems."

In the one study that directly examines state-level voting and state-level economic conditions, Chubb (1988, 149) finds that "state economic conditions and the assumption of gubernatorial responsibility for them have a significant impact on gubernatorial election outcomes" but concludes that the influence of state conditions is small in comparison with the effects of national economic conditions. Chubb interprets these results as providing little support for the notion that state politicians are held accountable for a state's economic performance (see also Peltzman 1987).

As with the early studies of national economic performance, Chubb's evidence was based on pooled time series data using states, not individuals, as the unit of analysis. It remains to be seen whether subjective assessments of state economic conditions have effects similar to those found at the national level. The individual-level mechanism through which national economic change renders national political consequences remains controversial, and at the state level it is altogether unexplored territory. Although the model in Figure 2 is stated in general terms, it is likely that people make the attribution link between political causes and personal consequences more easily at state or local levels; it is probably less of a mental leap to hold state or local officials responsible for losing one's job than to hold a president responsible.

Still, in interpreting the relative strengths of the pocketbook and sociotropic paths, it is important to note that these two measures, which have often been pitted against one another empirically, are on fundamentally different levels. Personal experiences are exogenous, objective things that happen to a person, while perceptions of economic change are subjective assessments of social conditions. Since subjective reality almost always predicts attitudes better than objective reality, the winner in these contests should be no surprise; it is indicated by the solid line in Figure 2.

Subjective Problem Perceptions

Personal experiences with economic problems are neither necessary nor sufficient conditions for viewing these issues as pressing personal problems (Kiewiet 1983); people who are currently employed or doing well financially may still be worried about these issues because they anticipate layoffs or salary cutbacks. With this problem in mind, I have incorporated in Figure 3 a

Figure 1   **Pocketbook Model of Relationship Between Economic Conditions and Evaluations of Incumbents**

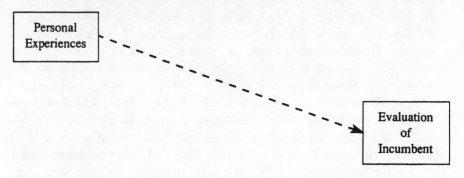

Figure 2   **Sociotropic Model of Relationship Between Economic Conditions and Evaluations of Incumbents**

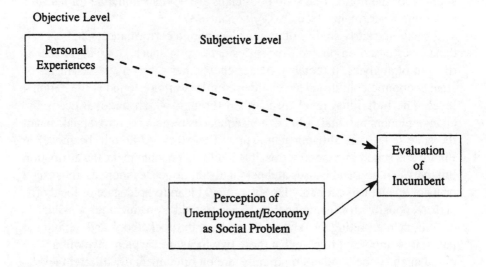

personal-level concept comparable to the social perception measure: perceptions of economic issues as problems in people's own lives. In previous studies, the investigator has usually defined some condition as a problem for the respondent using personal experience as an indicator (e.g., unemployment); here, by contrast, respondents are allowed to assess their own levels of personal economic concern.[2] I include prospective personal concerns at this position in the model, since they are the *result* of informational influences and thus endogenous to the model; anticipated or feared economic changes come about as a result of information gleaned from past personal experiences or from outside sources of information (see Fiorina 1981 for evidence on the effects of prospective evaluations).

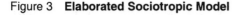

Figure 3   **Elaborated Sociotropic Model**

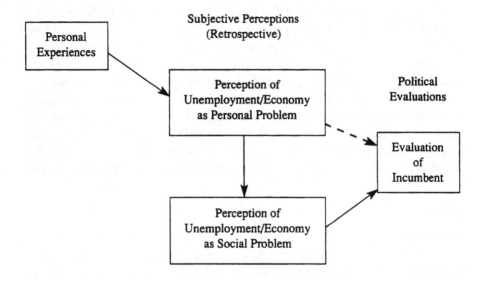

Since this concept incorporates future as well as past concerns as *subjectively* defined by the respondent, it is more likely to have a direct influence on incumbent evaluations than is an objective measure of personal experience, although the relationship between the subjective personal-level measure and incumbent evaluations is still not expected to exceed the strength of the sociotropic relationship. As Figure 3 illustrates, I hypothesize no direct relationship between personal experiences and incumbent evaluations, but personal experiences may have an indirect effect through their strong influence on perceptions of issues as personal problems.

The final, and most important step in building this model is to factor in the sources of economic perceptions at the collective level. What are the possible sources of information that lead to perceptions that economic conditions have gotten better or worse? To some extent, social perceptions may be generalized from perceptions of these problems at the personal level, as the central, downward arrow in Figure 3 indicates. Beyond generalizations from personal-level judgments, the two other possible sources of information on social conditions are mass media and other people.

Mass Media

The key factor that weakens the case for mass media effects with respect to economic issues in particular is that economic issues have "real world" consequences that researchers have long assumed to override potential media effects (e.g., Erbring, Goldenberg, and Miller 1980; Graber 1984; Weaver et al. 1981). Typically, "media dependency" theories downplay the potential for media effects in situations in which alternative information sources are available (see Ball-Rokeach and DeFleur 1976; Eyal, Winter, and DeGeorge 1981; McCombs and Shaw 1972; Palmgreen and Clarke 1977; Tipton, Haney, and Baseheart 1975; Zucker 1978). Inflation and unemployment in particular affect many people's lives on an everyday basis. Under these conditions, the media dependency literature suggests weak, if any, media effects on people's perceptions of economic issues, since there are highly credible, more easily accessible sources of information available in the form of people's own personal experiences (see, e.g., Ball-Rokeach and DeFleur 1976; Graber 1984). But to the extent that political behavior is based on perceptions of *collective* economic conditions, mass media may play an important role in this process.

Impersonal Influence

Recent evidence suggests that mass media's primary impact may be on social-level perceptions. Studies of agenda setting, for example, can be differentiated based on whether personal- or social-level definitions of audience agendas are used. McLeod, Becker, and Byrnes (1974) point out that mass media are typically found to have a greater impact on people's perceptions of the *collective* salience of issues than on the salience of the issues to individuals themselves (see also, Becker, McCombs, and McLeod 1975). In other words, a person may not perceive some problem as more important to him or her personally just because he or she has seen much news concerning it, but that person would be very likely to think that it is an important issue to other people and, thus, an important *social* problem (see also Hawkins and Pingree 1982).

Additional studies have demonstrated that mass-mediated information has an "impersonal impact" on perceptions of the frequency or severity of a problem, but not on personal judgments of concern or importance (Tyler and Cook 1984; Tyler 1980, 1984). Tyler (1980), for example, found that mass media coverage of crime influenced perceptions of crime as a social problem, but not as a personal one (see also Gordon and Heath 1981; Skogan and Maxfield 1981).

Studies of the "third-person effect" also suggest that people perceive others as influenced by mass media more than they themselves are (Davison 1983). Several examinations of this hypothesis have demonstrated that one major effect of exposure to mass media is to influence people's perceptions of what *others* think regardless of whether it influences individuals' personal perceptions (see also Cohen et al. 1988; Mutz 1989).

This collection of evidence suggests that despite the obtrusive nature of economic issues, mass media may still have some effect on perceptions of economic trends at the *collective* level. Very little research bears directly on questions about the effects of mass media reporting of economic news on perceptions of economic conditions. A few studies, however, indirectly address these questions and are well worth mentioning in this regard.

In an effort to understand the origins of perceptions of economic trends, Weatherford (1983a) compared people who relied heavily on newspapers for political information with those who did not and found that personal experiences weighed more heavily in voting considerations among the information-poor subgroup, while the information-rich relied on perceptions of collective economic conditions. These findings mesh well with Adoni and Cohen's (1978) suggestion that mass media use contributes to a subjective sense of economic knowledge; heavy media users in Weatherford's study relied on their subjective perceptions whether they were correct or not, while low media users relied on an information source of which they could be certain—their own personal experiences. The findings of Conover and colleagues (1986) loosely paralleled these results: those having inaccurate information about unemployment and inflation relied on personal experiences to form collective economic perceptions, while respondents with accurate unemployment and inflation knowledge did not. The extent to which people generalize collective or sociotropic evaluations from personal experiences seemingly depends on access to and assimilation of information about experiences beyond one's own; that is, in all likelihood, information from mass media.

Figure 4 assigns mass-mediated information a role consistent with these findings. As suggested by the literature on agenda setting, the impersonal impact hypothesis, and related studies, I expect mass-mediated information to have its greatest effects on perceptions of economic issues at the collective level. In the absence of mass-mediated information, personal and collective concerns would become less distinct, and people would default to personal experiences and more parochial sources as the basis of their perceptions of social change.

Interpersonal Sources

Although mass media influence has captured the bulk of researchers' attention as a potential source of economic information, some studies have also explored the flow of economic information in an interpersonal context.[3] Few, if any, studies have measured directly interpersonal discussion with respect to economic problems, but studies of "contextual" effects and group economic interests often suggest interpersonal communication as the underlying cause. As Weatherford (1983b, 870) noted, "The evaluation of economic conditions is a natural situation for contextual effects to operate through interpersonal contact; individuals are readily aware of co-workers and acquaintances who are unemployed, and shoppers in markets as diverse as food and real estate commonly compare their experiences with inflation" (see also Kinder, Rosenstone, and Hansen 1983). Results of the few studies that examine contextual effects and group-level economic interests do not argue for the superiority of these influences, but they suggest that interpersonally transmitted economic information may have an independent effect on political evaluations beyond the effects of personal experiences (see Conover 1985). Studies of issues outside the economic realm also have demonstrated that interpersonal discussion can influence both personal and social levels of judgment (Tyler 1980).

On the basis of these limited findings, the model assigns interpersonal communication the potential to influence both personal and social perceptions in Figure 4. This means that hearing about other people's economic problems can make people more aware that the problem is shared by others and thus an important social problem, and it also may make them more worried about their own personal situations. Nonetheless, the broken lines indicate that personal experience should be the strongest influence on perceptions of unemployment as a personal problem, and mass media should be the strongest influence on perceptions of unemployment as a social problem.

In Figure 4, the one remaining link that deserves explanation is the central arrow pointing upward from social- to personal-level perceptions. As previously mentioned, people may generalize from personal- to social-level concerns, but the recognition of a social problem may also trigger the reverse process; for example, national economic decline may lead people to believe that their own personal finances are in peril. Although one would expect the generalization from personal to social levels to be the dominant influence in the economic context, both directions are theoretically possible, and I test both possibilities in the context of the full model.

Methods

Unemployment was chosen as a narrowly defined economic issue appropriate for an initial examination of these ideas.[4] The data used to test the theoretical model illustrated in Figure 4 come from two surveys designed specifically for this purpose. For each wave of data, interviewers contacted a random sample of 300 Indiana residents by telephone using random digit dialing. This procedure resulted in two successive cross-sectional samples spaced at six-month intervals, in June and December 1987.[5]

Two of the three information source variables at the far left side of the model were assessed through survey questions. Personal experience with joblessness required that the respondent or someone in his or her immediate family had been laid off or had had trouble finding a job within the past year.[6] Instead of asking people how often they talked to others about some topic—the traditional measure of interpersonal communication—in this case they were asked how frequently others they knew *told them* about having trouble finding or keeping a job.[7] Constructing a measure of mass media exposure to information about unemployment involved combining survey responses on general media use with data derived from content analyses of respondents' newspapers.[8]

The questionnaire measured support for incumbents and retrospective perceptions of unemployment conditions at both state and national levels.[9] It also assessed subjective perceptions of unemployment change using parallel questions that addressed personal and collective levels of judgment. The personal-level measure of unemployment concern was designed to include those worried about job security and future layoffs as well as those with family members having actual experiences with these problems.[10]

At an operational level, care has been taken to ensure that the unidirectional arrows in Figure 4 are truly recursive relationships, with the exception of the one acknowledged reciprocal link;[11] I include control variables to partial out preexisting differences as much as, if not more than, is appropriate.[12] In addition to traditional controls, the analyses of both direct and indirect effects included one additional variable, the community unemployment context. This variable was operationalized using county-level unemployment statistics for the month preceding each wave of data collection. The design includes this variable to control for the possibility that people were responding to events in their community that were observed but not directly experienced, nor learned about through mediated sources; for example, when one observes long lines at the unemployment office.[13] In this way, the test for media influence controls for "real world cues" at both aggregate and individual levels. If the hypothesized relationships hold up under these stringent conditions with the small sample sizes used in this study, one can be assured that the findings represent relatively robust effects.

Findings

The presentation of results proceeds in four parts. First, the direct, additive effects of perceptions of unemployment on evaluations of incumbents are calculated using ordinary least squares regression. Next is an analysis of the origins of personal and collective retrospective perceptions of unemployment using two-stage least squares to examine influences on personal and social perceptions simultaneously. The third step evaluates the political importance of personal and collective perceptions with respect to the amount of unemployment coverage over time and exposure levels within subgroups of the population. Finally, a collapsed version of the model is considered to investigate further the potential for politicization of personal experiences.

At each stage in this progression, results are presented for the spring and fall waves of data at the state level and the fall wave at the national level. Testing three replications of the model allows over-time comparisons at the state level, and comparisons between state- and national-level unemployment effects at the same point in time.

Direct Effects on Incumbent Evaluations

As the unstandardized beta coefficients in Table 1 demonstrate, perceptions of unemployment at the social level have a consistently significant effect on

Figure 4   **General Model of Relationships Between Information Sources, Subjective Perceptions, and Evaluations of Incumbents**

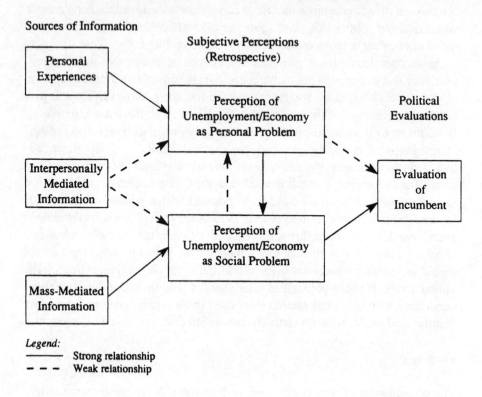

Sources of Information

Legend:
——— Strong relationship
– – – Weak relationship

approval of incumbents; this remains true across both waves for perceptions of state unemployment trends in relation to the incumbent gubernatorial administration and for perceptions of national unemployment trends in relation to the incumbent president.

As hypothesized in Figure 4, the sociotropic effect is the strongest direct influence on approval of incumbents outside the direct effects of party identification. Personal experiences with unemployment do not have direct effects, just as previous research would indicate. However, the measures of subjective perceptions of unemployment as a personal problem approach statistical significance in some cases, just as the weaker arrow in Figure 4 would suggest.

Origins of Retrospective Evaluations

Given the political importance of perceived unemployment trends, it becomes important to know on what kind of information these perceptions are based.

What sources of information contribute to the social- and personal-level perceptions that ultimately influence political attitudes?

To answer these questions, I used two-stage least squares to resolve the complications posed by the potential reciprocal relationship between perceptions of unemployment as a personal and social problem. Preliminary tests of the general model using ordinary least squares confirmed the two key instrumental variables indicated in the theoretical model and used in these analyses; personal experience uniquely identifies perceptions of unemployment as a personal problem across all three tests of the model, and exposure to newspaper coverage of unemployment trends uniquely identifies perceptions of unemployment as a social problem.[14]

The unstandardized betas in Table 2 illustrate the results of these efforts. At the state level, the pattern is clear; in both waves, personal perceptions significantly influence social-level perceptions, but not the other way around. At the national level, personal- and social-level concerns about unemployment remain virtually independent: personal concerns do not translate to social ones, and perceptions of unemployment as a national problem do not trigger concern at the personal level.

Table 2 also illustrates the consistent influence of personal experiences on personal concern, and mass media on social concern, just as the impersonal impact hypothesis would predict. Interpersonally mediated unemployment information represents the one inconsistent finding, demonstrating influence in two out of three cases.

These overall patterns suggest that personal experiences may indeed have an indirect influence on political evaluations at the state level by means of their influence on personal and ultimately social concerns. At the national level, however, the path that translates these concerns to political significance is incomplete.

The lack of connection between personal and social concern jibes well with many previous studies that find personal experiences and collective perceptions weakly, if at all, related. At the national level, the level of most research on sociotropic and pocketbook voting, there is not even an indirect path from personal experiences to political evaluations. This may overstate the case somewhat, since the subjective personal problem measures do approach significance in some analyses. Still, the overall pattern is clear: the experiences of others that reach one through mass and interpersonally mediated communication are weighted much more heavily in forming retrospective evaluations than are one's own personal experiences. It is mediated information, rather than information drawn from personal experiences, that is ultimately more important in bringing about the electoral effects of changes in unemployment at the national level. At the state level, personal experiences may play a more important role because social perceptions are to some extent generalized from personal-level perceptions.

Table 1

Predictors of Support for Incumbents

	Governor (Spring '87)	Governor (Fall '87)	President (Fall '87)
Subjective evaluations of unemployment			
Social problem (better)[a]	0.32 (0.14)*	0.41 (0.13)**	0.43 (0.19)*
Personal problem (better)	0.26 (0.15)	0.08 (0.13)	0.34 (0.18)
Sources of information			
Personal experience	-0.47 (0.33)	0.22 (0.33)	0.23 (0.45)
Interpersonally mediated information	-0.18 (0.12)	0.02 (0.13)	-0.31 (0.17)
Exposure to newspaper coverage of employment trends (bad news)	-0.01 (0.09)	0.06 (0.13)	-0.03 (0.03)
Community context	0.08 (0.09)	-0.00 (0.08)	0.18 (0.12)
Party identification			
Republican	0.41 (0.30)	0.64 (0.27)*	2.14 (0.41)***
Democrat	-0.78 (0.32)*	-0.74 (0.29)**	-0.61 (0.40)
R^2	0.20	0.26	0.16
N	(204)	(265)	(228)

Note: Entries are unstandardized betas with standard errors in parentheses. The dependent variable is evaluation of incumbent performance, where a high score indicates approval. This model represents conservative estimates of these relationships (see note 13); including both party and demographic variables produces considerably higher R^2 values, but does not change significantly the pattern of relationships.

[a]Direction of higher values indicated in parentheses.

*$p < .05$; **$p < .01$; ***$p < .001$, two-tailed tests.

Weighting of Personal and Collective Perceptions

The pattern of results in the fall and spring waves squares well with the changes in unemployment coverage that occurred during the study. Mass media coverage of unemployment went up considerably between waves 1 and 2, most likely due to the general media emphasis on economic issues brought on by "Black Monday," 19 October 1987. Subjective measures of the emphasis given to employment-related news increased by 70%; the number of column inches nearly doubled from an average of nine inches per sample of front page news in the spring to 17 inches in the fall.

Accordingly, the generalization of personal concern to state-level perceptions is much stronger in the first wave than the second wave, just as the theoretical model would lead one to expect; the closeness of the relationship between personal and social levels of judgment fluctuates according to the amount of outside information that reaches people through news coverage; mass mediated information is, after all, the only variable in the model capable of distinguishing social from personal judgments.

As personal and social levels of judgment became increasingly distinct, the weighting of these two factors in influencing attitudes toward incumbents also shifted. As a reexamination of Table 1 indicates, the weighting of perceptions of unemployment as a personal problem in predicting incumbent evaluations decreased considerably from wave 1 to wave 2 while the importance of social perceptions in evaluating incumbents increased. Although personal experiences did not have significant direct effects on incumbent evaluations in either wave, they came closest to having an impact during the first wave, again the time when media coverage was least.

The Sociotropic Priming Effect

To examine further the role of mass media in influencing the weighting of personal and social judgments, Table 3 shows these patterns separately for regular newspaper readers as opposed to occasional or nonreaders. Here the relationships become even more pronounced. As the top half of the table demonstrates, collective perceptions at either state or national levels clearly overwhelm the influences of personal concerns. On the other hand, among occasional and nonreaders, personal concerns, if anything, influence incumbent evaluations. It should be noted that this pattern is not simply a function of greater personal experiences with joblessness among the low readership group. These analyses included personal experiences, along with community employment context and a host of other controls.

A comparison of coefficients in the top and bottom of Table 3 further illustrates that the weights attached to personal unemployment concerns are consistently greater among occasional and nonreaders while precisely the opposite is true for collective unemployment concerns; here, coefficients are consistently larger among regular readers.

Table 2

Reciprocal Influences of Perceptions of Unemployment as Personal and Collective Problems

	Spring 1987		Fall 1987		Fall 1987	
	Personal problem	State problem	Personal problem	State problem	Personal problem	National problem
Endogenous variables						
Personal problem	—	0.65 (0.24)**	—	0.4 (0.15)**	—	0.09 (0.18)
State/nat'l problem	0.35 (0.36)	—	-.25 (0.34)	—	-.08 (0.39)	—
Exogenous sources of information						
Personal experience	-0.50 (0.20)*	—a	-0.28 (0.07)***	—a	-0.37 (0.07)***	—a
Interpersonally mediated information	-0.08 (0.08)	-0.08 (0.07)	-0.17 (0.12)	-0.20 (0.07)**	-0.12 (0.10)	-0.15 (0.08)*
Exposure to newspaper coverage of employment trends (bad news)	—a	-0.09 (0.04)*	—a	-0.14 (0.06)*	—a	-0.14 (0.06)*

Note: Table 2 shows the results of three independent simultaneous equation models using two-stage least squares. Cell entries indicate coefficients with their standard errors in parentheses. In addition to the variables of theoretical interest shown here, exogenous variables in these models included a block of demographic variables, party identification, retrospective assessment of change in family financial status, an indicator of the unemployment rate in the respondent's county of residence, and a variable that represented the change in unemployment within that county over the past 12 months.

aPersonal experience uniquely identifies personal problem, and newspaper coverage uniquely identifies social problem; thus these variables are omitted from the social problem and personal problem analyses, respectively.

*$p < .05$; **$p < .01$; ***$p < .001$, two-tailed tests.

The explanatory power of these models is also worth noting. Across all three columns, the regular readers register an *r*-square value five to 10 percentage points higher than the low readership group. Thus, the model accounts for incumbent evaluations better among regular readers than for others.

Clearly, media exposure heightens the salience of social-level judgments as well as informing collective evaluations. The former effect may be seen as a variant of Iyengar and Kinder's (1987) "priming" effect; by focusing on some issues more than others, media increase the importance attached to these issues in evaluating political figures. In this case, however, the effect is not simply the priming of all considerations surrounding an issue but rather "sociotropic priming": the priming of collective perceptions and a deemphasis on personal concerns. By heightening the importance of social concerns to political evaluations and decreasing the importance of personal concerns, mass media contribute to the depoliticization of personal experience.

Discussion

Reading in a newspaper that the unemployment rate has increased by a few percentage points seems a fundamentally different experience from receiving a pink slip that indicates that one has lost a job. Losing a job has an inescapable impact on an individual's everyday life; on the other hand, this study suggests that reading about unemployment in a newspaper may have greater consequences for U.S. political life.

Although they may be limited by time and locale,[15] these findings have implications for the study of economic influences on voting, and for analyses of mass media's role in the political process. First, these findings suggest that the answer to the question of what kind of information sustains the political impact of unemployment trends depends on the level of office being considered and on characteristics of the individual's information environment. At the presidential level, the general answer to this question clearly is mediated information. At the state level, personal perceptions influence social perceptions, and thus personal experiences indirectly enter into the process as well. Even at the national level, personal experiences may enter into these evaluations in the absence of other information. Just as Weatherford (1983a, 162) is correct in suggesting that "the dilemma of choosing between personal and national referents is more apparent than actual," the dilemma of choosing between personal experiences and mediated sources of information as a basis for political decisions is also contrived.

Contrary to the claims of Kramer (1983), these results demonstrate that individual-level variations in perceptions of unemployment conditions are, in fact, meaningful; they primarily demonstrate differences in the amount and type of information available to people. Those with much information from mass media sources will have perceptions of unemployment consistent with media presentations, while those relying on more parochial sources will have perceptions that reflect their immediate environments. These results further confirm the hypotheses of Weatherford (1983a) and Conover and colleagues (1986) that personal experiences are influential information sources among unknowledgeable people, but these findings also extend this general argument by demonstrating the sources of social perceptions among those who are knowledgeable.

The case against personal experiences in the literature on economic influences on voting has probably been overstated. Personal experiences do influence assessments of social conditions among the substantial proportion of the population that lacks alternative sources of information. Furthermore, when personal and social judgments move closer together in the absence of outside information, it becomes increasingly meaningless to distinguish between personal and social impacts, since one is simply an extension of the other. When a link does exist between personal and social levels of judgment as in the state-level model, personal experiences may influence social perceptions and thus, indirectly, political evaluations as well. Finally, even personal perceptions themselves, when measured subjectively, appear to have the potential for relatively weak, but significant direct effects on evaluations of incumbents.

On the whole, however, social perceptions and mediated information matter more. This is especially true when one takes into consideration the fact that the highly involved people who follow political news and form attitudes on a sociotropic basis are also most likely to be the ones voting. At the national level in particular, reading about unemployment in the newspaper or hearing about it from friends with employment problems may indeed have greater political consequences than personally losing a job. The closer to home the political contest, however, the stronger one would expect the personal-social link to become.

Perhaps the most surprising finding from this study in light of the conventional wisdom on mass media effects is that mediated information has any influence at all with an issue that so clearly affects individuals' everyday lives as unemployment does. The findings of this study suggest the exact inverse of what media dependency theories would suggest. Instead of arguing that mediated information sources will have effects in the absence of more personal information, this study suggests that for lack of more representative, social-level information from mediated sources, personal experiences will inform these judgments.

In addition to serving to inform social-level judgments, mass media also serve as an obstacle to the politicization of personal experience. Mass media coverage primes the sociotropic side of the general model and decreases the importance of the pocketbook path. This consistent pattern appears when we look at changes over time as media coverage increased and when we examine high- and low-exposure subgroups of these samples.

Understanding the normative implications of these findings is complex because mass media are functioning in two different capacities with respect

Table 3

Weighting of Personal and Collective Perceptions in Evaluating Incumbent Performance by Newspaper Readership

| | Spring 1987 | | Fall 1987 | | Fall 1987 | |
	Governor		Governor		President	
Regular readers[a]						
Personal problem	0.17	(0.19)	0.03	(0.23)	-.05	(0.28)
State/national problem	0.30**	(0.16)	0.49*	(0.23)	0.63*	(0.27)
R^2	0.20		0.43		0.30	
Occasional and nonreaders[a]						
Personal problem	0.28*	(0.12)	0.08	(0.17)	0.50*	(0.21)
State/national problem	0.06	(0.12)	0.18	(0.19)	0.34	(0.26)
R^2	0.14		0.25		0.33	

Note: Table 3 represents the results of six individual OLS regressions. In addition to the indicators of personal- and social-level concern shown here, each equation included demographic variables, party identification, community context, and all of the information sources appearing in the general model. Entries are unstandardized beta coefficients with standard errors in parentheses.

[a]Regular readers were defined as those who read a newspaper seven days a week. This group comprised 53% of the sample in the spring 1987 wave and 44% of the sample in the fall 1987 wave. The remainder were occasional and nonreaders.

* $p < .05$; ** $p < .10$, two-tailed tests.

to unemployment, each with different implications for the economic account-ability of incumbent leaders. On the one hand, mass media coverage of un-employment trends encourages accurate perceptions of social conditions.[16] This is a valuable function for mass media to serve, especially when citizens are relying primarily on social-level perceptions as a basis for political deci-sions. At the same time, mass media are an obstacle to the politicization of personal experiences because they provide a steady flow of information that establishes a social world beyond one's personal experiences and interper-sonal contacts. Widening the gap between personal and social judgments may be dysfunctional to the extent that people's social perceptions become inde-pendent of their aggregated personal experiences, and democratic accountability breaks down. Those who are not exposed enough to mass media to have accurate perceptions of state or national conditions may punish incumbents for economic declines that have not truly occurred, or reward incumbents for economic im-provements that have no basis in collective individual realities.

Appendix A

Sampling and Data Collection Procedures

Data collection was carried out by professional staff interviewers of Walker Research, Inc., as part of a biannual statewide poll. Telephone surveys were conducted between 1 and 5 June for the first wave, and between 7 and 11 December for the second wave. A random digit computer-generated sample was used with the number of telephone exchanges listed proportionate to the state population. An evening and weekend calling pattern was utilized with each number receiving three attempts. All respondents were at least 18 years old. The number of interviews conducted in each county was roughly propor-tionate to the county's percentage of the state population.

Appendix B

Wording of Survey Questions

Personal experience: "In the past year have you or anyone in your family been laid off or had trouble finding a job?" (No; Yes, respondent; Yes, family member). Coded (0) if no one in the immediate family has been unemployed, (1) if respondent or someone in family has been unemployed.

   Interpersonally mediated unemployment experiences: "How often do other people talk to you about their employment problems, that is having trouble finding or keeping a job? Would you say they talk to you about job security or unemployment problems everyday, 3 or 4 times a week, once or twice a week, or less often than that?" Coded as everyday (4), 3 or 4 times a week (3), once or twice a week (2), or less often than that (1).

Unemployment as a state/national problem: State level: "Let's talk about the employment situation here in Indiana. Would you say that over the past year people across our state have had a harder time finding enough work, an easier time, or have things stayed about the same? Is that a little harder/easier or a lot harder/easier?" Coded on a 5-point scale from a lot harder (1) to a lot easier (5). "Not sure" and "Don't know" recoded as (3). National level: "And what about the United States as a whole. Would you say that over the past year people across the United States have had a harder time finding enough work, an easier time, or have things stayed about the same? Is that a little harder/easier or a lot harder/easier?" (Wave 2 only). Coded on a 5-point scale from a lot harder (1) to a lot easier (5). "Not sure" and "Don't know" recoded as (3).

Unemployment as a personal problem: "How about you, or people in your own household. Over the past year, have you been more worried about finding a job or keeping the one you have, less worried about these things, or have things stayed about the same? Is that a little more/less worried or a lot more/less worried?" Coded on a 5-point scale from a lot more worried (1) to a lot less worried (5). "Not sure" and "Don't know" coded as (3).

Approval of incumbent administrations: "Overall do you approve or disapprove of the way (Name of governor/lt. governor) is doing his job as ___? Is that strongly approve/disapprove or somewhat approve/disapprove?" Additive index comprised of two 5-point approve-disapprove scales. Same questions repeated for presidential incumbents to form comparable scales corresponding to approval of state/national incumbent administrations.

Exposure to mass media coverage of employment trends: (A) Newspaper identification: "What one newspaper do you read most often?" Interviewers coded name and city of publication of newspaper. For each newspaper named by a respondent(s), a systematic content analysis was done of front pages appearing during two reconstructed weeks from the two months preceding each survey. (B) Frequency of exposure: "How many days in the past week did you read the front page news in a newspaper?" 0 to 7 raw scale recoded to 3-point scale representing nonreaders (0), occasional readers (1), and regular, 7-day-a-week readers (2).

Party identification: "Generally speaking, do you think of yourself as a Republican, a Democrat, an Independent or of some other political party?" Two party identification measures created representing whether respondent was Republican (1) or not (0), and Democrat (1) or not (0).

Unemployment knowledge: "Do you happen to know what the current unemployment rate is in the state of Indiana/the United States?" (If at first don't know, probe) "Could you take a guess?" Answers rounded to nearest whole number. Answers were counted as correct (1) if the respondent named a number that had been the actual state or national unemployment rate within the previous year (from 5% to 8%, when rounded), and incorrect (0) if the respondent was outside of this range or refused to guess.

Age: "Now I'm going to read some age groups. Please tell me into which group your age falls. Would that be 18–24 (1); 25–34 (2); 35–44 (3); 45–54 (4); 55–64 (5); 65 and over (6)."

Education: "What was the last grade of school that you, yourself, completed?" Grade school or less—grades 1–8 (1); some high school—grades 9–11 (2); graduated high school (3); some college/technical school (4); graduated college (5); postgraduate work (6).

Income: "Which of the following best represents your total annual household income? Under $10,000 (1); $10,000 to $20,000 (2); $20,000 to $30,000 (3); $30,000 to $40,000 (4); $40,000 or more (5)."

Race: "In order to ensure that all groups are properly represented in this survey, are you white, black, Hispanic American, American Indian, or some other nationality?" Coded as (0) for white, (1) for nonwhite.

Gender: Recorded by interviewer as male (1) or female (2).

Notes

1. A few studies have found evidence of directional effects (e.g., Haight and Brody 1977; Page, Shapiro, and Dempsey 1987), but this evidence remains primarily (if not entirely) at the aggregate level. The hazards of relying on such evidence for inferring individual-level effects are obvious.

2. Although Kiewiet (1983) tried to circumvent this problem by comparing open-ended responses to personal and collective "most important problem" questions, these questions clearly do not measure the same thing as personal and social-level retrospective economic evaluations.

3. Subsequent research on the two-step flow idea proposed by Katz and Lazarsfeld (1955) suggested that it was more the exception than the rule; most mass-mediated information reaches people directly rather than through an interpersonal network (see Chaffee 1972, 1982, for a review of this literature).

4. Methodological considerations also suggest that unemployment would provide a cleaner and more exacting test of the model than, say, changes in personal financial status (see Kramer 1983; Rosenstone, Hansen, and Kinder 1986).

5. For details on sampling and data collection procedures, consult Appendix A.

6. This question incorporated many more respondents into the personal experience category than would a measure of respondents' personal experiences alone. For example, although only 7% to 9% of respondents reported having been personally unemployed during the past year, more than 20% reported either themselves or someone in their immediate family had been personally affected within the past year.

7. Again, this indicator should be distinguished from the interpersonal communication measures traditionally included in election research in which interpersonal communication is conceived as a force in competition with mass-mediated information. Here, by contrast, it is seen as yet another channel through which information about unemployment (contrasting or, more likely, congruent information) may flow.

8. Although newspapers obviously do not cover the entire spectrum of mass media available to people, newspapers were chosen as the indicator of mass media content because some evidence has suggested that their effects are more reliable and enduring than effects of television news broadcasts. Furthermore, broadcast agendas tend to imitate newspaper agendas with a small time lag. (For more on television-newspaper comparisons, see Benton and Frazier 1976; Erbring 1980; Eyal 1981; McClure and Patterson 1976; Tipton, Haney, and Baseheart 1975.)

For each newspaper named by a respondent, a content analysis was done of 10 front pages appearing during two reconstructed weeks (weekday editions only) selected from the two months preceding each survey. Two coders measured the number of column inches for each identified unemployment-related article and noted the directional thrust of the article along a five-point good news/bad news scale. Amount-by-direction measures were summed, creating a single score for each newspaper for each wave. The intercoder reliability coefficient was .76. Intracoder reliability was .95 for the first coder, and .87 for the second coder. Discrepancies were resolved in favor of the more reliable coder. The final measure of Exposure to Newspaper Coverage of Employment Trends was created by standardizing the variable described above, and then multiplying it by a dummy variable representing the respondent's frequency of newspaper exposure (0 for nonreaders, 1 for occasional readers, and 2 for regular readers).

9. Both state and national assessments are parallel in the amount of time preceding an election. Further, both the gubernatorial and presidential incumbents were two-term Republicans who were not running for reelection.

10. Details on the operationalization of concepts in Figure 4 are described in Appendix B. To avoid problems resulting from priming respondents to think about economic issues in the context of the survey interview, the subjective unemployment-related questions were not asked in close proximity to questions dealing with evaluations of incumbents (see Sears and Lau 1983).

11. To avoid simultaneity problems, operationalizations of concepts purposely erred on the conservative side. For example, the coding procedure used in this study results in a very general measure of exposure to media coverage of unemployment news. Questions about attention to job-related news are not included as part of the measure. If questions were asked in more specific terms, information seeking that might result from social or personal perceptions of the issue-as-problem would make it necessary to draw causal arrows from subjective perceptions to attention to unemployment news as well as the other way around.

12. Controlling for party identification is one means of establishing a baseline that explains as much of the preexisting variation as possible; however, the usual party identification scale is likely to pick up short-term as well as long-term influences, so a model estimated with these controls would likely overcontrol for preexisting differences and underestimate the true effects of perceptions of unemployment trends (see, e.g., Brody 1977; Converse and Markus 1979; Fiorina 1981; Meier 1975; Page and Jones 1979; Shively 1977). Following Kiewiet (1983), this dilemma was resolved by using two multiple regression models, one using party identification and the other demographic variables, as upper and lower boundaries of the effects to be estimated. I have presented the more conservative estimates of these relationships in Table 1. The alternative models have greater explanatory power overall, but do not change the relationships between variables significantly. Both party identification and demographic controls are used in the remainder of the analyses in Tables 2 and 3.

13. These variables are likely to "overcontrol" for the influence of mass and interpersonally mediated messages. Areas with high unemployment rates, for example, are likely to have high levels of interpersonal discussion and high media coverage of this issue. Although much of this information will be conveyed to people through mediated channels, the community-level indicators will account for this same variance to the extent they mirror real world conditions.

14. Additional exogenous variables in the equations included interpersonally mediated information, demographic variables, party identification, retrospective assessments of family financial status, the unemployment rate in the respondent's county of residence, and indicators of change in unemployment within that county (see Table 2 for details).

15. For most purposes, a statewide sample does not pose generalizability problems for this kind of study, since hypotheses are about the processing of political information that is unlikely to differ systematically from state to state. But using a statewide sample does mean that the conclusions may be bound to the particular employment conditions found in the state at that particular time. By most standards, unemployment was low during the period of this study. Indiana's rate of unemployment had closely paralleled the national average for several years, including the period of this study. Moreover, the advantages of a statewide sample clearly outweigh the problems when the purpose is to look at variation in people's information environments. Studies using national samples typically have been forced to aggregate media content measures over time from a single, metropolitan source, such as the *New York Times* (see, e.g., Behr and Iyengar 1985; Funkhouser 1973a, 1973b; MacKuen and Coombs 1981). Such aggregation risks the same ecological fallacy that has slowed understanding of economic influences on voting.

16. Using the questions about estimated state and national unemployment rates as dependent variables, probit analysis indicated that daily newspaper reading did, in fact, encourage more accurate perceptions of unemployment conditions at both state and national levels, even beyond the effects of education and other demographic indicators. This probit regression included the three information source variables, party identification, race, gender, age, education, income, and the county unemployment rate in the respondent's community. Gender and newspaper exposure accounted for the bulk of variance in unemployment knowledge.

References

Adoni, Hannah, and Akiba A. Cohen. 1978. "Television Economic News and the Social Construction of Economic Reality." *Journal of Communication* 28:61–70.

Ball-Rokeach, Sandra J., and Melvin L. DeFleur. 1976. "A Dependency Model of Mass Media Effects." *Communication Research* 1:3–21.

Becker, Lee B., Maxwell E. McCombs, and Jack M. McLeod. 1975. "The Development of Political Cognitions." In *Political Communication: Issues and Strategies for Research,* ed. Steven H. Chaffee. Beverly Hills: Sage.

Behr, Roy L., and Shanto Iyengar. 1985. "Television News, Real World Cues, and Changes in the Public Agenda." *Public Opinion Quarterly* 49:38–57.

Benton, Marc, and P. Jean Frazier. 1976. "The Agenda-Setting Function of the Mass Media at Three Levels of Information Holding." *Communication Research* 3:261–74.

Brody, Richard A. 1977. "Stability and Change in Party Identification: Presidential to Off-Years." Presented at the annual meeting of the American Political Science Association, Washington, DC.

Chaffee, Steven H. 1972. "The Interpersonal Context of Mass Communication." In *Current Perspectives in Mass Communication Research,* ed. F. Gerald Kline and Phillip Tichenor. Beverly Hills: Sage.

———. 1982. "Mass Media and Interpersonal Channels: Competitive, Convergent, or Complementary?" In *Inter/Media: Interpersonal Communication in a Media World,* ed. Gary Gumpert and Robert Cathcart. New York: Oxford University Press.

Chaffee, Steven H., and Diana C. Mutz. 1988. "Comparing Mediated and Interpersonal Communication Data." In *Advancing Communication Science: Merging Mass and Interpersonal,* ed. Robert P. Hawkins, John M. Wiemann, and Suzanne Pingree. Newbury Park, CA: Sage.

Chubb, John E. 1988. "Institutions, the Economy, and the Dynamics of State Elections." *American Political Science Review* 82:133–54.

Cohen, Jeremy, Diana C. Mutz, Vincent Price, and Albert C. Gunther. 1988. "Perceived Impact of Defamation: An Experiment on Third Person Effects." *Public Opinion Quarterly* 52:161–73.

Conover, Pamela J. 1985. "The Impact of Group Economic Interests on Political Evaluations." *American Politics Quarterly* 13:139–66.

Conover, Pamela J., Stanley Feldman, and Kathleen Knight. 1986. "Judging Inflation and Unemployment: The Origins of Retrospective Evaluations." *Journal of Politics* 48:565–88.

Converse, Philip E., and Gregory B. Markus. 1979. "Plus ça Change . . .: The New CPS Election Study Panel." *American Political Science Review* 73:32–49.

Davison, W. Phillips. 1983. "The Third Person Effect in Communication." *Public Opinion Quarterly* 47:1–15.

Erbring, Lutz. 1980. "Media Monitoring and Public Opinion Change." Presented at the annual meeting of the American Political Science Association, Washington, DC.

Erbring, Lutz, Edie N. Goldenberg, and Arthur H. Miller. 1980. "Front-Page News and Real World Cues: A New Look at Agenda-Setting by the Media." *American Journal of Political Science* 24:16–47.

Eulau, Heinz, and Michael S. Lewis-Beck. 1985. *Economic Conditions and Electoral Outcomes: The United States and Western Europe.* New York: Agathon Press.

Eyal, Chaim H. 1981. "The Roles of Newspapers and Television in Agenda-Setting." *Mass Communication Review, Yearbook 2.* Beverly Hills: Sage.

Eyal, Chaim H., James P. Winter, and William F. DeGeorge. 1981. "The Concept of Time Frame in Agenda-Setting." *Mass Communication Review, Yearbook 2.* Beverly Hills: Sage.

Fiorina, Morris P. 1981. *Retrospective Voting in American National Elections.* New Haven: Yale University Press.

Funkhouser, G. Ray. 1973a. "The Issues of the Sixties: An Exploratory Study in the Dynamics of Public Opinion." *Public Opinion Quarterly* 37:62–75.

———. 1973b. "Trends in Media Coverage of the Issues of the '60s." *Journalism Quarterly* 50:533–38.

Gordon, Margaret T., and Linda Heath. 1981. "The News Business, Crime, and Fear." In *Reactions to Crime: Individual and Institutional Responses,* ed. Dan A. Lewis. Beverly Hills: Sage.

Graber, Doris A. 1984. *Processing the News.* New York: Longman.

Haight, Timothy, and Richard A. Brody. 1977. "The Mass Media and Presidential Popularity." *Communication Research* 4:41–60.

Hawkins, Robert P., and Suzanne Pingree. 1982. "Television's Influence on Social Reality." In *Television and Behavior,* vol. 2, ed. David Pearl, Lorraine Bouthilet, and Joyce Lazar. Rockville, MD: Government Printing Office.

Hinckley, Barbara, Richard Hofstetter, and John Kessel. 1974. "Information and the Vote: A Comparative Election Study." *American Politics Quarterly* 2:131–58.

Iyengar, Shanto, and Donald R. Kinder. 1987. *News That Matters.* Chicago: University of Chicago Press.

Jennings, M. Kent, and Harmon Zeigler. 1970. "The Salience of American State Politics." *American Political Science Review* 64:523–35.

Katz, Elihu, and Paul F. Lazarsfeld. 1955. *Personal Influence.* Glencoe, IL: Free Press.

Kiewiet, D. Roderick. 1983. *Macroeconomics and Micropolitics: The Electoral Effects of Economic Issues.* Chicago: University of Chicago Press.

Kinder, Donald R. 1981. "Presidents, Prosperity, and Public Opinion." *Public Opinion Quarterly* 45:1–21.

Kinder, Donald R., and D. Roderick Kiewiet. 1979. "Economic Discontent and Political Behavior: The Role of Personal Grievances and Collective Economic Judgments in Congressional Voting." *American Journal of Political Science* 23:495–527.

———. 1981. "Sociotropic Politics: The American Case." *British Journal of Political Science* 11:129–61.

Kinder, Donald R., Steven J. Rosenstone, and J. Mark Hansen. 1983. "Group Economic Well-Being and Political Choice." Pilot Study Report to the 1984 NES Planning Committee and NES Board.

Klorman, Ricardo. 1978. "Trend in Personal Finances and the Vote." *Public Opinion Quarterly* 42:31–48.

Kramer, Gerald H. 1983. "The Ecological Fallacy Revisited: Aggregate- Versus Individual-level Findings on Economics and Elections, and Sociotropic Voting." *American Political Science Review* 77:92–111.

Lazarsfeld, Paul F., Bernard Berelson, and Hazel Gaudet. 1944. *The People's Choice.* New York: Columbia University Press.

McClure, Robert D., and Thomas E. Patterson. 1976. "Setting the Political Agenda: Print vs. Network News." *Journal of Communication* 26:23–28.

McCombs, Maxwell E., and Donald L. Shaw. 1972. "The Agenda-Setting Function of the Mass Media." *Public Opinion Quarterly* 36:176–87.

MacKuen, Michael B., and Stephen L. Coombs. 1981. *More Than News: Media Power in Public Affairs.* Beverly Hills: Sage.

McLeod, Jack M., Lee B. Becker, and James E. Byrnes. 1974. "Another Look at the Agenda-Setting Function of the Press." *Communication Research* 1:131–66.

Meier, Kenneth J. 1975. "Party Identification and Vote Choice: The Causal Relationship." *Western Political Quarterly* 28:496–505.

Mutz, Diana C. 1989. "The Influence of Perceptions of Media Influence." *International Journal of Public Opinion Research* 1:3–24.

Page, Benjamin I., and Calvin C. Jones. 1979. "Reciprocal Effects of Policy Preferences, Party Loyalties, and the Vote." *American Political Science Review* 73:1071–89.

Page, Benjamin I., Robert Y. Shapiro, and Glenn R. Dempsey. 1987. "What Moves Public Opinion?" *American Political Science Review* 81:23–44.

Palmgreen, Phillip, and Peter Clarke. 1977. "Agenda Setting with Local and National Issues." *Communication Research* 4:435–52.

Peltzman, Sam. 1987. "Economic Conditions and Gubernatorial Elections." *American Economic Review* 77:293–97.

Piereson, James E. 1977. "District Economic Conditions and Congressional Elections." Presented at the annual meeting of the Midwest Political Science Association, Chicago.

Pollard, W. 1978. "Effects of Economic Conditions on Elections: A Study Controlling for Political Variables." Presented at the annual meeting of the Public Choice Society, New Orleans.

Rosenstone, Steven J., J. Mark Hansen, and Donald R. Kinder. 1986. "Measuring Change in Personal Economic Well Being." *Public Opinion Quarterly* 50:176–92.

Schlesinger, Joseph A. 1966. *Ambition and Politics: Political Careers in the United States.* Chicago: Rand McNally.

Schlozman, Kay L., and Sidney Verba. 1979. *Injury to Insult.* Cambridge: Harvard University Press.

Sears, David O., and Richard R. Lau. 1983. "Inducing Apparently Self-Interested Political Preferences." *American Journal of Political Science* 27:223–52.

Shively, W. Phillips. 1977. "Information Costs and the Partisan Life Cycle." Presented at the annual meeting of the American Political Science Association, Washington, DC.

Skogan, Wesley G., and Michael G. Maxfield. 1981. *Coping with Crime: Individual and Neighborhood Reactions.* Beverly Hills: Sage.

Tipton, Leonard, Roger Haney, and James Baseheart. 1975. "Media Agenda-Setting in City and State Election Campaigns." *Journalism Quarterly* 52:15–22.

Tyler, Tom R. 1980. "Impact of Directly and Indirectly Experienced Events: The Origin of Crime-Related Judgments and Behaviors." *Journal of Personality and Social Psychology* 39:13–28.

———. 1984. "Assessing the Risk of Crime Victimization: The Integration of Personal Victimization Experience and Socially Transmitted Information." *Journal of Social Issues* 40:27–38.

Tyler, Tom R., and Fay L. Cook. 1984. "The Mass Media and Judgments of Risk: Distinguishing Impact on Personal and Societal Level Judgments." *Journal of Personality and Social Psychology* 47:693–708.

Weatherford, M. Stephen. 1983a. "Economic Voting and the 'Symbolic Politics' Argument: A Reinterpretation and Synthesis." *American Political Science Review* 77:158–74.

———. 1983b. "Evaluating Economic Policy: A Contextual Model of the Opinion Formation Process." *Journal of Politics* 45:866–88.

Weaver, David H., Doris A. Graber, Maxwell E. McCombs, and Chaim H. Eyal. 1981. *Media Agenda Setting in a Presidential Election.* New York: Praeger.

Zucker, Harold G. 1978. "The Variable Nature of News Media Influence." In *Communication Yearbook 2,* ed. Brent D. Ruben. New Brunswick, NJ: Transaction Books.

Discussion Questions

1. If Mutz had simply measured the bivariate relationship between the respondent's perception of unemployment as a social problem and the respondent's support for the incumbent, what variable or variables could have made such a relationship spurious?

2. Can you think of other variables that you would like to have included in the multivariate analysis? What about personal income level? Age? Gender? If any of these factors are important influences on incumbent support, what effect would omitting them have on the study?

3. Mutz states that "losing a job has an inescapable impact on an individual's everyday life; on the other hand, this study suggests that reading about unemployment in a newspaper may have greater consequences for U.S. political life." What specific findings from her multivariate analysis support this statement?

4. Most of the variables used in the analysis involved reducing responses to numerical form (see Appendix B). What level data did this approach produce? What did Mutz have to assume in order to use these data in regression analysis?

5. The same questions that Mutz examined could also be examined in a study designed to measure the association between actual economic conditions (e.g., unemployment rate, inflation, growth rate) and voting. How would such a study be different from Mutz's study? What kinds of factors would have to be controlled for in the multivariate analysis of these variables?

Commentary

Mutz concludes that media coverage of national or state economic conditions is critically important. According to her study, people do not simply "vote their pocketbooks." Support for an incumbent is influenced by popular perceptions of how well the country (or state) is doing, and these perceptions are significantly affected by media coverage.

Mutz presented her findings in a generally simple and clear manner. In Table 1, the results indicate that the most important influences on the level of incumbent support were the repondent's perceptions of unemployment as a social problem and the respondent's party identification. The other factors, including the respondent's perception of his or her own unemployment problem, were not significantly related to incumbent support. Mutz reported the standard error for each regression coefficient, allowing the reader to see which coefficients were statistically significant.

For Table 2, Mutz reported that she used "two-stage least squares" regression "to resolve the complications posed by the potential reciprocal relationship between perceptions of unemployment as a personal and social problem." This method includes refinements to prevent the interaction between two independent variables from disturbing the accuracy of the regression coefficients.

Mutz reported the R^2 (the "coefficient of multiple determination") in Tables 1 and 3, indicating the proportion of the variation in the dependent variable that can be attributed to variation in the independent variables. The value of R^2 can vary from 0 to 1, higher values indicating that the independent variables accounted for a large portion of the variation in the dependent variable. The values of R^2 that Mutz obtained were rather low, suggesting that there are other influences on the dependent variable (support for incumbents) not included in the model. It is possible that the variables not included would, if included, change the relationships that Mutz identified. Determining if this is a cause of concern is one of the most important tasks of the researcher in multivariate analysis. Mutz has added to our knowledge by discovering the relationships she reported; subsequent research may refine her conclusions, perhaps by bringing additional variables into the model.

To be sure, the techniques employed in these excerpts—multiple regression and path analysis—are but two of a much broader range of statistical tools useful for multivariate analysis. Many other multivariate techniques are commonly employed in the social sciences. One of the more interesting of these is **partial correlation**, a mathematical technique that allows us to subtract the influence of the variable or variables for which we want to control from the explained variation in the dependent variable.[6]

The key point here is that tools such as multiple regression, path analysis, and partial correlation are often essential to our efforts to answer research questions involving complex relationships among many variables. They are commonly employed not to dazzle the uninitiated, but because they provide a basis for more accurate and useful conclusions. The complexity of political research requires that we nearly always use multivariate analysis in some form.

---

6. For a good discussion, see Jones (1971), pp. 146–152.

13 Scientific Principles in Political Study: Some Enduring Controversies

Scientific political inquiry involves the application of scientific principles and methods derived from mathematics and the natural sciences to politics. This book is based on the belief that such an effort is appropriate and useful. Scientific political research has generated many new insights and understandings that have replaced inaccurate suppositions, prejudices, and common-sense views about political life. The scientific study of politics has been a resounding success in many important areas.

From its inception, however, the scientific study of politics has aroused controversy and criticism. Critics have argued, and continue to argue, that human behavior, particularly *political* behavior, cannot and should not be studied in the same manner in which inanimate objects and physical forces are studied. The purpose of this chapter is to identify and explore some of the more common criticisms of scientific political research. As we understand and acknowledge these arguments, we will see that there may, in fact, be limits on the application of scientific principles to the study of politics.

Criticism 1. Scientific Political Research Is Impractical

The basic principles of scientific research were developed in the "hard" or natural sciences whose subject matter is very different from what we study in political science. Some scholars contend that the special nature of political phenomena makes it impractical, if not impossible, to use the scientific method to understand and predict behavior in political life.

Perhaps the most obvious difficulty is that, while political analysts seek empirical tests of verifiable hypotheses just as researchers in the hard sciences do, the quality of available political data is often poor. Political scientists have had to be creative and imaginative in designing measurements and data gathering techniques. It must be admitted that some of these measures and techniques are controversial and occasionally leave readers with doubts about their legitimacy. For example, when analysts wanted to determine which leaders were on the way up in the old Soviet Union, they sometimes counted the number and type of reports of applause included in public transcripts of each leader's official speeches. An official state newspaper report of "long and stormy" applause following a leader's speech has been cited as evidence that this leader's standing in the Politburo is higher than that of a leader whose statements were greeted with "polite applause." To put it in terms of our discussion in chapter 1, we often encounter validity problems in operationalizing political variables. Data are much more easily obtained and quantified in the realm of the natural sciences than in politics.

Perhaps even more important, the number of influences on political behavior is so large that our hypotheses may be fatally incomplete. Compared to experiments in physics or chemistry, where critical variables can be precisely measured and confounding factors controlled, political research often seems disturbingly imprecise. Our research problems involve a large number of variables and (usually) a relatively small number of cases. This makes causal inference very difficult. Often, even when a dependent variable appears to have been influenced by a particular independent variable, unknown factors may have been responsible.

Of course, the difficulties inherent in the scientific prediction of complex phenomena are not limited to the social sciences. Consider the case of a meteorologist who attempted to use a computer to predict weather patterns. He first constructed a mathematical model that incorporated several basic variables, each weighted in accordance with well-established practice. He then entered a set of initial conditions and ran his model, thereby generating a set of predicted changes in the weather for a specified period. Shortly thereafter, he ran the same problem again in an attempt to replicate his initial study. To his great surprise, the second set of predictions was identical to the first for only the first few days. Thereafter, the two sets of predictions were very different.

Upon further analysis, the meteorologist discovered that the differences in the two sets of predictions were caused by extremely minute differences in his set of initial conditions that were attributable to rounding of the numbers representing those conditions. A change in initial conditions so small as to be considered irrelevant profoundly affected the model's predictions. This discovery led to what has since come to be known as the "butterfly's wing" problem: The weather some months ahead may be significantly affected by the movement today of a butterfly's wing (Gleick 1987).

The meteorologist's objectives are similar to those of most political scientists. We attempt to predict the occurrence or outcome of extremely complex phenomena such as elections, the incidence of coups, and state economic growth rates. If predictions of rainfall can be completely wrong as a result of a minute error in specifying a single initial condition, what are the chances that a political scientist can predict the outbreak of a revolution or even which party will control Congress in four years? Political scientists were conspicuously unable to predict the dismantling of the

Berlin Wall or the demise of communism in even one of the Warsaw Pact nations in 1989, a set of events that was central to research in comparative government, international relations, and political development. Political scientists also failed to predict the Republican takeover of the House of Representatives in 1994 or the increased strength of the Democratic party in the House in 1998. As recently as June 2000, a distinguished group of political scientists predicted that Al Gore would win the 2000 presidential election by a comfortable margin. Can political research ever produce useful predictions?

One answer is that political scientists are very likely to be able to make useful predictions of a less exacting variety. Political scientists may never construct models that will allow them to predict precisely when and where political coups will occur. However, political research can significantly improve predictions that would otherwise be made on the basis of hunches or blind intuition. Robert Jackman's study of coups in Africa (Jackman 1978) demonstrated that knowledge of the relationship between coups and such factors as cultural pluralism, multipartyism, and social mobilization can be helpful. Even though Jackman's model does not predict political instability with great precision, corporations considering a major investment in these countries would almost certainly be interested in his findings regarding the conditions that are associated with a greater likelihood of violent political instability. In short, the best empirical studies demonstrate that scientific political research can have value even if it never allows us to predict the future with complete certainty.

Criticism 2. Political Research Is Subject to Misuse

The issues addressed by political research are necessarily controversial, and our findings are often subject to misinterpretation by those with political motives. Perhaps the most notable recent example of this problem is the controversy over *The Bell Curve* (Herrnstein and Murray 1994). The stated purpose of this study was to explore the ways in which intelligence, as measured by standardized tests, has become increasingly important in influencing career success and social stratification in modern society. However, the book contained some very controversial material regarding racial differences on intelligence tests, which may or may not have reflected the authors' views on race. Newspapers and television commentators focused almost exclusively on the book's data regarding racial differences, undoubtedly making other analysts reluctant to address this subject at all because of the possible harm done by such research to our society's basic consensus on human equality. Some critics argue that, in such areas as this, the danger of misinterpretation outweighs the potential benefits of research. Perhaps some questions simply should not be addressed with the tools of social science inquiry.

Of course, this problem is hardly unique to the social sciences. Scientific research in the areas of weapons development and pesticides, for example, has resulted in the creation of potentially catastrophic new weapons and chemicals. Whether political research might ever produce equally threatening results is difficult to say. What is clear is that the core issues and terminology of political research are directly involved with values. For this reason, they are highly susceptible to misinterpretation, whether deliberate or accidental.

Nonetheless, a strong case can be made that ignorance of political and social phenomena is at least as damaging as the findings of political scientists. Hitler's Nazis proclaimed sociological "truths" that would have been hilarious in their unsophistication if they had not served as the foundation for such unspeakable evils (Hitler once dismissed Einstein's theories as "Jewish physics," for example). When scientific research corrects error and ignorance, the results are almost always beneficial.

The crucial point is to maintain the openness of the political research process. As long as the research process is open to those with different points of view, and as long as research results are subject to scrutiny by a diverse community of scholars, the benefits of political research will usually outweigh the dangers of its misuse.

Criticism 3. The Application of Science to Political Issues Dulls Our Ethical and Moral Sensibilities

Political research is often concerned with revolutionary violence, war, racial injustice, and other matters that have profoundly important moral dimensions. Does the scientific method divert our attention from morality? Lawrence Tribe (1972), for one, has suggested that it does. Quantifying aspects of human aspirations and tragedy may be necessary for scientific analysis but doing so may make us lose sight of their complex moral aspects.

In a similar vein, it has been argued that finding solutions to our major social problems requires an emotional attachment to high moral and even spiritual values. As David Easton has argued, "the contemporary loss or confusion of faith by which men live has been hastened by the growth of scientific reasoning in the natural and social sciences" (Easton 1971, p. 19). These are challenging ideas. Essentially, we are told that an emphasis on science is detrimental to ethical, moral, and philosophical analysis. Numbed by his or her pursuit of quantifiable data, the scientific researcher falls victim to the delusion that political issues can be resolved by science.

Interestingly enough, this criticism of scientific research in the social sciences comes from both ends of the political spectrum. Liberals like Tribe argue that social science methods lead us to gloss over the serious human tragedy of, say, joblessness, by diverting our focus from the people whose daily lives are affected to the bloodless, impersonal, and "objective" indicators we use to measure unemployment.

Similarly, conservatives like Edward Banfield have argued that social science methodology deflects attention away from traditional social values that lie at the core of a functioning society (Banfield 1975). Science, they argue, can easily determine if a statistical relationship exists, but it cannot, by itself, provide moral guidance concerning how best to change or manage those relationships. To the extent that the answers to political problems lie in a moral plane, our quest for them is not advanced, and may even be retarded, by the application of science.

The solution is obvious to most social scientists. Good research is enlightening, even for moral discourse. We are better able to address moral and ethical problems when we operate from a factual basis. It cannot be seriously argued that judgment is enhanced by ignorance. If research is sometimes misleading, poorly designed, and misinterpreted, then we should pay greater attention to improving its quality. Neglecting research where factual questions are open will in no way promote progress in solving or understanding political problems, ethical or otherwise.

Criticisms 4. Scientific Research on Politics Is Restricted by the Existence of Free Will

There is a very old controversy in the social sciences regarding the problem of free will. The general point is straightforward. When a physicist develops and tests a theory of, say, quantum mechanics, the subjects of the study are driven by certain forces. If all the relevant variables are known, prediction becomes possible. However, political research attempts to predict human behavior, and, regardless of the forces that we think incline them in certain ways, humans can choose to act differently, even acting against their own interests, and thereby invalidate our predictions. Nonetheless, political research, like all scientific inquiry, rests on the assumption that behavior is ultimately understandable in terms of general laws. If we could exhaustively identify the variables, political behavior could be fully accounted for and predicted. The concept of free will is inconsistent with this assumption. Peter Winch (1958) argues the point with conviction:

> Even given a specific set of initial conditions, one will still not be able to predict any determinate outcome to a historical trend because the continuation or breaking off of that trend involves human decisions which are not determined by their antecedent conditions. . . . Think of the interplay between orthodoxy and heresy in the development of religion; or of the way in which the game of football was revolutionized by the Rugby boy who picked up the ball and ran. It would certainly not have been possible to predict that revolution from knowledge of the preceding state of the game any more than it would have been possible to predict the philosophy of Hume from the philosophies of his predecessors. (pp. 92–93)

The central point here is that many important political events are profoundly affected by the results of human decisions. Because of this, it is argued, we will never be able to predict those decisions in detail.

In response, even the staunchest defenders of the scientific approach have been willing to concede that the prediction of human behavior is more complicated than prediction in the natural sciences where subjects cannot choose their behavior. Yet, some have argued, perhaps this complexity is not due to free will itself, but to the fact that the number of environmental influences acting upon human beings is so large. An individual who appears to be making a choice explainable by nothing other than his or her own creative impulses is really being driven by influences that we simply have not identified. Those who hold to this position suggest that, in principle, human behavior *can* be predictable. We simply need to know all of the influences (including remote childhood experiences) that may be acting upon a person's observed behavior.

Happily, we do not have to resolve this thorny philosophical problem. Instead, we simply need to recognize that our predictions about political behavior are inevitably imprecise. Whether this is because of free will or the almost infinite number of influences acting on human behavior is not terribly important. What does matter is that even a limited science of politics is still extremely useful. It may be, for example, that we can only predict a person's party affiliation with 75 percent accuracy from knowledge of his or her income, education level, and other relevant factors. Nonetheless, such information is extremely useful, as both campaign managers and political analysts would be quick to attest.

Criticism 5. The Scientific Method Ignores Holistic Factors

It is often remarked that a group is more than the sum of its parts. At the most abstract level, this implies that some quality or characteristic of the group cannot be entirely accounted for in terms of the behavior or other characteristics of the group's members. This idea is called holism, and it is usually offered as a challenge to the principles of empirical research in social science.

May Brodbeck (1958) described the idea:

> If, for instance, the efficiency of a group is not some function of the behavior of its constituent individuals, then there must be something else that exhibits this efficiency, the group itself. And if there be such a super-entity as, say, a group mind, then it will have characteristics of its own: allegedly, it may have political opinions. (p. 283)

The implication for scientific research is clear—we cannot effectively study groups, classes, or other wholes by studying the individuals comprising them. The nature of the group itself will be overlooked or distorted in our research. If, as holistic thinkers believe, the group itself is important in some respects, we will have failed to take its effects into account in our observation and analysis of individual behavior.

The problem is that groups are not observable. We observe individuals.

Even when we use aggregate level data (e.g., state per capita income), we assume that the values involved are derived from measurements taken at the individual level. For this reason, most proponents of holism inevitably reject empirical scientific inquiry. Conversely, a scientific approach to political study must reject holism, at least in its more extreme forms.

Consider a discussion of "the German mind," a notion that many thinkers pondered after World War II and that others ponder now after German reunification has become a reality; the most likely empirical approach to the problem would be to conduct a survey of a representative sample of German individuals and compare their answers to those of a sample of persons from other countries. (See Almond and Verba 1963, for a classic study along these lines.) If the answers given by our German respondents were significantly different from those of others, we might conclude that a distinctive set of attitudes exists among the German people.

Such a conclusion would, however, be based on the opinions of German *individuals*. The holistic analyst could claim that "the German mind" is an entity that transcends the opinions of individual Germans. If so, we have a serious problem. Since "the German mind" cannot be observed except by observing individuals, we cannot treat the holistic concept scientifically: "The holistic assumption that there are group properties over and above the individuals making up the group, their properties, and the relations among them is counter to empiricism" (Brodbeck 1958, p. 283). An empirical, scientific approach requires that we deny the existence of an entity transcending individuals.

This does not mean, however, that we cannot study and compare aggregates, or even that we must reject the study of properties like culture or class consciousness that are widely shared by many people. Holistic thinkers may, moreover, contribute to our understanding by helping us to consider factors that *appear* to transcend individuals—they may help us to see the forest and not only the trees. However, when we embark on empirical research, we are limited to those concepts that can be analyzed by observation. In political science, this normally requires that we emphasize individual behavior and concepts derived from it.

Criticism 6. Scientific Methodology Has Led to the Disintegration of Political Science

During the middle part of the twentieth century, there was frequent conflict among members of political science departments, just as there is today, and just as there has always been in all academic departments. The conflict during that time was largely between the political scientists trained during an earlier period and a cadre of newly minted assistant professors who embraced the methods of behavioral science. Many scholars were convinced that when the behaviorally-oriented scholars became dominant, the discipline would be a substantially unified force working to produce new knowledge about political life.

One of the former presidents of the American Political Science Association, Warren E. Miller, entitled his 1980 Presidential Address "The Role of Research in the Unification of a Discipline." Miller argued that the growing acceptance of behavioral methodologies in leading political science graduate programs produced a helpful unification (Miller 1981). In earlier times, political scientists specializing in the study of, for example, the British Parliament had little in common with those specializing in Latin American politics. Each set of specialists did research on different sets of unique governmental institutions, different cultures, and different histories. The emergence of a common methodological framework would, according to Miller, bring political scientists together. Thus, political scientists doing research on the Israeli Knesset, the Japanese Diet, and the U.S. Congress would all be studying *legislative behavior*, and they would build on information and understanding generated in settings other than their own. While pre-behavioral approaches left scholars in isolation, focusing on the unique historical and legal features of their respective subjects, the application of scientific methodology would lead political scientists to see common variables, influences, and questions.

Although some unification has occurred, most political scientists are convinced that the discipline is more divided than ever, and largely because of methodological factors. A few years after Miller's Presidential Address, another political scientist wrote an essay entitled "Separate Tables." The name came from a 1955 Terence Rattigan play in which several different persons pursue very different, isolated lives while eating in the same restaurant. This appears to be a good characterization of contemporary political science, with its broad array of subfields that have largely ceased to communicate with each other.

The discipline was once divided between the old-fashioned "legal-institutional" specialists and the newer behavioralists, and people like Warren Miller felt that the latter group's inevitable dominance would generate a helpful unity in approach. Things have not worked out this way. Political science is now divided more deeply than ever along several different lines. With the emergence of rational choice theory, some political scientists now apply mathematical modeling to derive complex theories of political behavior. Their research style and methodologies rarely lead them to empirical testing of their ideas, which frustrates many behavioralists. Other political scientists reject the apolitical stance of behavioralism, embracing an explicitly political approach steeped in either left or right ideology. Some specialists in comparative politics embrace the study of language, culture, and history, rejecting the idea that genuine understanding can be produced by the quantitative study of behavior. Postmodernists seem to reject the idea of science itself.

To a significant extent, the new divisions are a consequence of the fact that behavioral methodologies gained a commanding presence in the discipline, while leaving many questions unanswered and unaddressed. Many political scientists became disenchanted with what they saw as a restrictive methodological focus that failed to develop a clear theoretical basis and that de-emphasized the partisan and ideological passions that brought them to the discipline. In response, some embraced rational choice theory while others were drawn to controversial problems in contemporary political philosophy.

Miller's optimism was thus founded on hopes that have not been fulfilled. The highly varied subject matter of political science makes it impossible for large segments of the discipline to accept even a roughly uniform methodology. The heated resistance to the partial dominance of behavioral science demonstrates that attempting to force such a unified framework on political science was probably counterproductive.

There are benefits to diversity in approach and method, however, and we must hope that a discipline with so many "separate tables" will nonetheless prosper through cross-fertilization.

Criticism 7. Political Research Is Excessively Quantified

In their efforts to use the most advanced statistical tools, political researchers have been criticized for their attraction to quantification. In the view of some critics, "If you cannot count it, it does not count" is the motto of the methodologically sophisticated political scientist.

There are at least two reasons why a bias toward quantification may distort our research findings. The first is that it may lead us to disregard factors that are relevant to the behavior in question when they are difficult to quantify. This is an especially intense controversy in comparative politics: The quantifiers argue that political development and stability can be explained by such quantifiable factors as the number of telephones per 100,000 population, literacy rates, or voting turnout, while their less quantitatively oriented colleagues claim that distinctive cultural characteristics and historical events are of paramount importance. If a penchant for quantification leads the analyst to ignore difficult-to-measure concepts that are nonetheless important to the question at hand, his or her research will be seriously flawed.

Second, quantification can lead to oversimplifying or even trivializing concepts. Abraham Kaplan (1998 [1964]) illustrated the problem with an amusing anecdote about the famous Kinsey report on sexual behavior:

> One of the subjects of [the Kinsey study] complained bitterly of the injury to his masculine ego. "No matter what I told him," he explained, "he just looked me straight in the eye and asked, 'How many times. . . ?'" Plainly the subject felt that what he had done was incomparably more significant than the frequency of its performance. (p. 171)

In a realm as complex as politics, the attempt to quantify unique events inevitably carries with it the risk of distortion. Every violent overthrow of a government, for example, is surely different in many important ways from all others. Yet one researcher (Jackman 1978) used a simple three-point rating scheme to classify and count them! The question here is whether an event involving a conspiracy of many important and unique individuals accompanied by acts of violence and intrigue can be meaningfully studied by assigning it a score of 2 while another similar event somewhere else receives a score of 1 or 3. Most observers would say it cannot.

We need not conclude from this that quantification is impossible, however. It seems more reasonable to suggest that: (a) we must be creative in devising ways to quantify difficult concepts; (b) we must incorporate qualitative variables into our research where appropriate; and (c) some aspects of politics may lie beyond the reach of quantitative research. Not every concept can be measured, perhaps, but where quantification is possible, a great deal can be done with the scientific method. Progress in political science will, to a large extent, be a matter of how effectively we can extend the limits of quantification while still finding meaningful ways to study important concepts.

Criticism 8. Scientific Political Research Obscures Subjective Judgment and Bias

Prescientific analysis of political issues is unabashedly subjective. We can easily perceive the author's biases and opinions in such research because they are often explicitly stated as such. It is sometimes argued that scientific analysis, although cloaked with a mantle of objectivity, is in fact no less subjective than any other type of analysis. It may thus be argued that the objective appearance of scientific research is highly deceptive and even dangerous. Unwary readers may be misled into believing that highly subjective conclusions are actually the result of objective research. The problem is suggested by the well-known expression that "figures don't lie, but liars figure."

The problem here, however, is not so much with the scientific method itself, as with the conduct of researchers and readers. To the extent that prejudices are conveyed as objective fact by deliberate distortion, the only defense is a thorough knowledge of scientific method. It is difficult to use science to deceive someone who understands statistics, causal inference, sampling, measurement, and operationalization.

Subjective judgments and prejudice actually constitute a more serious problem when they *unintentionally* find their way into a research design. Even a conscientious researcher may select measures and construct hypotheses in ways that enhance the chances that his or her preferred conclusion will be supported by the research. Because the results are presented as objective, and because the biases and prejudices are normally not made explicit (as they would be in nonscientific, philosophical discourse), readers may attach more weight to such findings than they deserve.

Bachrach and Baratz's classic essay still provides an instructive discussion of unintentional bias (Bachrach and Baratz 1962). They focused on studies of the extent to which political power in big U.S. cities is concentrated in the hands of a unified "elite." One study they criticized was completed by an analyst (Robert Dahl) who hoped to prove that political power was actually quite widely distributed. He had set about to study the problem by observing the process by which political decisions were publicly debated and decided. As Bachrach and Baratz pointed out, it should have been obvious that, even before data were gathered, such a strategy would tend to confirm the researcher's preexisting views. Almost surely, he or she would observe that no single faction won all the battles, that one faction might defeat another on one issue only to suffer a reverse on the next. And so the analyst could then gleefully conclude that no single elite dominated the decision-making process.

The study would, however, have overlooked those important issues that never reached the public agenda. Perhaps a very powerful elite uses its influence to keep certain issues from being effectively raised. If these issues had been considered by the researcher, the real power of a unified elite would have been apparent, but *the research design prevented these issues from being studied*. The choice of research design—focusing only on those issues that made it to the official agenda of the city council—led to a seemingly objective, yet predetermined, set of results that understated the extent to which political power is concentrated in the hands of a unified elite. Some people have reacted to the problem of subjectivity in scientific research by wholly rejecting the value of such research, insisting that "there are studies to support virtually any conclusion you want." Presumably, these people still have some basis for making policy choices and predictions, perhaps intuition or tradition or some other approach. Another contemporary reaction to the subjective element in science is that of the "postmodernists" who generally embrace a kind of radical subjectivity. Although the postmodern movement is hardly a coherent approach, it rejects behavioral, empirical analysis in social science and instead insists on seeing political agendas in the methodology of science itself.

There are two more constructive reactions to the inevitable presence of subjectivity in science. First, researchers must accept the basic idea of objectivity *as a principle*, even if it cannot be fully attained in practice. This was effectively stated by Heinz Eulau and James March in 1969:

> Whether the researcher seeks personal involvement in the policy process or prefers to observe it from the outside is a matter of individual choice. But whatever role the political scientist may take, his study of the policy process requires a high degree of judiciousness as a norm of *scientific* conduct. He must seek to balance as wisely as he can what his involvement in the policy making process may require. This balancing is far from easy, but it is an obligation that both political scientist and public policy maker appreciate and honor if political science is to continue as a scientific discipline and not become the handmaid of special interests. Its task, in short, is to be of service to all and subservient to none. (p. 43)

The second positive step that the profession can take is to ensure that political research remains an open enterprise in which a sufficient number of well-trained scholars approach the subject from a diverse array of perspectives. Partisan or ideological bias flourishes best in disciplines and departments in which only a single point of view is considered "acceptable." In genuinely diverse settings, especially where political diversity is coupled with strong methodological skills, biased research designs will be increasingly perceived as flawed, or, at the very least, their nonneutral elements will be identified and discussed. Moreover, as more analysts are involved in the research process, different approaches to research problems will be developed, and greater balance in perspective will be achieved. Indeed, this is one purpose of the peer review process used by professional associations and publishers to help them identify the material most worthy of publication.

There will never be a solution to the problem of subjectivity in political science, but progress within the discipline, along with its standing in society, depend on the strength of these principles among those in the profession.

Conclusion

Common sense once told us many things about politics. It told us that political independents know more about politics than strong party identifiers, that revolutions are more likely to occur when repression is at its worst, that those who are most dependent on government assistance will vote more regularly than more prosperous citizens. Tradition and prejudice once told us that certain racial groups are inferior. A hopeful idealism once told us that corruption and selfishness among public officials would be eliminated once women had the right to vote. Scientific political research has shown all of these suppositions to be false.

It is my firm conviction that, within important limits, the most reliable and productive (though by no means the only) path to political understanding is through empirical, scientific inquiry. The scientific study of politics has not only helped us set aside some longstanding errors in understanding politics and government, it has also provided a firmer foundation for ethical and moral discussion. No informed person can seriously doubt that we know much more about politics now than we did even a few decades ago.

While critics of scientific political research argue that science works best in physics, chemistry, and biology, the quantification and precise thinking associated with scientific principles may be particularly valuable in social science. Herbert Simon, a Nobel Prize winner in economics, made the point in the strongest terms:

> Mathematics has become the dominant language of the natural sciences not because it is quantitative—a common delusion—but primarily because it permits clear and rigorous reasoning about phenomena too complex to handle in words. This advantage of mathematics over cruder languages should prove of even greater signifi-

cance in the social sciences, which deal with phenomena of the greatest complexity, than it has in the natural sciences. (quoted in Buchanan 1988, p. 63)

Thus, the principles of scientific method may open doors to even greater progress in political research than they have in other fields. If so, we must consider political science as a discipline in its infancy. We have a long way to go, and the arguments raised in this chapter suggest we will probably never reach our ultimate objective of a set of universal laws of political behavior. However, a vast range of important questions is clearly within our reach. Striving to answer them scientifically will make us wiser in all our political thinking. When considering the true value of a scientific approach to the study of politics, we would do well to recall the words of Charles Beard:

> No one can deny that the idea is fascinating—the idea of subduing the phenomena of politics to the laws of causation, of penetrating to the mystery of its transformations, of symbolizing the trajectory of its future; in a word, of grasping destiny by the forelock and bringing it prostrate to earth. The very idea itself is worthy of the immortal god. . . . If nothing ever comes of it, its very existence will fertilize thought and enrich imagination. (quoted in Easton 1971, p. viii)

Glossary

additive index   an index constructed by adding several items together to produce a single score for each case

aggregate variables   variables that pertain to units made up of many individuals (e.g., nations or alliances)

association   a relationship between or among two or more variables; two variables are said to be associated when knowing the value of one variable for a given case increases the chances of guessing the value of the other variable for that case; also called "relationship"

bivariate analysis   the use of statistics that measure the relationship between two variables

causal relationship   a relationship in which one factor or influence affects another factor; such relationships are distinguished from relationships in which two factors simply vary together, perhaps as a result of some unknown factor

causation   the act of causing; to produce an effect or result; determining causation requires that the supposedly causative factor or variable precedes changes for which it is responsible, that there is an observable relationship between the causative factor and the changes it causes, and that no other factor is responsible for the observed changes

central tendency   measures of central tendency indicate the value of some variable for a set of cases that best represents the value of the whole set

chi-square   a measure designed to determine the statistical significance of a relationship between two nominal variables

classic experiment an experimental design in which one experimental group of subjects and one control group are selected, both of which are measured in some way before and after the experimental treatment is applied only to the experimental group; sometimes termed the "pre-test/post-test control group design"

cluster sampling an approach to sampling that involves the division of the population under study into a large number of subunits, a case from each of which is to be included in the analysis; also called multistage random area sampling

coefficient a measure of the extent to which two or more variables are related, and of the direction of that relationship

cohort survey a survey of a specified category or class of subjects at different points in time (e.g., people born in a particular year)

collective good something of value that is enjoyed by all members of a given group or category of persons, regardless of whether they contributed to obtaining it (e.g., citizens who enjoy recreational activities in wilderness areas benefit from the lobbying efforts of environmental organizations even if they do not contribute to those efforts)

composite indicator an indicator made up of several other indicators

conceptualization an idea about a complex problem that systematically identifies the important factors involved

confidence interval in tests of statistical significance, the range of values in which the value for the whole population must lie

confidence level in tests of statistical significance, the probability that the value for the whole population lies within the confidence interval

content analysis any method for quantifying aspects of the contents of documents

control the effort to isolate the effect of an independent variable on a dependent variable by holding the effects of other variables constant; control can be achieved in experimental design by the use of control groups, and in statistical approaches by multivariate analysis

control group   in an experiment, a group of subjects observed or measured but not exposed to an experimental treatment

Cramer's V   a measure of association for use with nominal level data

cross-sectional survey   a survey that analyses cases from different regions, groups, or classes taken at a single point in time

dependent variable   a variable whose values are expected to change in response to some other variable or variables

dispersion   the extent to which the values of some variable vary around the average value for the group

ecological fallacy   using information about an aggregate to draw conclusions about an individual case from that aggregate

empirical   having to do with observable and measurable reality

ex post facto design   a quasi-experimental design in which statistical methods are used to simulate the logic of control group designs

experimental design   the plan for selecting and grouping subjects and measuring variables in an experiment

experimental treatment   the influence or factor to which the experimental group in an experiment is exposed

experimentation   the research strategy in which the researcher has total control over the subjects and the experimental treatment; rarely achieved in political science

external validity   the extent to which the findings from a study can be generalized to the population in question; anything that makes the subjects studied different from those not studied can threaten external validity

field experiment   an experiment that takes place outside the laboratory

filter questions   questions added to a survey that enable the researcher to determine which respondents have enough information about a subject to make their answers meaningful

forced response items on a questionnaire, items that require the respondent to select from a list of answers

frequency a presentation of univariate data showing how many
distribution cases fall into each category or value of some variable

generalizability the ability of some finding to apply broadly, beyond the realm of a particular circumstance or event; a key component of scientific conclusions

Goodman and a measure of association for use with ordinal data
Kruskal's gamma

history effect influences on experimental subjects created by outside events that occur during the course of an experiment, possibly leading the researcher to conclude that the experimental treatment has had effects that were really caused by the history effect; one of the most important justifications for the use of control groups; a threat to the internal validity of a research design

hypothesis a verifiable statement about a relationship between or among two or more variables

hypothesis the process of forming a hypothesis; usually involves
construction refinement and specification of a theoretical idea

hypothesis testing the application of observation and empirical analysis to determine whether a hypothesis is true

independent variable a variable the values of which have been hypothesized to affect the values of another variable

index a composite indicator, made up of several more specific measures

indicator a specific, observable measure of a variable

intercoder reliability the extent of agreement among several independent observers assigning values to cases in an empirical study; a relevant concern when judgment is required in operationalizing data

internal validity the extent to which the logical structure of a research design enables the researcher to be confident that changes in the dependent variable are attributable to an independent variable

interval a kind of measure in which the values assigned indi-
measurement cate both the ordering of the cases and the distance between values

Kendall's tau	a measure of association for use with ordinal data
laboratory experiment	an experiment conducted within a laboratory setting
longitudinal survey	a study that compares the responses to a survey over several points in time
maturation effect	changes in the experimental subjects caused by the passage of time, possibly leading the researcher to conclude that the experimental treatment has had effects that were really caused by the subjects' maturation; one of the most important justifications for the use of control groups; a threat to the internal validity of a research design
mean	a measure of central tendency, computed by adding the values of all the cases and dividing by the number of cases; appropriate for interval data only
measures of association	any statistic that indicates the extent to which two or more variables are associated
median	when the values for some variable for a set of cases are arranged from lowest to highest, the value in the center (half are higher, half are lower); a measure of central tendency for either interval or ordinal data
mode	the most frequently encountered value for some variable among a set of cases; a measure of central tendency for interval, ordinal, or nominal data
modeling	creating an equation to represent a relationship to be tested through statistical analysis
multicollinearity	in regression analysis, a situation in which the independent variables are highly correlated; produces inaccurate regression coefficients
multidimensional	having more than one element; multidimensional concepts are often a source of difficulty in operationalization
multiple regression	regression analysis in which there is more than one independent variable
multiplicative index	an index created by multiplying several measures to produce a single score for each case
multistage random area sampling	(see cluster sampling)
multivariate	any statistic pertaining to more than two variables

multivariate analysis   an approach that allows the researcher to determine the effects on a dependent variable of several independent variables, while controlling for the effects of the others

negative relationship   the relationship between two variables that exists when cases with high values on one variable have low values on the other variable

nominal measurement   a kind of measurement in which the researcher is only able to place cases in different categories; there is no information as to which categories are "higher" or "lower" than other categories

normal curve   a symmetrical, unimodal distribution of values in which the most frequently encountered value (the mode) is also the median and the mean of the distribution

normative   having to do with judgments about obligation, duty, right and wrong, and justice

objectivity   a principle of scientific research holding that the analyst should design the study without bias regarding the results

operationalization   the process of translating concepts into observable and measurable indicators

ordinal measurement   a kind of measurement in which the values assigned indicate the rank or order of cases without any information about the distance between values

panel survey   a study that surveys the same subjects at several points in time

partial correlation   a measure of the association between two variables that remains after controlling for the effect of a third variable

Pearson's *r*   a measure of association for use with interval data

population   the set of cases in which the researcher is interested; also called "universe"

positive relationship   the relationship between two variables that exists when cases with high values on one variable have high values on the other variable

probability   a measure of how likely something is to occur

quantification   the process of transforming a concept into a form in which it can be reduced to numerical terms

quasi-experimental design	an approach to research design in which the analyst hopes to approximate the logic of real experiments by other means
ratio measurement	a kind of measurement in which the values assigned indicate the order among cases and the distance between values and in which the value of zero indicates the absence of any quantity of the variable
regression analysis	an approach to measuring association for interval data
relationship	(see association)
reliability	the extent to which a measurement technique produces consistent readings of a variable
research design	the plan for operationalizing concepts, gathering and analyzing data, and interpreting results in a scientific study
response rate	the number of subjects who return a completed survey divided by the total number of subjects who received one
sample	a group of cases drawn from a population for scientific study
sampling	the process of selecting cases to form the sample for a study
sampling error	the extent to which the sample of cases studied is different from the population that the sample is intended to represent
scientific political research	any approach to research that emphasizes empirical observation, objective measurement, and systematic, careful analysis
simple random sample	a sample of subjects selected in such a way that each case in the population had the same probability of being selected
Solomon four-group design	a design in which the subjects are divided randomly into four groups: the first two groups are treated exactly like the experimental and control groups in the classic experimental design (i.e., they are both observed, the experimental group is exposed to the experimental treatment, and then both groups are measured again to detect differences between them); the third and fourth groups are measured only after the

experimental treatment has been applied to one of them; this design controls for the interaction of the measurement or testing process and the experimental treatment because it contains a group that was exposed to the experimental treatment without first being measured

Spearman's rho   a measure of association for use with ordinal data

spurious relationship   a relationship between two variables caused by some other variable's influence

standard deviation   the basic measure of dispersion

standard error   a measure of the probable differences between the values measured in a sample and the values that actually characterize the population

standardization   the process of transforming measures so that they can be directly compared

standardized regression coefficients   a representation of the effect of an independent variable on the dependent variable in a regression equation in standard deviation units; in the basic regression equation, $Y = a + bX$, a standardized coefficient for b of .64 would indicate that as X increases by one standard deviation of X, Y increases by .64 standard deviations of Y

strata   portions of a population defined by their members' sharing some demographic, attitudinal, or behavioral characteristic

stratified sampling   an approach to sampling in which the population is first divided into strata that are particularly important to the study, and then cases are randomly selected from each stratum; the method ensures that a sufficient number of cases in the sample will be from each stratum

testing effect   changes in the experimental subjects caused by multiple exposures to measurement, possibly leading the researcher to conclude that the experimental treatment has had effects that were really caused by the subjects' heightened sensitivity created by their being repeatedly measured; a threat to the internal validity of a research design

tests of statistical significance   a statistical evaluation of the probability that a chance selection of sample cases led to an inaccurate conclusion about a population

time-series design   a research design that attempts to determine the existence of a causal relationship by taking measurements in several points in time

trend survey   a study that compares a specified population at different points in time

unidimensional   having only a single facet; unidimensional concepts are more easily operationalized than multidimensional concepts

univariate   any statistic pertaining to a single variable

universe   (see population)

validity   the extent to which an indicator is a meaningful, appropriate measure of a concept

variables   qualities or characteristics that can take on different values for different cases

verifiability   capability of being disproved; a key characteristic of a scientifically useful hypothesis

weighted index   an index in which some elements are considered more important than others; the more important elements are typically multiplied by some constant to make variations in them more influential than other elements in determining the index value

Bibliography

Almond, Gabriel A., and Sidney Verba. 1963. *The Civic Culture*. Boston: Little, Brown.

Arrow, Kenneth. 1951. *Social Choice and Individual Values*. New Haven, CT: Yale University Press.

Bachrach, Peter, and Morton S. Baratz. 1962. "The Two Faces of Power." *American Political Science Review* 56: 947–1053.

Banfield, Edward C. 1975. *The Unheavenly City Revisited*. Boston: Little, Brown.

Bishop, George F. et al. 1978. "The Changing Structure of Mass Belief Systems: Fact or Artifact?" *Journal of Politics* 40: 781–787.

Bohrnstedt, George W., and David Knoke. 1988. *Statistics for Social Data Analysis*. Itasca, IL: F.E. Peacock.

Brodbeck, May. 1958. "Methodological Individualism: Definition and Reduction." In *Readings in the Philosophy of the Social Sciences*, M. Brodbeck, ed. New York: Macmillan, pp. 280–303.

Buchanan, James M., and Gordon Tullock 1962. *The Calculus of Consent*. Ann Arbor: University of Michigan Press.

Buchanan, William. 1988. *Understanding Political Variables*, 4th ed. New York: Macmillan.

Campbell, Angus et al. 1960. *The American Voter*. New York: John Wiley.

Cook, Thomas D., and Donald T. Campbell. 1979. *Quasi-Experimentation: Design and Analysis Issues for Field Settings*. Chicago: Rand McNally.

Easton, David. 1971. *The Political System*, 2d ed. New York: Knopf.

Eulau, Heinz, and James G. March. 1969. *Political Science*. Englewood Cliffs, NJ: Prentice Hall.

Fiorina, Morris. 1989. *Congress: Keystone of the Washington Establishment*. New Haven, CT: Yale University Press.

Friedman, Jeffrey. 1996. *The Rational Choice Controversy*. New Haven, CT: Yale University Press.

Gleick, James. 1987. *Chaos: Making A New Science*. New York: Viking.

Green, Donald P., and Ian Shapiro. 1994. *Pathologies of Rational Choice Theory: A Critique of Applications in Political Science*. New Haven, CT: Yale University Press.

Herrnstein, Richard J., and Charles Murray. 1994. *The Bell Curve: Intelligence and Class Structure in American Life*. New York: Free Press.

Huntington, Samuel P. 1968. *Political Order in Changing Societies*. New Haven, CT: Yale University Press.

Jackman, Robert W. 1978. "The Predictability of Coups d'Etat: A Model with African Data." *American Political Science Review* 72: 1262–1275.

Jones, E. Terrence. 1971. *Conducting Political Research*. New York: Harper and Row.

Kaplan, Abraham. 1998 [originally published 1964]. *The Conduct of Inquiry: Methodology for Behavioral Science*. New Brunswick, NJ: Transaction.

Key, V.O., Jr. 1958. "The State of the Discipline." *American Political Science Review* 52: 961–971.

————. 1949. *Southern Politics*. New York: Knopf.

Leege, David C., and Wayne L. Francis. 1974. *Political Research*. New York: Basic Books.

Manheim, Jarol B., and Richard C. Rich. 1991. *Empirical Political Analysis: Research Methods in Political Science*, 3d ed. White Plains, NY: Longman.

McClosky, Herbert. 1958. "Conservatism and Personality." *American Political Science Review* 52: 27–45.

Miller, Warren E. 1981. "The Role of Research in the Unification of a Discipline." *American Political Science Review* 75: 9–16.

Nie, Norman M. et al. 1976. *The Changing American Voter.* Cambridge, MA: Harvard University Press.

O'Sullivan, Elizabeth Ann, and Gary R. Rassel. 1989. *Research Methods for Public Administrators*. White Plains, NY: Longman.

Olson, Mancur, Jr. 1982. *The Rise and Decline of Nations*. New Haven, CT: Yale University Press.

————.1965. *The Logic of Collective Action*. Cambridge, MA: Harvard University Press.

Pedhazur, Elazar J. 1982. "Multiple Regression." In *Behavioral Research*, 2d ed. New York: Holt, Rinehart and Winston.

Pye, Lucian W. 1990. "Political Science and the Crisis of Authoritarianism." *American Political Science Review* 84: 3–19.

Ranney, Austin. 1976. "Parties in State Politics." In *Politics in the American States*, 3d ed., Herbert Jacob and Kenneth Vines, eds. Boston: Little, Brown.

Tabachnick, Barbara G., and Linda S. Fidel. 1983. *Using Multivariate Statistics*. New York: Harper and Row.

Tribe, Lawrence. 1972. "Policy Science: Analysis or Ideology?" *Philosophy and Public Affairs* 2: 66–110.

Walker, Jack L. 1969. "The Diffusion of Innovations Among the American States." *American Political Science Review* 63: 880–899.

Winch, Peter. 1958. *The Idea of a Social Science and Its Relation to Philosophy*. London: Routledge and Kegan Paul.

Index

About the Editor

Marcus E. Ethridge is professor of political science at the University of Wisconsin-Milwaukee. His published work has addressed the effect of citizen participation and legislative oversight on administrative behavior and, more recently, issues relating to interest group power in American society. Although initially interested in the field of law, he decided on a career in political science after taking his first undergraduate course in government at Wake Forest University. Ethridge received his Ph.D. from Vanderbilt University. He regularly teaches a graduate seminar in interest group theory and the introduction to political science.

Ethridge is convinced that genuine knowledge about political life requires strong measures of both quantitative, empirical research *and* careful theorizing. In his classes he emphasizes a balanced approach, pointing out, on the one hand, "facts" about politics that have not withstood the scrutiny of empirical inquiry and, on the other hand, exhaustive data analysis that generated inadequate and simplistic conclusions. The enduring debate in political science among narrow-minded empiricists and defiant theorizers is, he feels, ultimately productive; each kind of scholar has something to offer, and each checks the excesses of the other.